W9-AWG-845

# PLAYING WITH GOD

# PLAYING
# WITH
# GOD

RELIGION

AND

MODERN

SPORT

William J. Baker

HARVARD UNIVERSITY PRESS

*Cambridge, Massachusetts*

*London, England*

*2007*

Cataloging-in-Publication Data available from the Library of Congress
Library of Congress catalog card number: 2006051531
ISBN-13: 978-0-674-02421-2 (alk. paper)
ISBN-10: 0-674-02421-4 (alk. paper)

For Tina
my rock,
my love

# CONTENTS

# ILLUSTRATIONS

# PLAYING WITH GOD

# INTRODUCTION

**S**port and religion dominated the North Georgia textile town where I came of age in the 1950s. Athletic events united mill hands and preachers. Surrounded by Protestant churches, our local mill produced nationally known "amateur" teams in softball and basketball, and provided gyms, ball fields, equipment, and supervision for youth sports. Spindles and spires spun out identical messages: work hard, play hard, play fairly, and win. In high school I played varsity baseball, basketball, and football, quarter-backing our Bulldogs to two consecutive state football championships. All the while, I engaged in youth evangelism and dreamed of becoming a Baptist minister. Before embarking on a seminary degree, I attended college on an athletic scholarship. For me, as for fellow southerner Deion Sanders, sport and religion went together "like peanut butter and jelly."[1]

Others view the connection more ironically. When Max Hellerman, a commentator for the Friday night fights on ESPN, argued with his younger brother, Sam, about the origins of athletic spectacles, Sam declared sport to be "man's joke on God": "You see, God says to man, 'I've created a universe where it seems like everything matters, where you'll have to grapple with life and death and in the end you'll die anyway, and it won't really matter.' So man says to God, 'Oh, yeah? Within your universe we're going to create a sub-universe called sports, one that absolutely doesn't matter, and we'll follow everything that happens in it as if it were life and death.'"[2]

Sam Hellerman got it right. In the subuniverse of sport, Americans follow their favorite players and teams as though it were a matter of life and death. Whatever natural disaster or war in the news, grown men eagerly turn to the early morning sports page and evening sports channels. Parents arrange and rearrange their lives around their children's ball games, swim meets, gymnastics practice, and track events. People are married in

Cubs, Packers, Steelers, or Red Sox uniforms; some are buried in them. Meanwhile, public displays of piety abound at every level of sport in the United States. Elite professionals and amateur high school athletes point heavenward in celebration of touchdowns and home runs. Impeccably attired golfers and rough-looking boxers have little in common, but both share their glory with God. On baseball diamonds, football gridirons, and basketball courts, coaches and athletes engage in pregame and postgame prayers, earnest midgame gestures of supplication, and televised nods to God for games won.

For all their differences, religion and sport seem to have been made in the image of each other. Both are bathed in myth and sustained by ritual; both reward faith and patience; both thrive on passion tempered with discipline. More than a century ago, social scientist Thorstein Veblen tried to explain the tendency of high-culture leisure activities, competitive sport, and religious belief to coexist in a mutually supportive fashion. In stilted academic prose, he insisted that "religious zeal" and "the sporting element" partook of the same temperament: the need for humans to distinguish themselves and the urge to believe in divine beneficence or mere good luck. As Veblen viewed the world on the eve of the twentieth century, "the habitation to sports, perhaps especially to athletic sports, acts to develop the propensities which find satisfaction in devout observances."[3]

Veblen might have drawn on the long history of Western civilization to illustrate this intimate connection between religion and sport. Except for rare periods of antagonism, sport has always been closely aligned with piety. Early ball courts and religious temples functioned side by side. Ancient Greeks assumed their athletic enthusiasm to be rooted *en theos,* inspired by a god. Surrounded by religious trappings, medieval and early modern sport evolved within the walls and on the grounds of cathedrals, monasteries, and churches. Sixteenth-century Puritans momentarily called a halt to this cooperative arrangement; but long before organized sport as we know it, competitive folk games passed from one generation to another among the same people who customarily accepted the institutional church and religious dogma without question.

Beginning in the mid-nineteenth century, shortly before most American sports took on written rules, leagues, and governing bodies, religious reformers embarked on a trail that featured unpredictable twists and turns.[4] Far from the security of inherited patterns of behavior, they filled this saga with debate, negotiation, and accommodation. Christians argued vigorously with each other, then with non-Christians, about the proper relation of religion to sport. In America, from 1850 to 1900 liberal Protestants and a few evangelicals adjusted their theological and institutional commitments to the newly emergent attractions of organized sport. Roughly from 1900 to 1950, more moderate Protestants joined Roman Catholic, Mormon, and Jewish endorsements of sport. Finally, in the l950s fundamentalist evangelicals baptized sport just as some American athletes started giving Allah the credit for knockouts and touchdowns.

Despite a heritage of Puritan prohibitions, today religious believers embrace sport because both religion and sport have changed, each making itself acceptable—even useful and desirable—to the other. Within the past two centuries, people of faith have modified many dogmatic assumptions and ethical restrictions. For example, Protestants have largely dispensed with the old Puritan requirement that Sundays be spent in quiet reflection, making Sunday a popular day for sports events. More important, religious folks of all stripes have learned to affirm the human body and the "pleasures of the flesh" vividly celebrated in the spectacle of modern sport. Religious institutions as well as individual believers have learned to capitalize on both the moral and commercial potential in sport.

Sport too has changed. From a disorderly, unstructured folk heritage of wonton violence, sport underwent a "civilizing process" through the development of explicit rules and governing bodies that balanced restraint and spontaneity, control and pleasure.[5] Sport has sanitized its games. Baseball's reluctance to induct Pete Rose into its Hall of Fame is but one example of the wary relation between playing fields and gambling halls. Gamblers are kept at arm's length from athletes not only because the game's integrity is at stake. So is its reputation, a point not lost in the perennial controversy surrounding steroids and performance-enhancing drugs. Market realities require a decent reputation. As sport has expanded its attraction beyond the unlettered masses on the one hand and the top-hat patricians on the other, it now appeals to the same middle-class, respectable folk who keep churches afloat.

The union of religion and sport began as a quest for physical and moral health, prime concerns of city folk in mid-nineteenth-century Britain and the United States. Muscular Christianity originated in the fervent belief that physical exercise and competitive games made for better digestion, lungs, and muscles, and that a stronger body would fortify the human spirit against the beguiling allurements of big-city life. Male middle-class anxieties weighed heavily in this equation. In addition to the practical measures of health and morality, a "manhood question" prompted Victorian reformers to resist the effeminacy that seemed to be resulting from too much urban ease. Competitive sport became a substitute for the rigors of physical labor, frontier dangers, and warfare, the customary measures of manhood. For much of modern history, males have dominated athletic clubs and sporting events because men have had the most to win in terms of self-respect and purpose.

In the religion-and-sport game, denominational colleges and universities also had much to win. The great majority of America's church-related institutions of higher learning originated in the same era that baseball, college football, basketball, and a host of other athletic games first took organized form. Sports teams provided student activity, institutional visibility, and alumni support. From the outset, religiously affiliated institutions mimicked other private and public colleges, integrating American academic and athletic programs in a fashion that is utterly foreign to the rest of the world. The athletic histories of places like Methodist Duke, Baptist Baylor, Catholic Notre Dame, Mormon Brigham Young University, Jewish Brandeis, and fundamentalist Liberty University thus figure heavily in the American accommodation of religion to sport.

What denominational colleges and universities did institutionally, American patriotism has done ideologically: making religion and sport interdependent. Early in the twentieth century, religious leaders and sportsmen teamed up to train immigrants in American folkways and loyal citizenship, then stayed in harness for more pressing patriotic purposes. During World War I, as churches and synagogues prayed for the Hun's defeat, major league baseball initiated its "tradition" of singing the National Anthem prior to the start of the game. By the end of the century, the Super Bowl topped the World Series as the nation's dominant sports event. Super Bowl Sunday is a spectacle so orchestrated with cherished beliefs and rituals that it approximates a religious festival.[6] Displays of the flag, the National Anthem, military flyovers, and bombastic rhetoric leave no doubt that the United States is a nation patriotically connected to both games and prayers.

Religion and sport especially are joined at the altar of commercial interest. As sports promoters seek publicity and lively attendance at their events, and as churches seek wholesome activities and a podium for their message, their marriage seems made in heaven. The recent introduction of Faith Nights in minor-league ball parks—featuring various combinations of gospel pop music, handouts of Bibles and bobble-head biblical figures, colorful Veggie Tales cartoon characters, and inspirational testimonies from local sports heroes—is a good example of the wedding of sport and religion. The idea originated in the office of Mike Snider, president of an entertainment and sports marketing company in Nashville, Tennessee. Snider convinced a vice-president of Nashville's AAA baseball team, the Sounds, that the club's need "to put more fannies in the seats" could well complement the needs of the 3,000 churches within driving distance of Nashville.

In 2001 busloads of church folk rolled in for the first Faith Nights; by 2006, some seventy Faith Nights in forty-four American cities spiced up indoor Arena Football games as well as minor-league baseball evenings. Still predominantly southern but no longer confined to the evangelical South, these promotional efforts now range from Bridgewater, New Jersey, to Spokane, Washington. Careful not to inflict "ambush evangelism" on unsympathetic fans, club owners nevertheless offer these low-cost, fun-filled, family-friendly events with the added incentive of promoting Jesus. As the marketing director of the minor-league Hagerstown (Maryland) Suns chortled upon boarding the Faith Night wagon, "Baseball, faith, and Americana, it's a perfect fit."[7]

Perfect or not, the modern American "fit" of faith and sport makes a complex, fascinating story.

# 1

## OLD GODS AND GAMES

**B**efore they could read or write, and before they learned to reason scientifically, humans created narratives and metaphors to explain both their physical world and their heartfelt longings. Deities filled their universe. By some accounts, gods created the heavens and the earth; in other versions, gods took the shape of mountains, rivers, and trees, and of the sun, moon, and stars. Wherever they might dwell, the gods determined the fate of mortals.

Familiar information, this. Not so well known is the fact that many old creation myths and religious dramas featured ball games and other physically competitive activities that would be wholly recognizable to today's sports fan. Religious rituals dramatized the myths; temples and churches gave the myths institutional credence, with holy days that doubled as sporting holidays. Seventeenth-century Puritans and their descendants assaulted this tandem of religion and sport, but Puritan complaints merely season the impression that prior to the emergence of modern sport in the nineteenth and twentieth centuries, religion and sport enjoyed a long and lively interaction.

### Getting the Gods to Smile

Through ceremonial dance, blood sacrifice, and prayer, our ancient forbears sought to win the favor of nature's unseen spirits, their deities. The stakes seemed high. People believed that only the gods could provide fertile wombs, good crops, successful hunts, and victorious wars. In addition to pious ritual, competitive games reportedly caused the gods to smile on the offering of a tribe's choice youths on the altar of physical contest.[1]

For many centuries before the arrival of Spanish conquistadors, Central

American Mayans and Aztecs built elaborate stone ball courts adjacent to their religious temples. Under the watchful eye of a priest, they competed fiercely in a ball game that was as much a cultic ritual as a competitive sport. They played with a solid rubber ball, hitting it only with their hips, not with hands or feet, through a stone or wooden hoop turned sideways on the wall.[2]

Thought to be a creation of the gods, this game supposedly reenacted the arc and descent of the sun into the underworld, then its resurrection to new strength and warmth. Often after a game, a player or a slave was beheaded and his heart cut from his body on the sacrificial altar. Stone carvings and vase drawings depict plants sprouting from severed heads, suggesting the fertile soil and fruitful mix of rain and sunshine that the ancients hoped would result from their rituals. Recently excavated ball courts all over Central America remind us of a day when religion and athleticism enjoyed an intimate, if gory, relationship.

Stories of competitive games dominate ancient creation myths. Aztecs and Mayans accounted for the sun and moon with a bizarre yarn about a ball game that took place at the dawn of civilization. Twin brothers challenged the gods to a game. Upon losing the game, the twins also lost their heads as a sacrifice to the gods. One of the heads, placed in a tree, spurted a stream of sperm when a young virgin passed that way. Impregnated, the girl bore twins. Once they were grown to young manhood, the twins challenged the gods to yet another ball game. This time the gods lost the game, whereupon the severed heads of the two original twins ascended into the heavens to become the sun and the moon.[3]

Native North Americans, too, linked physical competition to religious lore. Special formulas and procedures accompanied all sorts of hoop-and-pole contests, ring-and-pin games, and relay races. The southwestern Apaches, for example, associated the sun with animal masculinity and the moon with feminine vegetation, and "played out" these beliefs in seasonal relay races of young unmarried males. Ceremonies before, during, and after the races featured the use of pollen, saplings, ears of corn, eagles' feathers, and fire. No boundary separated faith from contest, religious ritual from sport, Allen Guttmann notes, "because the race was as religious as the drumming, the singing, and the pollinating."[4]

Especially mixed in its religious, cultural, and recreational functions was an ancient stick-and-ball game that came to be known as lacrosse. Appropriately, the term *lacrosse* originated with a later religious source: a French Jesuit missionary who thought the stick used in the game resembled a *cro-*

*sier* (small cross) that Catholic bishops carried in religious processions. In various forms and under many different names, lacrosse was popular throughout North America long before the arrival of Europeans. Whether the Huron to the north, the Iroquois in the east, the Dakotas in the upper midwest, or the Choctaw in the south, all thought their ball game a gift from the Great Spirit, the Creator.[5]

For Cherokees in the southern Appalachian mountains, ancient beliefs, taboos, and rituals swirled around lacrosse contests in the late summer and early autumn. Players abstained from certain foods and sex for seven days; the tribe danced and chanted taunts all night before the big game. On the morning of the event, the tribal priest (shaman) performed "mystic rites" of exorcism, hexed the opponents, ceremonially marked the players with scratches, and offered prayers to the birds and animals of the forest, asking for their assistance in the forthcoming contest. The red deer could lend his speed, the hawk his keen sight, and the rattlesnake his terrible venom against the foe.[6]

Like the Central American ball-court game, lacrosse spawned imaginative myths that helped people make sense of their physical and moral universe. According to a Cherokee legend, a player, eager to win, once picked up the ball with his hand (rather than with the leather-laced net at the end of his stick), in violation of the rules of the game. He tried to throw the ball at the far goal, but it went high into the air. Sticking on the sky, the ball became the moon. When the moon waned, small and pale, Cherokees were reminded of the negative results of cheating.[7]

Early Africans and Europeans, too, found both moral and metaphysical meaning in physical contests. Highly ritualized wrestling especially flourished in ancient Egypt, among the Nuba people in the Sudan, and in Nigerian Ibo villages. For three months or so during their rainy yam-growing season, the Ibos promoted wrestling matches every eighth day, then finished with an entire day devoted to prayers, dances, and wrestling contests in honor of the corn deity. Fearful of displeasing the gods and thus causing the crops to go bad, the Ibo wrestler was forbidden to become fatigued or angry during his match.[8]

Throughout the ancient world, ancestor worship and fertility rites combined to produce funeral games in honor of deceased kinsmen and chieftains. Tests of speed and strength celebrated the vigor of the departed; commemorative festivals kept fame alive. Portraying Greek life around 1000 B.C., Homer's *Iliad* provides a richly detailed account of funeral games held in honor of a Greek soldier slain in battle at the gates of Troy. As they competed in chariot races, boxing and wrestling matches, and discus and javelin throws, young warrior-athletes affirmed life in the face of death.

According to Homer, the gods took an active interest in the events. Like modern athletes who chalk up wins or losses to the will of God, young Greeks blamed or praised the gods according to the contest's outcome. An archer was said to have missed his target because he had failed to promise Apollo a sacrificial offering. Presumably Apollo begrudged him victory. When a chariot driver momentarily dropped his whip in the midst of a race, he blamed Apollo for knocking it out of his hand but thanked the goddess Athena for helping him retrieve it. These early athletes looked to the heavens for assistance. Eager to win the prize for the footrace, Odysseus charged down the stretch praying to Athena, "Hear me, goddess: come, bless me with speed!"[9]

Sport was first organized on a religious basis in ancient Greece. Hundreds of local religious-athletic festivals thrived around the Greek-dominated rim of the Mediterranean, each one in honor of some Greek god. For all their emphasis on rationality and human achievement, the Greeks were polytheists. They looked to particular gods for assistance in specific spheres of life. They appealed to Artemis for assistance in the hunt, to Poseidon when they sailed the seas, to Aphrodite in matters of love. The Greeks firmly believed that all the gods, whatever their specialty, looked with favor on the male warrior virtues of physical strength, agility, and endurance.

Warrior skills were best taught and practiced in athletic contests such as wrestling, chariot racing, and the throwing of the discus and javelin. These events were featured in numerous local religious-athletic festivals. By the fifth century B.C., four major festivals dominated the Greek circuit: the Pythian Games at Delphi in homage to Apollo, the Isthmian Games honoring Poseidon at Corinth, the Nemean Games at Nemea in honor of the mighty Zeus, and the Olympic Games at Olympia, also in the name of Zeus.[10]

Reckoned to be a vigorous warrior god who cast thunderbolts like javelins from the sky, Zeus bestrode the Greek pantheon just as surely as the Olympic games dominated the athletic circuit. Sometime around 1000 B.C., Greek ritual and myth established Zeus as the patron deity at Olympia. Some evidence suggests that he usurped his sister-wife Hera, whose earlier Heraean games featured women athletes, manifestations of an early matriarchal society. The actual origins of the Olympic games are shrouded in mystery, but one legend depicts Zeus and a rival god, Cronus, engaged in a wrestling match in the hills above Olympia. Zeus won the tussle, and his victory inspired religious ceremonies and quadrennial athletic contests as testimonies to his prowess. By the supposed authority of Zeus, athletes, trainers, and spectators were guaranteed safe passage every four years to Olympia, even in times of war.[11]

Once they arrived at Olympia, athletes had to swear by Zeus that they had been in training for the past ten months and that they would play fair and obey all the rules. If they broke their oaths, they were required to pay fines, which went toward the building of statues in honor of Zeus. During the fifth century B.C., a huge temple was constructed of local limestone for the worship of Zeus. Shortly thereafter the most famous sculptor of the day, Phidias, erected a magnificent statue seven times larger than life, encased in gold, silver, and ivory. It depicted Zeus sitting on a throne in the inner chamber of the temple. Visitors never failed to comment on its memorable finery and proportions. Admirers thought it one of the Seven Wonders of the World; critics complained about the outlandish size. If Zeus stood up, they noted, he would poke his head through the roof.

Of the five-day program of Olympic events that became fixed during the fifth century B.C., athletic contests took only two and a half days. The first day was devoted entirely to religious rituals. A prolonged opening ceremony featured athletes and their trainers offering oaths, prayers, and sacrifices to Zeus. They presented gifts at the statues of past Olympic victors who had been deified, at the shrines of various lesser gods, and especially at the altars and statues of Zeus. In the evening of that first day, Olympic participants marched in solemn processions and sang hymns of praise and devotion.

Then came a full day of athletic contests: chariot races and horse races in the morning, the pentathlon (discus and javelin throws, long jump, sprint, and wrestling) in the afternoon. As soon as the sun set, however, attention shifted back to religious activities. By the light of a midsummer full moon, a ram was slain and burned as a sacrifice, to the accompaniment of prayers and hymns. On the following morning, priests led Olympic judges, Greek city-state officials, and athletes and their trainers in a colorful procession to the altar of Zeus, where one hundred oxen were ceremoniously slain. The animals' legs were burned in homage to the gods; their carcasses were roasted for a big banquet on the last day of the festival. Lauding this union of piety and athleticism, Greek poet Pindar noted "the expense and toil" that enabled the athlete to take advantage of "high gifts shaped by the gods." The victorious athlete, added Pindar, "cast his anchor at the furthest shore of happiness, honored of heaven."[12]

Long before the Greek Olympics came to an end in the fifth century A.D., faith in the old gods waned to such an extent that Olympia's religious trappings lost much of their original meaning. Yet other gods beckoned in the Graeco-Roman world. The Romans took their gods largely from the Greeks, changing merely the names. In Roman hands, Zeus became Jupiter, but with a difference: Jupiter never became associated with competitive sport. Rome's gladiatorial and chariot-racing spectacles originated as funeral games based on ancient religious festivals, culminating in the brutality of the Colosseum and the gambling frenzy that surrounded the Circus Maximus.[13]

## Sport and Spire

Early Christians generally accepted Greek athletics. The Apostle Paul frequently cited them as illustrations of the spiritual race to be run and the incorruptible prize to be won by Christians. Roman sport was another matter. For well over two centuries, Christians were unwilling participants in Roman spectacles. Thrown into the arena as punishment for their unorthodox religious beliefs, they inevitably lost the lions-versus-Christians game. Yet even when the persecution ceased, Christian leaders continued castigating Roman sport's "pagan" basis, its open association with gambling and prostitution, and its inhumane brutality.[14]

Tertullian of Carthage, an eminent theologian, was the harshest critic of all. In a treatise entitled *On Spectacles,* written around 200 A.D., he urged Christians to have "nothing to do, in speech, sight, or hearing, with the madness of the circus [chariot races]" or "the savagery of the arena." The "spectacles," he insisted, originated in idolatrous worship of deceased ancestors or pre-Christian deities, rewarded injurious or useless displays of strength, caused unholy outbursts of enthusiasm, and put Christians in the bad company of prostitutes and gamblers. "It is our duty," concluded Tertullian, "to hate these assemblies and gatherings of the heathen, were it only that there the name of God is blasphemed . . . and that there temptation has its base."[15]

Tertullian was by no means a lone Christian leader crying against Roman spectacles. His shrill tone, however, suggests that many Christians did not necessarily follow their leaders in these matters. "I find you sighing for goal-posts, the stage, the dust, the arena," lamented Tertullian. Exaggerated denunciations probably say as much about the audience and their activities as they do about the highly principled Tertullian and his kind.[16]

With the collapse of the Roman empire, the lively interaction of religion

praicl ki eltoir desoue
7 auoec lui estoient li
s hommes. LA DAMOI

**Medieval games.** Medieval churchmen decorated manuscripts with marginalia featuring people throwing and hitting balls. Some wield sticks that look like cricket or baseball bats; others use only their hands. Off the walls of monasteries, monks devised a game of handball, a forerunner of tennis before the invention of rackets. (Author's collection.)

and sport shifted to northern Europe. Ancient games such as German *kegels* (bowling), French *soule* (football), and the stick-and-ball games of Irish hurling and Scottish shinty all had religious associations akin to the competitive fertility rites of ancient peoples. Light toyed with darkness, warmth with cold, life with death in the pre-Christian mythologies of Europe. Moslems enriched the mix in the eighth century when they brought old Egyptian fertility rituals across the narrow western neck of the Mediterranean into Spain. For several centuries Muslim, Christian, and pre-Christian practices blended harmoniously, especially around the annual rites of spring renewal that Christians called Easter.[17]

Various forms of ball play became an integral part of Easter season ceremonies all over medieval Europe. Colorfully garbed French priests near Paris chanted a traditional liturgy and passed a ball back and forth as they danced down the church aisle celebrating springtime signs of Christ's resurrection. An archbishop near Lyon participated in a ball game immediately after an Easter meal. As late as 1165 a theologian at the University of Paris saw the need to denounce church-sponsored ball play at Poitiers and

Rheims. It derived from old pagan customs, he complained. He was right, of course, but no one seemed to share his alarm.

While incorporating ball play within its religious program, the medieval church helped to popularize ball games and other recreational activities. For one thing, the church provided a time for parishioners to play. For six days of the week peasants and household servants worked, and on Sunday they were expected to worship at the village church. Yet no puritan pall hovered over medieval Sundays. After the morning sermon and sacraments, villagers lounged or played on Sunday afternoons. Moreover, as the church's holy days aligned with ancient seasonal holidays, villagers also played at festive occasions around Easter, during the harvest season, and at Christmastime. Various regional versions of competitive sport flourished on holidays blessed by the local clergy. Italians regularly scheduled horse races *(palio)* on several of their many saints' days; each spring in England, peasant football thrived around the food, drink, music, and dance of Shrove Tuesday, just before the onset of Lent and its austere code of abstinence.

In addition to a calendar that allowed time for play, the medieval church provided physical space that otherwise would have been unavailable for popular recreation. In the days before public parks, playgrounds, and school yards, villagers usually played on a village green or some other "commons" normally set aside for grazing cattle. In villages that had no commons, the churchyard or cloisters often made mass recreation possible. Spires and stained-glass windows served as backdrops for wrestling matches, juggling exhibitions, and board games. A fourteenth-century English clergyman unintentionally admitted the popularity of these practices when he attempted to banish "dancing, playing at quoits, bowling, tennis-playing, handball, football, stoolball, and all sorts of other games" from church property.[18]

Peasant football, an ill-organized, uncodified game that had no physical boundaries or limits on team size, required open countryside. Likely as not, the land was owned by the church and rented out to wealthy landlords, who traditionally turned it over to peasant sport shortly before spring crop planting and just after the autumn harvest. English and French clerics frequently complained about property being damaged by hordes of drunken football players. A few critics pointed to the roughness of the game, but the most severe prohibitions came from bishops and kings eager for common folk to spend their time practicing archery—a military necessity—rather than playing football.[19]

Medieval church leaders looked more benignly on upper-class sport. Like modern ministers who cater to early Sunday morning golfers, some priests happily dispensed quickie communion at the break of dawn to aristocrats eager to get to the fields for hunting and hawking. Although the Church tried to ban tournaments in some parts of Europe, bishops often sat jowl to jowl with the castle crowd at ceremonious jousting contests. Churchmen especially looked with favor on royal ("real") tennis, for the game apparently originated with French monks, abbots, and priests in monastic and church cloisters. Players hit a small ball with their open hand *(le jeu de paume)* over a rope stretched across the middle of the space available. They played the ball off walls and onto sloping roofs that efficiently kept the ball in play. According to legend, a French king visited a monastery, saw a game of tennis, and admired it so much that he had it copied in his royal palace. The term "tennis court" probably derives from the game's early location in the courts of European monarchs.

Renaissance churchmen enthusiastically linked tennis to the Renaissance ideal of well-balanced mental and physical skills. Christian humanist Desiderius Erasmus, a former monk, lauded tennis as an ideal game for exercising all parts of the body; England's Cardinal Thomas Wolsey arranged the construction of an indoor tennis court for King Henry VIII at Hampton Court. An Italian monk, Antonio Scaino da Salo, produced a treatise in 1555 that established the first simple set of written rules, a standard court size, and a scoring system. Monks and aristocrats enthusiastically played tennis as a means of health and refinement.[20]

## The Changing of the Guardians

Protestant reformers gave a more mixed message about sport. Martin Luther encouraged his followers to participate in "honorable and useful modes of exercise," such as dancing, archery, fencing, and wrestling.[21] For his own exercise, Luther engaged in the old German game of bowling (kegels). When the bowling ball banged against the pins, it reminded him of the Christian's duty to knock down the devil. Passionately protestant but crude of speech and manners, Martin Luther was too much a man of the soil to prohibit traditional pleasures of the flesh.

The more urbane, legalistic John Calvin blew a more uncertain trumpet. Like Luther, Calvin enjoyed bowling. He also played quoits, a medieval game in which players threw iron rings onto a peg, similar to the American frontier game of horseshoes. But the censorious Calvin was critical of most other sports. Eager to remove the fleshpots from the city of Geneva, he saw sport as a hindrance to holy living. Most games seemed too intimately associated with "carnal pleasure," such as drunkenness and sexual indulgence. Competitive games frequently spawned gambling and desecration of the Christian Sabbath, two of Calvin's great taboos. For Geneva's public policy as well as private piety, Calvin was quite prepared to lump most sports with thievery and prostitution, and to ban them all.

Protestant exiles from England, Scotland, and Holland flocked to Geneva, where they imbibed Calvin's ethical mandates as well as his theological beliefs. Most of all, they assumed the supreme self-confidence that came from believing oneself selected by God for salvation and thus for serving as God's moral monitor in the war against evil. When they turned northward to home, these converts to Calvinism put their shoulders to the task of moral reform. English Calvinists led the way. Their zealous crusade to purify both church and society provoked people to call them Puritans.

Yet the Puritans represented no monolithic bloc of opinion or practice. They often disagreed with each other on various points of doctrine, and especially on specific evils that needed to be eradicated. Puritan merchants and businessmen thought and acted quite differently from village farm laborers. Ministers sometimes preached one thing while their congregations did something else. When a preacher denounced "wakes or feasts, may-games, sports and plays, and shows, which trained up people to vanity and looseness, and led them from the fear of God," one could be sure that many in England were still finding pleasure in these traditional pastimes.[22]

Popular or not, folk games emitted strong whiffs of pre-Christian fertility rites and Roman Catholic holy days, prompting the Puritans all the more to suppress them. Puritans first tried moral preachments in the home, at church, and in the marketplace. When sermonizing met with negligible success, they pursued political means of reform. In the early seventeenth century they put themselves forward as city councilors, mayors, and members of Parliament, eager to prohibit everything from traditional peasant games such as "futbol" to old sportive holidays such as Easter and Christmas.

Puritan zealotry provoked a backlash in the form of some "Olympick Games" organized by a wealthy royalist, Robert Dover, whose estate in the Cotswolds became the center of an annual two-day orgy of dance, food, drink, folk games, and horse races. Garbed in a colorful cloak with a feather in his hat, Dover oversaw the activities on horseback. Thumbing his nose at Puritan moralists, he openly encouraged gambling on housewives' footraces and hare hunts as well as horse races. It was a scene designed to please the pagan god Bacchus, not the Old Testament Yahweh to whom the Puritans bowed.

In political terms, the conflict was between reformist Protestants (Puritans) and conservative Anglicans and Catholics. England's first Stuart monarch, James I, virtually captained the latter team. When some Puritan magistrates issued prohibitions against recreational activities on Sunday in the large northern county of Lancashire, James responded with a rousing *Declaration on Lawful Sports* (1617). He decreed that once the Sunday morning service of worship was finished, none of his subjects should be prevented from enjoying "harmless recreation" such as dancing, archery, leaping, and vaulting. Even May Day games and ceremonies were to be allowed on Sunday so long as they caused no "impediment or neglect of Divine Service." One can imagine the irritation felt by Puritan divines when they were informed that all clergy must read the entire text of James's *Declaration* from the pulpit. Popularly called *The King's Book of Sports,* this anti-Puritan mandate was reissued under Charles I in 1633.[23]

Just nine years later, while King Charles played golf on the links of Leith near Edinburgh, the English civil war began. Victorious in battle, the Puritans ruled the nation for a decade at midcentury. Appointing army officers to serve as guardians of public morality, they struck at the heart of old church festivals and folk games by leveling fines and imprisonment against any display of public intoxication or gambling and against any desecration of the Sabbath. Yet people clung to their playful ways. Rigid prohibitions occasionally stirred hostile protests. According to a report from an Essex village, when the local Puritan vicar began the Sunday morning service in the parish church, "the people did usually go out of church to play at football, and to the alehouse and there continued till they were drunk, and it was no matter if they were hanged."[24]

This rural resistance to Puritan reform eventually won the day. English villagers continued living out their lives in seasonal cycles, with periodic festivals and games compensating for times of intense agricultural labor. Puritanism, largely confined to urban merchants and business classes for whom moral discipline and the work ethic made sense, was to enjoy a renewal among the urban Victorian middle class, but it was much too self-denying for the more traditional, casual life of preindustrial England. In the end, only the Puritan Sunday survived the Restoration of 1660. Sunday became sacrosanct in a fashion that distinguished English society from its Continental counterparts. For the better part of three centuries, Sunday in

England would remain free of public amusements and sports as well as commercial activity.

## Godly Games Abroad

Puritan zeal also met with mixed success in New England. There, ideology linked up with practical requirements of survival in an alien environment. The need for shelter, food, and peaceable relations with native inhabitants inspired the Pilgrims and their fellow immigrants to emphasize hard work and an orderly, disciplined life. But practicalities did not preclude principles: God-talk and prescriptions for godliness remained paramount. From the outset, the Puritans banned Sunday sport in North America and were similarly severe in their opposition to activities associated with gambling and drunkenness. By 1650 card games, shuffleboard, bowling, and horse races headed the list of prohibited pastimes in Massachusetts and Connecticut.[25]

Yet the Puritans were not the dour spoilsports that subsequent moralists and pundits have made them out to be. From Nathaniel Hawthorne to H. L. Mencken, the early Puritans have served as convenient whipping boys for progressive thinkers impatient with hypocrisy and repression in modern life. Surely we can blame the Puritans for all our work ethic and guilt-ridden inability to have fun. As Mencken memorably framed the image, at the heart of Puritanism was "the haunting fear that someone, somewhere, may be happy."[26]

In truth, the Puritan posture on sport was complex, ambivalent, and inconsistent. As in the Old Country, Puritans in New England never achieved a consensus on doctrines, nor did they ever reach unanimity on what popular pastimes were permissible. John Winthrop, the first governor of the Massachusetts Bay Colony, thought moderate exercise and recreation useful for the prevention of "great dullness and discontent" of the spirit. Winthrop worried, however, that he might take too easily to unnecessary or unwholesome recreation and thus become ensnared "in worldly delights" that would "cool the graces of the spirit." Ambivalent at best, Winthrop and his kind pragmatically accepted physical recreation and even some sport as antidotes to lethargy.[27]

Calvinist principles sometimes clashed with scripted behavior. For Puritans who firmly believed themselves called of God to work hard, invest time and money wisely, and expect financial success as an appropriate sign of their stewardship, problems arose when they and their neighbors realized that sport was a good business investment. Recreational goods and services provided a limited but steady market for the "industrious sort." At first these goods were imported from England; soon Yankee craftsmen turned out their own products. Native printers produced playing cards, gardeners groomed bowling greens, and promoters arranged horse races. Within a generation of the first settlers, packs of cards sold for three shillings apiece in Suffolk County, Massachusetts. Despite harangues from the pulpit, lotteries proliferated.[28]

New England's innkeepers especially mastered the entrepreneurial art of making money from the human hunger for pleasure. Whatever the legal prohibitions, at roadside taverns one could usually find strong drink, dice and card games, dancing, bowling, shuffleboard, wrestling matches, horse races, and even an occasional cockfight. Ironically, these "unethical" activities derived from the Protestant ethic, which favored capitalist enterprise.[29]

While the work ethic flourished, time and circumstance tempered anti-sport attitudes in New England. A second-generation Puritan divine, Increase Mather, observed that the Christian use of recreation was "very lawful, and in some cases a great duty." Musters, or militia training days, constituted one of those cases of dutiful sport. All males between sixteen and sixty years of age were expected to gather several times a year on the village green or in an open field for military training. Beginning in 1639, the voluntary defense units of Massachusetts added formal physical exercise and athletic competitions to their usual parades and mock battlefield maneuvers. Crowds gathered to watch military drills in the morning, then foot races, wrestling matches, and "shooting at the mark" contests in the afternoon. By 1704 the athletic portion of these militia days had become so dominant that one observer called them "Olympiack games."[30]

As the threat of wilderness warfare required hand-to-hand combat tactics, wrestling bouts became a favorite means of training that not even the strictest Puritan conscience could oppose. Three Congregationalist ministers emerged as the most memorable wrestlers in seventeenth-century New England. The Reverend Henry Smith of Wethersfield, Connecticut, reportedly preached brilliant sermons and courageously opposed the Anglican church hierarchy, but was best known for taking "delight in sports of strength" on militia days. Another Connecticut cleric, John Trumbull of Waterbury, became a local legend by conquering the militia champion from the nearby town of Westbury in a long evening bout. Yet another "famous wrestler" was the Reverend John Wise, a Harvard graduate of 1673.[31]

If militia days afforded "lawful recreation" for local communities, two new colleges did the same for a privileged set of young men who benefited from the Puritan zeal for education. Harvard College, founded in 1636 as a means to prevent "an illiterate ministry to the churches," and Yale College, founded for similarly pious purposes in 1701, became sanctuaries for youthful high jinks that contrasted sharply with Puritan values. Intramural snowball fights, wrestling matches, and football games seemed innocent enough when compared to the more frequent undergraduate binges of smoking, drinking, gambling, and dancing.[32]

In the 1650s the Harvard faculty attempted to define acceptable student behavior, prescribing even the time of day when recreational sport could be pursued. But at a distance from the censorious scrutiny of parents and local parsons, undergraduates easily found ways to bend, and to break, strict college rules. In 1696, in response to the drowning deaths of two Harvard students in an ice-skating accident on Fresh Pond, President Increase Mather uttered a last gasp of the older Puritan ambivalence when he reminded the parents of the deceased that "although death found them using recreations (which students need for their health's sake), they were lawful recreations."[33]

Despite Puritan misgivings, New England nursed variants of two old English village ball games that were destined to become central features of the American athletic landscape. One came to be known as the Boston game, which was adapted years later into American football; the other was called the Massachusetts, or New England, game, a distant forerunner of baseball. Of the two, football was by far the most controversial within religious circles. The first mention of a football game in New England occurred in 1686, when an English visitor reported "a great game of football" on a sandy beach at Rowley, Massachusetts. Impressed that the players were "not so apt to trip up one another's heels and quarrel, as I have seen 'em in England," the observer mildly echoed an old English Puritan indictment of peasant football's rough, disorderly, and vulgar tendencies. A New England diarist, William Bentley, thought the game had changed little in its transatlantic passage. Football's wonton violence rendered it "rather disgraceful" for young men "of better education," he insisted.[34]

This bias in favor of "better education" was not confined to Puritan New England, nor was the pious suspicion that sport might work to the detriment of such education. At the College of New Jersey, founded by Presbyterian Scots in 1746, the faculty banned field hockey (known as shinny, or bandy) in 1787 as an activity "low and unbecoming gentlemen and scholars." Not surprisingly, young gentlemen and scholars not only delighted in that forbidden fruit but also in wrestling, quoits, bowls, "baste ball," football, and a winter stick-and-ball game that seems to have been an early version of ice hockey. When the College of New Jersey was officially renamed Princeton University in 1896, it could rightfully claim a long history of campus sport, albeit loosely organized.[35]

In the South, plantation owners in Maryland, Virginia, and the Carolinas enthusiastically pursued the older aristocratic pastimes of hunting, horse racing, and cockfights. At the College of William and Mary, founded in 1693 in Williamsburg, Virginia, for the sons and grandsons of transplanted Englishmen, Oxford-trained professors made halfhearted efforts to prohibit undergraduates from participating in these activities. They met with little success. Virginia parsons had even less interest in taking a puritanical stance against popular pastimes. At Rappahannock, horse races were regularly run on Sundays in a field just beside a church, shortly after the hour of worship. Occasionally the minister and his congregation turned out to watch the races.[36]

A visitor from sober, restrained New England would have surely dismissed these Tidewater Sunday horse races as worldly indulgences. A far more horrific "sports" scene assaulted the senses of visitors in the southern Appalachian backcountry of western Virginia and the Carolinas, eastern Kentucky and Tennessee, and North Georgia. Male Scots-Irish mountaineers drank heavily and gambled fiercely at informal horse races and cockfights, but saved their most savage tendencies for rough-and-tumble fights. The fighters' motives ranged from revenge for an insult to a mere defense of honor in response to a verbal challenge. For spectators, these events broke the boredom of isolation in small hamlets poorly connected by badly kept roads.

The ordeal was a no-holds-barred fight to the finish. Men slapped and feinted, hit with bare fists, and kicked and kneed each other. As they grappled and rolled in the dust or mud, they groped for testicles and intentionally bit off their opponents' nose, ear, or lip. Worst of all, they attempted to gouge out eyes, leaving the opponent's eyeball hanging on his cheek unless the victor had sharpened his fingernails so well (as some fighters did) that their razor-sharp edges cleanly severed the connecting tissues that held the eye in its socket. This crude, unruly sport reflected the harsh, unpredictable tenor of mountain life. As historian Elliott Gorn explains, "The touchstone of masculinity was unflinching toughness, not civility, duty, or piety."[37]

Piety penetrated the Appalachians in the form of religious revivals in the late eighteenth and early nineteenth centuries, inspiring small backwoods churches to crusade against the evils of strong drink, gambling, whoring, cursing, and male rough-and-tumble orgies, which were said to encourage these evils. "But conversion was far from universal," Gorn notes. In many backcountry settlements, "the evangelical idiom remained a foreign country."[38] On the eve of the modern world, and most certainly at its cultural fringes, sport still behaved like a wild, unharnessed horse. To tame it, nothing less than a crusade would be required.

# 2

## THE ROAD TO BRAWNVILLE

Three major revolutions gave birth to the modern era of world history. The industrial revolution, which began in eighteenth-century Britain, replaced the use of human and animal muscle with machines and steam engines. At a more precise date, 1776, the American Revolution erupted to reject European colonial rule. Shortly thereafter, in 1789 French radicals began ousting its own traditional monarchy and aristocracy in favor of mass opinion and representative government. The fruits of these three revolutionary streams mingled, becoming a potent cocktail in the early years of the nineteenth century.

Intoxicated with the prospect of a better life, people moved from cottage to factory, from the rural countryside into cities, from cultural isolation to community consciousness. Some left behind ignorance and passivity to become informed, politically active citizens. Many more sought the pleasures made newly available by the tempo of factory work and the bright lights of the city. Another kind of revolution, a leisure revolution, followed closely on the heels of the great economic and political upheavals of the age. People in proximity to each other, with time on their hands and money to spend, sought diversions that had been unavailable to their fathers and mothers.

Competitive sport was one of many leisure-time possibilities. Some could actively participate; many more could watch. But an updated, urbanized form of sport was required. England's peasant football, for example, had flourished for centuries with local, unwritten rules that designated whatever objects were available to be used as goals; but such lack of physical boundaries made it unsuitable for town or city play. So did the uncertain amount of time required for a game. Sometimes lasting all day but at other times ending abruptly when a player scored quickly, old-style football was not an option for people whose lives were being newly structured by the constraints of factory and shop schedules. Nor was old-style cricket, England's other great gift to the world of team sports.

To be sure, the first signs of what we now recognize as modern sport first appeared in eighteenth-century Britain well before industrial growth transformed the landscape. By around 1800, horse racing, cricket, prize-fighting, yachting, and golf had all taken on written rules, clubs, and governing bodies.[1] As in so much else, young America quickly followed Britain's lead. Baseball's first written rules and organized clubs appeared in the 1840s; America's distinctive gridiron game, adapted from English rugby, took shape in the 1870s and '80s. The invention of basketball in 1891 completed the American Big Three of sport, codified, controlled, and promoted as the gods' gift to modern life.

The birth of modern sport forced believers in the oldest of human concerns, religion, to adjust their principles to this newcomer. No longer did people welcome long-winded theological orations or negative dismissals of popular pastimes. Pulpits increasingly featured nuanced views on the vice or virtues of certain amusements and sports. The term "muscular Christianity" became a mantra to be accepted, modified, or rejected. As they approached the new sports scene, religious folk found the road to Brawnville to be twisting and uneven.

## Sins of the Fathers

Extraordinary measures require extraordinary rationales. Like politicians jockeying for office, reformers frequently portray their predecessors in the worst possible light. Otherwise, reform would not seem so urgent. John the Baptist bewailed the crooked paths that needed to be set straight. Renaissance and Reformation leaders castigated medieval "dark ages" supposedly filled with superstitious monks and ignorant priests. In the service of faith and feeling, early nineteenth-century romantics lamented the apparent impiety and cold logic of their rationalistic forebears. We should therefore not be surprised to find mid-nineteenth-century crusaders for a new sports creed behaving in similar fashion: creating negative stereotypes by ridiculing the supposedly colorless, humorless tenor of life endured by their ancestors. In building their case, they found compliant texts in old Puritan sermons, essays, and diaries that called down the wrath of God on frivolous behavior. Thinking (or wishing) the worst of their ancestors, Victorian reformers dispensed with nuance.

Reformist sons especially like to set their projects in contrast to the values of their own fathers. Liberal clergyman Henry Ward Beecher, for example, thought that to give city youths "the means of physical vigor and health" would constitute a "valuable reformation" amounting to "a very gospel" altogether different from the gospel preached by his father, Presbyterian clergyman Lyman Beecher. The elder Beecher (1775–1863) rejected the old Calvinist doctrine of predestination but puritanically opposed dancing, card playing, the theater, and novels. Of course he rejected any activity that might tend to gambling or desecration of the Sabbath.[2] Such a dour image weighed heavily in the son's complaint, years later, that to fulfill society's expectations for a clergyman he would have to rise early each morning, "put on a black coat, a black hat, and a pair of well-polished boots, and, with stately and ministerial step, walk a mile and back before breakfast, and then, with a devout face, call it amusement."[3]

Another midcentury Yankee reformer, Thomas Wentworth Higginson, similarly blamed his immediate forebears for the "deficiency" in sport that he and his contemporaries sought to rectify. A descendant of the first clergyman in the Massachusetts Bay Colony, Higginson thought it unfair to accuse the Puritans of old. "They are not even answerable for Massachusetts," he insisted, "for there is no doubt that athletic exercises, of some sort, were far more generally practised in this community before the Revolution than at present." Higginson suggested that the early danger of "almost constant Indian warfare" required the "muscle and agility" provided by exercise and sport. Once that danger ceased, Higginson concluded, concern for health and physical vigor languished.[4]

Yet another reformer, Boston Unitarian minister Edward Everett Hale, pointed a judgmental finger at his hometown rather than at his father. Recalling the amusements available in the Boston of his youth, "a brisk commercial town of about forty-five thousand people" in the 1820s, Hale mentioned swimming, boating, walking, kicking pails in the street, and playing tug-of-war, but no organized sports. He also remembered a gymnasium, newly opened by German immigrants Charles Beck and Francis Lieber. Primarily associated with German and Swedish patriots, the gymnastics movement had originated among Lutheran theology students, clergymen, and teachers eager to spread the gospel of nature and physical exercise—a German version of muscular Christianity. In Boston, however, the appeal of gymnastics waxed and waned. In the first two years of Beck and Lieber's gym, several hundred people signed up; in its third year, however, only four pupils enrolled. A complex set of ropes, rings, ladders, pulleys, and other gymnastics apparatus was set up in the yard behind Boston's Latin School, but when Edward Everett Hale enrolled there in 1831 only a vaulting-horse and parallel bars remained. They too soon disappeared.[5]

For both Hale and Higginson, Harvard athletics in the 1830s suffered from an "utter lack of system." Undergraduates "had base-ball," Hale recalled sixty years later, "in utter ignorance that there were ever to be written rules for base-ball, or organized clubs for playing it; and we had cricket, in a way." Higginson, Hale's contemporary at Harvard, played "cricket of the old-fashioned kind with large bats and heavy balls." Higginson also went for long walks, rode horseback, bowled ninepins, took boxing lessons, and swam in summer and ice-skated in winter at a nearby pond.[6] Brimming with energy, neither Higginson nor Hale let the lack of organized sport deter them from finding outlets for their physically active impulses.

Both eagerly took to "old time football" at Harvard. Higginson "kicked football assiduously in the autumn," often by moonlight before the snow fell. In one of his most enduring campus memories, his freshman team beat a sophomore squad. Hale remembered "tumultuous throngs" of players engaged in a game without written rules or special equipment, featuring an indiscriminate mixture of kicking and handling the ball. Even in that day, prior to intercollegiate football, the game could get fiercely competitive. Hale once had a coattail torn halfway off. On another occasion, he slammed into an opponent so hard that he suffered chest pains all evening.[7]

Occasional and ill-organized as it might still have been by the early nineteenth century, competitive sport could be found on the streets, fields, and campuses of New England. People played, but with some misgivings. Negative attitudes, not the mere presence of sport, was the issue. As younger, outspoken Yankees framed the argument, the older generation still trailed moralistic clouds of Puritan restraint.

Yet young and old joined forces in opposition to one sport, prizefighting, for it linked all the traditional religious arguments to an elitist bias based on superior wealth, old family ties, and education. Prior to the Civil War, bare-knuckle prizefights attracted more spectators, press coverage, and controversy than any sport in the United States. At midcentury, New York became the capital of pugilism, with St. Louis and New Orleans key centers in the hinterlands. Before the 1840s, English immigrants dominated the ring; between 1845 and 1850, half a million Irish immigrants provided combatants hungry for success and acclaim. Spectators, virtually all males from the extremes of society—the laboring poor and the wealthy "smart set"—loved to watch bare-knuckled ethnic rivals pound each other senseless. Respectable middle-class folk stayed away, often provoking the wrath of boxing enthusiasts. When native-born American Tom Hyers fought Irish immigrant James "Yankee" Sullivan in 1849, a New York journalist registered excitement throughout the "vast community" of New York, except for "the rigidly righteous, the pious, the saints, the puritans, or those who had no time to spare from their private rogueries or pious prayers, to public matters."[8]

Unfair as that aside might have been, most Christian criticisms of the prizefighting combined class prejudice and religious piety. For example, a Methodist weekly, the *Christian Advocate,* slammed the "painful and humiliating" mob scenes on the streets of New York after the Hyers-Sullivan fight. That chaotic street scene contrasted sharply with a "neatly and uniformly attired" children's choir that was simultaneously singing hymns in the Broadway Tabernacle, it insisted. "Here was a telling contrast," comments one historian: "Bowery depravity versus uptown righteousness." Little wonder that a fictitious pugilist of the day blurted out to a religious critic of prizefighting, "Come, come: none of your d—— methodism here! Go on with your business! Stick to your shop!"[9]

## A Liberal Bend to the Oar

Scarcely could Methodists stick to their shop, for the world was their business. Like evangelical Protestants of all denominational persuasions in nineteenth-century America, they harnessed an intensely personal faith to a vision of moral renewal. Some fought for social justice and human rights; others moralistically quibbled over trifles. Most did both. Nor were the evangelicals unique. Liberal Unitarians and later "social gospel" folk joined them in the great task of making the church "a working-place in the world," as Unitarian minister Edward Everett Hale put it, "of men and women who want to bring in God's Kingdom" rather than remaining "a club of well-to-do Christians who have associated for their profit and pleasure."[10]

As American liberals and evangelicals negotiated the meaning of "God's Kingdom" on earth, sport became a common metaphor of struggle and progress. Before the dominance of baseball and football, rowing was a favorite reference. "I bend to that oar," Hale often said when agreeing with an opinion. He thought of religious and secular agencies cooperatively engaged in a single purpose like oarsmen in a racing boat, "engaged in a common effort to get the world ahead." Toward the goal of human progress, each person had to strive mightily in order for the boat to "go ahead and not be driven around in a circle."[11]

At Hale's Harvard of the early nineteenth century, however, religion seemed anything but progressive. It was even more quaint than "old time" sport. Each morning students were required to crawl out of bed for chapel prayers at 6:00 A.M. Chapel sermons regularly touched on weighty theological and philosophical issues with seldom a word about contemporary life. Once young Hale was summoned to the president's office to be fined for wearing too colorful a coat on Sunday. It all smacked of traditional Calvinistic, Puritan piety, and that it was. But it was an outmoded code of behavior, because Harvard had long since cast off its Calvinistic theology in favor of a more liberal, progressive way of thinking.[12]

During the first half of the nineteenth century, most Harvard presidents, faculty, and students became "essentially and conscientiously Unitarian." As one wag observed, Unitarianism meant "the fatherhood of God, the brotherhood of man, and the neighborhood of Boston." Boston and nearby Cambridge did in fact become the hub, if not the whole, of the Unitarian movement. Beyond the Hub, and especially outside New England, Unitarian churches struggled like isolated colonies in alien territory.[13] Curiously, the three American universities that were destined to play crucial roles in the beginnings of intercollegiate sport—Harvard, Yale, and Princeton—each took different paths in the early nineteenth century as they readjusted to America's Puritan religious heritage. While Harvard's Unitarians occupied the liberal fringe, adamantly orthodox Presbyterians (largely unreconstructed Calvinists) staked out the conservative end of the spectrum for Princeton.

Yale took a middle road: a so-called "New Divinity" that poured new interpretations—supposedly more flexible than the Calvinists, more substantial than the Unitarians—into old theological ideas and terms. Congregationalists and Presbyterians led their evangelical charge along Bible-quoting, logic-splitting, commonsensical, moralistic lines. At the head of the parade stood Timothy Dwight, a grandson of the famous old Calvinist preacher Jonathan Edwards. Serving as president of Yale from 1795 to 1817, Dwight sent numerous graduates as clergymen into the Connecticut Valley and all points westward, eagerly dispensing a fresh dose of Christian doctrine and duty.[14]

Congregationalist clergymen became key players in the so-called Second

Great Awakening, a revivalistic fervor that swept across America during the first four decades of the nineteenth century. As Baptists, Methodists, and Disciples of Christ joined the evangelical army, they urged a style of public declaration of religious conversion that is still practiced in some evangelical quarters. Utterly new in the early years of the nineteenth century, this kind of churchmanship bred new techniques of passionate, colloquial oratory, emotionally charged audience participation, and prolonged camp meetings. At the parish level, one of Timothy Dwight's protégés, Lyman Beecher, mastered the revivalist art in Litchfield, Connecticut; the master of evangelistic tours was a former upstate New York lawyer, Charles Grandison Finney.[15]

Revivalists emphasized personal sin and spiritual conversion ("saved souls"), but all the while remained true to an older Puritan mentality that sought to impose social values. "As latter-day Puritans," explains Martin Marty, "they followed their fathers in the habit of tending to claim a monopoly on morality." They were motivated in large measure by a "postmillennial" belief that their work toward a moral world would prepare the way for the Second Coming of Christ and his reign of justice and peace for a thousand years. In 1831 the masthead of the *New York Evangelist* announced that the editors would be concerned primarily with revivals, doctrinal issues, and general "religious intelligence"; in 1835 they extended their purposes to "practical godliness" and "human rights."[16]

At worst, this evangelical view of the world reasserted old Puritan taboos against gambling and Sabbath abuse and created new taboos against dancing, strong drink, profanity, and any activity or place that allowed them. At best, it generated crusades on behalf of women's rights and against the evils of slavery, inadequate diet, and disease. Evangelicals often debated, and sometimes divided, over these issues.[17] But while they disagreed with each other over the means of bringing Christ's kingdom to earth, they occasionally linked arms with the very people whose theological liberalism they had rejected in the first place.

For all their ideological differences, rational Unitarians and reformist evangelicals preached a similar ethic. Unitarian William Ellery Channing, whom Emerson once called the "bishop" of early Transcendentalism, worked for "the elevation of men into nobler beings" because he believed in "the perfection of human nature";[18] Charles Finney worked toward the millennium because he believed in human perfectibility by divine grace. In practical terms, both amounted to the same thing: a highly moralized concern for self-improvement and an optimistic commitment to the cause of creating a "righteous empire" of spiritual, moral, and physical health. From this marriage of evangelical and liberal opinion, a sports creed was born in mid-nineteenth-century America.

Henry Ward Beecher, the most popular preacher of the day, exemplified that new birth. For years he lived under the shadow of his father's Calvinistic doctrines and moralistic precepts. Laden with morbid fears of damnation, as a "wretched" youth he was so hesitant of speech that he could hardly be understood. Upon graduating from Amherst College, he followed the line of least resistance to Cincinnati, entering Lane Theological Seminary, where his father had recently become president. Finally rejecting his father's stern teachings about human depravity and damnation, in 1839 Beecher became pastor of the Second Presbyterian Church of Indianapolis. His early sermons reflected a theology strikingly more moderate than his father's, but still rather harsh, narrowly anti-intellectual, and ethically puritanical. In his first book of sermons, published in 1844, Beecher railed against idleness, gambling, prostitution, intemperance, theaters, circuses, horse races, and various other popular forms of amusement. His zealous defense of traditional values—industry and thrift, purity and piety—must have made his old father proud.[19]

Beecher's message appealed to wealthy Bostonians and New Yorkers, whose cultures were being disrupted by the strange ways of Irish and German immigrants. In 1847 Beecher received calls from two prominent Boston churches and from the newly organized Plymouth Church in Brooklyn. Although reluctant to leave the revivalist opportunities in the West, he accepted the appointment at Plymouth Church. There he remained for forty years, to the end of his life preaching and lecturing to vast audiences, writing essays, and editing a newspaper for thousands of readers. He was a key figure in the transformation of nineteenth-century American Protestantism from an other-worldly to a this-worldly perspective, from evangelical dogmatism to a liberal middle-class emphasis on self-reliance, Darwinian science, and progressive social attitudes.[20]

No doubt the cosmopolitan culture of Brooklyn and New York contributed to the shaping of Beecher's views. His attitudes toward sports and amusements began to change in the 1850s. For purposes of health as well as pleasure, he recommended "muscular games" and "various wholesome exercises" for city youths. He admitted to a change of attitude toward billiards and bowling. Earlier he had denounced them; now he praised their "gentle excitement and exercise." Although he still lamented their associations with gambling and strong drink, he stood far removed from his father's negative judgments. "There is no more natural thirst in rolling ten-pins," Beecher observed, "than in hoeing in a flower-garden."[21]

Beecher even confessed to his congregation that he now did the "naughty" thing of regularly reading not only about prizefights but also about the training habits of the contestants. As usual, his confession introduced an admonition. Just as boxers refrained from dietary and sexual excess in preparation for their fights, Beecher wanted Christians to follow the Pauline injunction to be "temperate in all things" in order to win the "incorruptible" crown.[22] Until a sex scandal ruined him, Henry Ward Beecher was a walking, talking testimony to the compatibility of religion and sport.

## Broad Doctrines and Broad Shoulders

Some called this marriage of religion and sport "muscular Christianity," a term imported from Victorian England. It was first associated with a liberal Anglican clergyman, novelist, and social reformer named Charles Kingsley. A man of immense nervous energy and strong opinions, Kingsley liked nothing more than to hike for miles in the face of a blustery wind, or to ride, row, fish, or hunt all day. Once he impulsively walked from Cambridge to London, fifty-two miles, in a single day. As one of his contemporaries shrewdly observed, Kingsley "would probably have been a gladiator if he had not been a Christian. He revels in the description of every species of athletic exercise and desperate strife. Accordingly, all his heroes are men of surpassing animal strength, all bone and muscle, marvels of agility, boiling over with exulting and abounding life, and usually miracles of physical beauty likewise."[23]

Yet Kingsley was much more than a man of raw energy and physical activity. He was a friend and student of essayist Thomas Carlyle and of "Broad Church" (liberal) theologian Frederick Denison Maurice. From Carlyle he learned the virtues of self-reliance and courage; in the spirit of Maurice, he practiced tolerance and service for humanity, and for a time considered himself a Christian Socialist. In novels such as *Yeast* (1848), *Alton Locke* (1850), *Hypatia* (1853), *Westward Ho!* (1855), and *Two Years Ago* (1857), Kingsley demonstrated an infectious enthusiasm for God and country,[24] and for social justice as well as sport. Versatility incarnate, he served as the first professor of modern history at Cambridge University.

Kingsley's varied skills and interests became obscured after the invention of the phrase "muscular Christianity" by a London reviewer, T. C. Sandars, in 1857. Kingsley's latest novel, *Two Years Ago*, was "spreading the knowledge and fostering the love of a muscular Christianity," declared Sandars. "His ideal is a man who fears God and can walk a thousand miles in a thousand hours—who, in the language which Mr. Kingsley has made popular, breathes God's free air on God's rich earth, and at the same time can hit a woodcock, doctor a horse, and twist a poker round his fingers." Confronted with that rather eccentric definition, Kingsley rejected "muscular Christianity" as "a painful, if not offensive, term," an "impertinent" tag that could best be dispensed with.[25]

Yet the term stuck, and with a vengeance with the popularity of *Tom Brown's Schooldays,* published in the same year that the term "muscular Christianity" was coined.[26] Tom Brown, a creation of Kingsley's friend, Thomas Hughes, enjoyed the pleasures of "big-side" football, cricket, hare-and-hound games, and occasional fistfights at Rugby School. In Hughes's story, headmaster Dr. Thomas Arnold warmly encouraged athletics as a means of teaching teamwork, discipline, and sportsmanship. Actually, Arnold was much more concerned with academic studies and the spiritual aspects of Christian gentlemanliness than with sports during his headmastership at Rugby (1828–1842). Hughes simply put his own mid-Victorian enthusiasm for sports into the person of Dr. Arnold.[27]

At Tom Brown's Rugby School, team games, godliness, and good learning lived comfortably together. After Rugby, Tom Brown enjoyed more of the same at Oxford University.[28] Games tended to overwhelm the piety and the scholarship, convincing at least one historian that Hughes "severely distorted" Charles Kingsley's ideals of Christian manliness.[29] The supposed distortion escaped Kingsley, however, for he himself thought competitive sport a boon to moral and spiritual values. Expounding a theme that was soon to become commonplace, he declared that games contributed "not merely to physical, but to moral health." On the playing fields, boys acquired virtues that no prayers or books could provide, insisted Kingsley: "not merely daring and endurance, but, better still, temper, self-restraint, fairness, honour, unenvious approbation of another's success, and all that 'give and take' of life which stand a man in good stead when he goes forth into the world, and without which, indeed, his success is always maimed and partial."[30]

That muscular Christian "games ethic" thrived in Britain's elite private schools (called "public" schools because of their origins), such as Rugby, Winchester, Marlborough, Eton, and Harrow.[31] As those same schools produced the officers and administrators of the British Empire, Britons transplanted cricket, rugby, soccer, tennis, golf, and other games—all organized

**Spires and sport.** Anglican church spires recede into the background as a scrum half awaits the ball from the scrum. A referee in bowler hat, with cane in hand, keeps a watchful eye on this Victorian game of rugby, the favorite expression of moral muscularity at England's elite schools. (From Montague Shearman, *Athletics and Football,* 1899.)

in Britain, "the cradle of modern sport"—throughout the world. Britons not only taught the world to play; they also taught the world *how* to play with moral purpose. To Asia, Africa, the Antipodes, and North America, Tom Brown carried the flag of muscular Christianity in one hand and the Union Jack in the other.[32]

Although politically independent, the United States was highly susceptible to British influence. Long after the American Revolution, the youthful republic remained dependent on British investment, literature, and opinion. Americans fawned over British visitors and chafed at their harsh criticisms of New World habits and values. Evangelical parents regularly served up hefty portions of John Milton and John Bunyan for family consumption;[33] in many homes, Scott and Dickens far outranked Irving and Hawthorne, and Emerson took a back seat to Tennyson.

When old Britain sneezed, it seems, young America caught a cold. Temperance, antislavery, and feminist crusades began in England and made immediate transatlantic passage.[34] Americans also adopted their sports and games from Britain. Even baseball, the game destined to be America's "national pastime," came from the old country, an adaptation of a children's game, rounders. Years later, college boys turned English rugby into American football. When Tom Brown broke from the scrum in midcentury America, he saw nothing but an open field.

All the major American advocates of muscular Christianity admired the "breadth of shoulders, as well as of doctrines" in the Anglican Broad Church coterie of F. D. Maurice, Charles Kingsley, and Thomas Hughes.[35] Edward Everett Hale, for example, lauded Maurice's insistence on reading the Bible "like a man reading a book, and not like a bigot confirming or finding proof for a system"; he cheered Maurice for upsetting the "old-fashioned wings" of the Church of England by "setting the old machinery of the church to work for some vital purposes, as if it were a new dissenting chapel,—instead of letting it mull on in its old self-approved sleepy fashion." Hale also praised the sermons of "Yeast Kingsley" and frequently mentioned Thomas Hughes and Tom Brown.[36]

Educator and clergyman Moses Coit Tyler was even more attuned to England's muscular Christian movement. In the same year that *Tom Brown's Schooldays* and the muscular Christian label appeared, Tyler graduated from Yale; he then briefly attended Yale and Andover theological seminaries. Without a seminary degree, in 1859 he was ordained into the Congregationalist ministry and became an ardent disciple of Henry Ward Beecher. After short tenures at churches in Oswego and Poughkeepsie, New York, Tyler resigned in 1862, dissatisfied with orthodox theology. The frustrated theologian became a successful academic. For fourteen years he taught rhetoric and English literature at the University of Michigan and in 1881 went to Cornell as the nation's first chaired professor of American history. From that prestigious post he introduced graduate students to German critical standards of scholarship, published widely in colonial American literature and history, and led in the founding of the American Historical Association.

In the same year that Tyler took the chair in American history at Cornell he also "took orders" as a deacon in the Protestant Episcopal Church. He was ordained priest in 1883, capping a lifelong combination of Anglophilia and muscular Christianity. After leaving the Congregationalist ministry in the early 1860s, he had gone to Boston's Normal Institute for Physical Education, where he studied Dio Lewis's program of light gymnastics for ten weeks. At Lewis's suggestion, Tyler went to England as a propagandist for physical education. For three years he rubbed shoulders with Maurice,

Kingsley, Hughes, and their muscular Christian kind. In 1865–1866 he saw Kingsley and Hughes part company over a Jamaican rebellion and its savage repression by British colonial authorities. Kingsley defended the colonial governor, Edward Eyre, provoking the liberal Tyler to dismiss Kingsley as a "*once glorious* Muscular Christian" who had become "a toady to Toryism."[37]

For Tyler, though, muscular Christianity remained an obsession. Before he left England in 1866, he sent three essays back to an American journal, the *Herald of Health and Journal of Physical Culture,* extolling English pluck, schoolboy athleticism, and the character-building possibilities in sport.[38] Beginning in April 1867, Tyler contributed nine monthly essays to the *Herald,* fictitious minutes of the "Brawnville Athletic Club" that were speedily revised and published as a separate volume. In all this flurry of literary activity, Tyler displayed unabashed admiration for *Tom Brown's Schooldays,* encouraging one to agree with William Blaike's suggestion that the influence of Tom Brown on American sport "has been greater, perhaps, than that of any other Englishman."[39]

In truth, the supposed English influence on American muscular Christianity needs to be reconsidered. According to most accounts (some explicit, most tacit), the package as well as the label was manufactured in England; shipped out through books, magazines, and transatlantic friendships; and sold whole cloth in the United States. Yet influence never works that decisively, so cleanly dividing active propagators from passive receivers. In weighing influence, one must concentrate more on the persons being influenced than on the source of the idea or movement: what the receivers took, and what they rejected; what they chose to emphasize, and what they muted; what was mere surface dressing, and what was fundamental. In brief, Americans borrowed from England merely the term, not the movement, of muscular Christianity. The movement itself originated simultaneously in Great Britain and the United States, largely because moral leaders in both countries responded similarly to similar urban problems of physical congestion, poor health, and changing attitudes toward religion, work, and play.

In many ways, *Tom Brown's Schooldays* was a book utterly alien to American readers, for whom not even private schools like Exeter and Andover existed in the 1850s. Yankee readers might have been charmed by Rugby School's administrative style, student hierarchy, and playing-field banter, but charm does not influence make. Specific responses to *Tom Brown's Schooldays* suggest that Americans took what they needed, what they wanted for their own purposes, and left the rest alone. For example, Thomas Wentworth Higginson liked Tom Brown because he exemplified a "healthy boys' life" full of inner zest and outdoor games that Higginson thought necessary for "healthier, larger, freer, stronger" souls as well as bodies.[40]

Adding his own spin to Thomas Hughes's original spin on the late Dr. Thomas Arnold, Moses Coit Tyler lauded Arnold for denouncing "as an impiety, the whole system of cultivating one part of our nature at the expense of another." Arnold "fought it in the class-room and in the chapel," declared Tyler; "he talked against it, wrote against it, lectured against it, preached against it." By then, of course, Tyler himself was preaching rather than parsing. As viewed through Tyler's spectacles, Dr. Arnold told his Rugby boys "that good health was of more consequence to them than a knowledge of the Binomial Theorem, or than facility in the manufacture of Latin hexameters; that sound lungs and capable stomachs were the necessary conditions of useful scholarship; and that they would be displeasing him, disappointing their friends, and disobeying God, if they postponed bodily vigors to the mistaken requirements of literary ambition."[41]

For all his liberality of mind, Dr. Arnold said nothing of the sort. He was a man of an earlier age, advocating church reform rather than health reform, academic achievement rather than competitive athletics. But little did it matter to American readers of *Tom Brown's Schooldays*. For their own purposes they happily embellished Thomas Hughes's embellishments of the good Dr. Arnold. From Tom Brown they sought confirmation, not direction.

## The Gospel of Healthy Games

In both Britain and the United States, the muscular Christian movement began not as a passion for competitive games but rather as a concern for healthy diet, fresh air, and firm muscles. Good health seemed especially scarce in England's industrial cities, which grew like mushrooms in the early nineteenth century. Across the sea, industrial and commercial interests combined to enlarge New York City tenfold, from 60,000 inhabitants in 1800 to 600,000 in 1860. During that same period, inland cities such as Pittsburgh, Cincinnati, Cleveland, Detroit, Louisville, and St. Louis tripled or quadrupled in size. For migrants from the rural countryside as well as for immigrants from abroad, the city offered distinct economic and social opportunities. But rapid urban growth also produced problems of food supply, unclean water, inadequate sanitation, and congested housing, not to mention drunkenness, violence, and crime. City life meant, in Edward Everett Hale's words, "the contagion of large masses of men acting on each other" for good or ill.[42]

As the specter of cholera, tuberculosis, and pneumonia stalked the cities, fears of disease nudged out old religious preoccupations. "Ill health and physical weakness," as Anthony Rotundo neatly frames it, "filled men with apprehension, just as sin and spiritual weakness had inspired fear in so many of their ancestors." Medical authority waxed while ministerial authority waned in the city—or so it seemed.[43] Yet the changing of the guard was not so decisive. The day of the Protestant minister was far from past. Ministers led the crusade for hygienic reform by bending earlier views of evil, sin, salvation, and moral duty in the direction of the gospel of health.

They thought of ill health as an evil to be combated, a demonic force to be defeated. "Next to Satan and Beelzebub, the two great enemies of mankind are dyspepsia and the headache. Keep clear of them!" declared a religious magazine editor to a group of Brooklyn youths. Many of the demons that afflicted the spirit were in fact to be found in the blood and digestive tract, insisted a Massachusetts minister, O. B. Frothingham. Atheism and skepticism, he believed, could best be countered not by consultation and prayer in the vestry room, but rather by a better diet, a run in the fields, or a workout in a gymnasium.[44]

Health crusaders considered the body a sacred temple of God, requiring regular attention and cleansing. Admittedly, some diseases were unavoidable, but most physical debility could be traced to a violation of nature's laws pertaining to proper diet, sufficient exercise, and cleanliness. J. C. Holbrook, trained both medically and theologically, thought sickness a sin "when by any possibility" it could be avoided. Henry Ward Beecher joined the refrain. "Far be it from me to say that all sickness is disgraceful," he observed, but then insisted in the next breath that sickness defiled the temple of God, wrecked its roof, shattered its statues, and cast down its pillars. "Sickness is a sign of disobedience and sin," concluded Beecher, "and good health is a sign of obedience and virtue."[45]

Concurring in this health-based dualism of sin and salvation, Moses Coit Tyler observed that to grow up "puny, frail, sickly, mis-shapen, homely" was to sin against "the Giver of the body." Round shoulders and narrow chests were "states of criminality." Dyspepsia was a modern form of heresy; a headache signaled infidelity. "It is as truly a man's moral duty to have a good digestion, and sweet breath, and strong arms, and stalwart legs, and an erect bearing," declared Tyler, "as it is to read his Bible, or say his prayers, or love his neighbor as himself." To Tyler, the muscular Christian creed was brief but sublime:

> All attainable health is a duty.
> All avoidable sickness is a sin.[46]

In good revivalistic fashion, preachers of the gospel of good health opened wide the gates of heaven, inviting everyone to partake of salvation. Folks rich or poor, young or old, male or female could turn from their "sinful" unhealthy ways to claim the blessings of Nature and Nature's God. This emphasis on the freedom and power of the human will produced a kind of "physical Arminianism," as one historian phrases it: "a belief that bodily salvation might be open to all who struggled to win it, and that disease and early death were not an ineradicable part of the earthly passage." Claimants of that "bodily salvation" became in turn "physiological missionaries, bearers of a light man's burden to spread the gospel of health to the gluttonous and indolent heathen of the world."[47]

Of all the "physiological missionaries" roving the land, Moses Coit Tyler was the one most ready to put old religious concepts and structures at the service of this new gospel. In his *Brawnville Papers,* Tyler proposed that every village with two churches should simply combine the two congregations for worship in one church, and convert the other building into a gymnasium. Regular exercise would render men and women more prayerful, more charitable, and more virtuous, promised Tyler, because they would then have "a more regular supply of the gastric fluids, and less torpidity in the liver, and fewer obstructions in the intestinal canal." Most of all, people needed "the grace of a vigorous circulation and a sound digestion."[48]

Not surprisingly, Tyler's fictitious Brawnville minister was an outrageously idealized muscular Christian who could "out-walk, out-run, out-jump, out-skate, out-swim, out-fish, out-hunt, and out-preach" anyone in his neck of the woods. With consummate charm and presumably with sweet breath and graceful physique, he enticed the young men of his parish to participate in gymnastic exercises, boating, and ball games.[49] Yet Tyler's heart was not in competitive sports. He well knew the English emphasis on games for the building of character, but little of that spirit lived in Brawnville. Nor did the pursuit of sport for the sheer enjoyment of it. For Tyler, sports were mostly useful for healthy exercise.

That attitude was common among the early American advocates of muscular Christianity. The Reverend Dr. Kirk of Boston, for example, valued "all gymnastic exercises," but "chiefly as they strengthen the muscles which keep the spine erect and the chest expanded." Gym "workouts" were all well and good, observed the editor of the *Herald of Health,* M. L. Holbrook, but they failed to spark enthusiasm in youth. Holbrook recommended baseball and cricket games not only because throwing, catching, batting, and running gave "an almost infinite variety and intensity to muscular exertion," but also because athletic games were fun and therefore attractive to young people. "In all our efforts toward physical culture," Holbrook reminded his health-hungry readers, "we should not forget the more completely we can make our exercises a sport, a play, and pleasurable, the more likely we will be to make them useful."[50]

No one had to convince Thomas Wentworth Higginson of the enjoyable nature of sport. As the youngest of ten children of a prosperous Boston merchant, he was given free rein on his play impulses. True to his Puritan heritage, however, he grew up as a high-achieving, earnest sort of fellow. In his youth he read voraciously, entered Harvard at the age of thirteen, and four years later graduated second in his class. In 1847 he finished a further course of theological study at Harvard, and for the next fourteen years served as a minister of Unitarian churches in Newburyport and Worcester, Massachusetts. Unable to "settle down into the quiet though noble duties of a minister," he craved action, "unbounded action" in public causes.[51] Prior to the Civil War, he plunged into virtually every liberal reform movement of the day, crusading for temperance, women's suffrage, the abolition of slavery, school reform, and health reform.

Amidst all these good works, Higginson regularly rekindled his love of play. The more intense the work, the greater his need for the refreshment that came from hiking in the mountains, paddling around in a boat, swimming in the river, playing on a cricket field, or exercising in a gym. While pastor of the Free Church in Worcester, he organized a boat club and arranged open-country walks for his parishioners. He also served as president of Worcester's athletic club, skating club, and cricket club. Once he played all day in a cricket match, then took a swim in the river before dinner. He was a most unusual minister.[52]

Yet Higginson not only exemplified muscular Christianity; he also articulated its theoretical basis and implications. From 1858 to 1862 he contributed nine essays to a newly founded journal of opinion, the *Atlantic Monthly,* hanging the twin banners of health and athletics high for all to see. The first essay, "Saints, and Their Bodies," constituted a definitive turning point in the long history of an uneasy relationship between religion and sport. In a somewhat disorderly but nonetheless effective fashion, Higginson brought "physical vigor and spiritual sanctity" together, rejecting the view that "athletic capacity" was "in inverse ratio to the sanctity" expected of Christians.[53]

No one could question the compatibility of Christianity and health reform, but sport was quite another matter. Anticipating Thorstein Veblen's later dismissal of athletics as a form of arrested development, some critics accused Higginson of irresponsibly promoting "boyish" games that were neither wholesome nor useful. "Athletic sports are 'boyish,' are they? Then they are precisely what we want," Higginson retorted. "We Americans certainly do not have much boyhood under the age of twenty, and we must take it afterwards or not at all." Shrewdly he turned the accusation into an accolade. Athletics refresh the mind and renew the muscles, leaving the athlete free, insisted Higginson, "as boys and birds are free."[54]

Boys and birds are especially free in nature, and Higginson favored outdoor activities and games. A child of the romantic movement and a friend of Emerson and Thoreau, he frequently hiked and camped in the White Mountains of New Hampshire and on Mt. Katahdin in Maine. Water and field sports, not indoor gymnastics, attracted him most. Whether organized or unorganized, sport in the open air, under the sun, allowed Nature to work on the athlete "by indirection," Higginson believed. As he saw it, one could "meet Nature on the cricket-ground or at the regatta; swim with her, ride with her, run with her, and she gladly takes you back once more within the horizon of her magic, and your heart of manhood is born again into more than the fresh happiness of the boy."[55]

Higginson retained that boyish enthusiasm for nature and sport for the duration of his long life. In 1862 he bade farewell to the Unitarian ministry and went off to command a regiment of African-American volunteers in the Civil War. Two years later he returned home, wounded by a shell burst, and immediately took up sailing, rowing, swimming, and walking on a daily basis. Despite his "army ailment," he learned to ride the velocipede, and at Newport, Rhode Island, he founded a gymnasium and led a large exercise class. In 1880 he celebrated his fifty-seventh birthday by skating on Fresh Pond, near his old home in Cambridge. All the while he took a "perennial interest" in football games at Harvard, seldom missing a game. Finally, unable any longer to cope with the stadium crowd, he went to Harvard Square each Saturday afternoon to follow the progress of the game on billboards.[56]

At seventy years of age, in 1892, Higginson observed "the immense advance made in athletic habits among us within half a century."[57] During his lifetime, sports had taken organizational shape in terms of codified rules and governing bureaucracies. Though major league baseball and college football were only about fifteen years old by the early 1890s, both thrived and would soon be joined by yet another game, basketball, filling out the team-sports calendar. All the while, track and field athletics, golf, lawn tennis, croquet, and badminton boomed in popularity; and a new winter game called ice hockey attracted attention in the northern states, which had more in common with Canada than with states in the Deep South. Thomas Wentworth Higginson lived to see the United States become what he predicted in the very first essay he wrote in 1858 for the *Atlantic Monthly:* "a nation of athletes."[58] Urban growth, industrial expansion, and commercial ambition caused that dramatic transformation; Higginson and his muscular Christian friends gave it a moral, religious rationale.

# 3

## PRAYING AND PLAYING IN THE YMCA

The ideological trailblazers of muscular Christianity were not run-of-the-mill folk. Most came from highly privileged backgrounds, were trained in the classics at private boys' schools, and received degrees from Oxford or Cambridge, Harvard or Yale. Informed and articulate, they moved comfortably in the company of clergymen, lawyers, and professors, not with laborers and servants.

What Thomas Wentworth Higginson and Moses Coit Tyler announced from their elite perch the Young Men's Christian Association (YMCA) implemented on the Main Street of American life. One can scarcely imagine a more unlikely tandem. Aristocracy meets petite bourgeoisie. Cool High Church kneels down to pray with fiery Low Church, and in the end the Low makes effective what the High could only talk about. In brief, the YMCA democratized the tenets of muscular Christianity.

Not that the YMCA was an easy convert to the gospel of sport. The Y was born of Protestant piety, not playfulness. In England, the land of its birth, it barely endorsed physical exercise programs, leaving organized sports to schoolboys, college men, and sports clubs. Americans chose a different path. In the process, they created a principled but flexible institution run by highly motivated, well-trained personnel, an institution equipped to carry the gospel of sport all over the world.

### Narrow Grooves of Change

Prior to the YMCA's emergence as an athletic center, American muscular Christianity existed on a limited, narrow basis. Regionally, it was confined to the Northeast—largely New England, with substantial support in New York. On the eve of the Civil War, while northern pulpits and periodicals sounded the liberal gospel of human rights and healthy sports, not a peep of muscular Christianity came out of the American South. Finally, two years after the war, a Presbyterian magazine in North Carolina endorsed muscular Christianity's emphasis on "robustness and vigor" as virtues of "those who are strong in the Lord and the power of His might." The Protestant South, destined to emphasize the union of Christianity and muscularity more than any other region in the United States, at first interpreted it wholly in spiritual terms. For Carolina Presbyterians, the movement meant neither sport nor health-oriented gymnastic exercises, but rather a spirituality that found its highest development in "those who neither run uncertainly, nor fight as those who beat the air, but who, in their resolute purpose, take no denial of the blessings they seek, wrestling until their petitions are granted and their peculiar mission thoroughly and successfully accomplished."[1]

The Upper Midwest also failed to produce any notable contributors to early muscular Christian thought. In 1855 a Unitarian minister in Cincinnati, Abiel Abbot Livermore, submitted an essay on gymnastics to the *North American Review* in which he lauded the ancient Greeks for their emphasis on physical as well as mental excellence, and as models of the "strength, health, and beauty" that could now "be quarried out of the rich materials stored away in human nature by a bountiful Creator."[2] Finally, it seemed, muscular Christianity was making its way beyond the Northeast perimeter. In truth, though, Livermore was a graduate of Phillips Exeter Academy and Harvard and a former pastor of a Congregational church in Keene, New Hampshire. He remained only six years in Ohio before returning east to a church in Yonkers, New York, then served for almost thirty years as president of a Unitarian theological school in Meadville, Pennsylvania. That Livermore's was the only significant voice on behalf of muscular Christianity outside the Northeast underscores the regionally specific roots of the movement.

It was also class specific—of, by, and largely for the urban middle class. All the leading advocates of muscular Christianity were white, Anglo-Saxon, and Protestant. They were all college graduates, an elite minority in that day when fewer than 1 percent of all Americans set foot in the halls of higher learning. Moses Coit Tyler's "emaciated, long-haired, big-eyed, pious and mooney young gentlemen, who excelled in Homer and hypochondria" were definitely of the college set. They cultivated prayer, poesy, and dyspepsia, complained Tyler, when they should have been outdoors kicking a football.[3]

Farm boys worked outdoors, and so did native and immigrant laborers who hauled the supplies, dug the foundations, and laid the bricks in the building of urban America. Scarcely did they need directions to exercise and fresh air. Not by coincidence, Thomas Wentworth Higginson's dyspeptic was a man in the retail business who paid an Irishman to split his wood. While that Irishman resisted "rational recreation" and other forms of respectable middle-class behavior, brokers and lawyers joined Higginson's "anxious merchant-prince in his counting-room" and the "bookworm in his library" as peas in the same sedentary pod. Henry Ward Beecher extended the list but retained the middle-class focus. He preached his gospel of good health and wholesome exercise primarily to "professional men—lawyers, physicians, teachers, and above all, ministers of the Gospel."[4]

This middle-class character of muscular Christianity guaranteed a moral veneer on sport as it became organized during the second half of the nineteenth century. Old Puritan prohibitions against gambling, Sunday play, and public drunkenness reappeared under the guise of respectability. Fearful of the great unwashed, some middle-class muscular Christians denounced spectator sports. They also lent a moral imperative to the emerging idealization of amateur athletics. In depicting amateurs as somehow more "pure" than professionals, playing the game for the game's sake rather than for the acquisition of filthy lucre, they obscured a fundamental issue of social class: a laborer-athlete simply could not afford to pay for equipment, time off from work, and travel to distant games without some sort of remuneration. Ignoring that fact by taking the high road of amateurism, muscular Christians in the United States faithfully reproduced a highly class-conscious attitude that was born and bred in Britain.[5]

With Britons the American muscular Christians also shared a pronounced gender bias. Tom Brown's private-school world was a boy's and man's world, dominated by rough, competitive games. In the absence of such severe segregation of the sexes, American males argued all the more vehemently for male Christian muscularity. They assumed that both women and men could benefit from proper diets, healthy walks, and mild gymnastic exercises, but that competitive sports was not the "proper sphere" for a mid-nineteenth-century woman. Even Catharine Beecher, a sister of Henry Ward Beecher and the most outspoken advocate of "robust" womanhood, thought strenuous athletic exercises were "suited to the stronger sex" but not to "the female constitution." A female muscular Christian was a contradiction in terms. "For muscle and manhood run together by nature," wrote Eliza Archard for the *Herald of Health and Journal of Physical Cul-*

*ture;* "But who ever heard of muscular womanhood?" The stronger the emphasis on competitive sport, the greater the identification of muscular Christianity with manliness.[6]

Assumptions of gender differences were so embedded in mid-nineteenth-century American life that muscular Christian apologists seldom confronted them directly.[7] Occasionally they referred to "effeminacy" or "effeminate" qualities, always in a negative, dismissive tone. But usually they simply omitted any references to women in their sermons and essays on behalf of exercise and sport. For examples of "English pluck," Moses Coit Tyler cited the Puritan warrior Oliver Cromwell; the bluff, highly opinionated Dr. Samuel Johnson; pugilist Tom Sayers, bloodied but not beaten; and a Scotsman whose missionary son was eaten by cannibals. Men, not women, exemplified pluck just as surely as men dominated the heroic tales from ancient Greece and Rome, "when the poets, statesmen, artists, orators, and scholars of the age," as Tyler put it, "were men of magnificent athletic proportions."[8] Trained in the classics, Tyler, Higginson, and their kind instinctively turned to Greek boxers Pythagoras and Cleanthes and to wrestler-philosopher Plato as "examples of the union of saintly souls and strong bodies."[9] In turning to the Greeks, they selected male exemplars whom they had studied under male authors and professors.

Yet the heavy male flavor of Christian muscularity derived from something more than the Victorian, patriarchal temper of the times. Muscular Christianity represented a reaction against the "feminization" of American middle-class culture that occurred during the first half of the nineteenth century. As American males attended to the competitive worlds of politics and business, they largely left family and religious matters to the women. Child rearing became less patriarchal and more maternally affectionate and nourishing; children came to be seen as innocents in need of emotional support and instruction rather than as little reprobates doomed to hell because of original sin. As Calvinism languished on the hearth, not merely in the minds of theologians, the image of Christ changed from a stern, divine authority to a meek-and-mild human figure, a sacrificial lamb strikingly similar to female victims in much of the art and literature of the day.[10]

Although male hierarchies of ministers, deacons, and elders remained intact, women increasingly played key roles in the day-to-day life of Protestant churches. Women far outnumbered men as revival converts and in church attendance. They taught Sunday School, joined voluntary societies, collected money for missionaries, assisted at revivals, visited the sick, and generally supported the minister in ways that busy businessmen and male public figures could not or would not. After an extended visit to the United States in the late 1820s, British traveler Frances Trollope observed that she "never saw, or read, of any country where religion had so strong a hold upon the women, or a slighter hold upon the men."[11]

At midcentury, muscular Christians attempted to reestablish their grip on the religious sphere, or at the least to dispel the image of a weak and timid Jesus who could attract only women and effeminate men. To that end, they framed their case in unmistakably male terms. Health was one of their motives, easily recognized; hubris was another, largely hidden from view. Muscular Christianity denoted a certain kind of manliness, having as much to do with gender as with religion and sport. Appropriately, it was best exemplified in the Young Men's Christian Association, yet another Anglo-American movement that originated in the mid-nineteenth century.

## Enthused but Not Amused

Like so much of modern sport, the YMCA began in England, in response to the urbanization that accompanied the industrial revolution. Founded in London in 1844, the Y was one of many evangelical alliances, associations, institutes, self-improvement societies, and city missions catering to the moral and religious needs of young men recently arrived in the city.[12]

The prime mover, George Williams, was the son of a Somerset farmer. After an apprenticeship with a local draper, at age twenty he went to London and found a job as a clerk in a retail cloth shop. London threw Williams into severe culture shock. Having been reared on a simple chapel diet of daily prayers, Bible classes, temperance meetings, and exhortations to sexual purity, he found the city an ungodly, intimidating place. In contrast to the small, quiet village of his West Country youth, London was populous and noisy, brimming with variety and options. For Williams, those attractions amounted to "intemperance and dissolute living," temptations to be resisted. Taking refuge in an upstairs room provided by his employer, he soon began meeting regularly with other young clerks and apprentices at the firm who shared his provincial, religious background. They found mutual support in prayer, Bible study, and discussions. Encouraged by their boss, George Hitchcock, the young men distributed gospel tracts in the vicinity of the firm, and for a while called themselves the Drapers' Evangelical Association.

For three years they functioned without formal organization, but in early June 1844, a dozen or so members of the group agreed to designate themselves the Young Men's Christian Association. Their purpose, in the words of the minutes of their meeting, was to arouse converted men "to a sense of their obligation and responsibility as Christians in diffusing religious knowledge to those around them either through the medium of prayer meetings or any other meetings they think proper."[13] Thus, from the outset the evangelical purpose of the YMCA was clear and firm, the methods flexible.

Too flexible for some. Most self-improvement societies of that day set up small libraries ("reading rooms") and sponsored lectures to propagate their views, but several members of the Y adamantly opposed those "secular" measures. One, William Edwyn Shipton, railed for years against any dilution of the Y's central function as a center of Bible study, prayer, and missionary work. Deeply suspicious of education, Shipton exhorted London Y leaders to "confine themselves entirely to those religious agencies which were peculiarly the work of the Association." The YMCA, he insisted, should "seek to do first of all, last of all, and entirely, SPIRITUAL WORK" until all those sinners "now scattered up and down this naughty world" were brought into the fold. George Hitchcock agreed. Believing that one should pray before sitting down to read a book (for divine guidance through the book's erroneous parts), he wanted "as few secular things as possible" in the first YMCA buildings he helped furnish.[14]

If libraries and lectures were suspect to some early Y leaders, "mere amusements" were anathema to all. In November 1845, the first annual report of the London YMCA beckoned young men "to the library of useful knowledge, rather than to cards and billiards, the cigar divan and concert-room, the theatre, and the seducting and polluting retreat." The Y, after all, existed to keep young men off the "broad path" of city pleasures that led to destruction. To bring those worldly games and recreational activities into the YMCA parlor would risk ruin, or so the founders believed. Confronted with a proposal for a chess room in the Leamington branch of the YMCA, W. E. Skipton in 1862 had the last word in this opening round of debate: "I do not think it is part of the Association's work to provide any man with amusements."[15]

This negative attitude, common among the English founders of the YMCA, derived in part from a native Puritan tradition that included John Bunyan and seventeenth-century dissent, John Wesley and eighteenth-century Methodism, and Hannah More and early nineteenth-century evangelicalism—all fearful that frivolous pleasures and carnal allurements would damn the soul.[16] More immediate inspiration came from abroad. English Congregationalists, Presbyterians, Methodists, and evangelical Anglicans (the prime sources of YMCA enthusiasm) all responded warmly to the intensely personal, evangelistic, and moralistic message of an American revivalist, Charles G. Finney. They devoured Finney's *Lectures to Professing Christians* (1837) and *Lectures on Revivals of Religion* (1840); in 1849–1850, and again in 1858–1860, they eagerly welcomed his evangelistic crusades to the British Isles.[17]

Charles G. Finney was their kind of man, speaking their kind of message. From their lower-middle rungs on the pecking order of British society, they applauded Finney's condemnation of "parties of pleasure, balls, novel-reading, and other methods of wasting time." Christians should happily claim the title of "a peculiar people," Finney assured them, "and thus pour contempt on the fashions of the ungodly in which they are dancing their way to hell."[18] According to George Williams's biographer, the secret of Williams's "certainty of belief" and "absorbing passion for souls and for the work that wins souls" lay in Finney's emphasis on prayer, conversion, and holy living.[19] Finney's teachings were certainly one of the keys to the London YMCA's niggardly attitudes towards amusements.

In search of familiar moorings among the fleshpots, religious young men from the hinterlands were attracted, not deterred, by the strict standards of the YMCA. By the time of the Great Exhibition of 1851, seven branches of the Y were thriving in London, and fourteen more were spread around the United Kingdom. Several American and Canadian visitors to the Great Exhibition took the opportunity to examine the Y at first hand. Duly impressed, they returned home determined—as an editor of a Boston Congregationalist magazine put it—"to transplant it hither." In November 1851, the first YMCA in North America was founded in Montreal; just a month later, Boston seized the honor of having the first in the United States. In the early summer of 1852 a YMCA was organized in New York City for "the improvement of the spiritual, mental and social condition of young men" and "to promote evangelical religion among the young men of this city and its vicinity." By 1856 no fewer than fifty-six YMCAs could be found in North American cities, from Halifax, Nova Scotia, and Savannah, Georgia, on the east coast to San Francisco and Stockton, California, on the west.[20]

As local branches proliferated they were everywhere the same in evangelical intent but everywhere different in emphasis and clientele. In Louisville, Kentucky, for example, diverse interests converged on the creation of a YMCA in 1853. Protestant ministers wanted evangelistic assistance in winning the city's "irreligious element" to Christianity, while local businessmen welcomed the Y's emphasis on discipline and hard work as antidotes to the spirit of indolence that seemed to threaten the economic life of Louisville, and the city's German Protestant community sought institutional support for the moral and intellectual improvement of young German immigrants.[21]

Then as now, the YMCA offered something for everybody. In addition to Bible classes, prayer groups, and evangelistic services, most Y's provided reading rooms, public lectures, and debating societies. Before they bought their own buildings and converted them into sleeping quarters for homeless or lonely young men, local branches posted lists of respectable boarding houses beside lists of employment opportunities. They also assisted charitable organizations, especially for poor relief and the more occasional flood relief. Further diversifying in a way that the YMCA in England never did, American branches linked up with colleges and universities. The great day of the YMCA student movement lay in the post–Civil War era, but campus organizations appeared in 1858 at the universities of Michigan and Virginia.[22]

An English visitor to the United States saw these innovations as evidence of the "peculiar practicalness of endeavour" that characterized the American YMCA on the eve of the Civil War. Americans were developing "more of the secular element than in England," thought Thomas H. Gladstone, a patron of the London YMCA.[23] Had he inquired more closely, Gladstone would have even found a more secular, practical attitude toward "fashionable amusements." As a new YMCA organ of opinion, the *Young Men's Magazine*, put it in 1857, amusements like card playing, dancing, and novel reading were best confined to one's juvenile years and the privacy of the home, but these amusements were useful—and therefore reluctantly to be accepted—if they restored the mind and body for work. Otherwise, they were a waste of time, "and time wasted is a plunge downward," added the editor as he maneuvered back onto a familiar Puritan track.[24]

The "amusement question" was hardly settled prior to the Civil War. In 1867, at the twelfth annual North American YMCA convention, a Methodist clergyman threatened to withdraw his church from Y sponsorship "if a resolution favoring amusements were adopted." Reportedly, the threat was "received with anything but favor," but no pro-amusements resolution was adopted. As late as 1875 the editors of a national YMCA journal, *The*

*Watchman,* reminded their readers that the purpose of the Association was "not the providing of even rational, or elevating amusements."[25]

## Lords of the Gym

Sociable amusement was one thing; a physical activity program was a different matter. In the 1850s a number of voices insisted that a physical dimension be added to the YMCA's moral, spiritual, and intellectual emphases.[26] The loudest, yet most reasonable arguments came from Brooklyn, New York, where muscular Christian apologist Henry Ward Beecher pastored the Plymouth Church. "There ought to be gymnastic grounds and good bowling alleys, in connection with reading rooms" in every YMCA in order "to give to the young men of our cities the means of physical vigor and health, separate from temptations and vice," declared Beecher. Yet he saved his finest nudge for a gathering of Boston YMCA friends in 1857. Impishly observing that the Boston Y regularly sponsored two "amusements," lectures and social teas, he lauded starchy-stiff Bostonians for being ahead of New York and Philadelphia in these matters. But he wanted more: health-giving activities, physical exercise that put "muscle on a man." Why shouldn't the YMCA promote boating, running, quoiting, and javelin throwing? All would be "advantageous and innocent in practice," promised Beecher.[27]

In 1860 the leaders of more than 200 American and Canadian YMCAs, representing some 25,000 members, gathered in New Orleans for their seventh annual convention. They unanimously agreed on "the importance and necessity of a place of rational and innocent amusement and recreation for young men, especially in large cities and towns," and resolved that each local branch of the YMCA should build a gymnasium with all due haste. Unfortunately, that resolution fell victim to the guns that opened fire on Fort Sumter. During the Civil War, as the YMCA helped provide food, shelter, clothing, and spiritual counsel for combatants, the gymnasium question was momentarily put aside.[28]

At the end of the war, in 1865, most YMCAs were located in church basements or in some downtown rented building. Not a single one had a gymnasium. By 1890, however, about 400 YMCA gyms dotted the North American landscape, half of them with paid supervisors of physical activity. This phenomenal growth of buildings and professionally trained physical directors transformed the YMCA into the institution that we know today.[29]

The New York City YMCA led the way. Its director, Robert R. McBurney, a Protestant immigrant from Northern Ireland, barely waited for the smoke to clear from the Civil War battlefields before he launched a fund-raising campaign for the construction of a magnificent building on Twenty-third Street at Fourth Avenue. He especially wanted a gym. Knowing that to be a novel, controversial idea, McBurney directed a committee to prepare a "scientific" survey of the moral and physical dangers facing young men in the city in order to make apparent the need for physical fitness. In 1866 he orchestrated a change in the constitution of the New York YMCA, making it the first Y in the world to use the word "physical" to describe one of its fundamental goals of self-improvement.[30]

In the autumn of 1869 new YMCA buildings, with gyms, opened in Washington and San Francisco. Finally, in December of the same year, the New York building officially opened to much fanfare as "the only one planned, erected, and equipped" for physical activity. It was certainly the largest and finest built of the three. Whereas Washington's "magnificent building" was completed for $200,000 and San Francisco's (with a bowling alley as well as a gym) for just $57,000, New York's four-story stone edifice cost $487,000. For years it reigned as the model for YMCA architecture. Yet by today's standards, the gym was a mere exercise room, small and poorly equipped. Seventy feet long and fifty feet wide, it was cluttered with a wooden horse, parallel bars, a springboard, and ladders at various angles from the walls. Flying rings, pulleys, a trapeze, and a punching bag hung suspended from the ceiling. Lumpy mats covered portions of the floor reserved for wrestling and tumbling.[31]

New Yorkers apparently loved it. Despite a silly warm-up drill in which participants lined up, marched around the room, and stopped at designated painted circles on the floor (a kind of musical chairs with neither music nor chairs), the gym was regularly filled to overflowing. According to McBurney's annual report of 1870, only the Y's bowling alleys rivaled the gym in popularity. By 1876 gym attendance averaged 300 men daily; all 879 "dressing boxes" (open lockers) were rented, and more were needed.[32]

Meanwhile, enthusiasm for the gym grew slowly but surely throughout North America. In 1872 the Boston YMCA purchased the Tremont Gymnasium on Eliot Street, a large, old building that had long been used as a commercial, fee-paying place of exercise for urban "gentlemen of the ledger." In the following year, the oldest YMCA on the continent, Montreal, completed the construction of fine new quarters. A spacious, well-equipped gymnasium set Montreal at the head of a Canadian gymnasium mania that would take off in the 1880s.[33]

Unique circumstance caused the Chicago YMCA to lag behind in the race to facilitate "physical work." In brief, that circumstance was the heavy presence of revivalist Dwight L. Moody. From a rural village in western Massachusetts, Moody first made his way to Boston, where he worked as a boot and shoe salesman, joined the YMCA, and underwent a religious conversion. He moved to Chicago in 1856 in quest of economic opportunity, and virtually became a charter member of the Chicago YMCA at its birth in 1858. Moody energetically plunged into the evangelistic work of the downtown Y. He led noontime prayer meetings, distributed gospel tracts on the streets, and bluntly accosted street people and church people alike with the question "Are you a Christian?"[34]

In 1860 Moody abandoned his business as a leather-goods salesman to devote himself entirely to religious work. For the next decade he worked in and for the YMCA. As an agent of the Association, he ministered to the wounded and dying during the Civil War. For four years, 1866–1870, he served as president of the Chicago Association's board of directors. From wealthy businessmen, including copper magnate William E. Dodge, banker J. P. Morgan, meat packer J. F. Armour, and industrialist Cyrus H. McCormick, he raised money for the construction of three YMCA buildings (the first two were destroyed by fire).

Through the YMCA Moody met the man who would be singularly instrumental in his turn to evangelistic ministry. In 1870, at an international Y convention in Indianapolis, the ability and zeal of songleader Ira D. Sankey convinced Moody to invite him to Chicago. They worked well together, and in 1873 departed for a successful two-year gospel crusade in Britain. Returning home, they renewed the revival fires stirred earlier by Charles G. Finney throughout North America. Yet Moody remained a lifelong friend of the YMCA, and on several occasions raised funds for specific branches. To the end of his days he claimed that the YMCA did "more, under God, in developing me for Christian work than any other agency."[35]

Moody left the Chicago YMCA structurally and ideologically committed to evangelism, not to "physical work." He and Robert McBurney once engaged in a public debate over the best means of appealing to young men. McBurney wanted a gym; Moody wanted more Bible classes, sermons, and edifying lectures. He got his way. As one visitor recalled, the "principal feature" of the Chicago YMCA building was a huge lecture hall filled to capacity each Sunday for a sermon by Moody. None of the funds he raised ever went into the building of a gymnasium.[36]

The first general secretary of the Chicago YMCA, A. T. Hemmingway, was a man after Moody's heart: warmly supportive of evangelistic activities, cool to demands for programs of physical exercise. "Such work," recalled a Chicagoan years later, "was known as worldly activities."[37] Under great pressure from his members, however, Hemmingway appointed a committee to study the feasibility of going the gym route. Finally, in 1879 a second-floor room formerly used for prayer meetings was converted into a gymnasium. By then, Moody himself was recommending "a gymnasium, classes, medical lectures, social receptions, music and all unobjectionable agencies" rather than "simply evangelistic meetings" in the YMCA.[38] But his change of mind came too late to erase the shabbiness of the Chicago gym. An old-timer later sadly remembered it as "a large, dirty, smoky walled room with a few parallel bars, rings attached to ropes fastened to the ceiling, and a few pairs of dirty boxing gloves. That was all."[39]

While Chicago dragged its feet, other Y's dashed ahead in the building or renting of gyms and in the hiring of "physical directors" to supervise their use. In supervision, as in gym construction, the New York YMCA led the way. Shortly after opening its new gym in 1869, the organization hired William E. Wood as the first full-time YMCA physical director. An English immigrant, Wood had owned and operated several commercial gyms in New York before casting his lot with the YMCA. Although he reportedly functioned "without relation to the YMCA [religious] purpose," the earnest, gentlemanly, and physically fit Wood aptly demonstrated the newly emergent image of YMCA manliness.[40]

One of Wood's major concerns was gym safety. In the early years, circus performers, weight lifters, and pugilists found Y gyms cheaper and sometimes better equipped than athletic clubs as places to keep fit between professional engagements. Their flamboyant antics invited imitation.[41] The Boston YMCA was especially vulnerable to mishap because a large troupe of circus performers wintered in the area, filling the Tremont Gymnasium with circus acrobats, tumblers, and trapeze artists practicing their stunts. In the Tremont's very first year as a YMCA site, a young man killed himself trying to perform a double forward somersault off a springboard. Shortly thereafter the board of directors hired a circus rope walker to supervise the gymnasium, reasoning that a circus man could best curtail circus antics. He lasted just two years; his successor was a retired circus acrobat and tumbler.[42]

In 1876 the Boston YMCA did an about-face, appointing a devout Baptist, Robert J. Roberts, as gymnasium superintendent. A wood turner and mechanic by trade, the twenty-seven-year-old Roberts had achieved some local fame as a rower, swimmer, gymnast, and weight lifter. In 1864 he joined the Tremont Gymnasium (eight years before the YMCA took it over), and often went across the street to work out with heavy weights at a private gymnasium run by Dr. George B. Windship. Only five feet five inches tall with a forty-three-inch chest and a thirty-two-inch waist, Roberts proudly lifted 2,200 pounds with a yoke, raised a 120-pound dumbbell over his head with either hand, and dead lifted 550 pounds from the floor with one finger.[43]

Still, when Roberts coined the term "body building," he meant something other than the efforts of a bulky weight lifter. For popular YMCA use, he recommended light, simple apparatus as a compromise between the "fancy gymnastics" of the circus variety and the "heavy work" espoused by Dr. Windship. Pioneering in the use of dumbbells, indoor running tracks, medicine balls, and physical examinations, Roberts urged "safe, easy, short, beneficial and pleasing" exercises for purposes of health and agility. In 1881 he appeared on the program of the YMCA international convention in Cleveland, Ohio, in full gym uniform, demonstrating his dumbbell drill. That was the first time the convention had ever made a place on its program for the gymnasium question, and YMCA historians mark it as the turning point in the Y's larger interest in physical development.[44]

Prior to his address and demonstration, Roberts offered "a fervent and simple prayer," a gesture not lost on his audience. For several years YMCA leaders had feared that the gymnasium was secularizing the Association rather than the Association Christianizing the gym. Roberts's work, coupled with his regular column in *The Watchman,* allayed those fears. He presented himself as a Christian who directed physical activities, not a physical director who happened to be a Christian (or, worse still, non-Christian). As the Boston YMCA secretary happily observed, Roberts was "a Christian worker" who stationed himself "on the floor and mat of the gymnasium primarily to promote the coming of young men into the Christian life."[45]

Before young men could be won to Christianity, however, they had to be enticed into the YMCA itself—and for some YMCA supporters, that was reason enough to build, equip, and supervise gymnasiums. In one case, a gymnasium apparently saved an Association from extinction. The Dayton, Ohio, YMCA began in 1858 only to collapse at the onset of the Civil War. Resurrected in 1870, its membership list later declined so badly that it could scarcely pay the bills. Finally, the secretary identified the problem: there was no incentive for a young man to buy a membership if he was not interested in religion or reading. With only fifty members in 1885, he announced plans for a gymnasium and immediately received membership pledges of $10 each from 300 young men.[46] Practical and idealistic motives blended freely in the YMCA's baptism of the gymnasium.[47]

Yet one should not dismiss the gym mania as simply a way to ensure the institution's existence. Granted, in 1888 most YMCA men agreed with Luther Gulick, who reminded them that the gymnasium should always be a means to the end "of leading men to Christ"; but for evangelicals everything was a means to that end.[48] By the mid-1880s YMCA leaders were affirming, not merely accepting, the gym, and for principled as well as opportunistic reasons. At the annual international convention of 1887, in San Francisco, policy makers bowed to Lord Gym as "an integral part" of the Association's fourfold purpose: "Physically, the gymnasium should be a distinct department of our work; morally, it should be conducted on the purest principles of the Association; intellectually, it should be made educational; spiritually, it should be a place where active and associate members meet and where Christian influence prevails."[49]

## Doing Good with Games

By 1886, some 1,066 YMCA local branches in North America had 101 gymnasiums but only thirty-five physical directors.[50] Likely as not, those directors were all trained in some variation of the "hands-on" method perfected by Robert J. Roberts, who reportedly recruited and trained twenty to thirty instructors at the Tremont Gymnasium in Boston. Probably not one of them had a college degree, much less special religious or professional training. In this regard, they were little different from the first YMCA secretaries.

Beginning in the mid-1880s, secretaries and physical directors embarked on a process of professionalization akin to the route taken by lawyers, doctors, clergymen, and university professors in the late nineteenth century: theoretical study and supervised practical application in professional schools founded specifically for the task.[51] Compared to these other professions, of course, the YMCA functioned humbly. Aspiring secretaries first found training in summer institutes at Lake Geneva, Wisconsin. Then in 1885 an ambitious pastor of a Congregational church in Springfield, Massachusetts, opened a new School for Christian Workers. The original intent was to train YMCA secretaries, Sunday School superintendents, and pastors' assistants, but the Association focus quickly became dominant.[52] In

1890 the name was changed to the International Young Men's Christian Association Training School, in part to distinguish it from a similar new school in Chicago. Later the Springfield school would take on yet another name, Springfield College, and become known for its emphasis on physical education and social work.[53]

Instruction in physical education began in 1887 as a two-year course combining philosophical foundations and practical techniques. To teach the latter, Robert J. Roberts moved—with dumbbells in hand—from Boston to Springfield. For the more theoretical pedagogy, twenty-one-year-old Luther Halsey Gulick joined the staff. Born of missionary parents in Honolulu, Gulick attended Oberlin preparatory school in Ohio and the Sargent School of Physical Training in Cambridge, Massachusetts. Just a year before he accepted the Springfield job, he began medical school at New York University. Concerned primarily with hygiene and exercise for the prevention of disease, he completed his medical degree in 1889 eager to explore "the relation of good bodies to good morals."[54]

He did more than that. To the service of the YMCA (or, as he put it, to Christ) Gulick committed the most reflective, best-read, and widest-ranging mind in the entire history of the Association. During his thirteen-year tenure at Springfield, he taught philosophy, psychology, and history of physical training; physiology, hygiene, and anthropometry (scientific measurements); plus gymnastics and athletics. Students came into his classes with serious plans to be future gym directors; they left with a "recreative" imperative added to their "educative" schemes. Most of all, Gulick sealed the place of the gymnasium with a solid rationale and opened up YMCA thought to a new era by insisting on the potential benefits of athletic competition.

Unfortunately, the issue of athletics brought him into conflict with his Springfield colleague, Robert J. Roberts. The two men were vastly different in temperament and style. Gulick was quick-witted, imaginative, and experimental; Roberts was methodical, conservative, and predictable.[55] They thought differently, especially about the way the YMCA should relate to the competitive sports that were sweeping the country in the 1880s. Roberts forbade any competitive activities in his Boston gym and refused to teach advanced recreational courses at Springfield. He advised young men "*never* to enter competitive sports." At the least, they should refrain until age twenty-two, and then compete only under the care of a doctor and athletic trainer—and without the blessing of the YMCA. The "spirit of competition" should be altogether removed from Y-sponsored activities, argued Roberts. Only if young men learned to exercise for purposes of health rather than "for the sake of competition" would they "live the longer to do better work for God and humanity."[56]

Similarly enthusiastic for health, God's work, and service to humanity, Gulick differed sharply on the place of competition in the grand scheme of things. Sixteen years younger than Roberts, Gulick came of age with competitive rowing, baseball, football, lawn tennis, and a host of lesser sports.[57] A contemporary recalled him as a baseball pitcher with "a swift underhand ball,"[58] but in truth Gulick did not distinguish himself as an athlete. Unlike Roberts, he observed and directed better than he performed, and in the late 1880s he observed that YMCAs all over North America were purchasing or renting nearby open land for baseball and football games, track meets, bicycle races, tennis matches, and horseshoe games. The official historian of the YMCA exaggerated when he said that Gulick "found the Y.M.C.A. doing calisthenics and left it on the basketball court and playing field," but not by much.[59] Gulick found the YMCA timidly stepping onto the playing field, uncertain of its right to be there; from the podium and with the pen, he removed the doubts.

Gulick's effectiveness can best be gauged in the changing character of *The Watchman* and its successor, the *Young Men's Era*. For several years after its first edition in 1874, *The Watchman* carried scattered, infrequent references to gymnasium issues, and even fewer to competitive sports. Early in 1889, a "Physical Department" section appeared, but contained only brief reports from around the nation and took up less than half a column of a three-column page. In October 1889, however, Gulick became editor of the Physical Department section and immediately enlarged it to an entire page. Announcements and scores of games appeared beside reflective essays such as "Athletics in Paul's Writings" by Hartford Theological Seminary professor C. S. Beardsley.[60] The *Young Men's Era* succeeded *The Watchman* in 1890; by the end of 1892 the Physical Department section averaged three to four pages each issue. The issue of December 18, 1892, devoted seven full pages to gymnastics and sports.

Notices of games and scores ranged from handball to pentathlons, but commentary focused primarily on baseball, football, and basketball. For YMCA leaders, baseball was something of a disputed territory. Many agreed with the general secretary of the Cleveland, Ohio, Association, who thought it "worthy of being called our 'national game'" because it was "clean, healthful, invigorating and recreative, both to the player and the spectator." Others refused to endorse baseball as a YMCA-sponsored game because of its "pernicious habits, such as Sabbath playing, betting, drinking and the like," as the Y state secretary of Ohio put it.[61] More subtly, some thought baseball failed to contribute to the well-rounded development of lungs, muscles, and total health that was the hallmark of the Y's physical ideology. Worst of all, baseball was the one team sport that had gone professional, disqualifying it as a game that YMCA leaders could encourage unreservedly. "Professionalism aims at money and even sacrifices health and morals to obtain it," the *Young Men's Era* reminded its readers—for whom health and morals were paramount.[62]

Billy Sunday's story confirmed the YMCA's ambivalence toward baseball.[63] A "rube" from the fields of Iowa, Sunday signed as an outfielder with the Chicago White Stockings in 1883. For five years he wielded a weak bat but displayed good speed and daring on the bases for the White Stockings, then moved on for three more years as a professional ballplayer with Pittsburgh and Philadelphia. As Sunday himself often told the story, one evening in 1887 he and five fellow ballplayers staggered out of a saloon to encounter a noisy brass band making its way down the street to the headquarters of the local Rescue Mission. Sunday followed the band, heard the gospel preached, and was "saved" on the spot. In the classic style of the evangelically converted, he turned his back on alcohol, swearing, gambling, and the theater. Refusing to play any more Sunday baseball, on Sundays he gave inspirational messages to boys at the YMCA in whatever city the team happened to be.

Finally, nudged by a pious wife, Billy Sunday hung up his baseball gear in exchange for an assignment as a YMCA secretary, taking a hefty cut in salary that year to do so. As he followed the revivalist trail blazed by Dwight L. Moody, he kept audiences on the edge of their seats with his athletic antics. According to one observer, Sunday underwent "gruelling exertions," racing back and forth across the podium like a "restless gymnast." Sliding safely home seems to have been his favorite means of illustrating salvation. His favorite homily—"You can't measure manhood with a tape line around the biceps"—was taken right out of the YMCA gym. Warnings about sin and destruction often came in the form of yarns from his hell-raising days in major league baseball.[64]

Unlike baseball, football was a highly respectable campus sport whose tacit professionalism was hidden from view.[65] In the 1880s Americans adapted the British game of rugby into the much rougher, more dangerous game of football.[66] Yet football appealed to YMCA leaders because of its potential for "all around" physical development. Legs and arms, lungs and loins—all were exercised "in the writing and twisting and pushing of the rush line," noted one contributor to the *Young Men's Era*. Unlike baseball, football demanded constant motion and innovation rather than long periods of inactivity punctuated by repetitious moves. Best of all for aspiring middle-class YMCA men, football rewarded hard work—gritty effort more than natural talent.[67]

Strange (or even impossible) as it might now seem, innumerable local YMCAs sponsored football teams in the late nineteenth century. Before equipment, coaching, and insurance became prohibitively expensive, YMCA squads competed against teams from other Y branches, athletic clubs, colleges, prep schools, and seminaries. Leaders endlessly debated the "brutishness" of the game, but a sure sign of the YMCA's acceptance of football appeared in the autumn of 1890, when the Springfield Training School first fielded a team.

Amos Alonzo Stagg, a former football and baseball star at Yale, created and captained the Springfield team. At the outset, Stagg faced the formidable task of finding eleven decent players from a student body that numbered fewer than fifty. He succeeded brilliantly. In its first season, Springfield won five of eight games, finishing with a splendid performance in a 16–10 loss to the national champions, Yale. Facing a much tougher schedule the next year, Springfield won five, lost eight, and tied one. Again led by the quick, stocky Stagg, the 1891 squad averaged a mere 151 pounds; the players were less than five feet, eight inches tall on the average, earning them the nickname of the "Stubby Christians."[68]

More than Gulick's essays, Stagg's athletic exploits and coaching skills momentarily sealed the YMCA's connection to the gridiron. From Springfield, Stagg went directly to the new University of Chicago as athletic director and head football and baseball coach, and from that prominent perch he frequently preached the gospel of games and good sportsmanship.[69] As he explained shortly after arriving at Chicago, years earlier he had gone to Yale intending to become a Presbyterian minister, but had changed his vocational course as he came to see that his opportunities "for doing spiritual good" were better in athletics and student work than in a pastorate. In fact, he "deliberately concluded" that he "would be going away from rather than into the vineyard by being ordained."[70]

Another YMCA worker in the vineyard of the Lord, James Naismith, arrived at Springfield on a route remarkably similar to Alonzo Stagg's. Like Stagg, he grew up in a Presbyterian home (in Ontario, Canada) that was strong on moral precepts; like Stagg, he went off to college (McGill Univer-

sity in Montreal) confidently feeling "called" to study for the Christian ministry. Naismith, too, was a notable athlete, anchoring the front line of McGill's rugby football team even though "it was not thought proper for a 'theolog'" to engage in that sort of activity.[71]

During his undergraduate years, Naismith regularly worked out at the Montreal YMCA, near the McGill campus, and continued to do so during his three years of theological studies at a Presbyterian seminary in Montreal. In conversation with the Montreal YMCA secretary, he began airing the possibility "that there might be other effective ways of doing good besides preaching."[72] Although he finished his program of theological study and in 1890 was licensed for the ministry, the prospect of a career that would combine religion and athletics sent him to Springfield to prepare for YMCA work.

At Springfield Naismith distinguished himself in the classroom as well as on the football field. And he invented basketball—one of the few modern games without ancient roots. In response to Luther Gulick's suggestion that some sort of indoor team competition was needed to fill out the sports calendar between football and baseball seasons, Naismith drew up thirteen simple rules to govern a game that featured the tossing of a soccer ball into peach baskets suspended from the balcony railing at each end of the gym. The first game of basketball was played in December 1891; from Springfield it spread quickly throughout North America, and around the world, by means of YMCA literature and Springfield-trained personnel.[73]

The attractiveness of basketball brought an end to the YMCA argument over competitive sports. As American colleges and high schools took to the game, Luther Gulick observed that Y-sponsored athletics held far more promise than gymnastics because athletics were "more interesting to the average man."[74] While Gulick served as the first head of an Athletic League formed in 1895 to control YMCA competition, he and his colleagues repeatedly reminded themselves that they were promoting physical and spiritual health, not "mere sport as such."[75] Sport, they insisted, was a means to moral ends.

**A game for good.** Dating from a cold day in December 1891, basketball is one of the few games created instantaneously, without a long evolutionary history. As this cartoon suggests, basketball is also one of the few games devised consciously—by Canadian James Naismith—as a means of improving both the health and the morals of its participants. (From the Kautz Family Archives, YMCA of the USA.)

One of those ends was the reassertion of manliness, which seems to have been a constant worry in nineteenth-century America. Despite all the blood and bluster of the Civil War, the American male's "fear of feminization" did not abate. If anything, during the last quarter of the century it intensified among young men who had been too young to fight for the Blue or Gray. By the 1880s and '90s, they could only wonder anxiously if they would have displayed the bravery of their fathers, uncles, and older brothers. Moreover, the rise of corporate government, big business, and the bureaucratic workplace robbed middle-class men of outlets for creative individuality and self-assertion that their fathers had enjoyed. Little wonder that Theodore Roosevelt's vision of "the strenuous life" and heavyweight champion John L. Sullivan's emergence as America's first national sports hero coincided with the YMCA's commitment to competitive athletics. American masculinity was at stake, or so it seemed.[76]

Different needs fueled the Young Women's Christian Association. Like the YMCA, the YWCA originated as a group of prayerful youths eager to avoid the evils of the big city. In the 1850s several women's organizations sprang up in London and New York; the first to call itself a Young Women's Christian Association appeared in Boston in 1866. Assuming the importance of prayer, Bible study, and Christian witness, the first YWCA concerned itself with decent housing for women, then with job training. At the Y a young woman could obtain instructions to become a seamstress, stenographer, bookkeeper, typist, or telegraph or telephone operator. Physical culture was never a prominent part of the YWCA program. The first class in calisthenics was held in the Boston Y in 1877; the first YWCA gym appeared seven years later, also in Boston. Still, by 1893 only nine gyms could be found in the fifty-two city YWCAs scattered throughout North America. Sport figured marginally in the late-nineteenth-century YWCA because it occupied no central place in the definition of womanhood.[77]

For quite different reasons, the British YMCA also took half-heartedly to sport. Not one of the founders of the YMCA went to a British "public school," where sports became the rage in the middle years of the nineteenth century. George Williams, George Hitchcock, W. E. Shipton, and their friends were all pious businessmen, not athletes. As youths, they had no opportunity to play organized games; as serious, money-making, God-fearing adults, they had no inclination to join their less earnest contemporaries in watching rowing, cricket, rugby, and soccer matches. In the British Isles, competitive athletics never figured into the YMCA equation as it did in North America.

Even Thomas Hughes, the great English popularizer of muscular Christianity, was ambivalent regarding athletics. In 1873, sixteen years after the publication of *Tom Brown's Schooldays,* Hughes admitted to a reluctance in talking about athletic games because "these things are made too much of nowadays, until the training and competitions for them outrun all rational bounds." Apparently the late-Victorian games fetish knocked Hughes off his kilter. He pined for "a revival of the muscular Christianity of twenty-five years ago," which probably meant more Christianity and less muscularity. Athleticism was still "a good thing if kept in its place," he concluded in 1880, "but it has come to be very much over-praised and over-valued amongst us." These words appeared in a Hughes treatise entitled *The Manliness of Christ.*[78]

Few such misgivings colored American YMCA attitudes toward organized sport. By the end of the nineteenth century, the American Y fielded football and baseball teams, promoted volleyball tournaments and swim meets, and nourished its own brainchild, basketball. The organizational structure of the YMCA meant that this ball-bouncing brand of muscular Christianity would soon conquer remote pockets of American opinion previously untouched by the movement's elite New England advocates.

# 4

## SWEETENING THE GOSPEL WITH SPORT

**D**uring the last quarter of the nineteenth century, cities grew in size and technological complexity throughout the western industrialized world. Between 1873 and 1896, three severe economic slumps fueled enmity between industrial labor and capital. Squalid slums sprang up alongside corporate monopolies, provoking some Protestant ministers to preach a new social gospel, taking the side of the laboring masses in the name of justice and a benevolent Jesus. At one level, the social gospel was a search for moral order amid the chaos of urban industrial growth.[1]

From another angle, the social gospel was merely the latest adaptation of a Protestant set of beliefs that was always the same yet always changing, helping the faithful find fresh ways to deal with new problems.[2] Washington Gladden, Richard T. Ely, and Walter Rauschenbusch led in redefining the Kingdom of God as an earthly, attainable world of compassion and justice. They sought to abolish the traditional distinction between the sacred and the secular. "All work, all study, all social service, rightly performed, are sacred," declared Gladden. For him and his progressive friends, "social Christianity" meant "that Christ has redeemed the whole world, that it all belongs to him—its industries, its pleasures, its arts, its social institutions—and that it is the duty of the Church to claim it all for him and use it in his honor."[3]

That broad agenda included recreation and sport. Taking a cue from the physical programs at the local YMCA, churches began building gyms and sponsoring sports teams and leagues. By the early years of the twentieth century, many churches assumed both the intrinsic value and the practical usefulness of sports programs.

## Sporting Parsons

Like the more general marriage of religious ideology and sport, the institutionalized union of sport and churches first appeared in Britain. The Anglican path to ordination usually lay through "public" (private) schools and Cambridge or Oxford University, where sport became highly popular in the second half of the century. When those ordained young men went into parishes, they happily assisted in the forming of cricket and soccer teams. By 1867 about one-third of all the cricket clubs in Bolton, Lancashire, were connected to Anglican churches or nonconformist chapels. Between 1870 and 1885, one-fifth of all cricket clubs and one-fourth of all soccer teams in Birmingham were tied to some church. The soccer club of Aston Villa began in 1874 in a Wesleyan chapel Bible class. By the mid-1880s, nineteen clubs connected with Nottingham churches had formed their own city soccer league.[4]

Far from the urban crowds, rural folk played on the village green on Saturday, then prayed in the village church on Sunday. Cricket bestrode both worlds, recalling earlier, simpler days before the intrusion of technological growth and urban problems. Cricket metaphors popped up frequently in late Victorian sermons. "Put your whole soul into the game and make it your very life," exhorted one vicar; "hit clean and hard at every loose ball, for the least bit of work that helps anyone nearer God is blessed work and gladdens the Captain's heart." The "sporting parson" became a stock figure in the popular culture of the day. Likely as not, he could be found in a cricketer's garb. The rector of Handsworth (1860–1873), H. R. Peel, was reportedly "an ardent and skilful cricketer." So was the Reverend Vernon Royle. From 1873 to 1881 he played regularly in the county championships for Lancashire. Yet another Anglican clergyman, the Reverend J. R. Napier, contributed his expertise as a fast bowler and good batsman towards Lancashire's 1888 victory over Yorkshire, then to the defeat of a touring Australian team.[5]

When without a cricket bat in hand, the late-nineteenth-century sporting parson wielded a tennis racket or a golf club, subtle reminders of the great class difference between Oxbridge-trained clergymen and most of their parishioners. That culture gap seemed a chasm in the industrial cities, where the laboring masses worked, dressed, ate, drank, and played outside the pale of respectable opinion. Appalled at what they saw, Victorian middle-class reformers attempted to impose "rational recreation" on their

Vincent Brooks, Day & Son Ltd lith

"In his lighter moments"

social inferiors. From blue-nosed Tory to red-shirted socialist, paternalistic schemes hovered over the recreational life of the masses.[6]

Evangelicals led the crusade for rational recreation, but their constricted Calvinism ultimately rendered economic and social differences of little consequence. Evangelicals saw human beings primarily as individual souls in need of spiritual redemption, not as corporal beings shaped by material culture. Evangelicals fed the hungry and clothed the naked "in a purely charitable way," recalled an Anglican who worked in the East End of London, "but the appeal was wholly to the soul; the body was lost sight of." Cutting across denominational lines, this narrow mentality—held by some Anglicans as well as Baptists, Methodists, and Congregationalists—proved a great impediment to social reform in late Victorian Britain.[7]

To the end of the century, evangelicals remained fundamentally suspicious of popular amusements and sport, though they no longer forbade novels, concerts, theatrical drama, and social dancing, as their parents had done. In 1885 the chairman of the Congregation Union was still warning that amusements often "unfit a man for spiritual work, and tend to estrange his mind from spiritual realities." Several years later, his successor lamented recreation's role in the blurring of "the line that once divided the world from the church." Some turn-of-the-century Wesleyan chapels sponsored cycling clubs, and one Baptist minister set aside a special pew for visiting cyclists; but even the most liberal of the Congregationalist leaders, R. W. Dale of Birmingham, refused to endorse sports and amusements because they did not "surround the moral life with a certain environment favourable to the development of the graver and more serious virtues."[8]

For consistent religious support of sport, one must look to the "broad church" heirs of F. D. Maurice, Charles Kingsley, and Thomas Hughes, whose liberal theology encompassed a wide range of beliefs and activities. By the 1880s some of those old liberals were dabbling in a "religion of socialism," identifying Christian principles with socialist ideals.[9] Religious pews and athletic playing fields attracted strange soul mates. John Trevor, a former Baptist who later converted to Unitarianism, even founded a short-lived Labour Church with a specific recreational as well as political pro-

---

**A bishop at play.** Amid his official duties, Arthur Foley Winnington-Ingram, a late-Victorian Bishop of London, filled his lighter moments with active recreation. Embodying the original purposes of muscular Christianity, Winnington-Ingram enjoyed sound health and vigorously played tennis, field hockey, and golf to the end of his long life. (From *Vanity Fair*, 1912, supplement, "Men of the Day," no. 2273.)

gram. Mostly, though, England's Christian socialists directed their zeal for rational recreation to the chambers of city government, beyond the confines of the local church. In 1891 the Reverend Joseph Wood of Birmingham addressed the Fabian Society, making a strong case for municipal playgrounds, gyms, swimming pools, and public concerts. The national secretary of the Labor Church, Fred Brocklehurst, proposed similar municipal recreational facilities for the vast industrial sprawl of Manchester. As a Manchester town councilor, Brocklehurst presumably put feet on his piety.[10]

Physical exercise and sport fit comfortably into Christian socialist and "new liberal" views of society as an organic whole. For quite different reasons, Anglican high-church ritualists similarly baptized sport at the opposite end of the liturgical scale. For the ritualists, the physical world was the sacramental stuff through which individuals came to know God; no great gulf divided the spiritual and material realms, the sacred and the profane. In "outcast" London, especially, Anglo-Catholic churchmen added a variety of sociable activities to incense, vestments, and candles in the creation of a "social gospel." South London's St. Katherine's Rotherhithe, for example, began in 1880 as a mission to dockers, sailors, and prostitutes. Two years later a new edifice was completed, and by 1900 the new church offered a gymnasium, cricket and football clubs, a large Sunday school, a temperance society, an orchestra, a military band, and a "penny bank" for its members.[11]

In Scotland, churches played a less direct role in the sponsorship of recreation, sport, and social services. Instead, some ministers assisted in the creation of local teams and tournaments. For example, in 1879 the Reverend W. H. Churchill spearheaded the formation of a soccer club in the town of Moffat, on the central southern border of Scotland. Himself a former soccer captain at Cambridge University, Churchill played on the Moffat team. Saturday games apparently warmed him up for Sunday sermons. Soon, however, he moved to Reigate, near London, but was so concerned for the continuation of soccer in the Moffat area that he and his family donated a "Churchill Cup" for the winners of a tournament in the southern counties of Scotland. For several years local ministers supervised the tournament, giving the gate receipts to charity.[12]

The parochial character of the Churchill tournament accurately represented the fragmentation of Scottish sport into separate regions and social classes. While the older camen (shinty) and caber (Highland Games) remained in the mountains, soccer became king of the industrial cities in the late nineteenth century. Soccer was "the people's game," simple and safe enough for working-class children to play in the streets, colorful enough to thrill the masses at the stadium. Rugby, by contrast, became the preferred game of culturally elite private school and university graduates, as it was in England. Whether Scottish clergymen approved or not, they could hardly ignore this new sports mania. Some ministers and presbyters actively supported sports; others agreed with a Dumbarton presbytery's lament that men seemed to do nothing on Saturday afternoons "but attend or discuss sports" and that the Saturday evening sporting paper was "the young man's Bible and sermon."[13]

In British North America, late-nineteenth-century religious leaders promoted "manly" sport with less hesitation. Protestant pioneers on Canada's western plains encouraged rugged outdoor competition as a means of developing the firmness of muscle and character deemed necessary for frontier survival, and also as a way of establishing British culture in an alien land.[14] Until the turn of the century, nearly all of Canada's private schools were modeled on Britain's "public" schools: church-affiliated, with clerical headmasters preaching the gospel of muscular Christianity in chapel and cheering it on the playing fields.[15]

Canadian clerics also gave their blessing to competitive sport on icy lakes and rivers, where the winter games of curling and ice hockey thrived. Predictably, the old Scottish sport of curling was closely connected to the Presbyterian church in Canada. Presbyterian ministers served as club chaplains, wrapping religious ritual and rhetoric around the game's social event of the year, an outdoor combination of curling tournament and party that came to be known as a *bonspiel*. On the eve of the *bonspiel*, the chaplain often invited the entire club to his church for a service featuring a sermon on the spiritual significance of curling. At Saint Andrews Church in Lindsay, Ontario, in 1895 the Reverend Robert Johnston eulogized curling as a game requiring diligence, faith, and obedience, the "foundation principles" of life.[16]

In the 1890s, new women's curling clubs were beginning to make dents in the old "curling fraternity,"[17] but curling retained a masculine flavor little different from other Canadian sports. In 1900 the editor of an Anglican periodical, the *Canadian Churchman*, complained that the terms "manly" and "manliness" were being uttered with "wearisome frequency" in sermons and religious periodicals.[18] As usual, male clergymen were attuned to male concerns and to the assumed importance of sport in the making of Christian manliness. Ministers anxiously surveyed their congregations for men, but found few. At an Epworth League rally in 1901, Methodist minister T. E. Shore recalled an earlier youth assembly when males—most of them "delicate looking specimens of the genus homo"—numbered fewer than 100 of the 1,800 people present. "Where were the young men of vigor and strength? Where were the young men of athletics and sport?" he asked, as a prelude to a prescription: "Wherever they were, they were not in the church, and they never will be until we go after them, and adopt our methods of work to their conditions and needs."[19]

Significant segments of the three major Protestant denominations in Canada—Anglicans, Methodists, and Presbyterians—decided to "go after" their young men through church sponsorship of sports teams and leagues. In 1906 seven Anglican churches in Ottawa formed the Anglican Amateur Athletic Association for the supervision of track meets, tennis matches, and baseball, softball, basketball, and ice hockey games. At the apex of direct church involvement in organized sport, Toronto's Protestant and Catholic churches put 128 hockey squads on the ice in interchurch leagues, accounting for about one-third of the total number of teams in the entire Toronto Amateur Hockey Association.[20]

For less gender-specific recreation, Methodist and Presbyterian assemblies debated "the recreative life" of their churches. More decisively, the Annette Street Methodist Church in Toronto spent $1,000 to level a site beside the church, enclosing the area with a fence for use as an ice-skating rink. As one proud member of the church put it, their "up-to-date" facilities were "lit by hundreds of incandescent electric lights, making the scene a veritable fairyland, yet, withal operated within the pale of the church and Christian influence—no smoking, no swearing, all wholesome."[21]

## Recreational Means of Grace

Enthusiasm for wholesome, church-sponsored recreation derived from a complex mesh of athletic, theological, and personal factors. The experience of Washington Gladden is a good example. Variously called the "father" or "prophet" of the American social gospel, Gladden was born in Oswego, New York, in 1836, prior to the first murmurs of muscular Christianity. At age twelve he wanted to join the local Presbyterian church, but feared that religious conversion would require his giving up "boyish sports—ballplaying, coasting, fishing." A greater fear of hellfire made him willing to make that sacrifice; several years later, he joined a Congregationalist church.[22] An undergraduate at Williams College when Thomas Wentworth

Higginson first began preaching the gospel of health and athletics, Gladden returned home to Oswego in August 1859—the same month that another propagandist for Christian muscularity, Moses Coit Tyler, became pastor of the Oswego Congregational Church. For several months—until Tyler married and Gladden moved away to become pastor of a rural church in Pennsylvania—the two men lived in the same boarding house. They became close friends, bouncing ideas off each other. Apparently they discussed an issue that was then becoming important to Tyler: which amusements and recreational activities were permissible to Christians. Several years later, when Gladden preached and published a controversial sermon entitled "Amusements: Their Uses and Their Abuses," Tyler cheered him from afar.[23]

Gladden delivered that sermon in 1866 in the small western Massachusetts town of North Adams, within a year of his arrival as pastor of the Congregational church. The local Young Men's Christian Association, newly organized under church sponsorship, invited all the town's clergymen to meet with a few leading laymen to discuss the amusements that should be allowed in the YMCA. Everyone agreed that bowling and billiards had too many foul associations to be acceptable in a church-related institution. Gladden joined several laymen, however, in recommending checkers, chess, and backgammon, to the utter dismay of his ministerial colleagues. As Gladden recalled the scene many years later, the opposition insisted "that a truly converted man needed no diversions" and "that the joys of religion alone should satisfy the soul."[24]

Gladden's unorthodox views became the talk of the town. Thinking himself misquoted, he decided to clarify his views on amusements in a Sunday night sermon at his church. Yet hearsay still flourished until the sermon was put into pamphlet form for all to read. All over North Adams, eyes popped at the young pastor's proposal to "Christianize" dancing and card playing, as well as bowling alleys and billiards rooms. Gladden insisted that "sport, fun, glee, not the dismal, repressed, shame-faced variety, but the real hilarious, exuberant sort" should be encouraged by church folks. Borrowing a line from his old friend, Moses Coit Tyler, he especially approved of "the various athletic sports," which seemed "so useful in cultivating the physical nature." Not far in the future, he predicted, physical culture would be considered a Christian duty.[25]

In 1871 Gladden left North Adams for New York City, to take an assignment as religion editor of a Congregationalist weekly, the *Independent*. There he continued his crusade for more flexible Christian attitudes toward amusements and sports, the editorial column of the *Independent* allowing him to disseminate his views to a much larger audience. To evangelist Charles G. Finney's pronouncement that conversion would remove all desire for amusements, Gladden replied that Christian faith did not "deplete and maim," but rather completed and enlarged human nature. Confronting a petty tirade against croquet by President Jonathan Blanchard of Wheaton College, Gladden wittily satirized the supposed evils of the offending game: "Travel where you will, and you see the signs of its ravages. In every country dooryard you are greeted by the wicked wicket and the satanic stake, the malicious mallet and the baleful ball." The "righteous soul" of President Blanchard could rest assured "that all the devotees of this diabolical game are sure to come to the stake at last—if they play well enough."[26]

In a more somber vein, Gladden linked the amusement question with the larger economic issues to which he and other proponents of the social gospel would soon be devoting much attention. In an editorial entitled "Protestant Monasticism," he assaulted the inconsistency of those church ministers, deacons, and elders who ejected a man from the church for playing "a rubber of whist with his wife in the evening" while they reserved a pew of honor for "the hoary stock-gambler who has wrung millions of dollars from his fellow-men by knavish overreaching."[27] That editorial comment appeared in 1873, a year of severe economic depression; but economic evils became even more apparent to Gladden after his move in 1875 to the pastorate of the North Church in Springfield, Massachusetts. Yet another (and final) move seven years later, to the First Congregational Church in Columbus, Ohio, put Gladden in proximity to lively labor issues in Ohio's coal and iron strikes.

Amid all his social and theological concerns, references to amusements and sports regularly punctuated Gladden's conversations, sermons, and writings. In Columbus he sought an assistant minister "to share the oars"[28] in Christianizing play as well as work, amusements as well as business and politics.[29] In contrast to some of his peers, he saw sports not as "mere expedients or baits" to get young people into church. "They are not merely means of getting people under religious influences," he wrote. "They are means of grace, every one of them—helps to a godly life—just as truly as is the prayer meeting itself." Jesus was truly present with his followers, insisted Gladden, "not only when they are in the devotional meeting, but also in the recreation room."[30]

Jesus was on the baseball diamond, too. Having grown up as the game became organized, Gladden believed that baseball mirrored the social gospel's emphasis on the self in relation to society. No one could learn and play baseball alone, just as no one could be "soundly converted" in isolation, oblivious to social needs and responsibilities. One had to learn how to hit, catch, and throw from other baseball players; and only from other Christians and would-be Christians could one learn the secrets of Christian living. "The team work is the whole of it," concluded Gladden on behalf of socially responsible churches and communities.[31]

Gladden backed away, however, when friends and parishioners proposed that the church should become a direct sponsor of ball teams and recreation rooms. Not even for larger reformist causes did he think it the proper business of the church "to fashion or to run the social and political machinery." Rather, the church should inspire, provoke, and serve as a conscience for secular agencies to bring Christian principles to bear upon social conduct.[32] "When it is said that the Church ought to provide wholesome diversions for the people, it is meant, therefore, that the Church ought to stir up the intelligent and benevolent men and women under its influence to attend to this matter, and ought to make them feel that this is one of the duties resting on them as Christians."[33]

Gladden's Columbus church produced an occasional "church sociable" and in 1905 opened a settlement house that offered gymnastics classes along with a kindergarten, reading room, nursing services, domestic science, and music and dramatic clubs. But those gymnastics classes were held in normal rooms, not in a gymnasium specially built and equipped for vigorous exercise. At any rate, the settlement house was physically separate from the church, leaving intact Gladden's rather outdated belief (by turn-of-the-century social gospel standards) that "the proper function of the Church" was solely "teaching and moral influence." Some thirty-two years after he first confronted the amusements issue in the North Adams YMCA, Gladden observed that a church should count itself blessed if a nearby YMCA spared it the need to open a gym or reading room.[34]

Most churches were not so blessed, of course. During the last two decades of the nineteenth century, a new kind of urban church emerged, sensitive to the social and "amusemental" as well as the more narrowly defined religious needs of people.[35] It was an "open" church, dispensing with old rented pews and quite literally opening its doors seven days and seven nights a week rather than the customary one or two. It built kitchens to provide sociable food and drink, rooms for domestic and industrial training, and a gymnasium for vigorous exercise and games. It gave space, leadership, and institutional blessings to kindergartens, Boys' Brigade, Boy Scouts, and Girl Scouts. It sponsored basketball, baseball, and softball teams.[36]

If this new kind of church made Washington Gladden uneasy, it made some of the older generation outright hostile. In 1887 the Reverend Charles A. Dickinson accepted the pastorate of Berkeley Temple, a down-at-the-heels church in the South End of Boston. Within a decade, its membership jumped from 300 to 1,000, largely because the doors were flung open to innumerable groups; activities such as music, lectures, and sewing and mechanics classes; and sport as well as sermons and prayers. According to one estimate, Dickinson and two assistants oversaw more than three dozen weekly gatherings. Baffled old-timers were especially alarmed by the church's endorsement of sports and games, provoking Dickinson to answer simply that if church-sponsored recreation would keep young men "from the streets and the saloons," then every church should have a gymnasium and a ball field.[37]

## Swimming with the Tide

The standard history of the social gospel rightly dismisses the saloon as "a primary concern of what is generally meant by the social gospel,"[38] but the specter of the saloon stood tall over church-sponsored recreational programs. Religious attitudes toward Demon Rum combined pietistic moralism and class prejudice with realistic assessments of the disastrous effects of strong drink on family economies and relationships. Moreover, the saloon reigned as public enemy number one with church folks because its smoky atmosphere bred gambling and prostitution as well as drunkenness. Decent, attractive alternatives were needed, but downtown churches found themselves at great disadvantage. Churches customarily opened for no more than one or two nights a week, and even then their predominantly middle-class membership did not know how to cater to working-class needs. As one character in Worcester, Massachusetts, put it, while the saloon offered "unrestrained gayety," the church seemed "about as cheerful as a mausoleum."[39]

Certainly the saloon, not the church, stood at the center of male working-class life in Worcester. Saloons provided physical warmth, tasty food and drink, public toilets, male conversation and song, and even competitive games and a sportive atmosphere. As likely as not, saloon owners and bartenders were retired pugilists. Photographs of heavyweight champion

John L. Sullivan adorned the walls of many a saloon in the late nineteenth century, especially in the Irish working-class section of town.[40] Grog, grit, and grandeur made a trinity whose popularity was tough to beat.

Of all the churches that tried, few could rival the success of the Plymouth Congregational Church in Oakland, California. Their 800 members eagerly followed the lead of the Reverend Albert W. Palmer in supplying a gymnasium, bowling alley, billiard tables, and shuffleboard in the fight against saloons. "We have kept saloons out of our part of the city by fighting all applications [for liquor licenses] and by providing something better," the pastor proudly reported. By his own admission, that victory occurred in a "mostly well-to-do district with a fair proportion of needy families."[41]

Against quite a different social background, the First Congregationalist Tabernacle Church in Jersey City, New Jersey, also successfully fought the saloons with sport. When John L. Scudder arrived there as minister in the mid-1880s, he found decrepit housing, crime, and drunkenness worse than anything he had ever seen in India, where he was born of missionary parents. Tabernacle Church stood near the docks, between the canals and railways, in a neighborhood of 40,000 that supported nearly 300 saloons. Eager to create counter-attractions for youths, Scudder cleared out the basement of the church and constructed a bowling alley at his own expense. His board of deacons chafed at that unorthodox arrangement and for a time considered the bowling alley on probation. By the third month, however, deacons were rolling tenpins with young men who had "already forsaken the saloon in great numbers." Better still, a young man approached the pastor to profess his faith in Christ, explaining that the friendly bowling crowd made him feel welcomed to the church. "Through the ten-pin alley," he said, "I was brought to Christ."[42]

Encouraged, Scudder cajoled the church into purchasing a four-acre lot across the street for outdoor games and for the eventual construction of a huge brick edifice that came to be known as the People's Palace. By 1895 a billiards room, bowling alley, gymnasium, and swimming pool headed the list of attractions for 2,500 monthly participants. Each person paid a penny per day for use of the facilities. A lunch counter served cheap, tasty food and nonalcoholic drinks. For keeping people off "the road to perdition," the Reverend Scudder had a simple formula: "If Satan provides billiards for forty cents an hour and we charge only twenty, we can undersell him and capture much of his trade. If he gives the popular game of pool at the rate of five cents a cue, we beat him by giving 'two for five.'"[43]

That semicommercial basis of operation freed Scudder from the need to require church attendance of the youths who used the recreational facilities at the People's Palace. Yet never did the pastor lose sight of the fundamental purposes of the place. He wanted "legitimate sports" to "predispose young people in favor of religion and help mightily to build up the Church." To that end, he assured the adults in Tabernacle Church that the People's Palace would provide "a pond well stocked with fish" where evangelical members could "angle at their leisure" to hook lost souls for Christ. To the more progressively minded of his congregation, he insisted that his innovative program stood for an idea: a "genial, broad-gauge, common-sense religion" that needed to be "felt at every point where it comes in contact with men." Himself a complex mixture of evangelical and liberal principles, Scudder often said to youths as he pointed from the People's Palace to the church across the street, "Play here or pray there, but keep away from the saloon and the gambling den."[44]

Yet another pastoral proponent of church-sponsored sport, the Reverend William S. Rainsford of St. George's Episcopal Church on the Lower East Side of Manhattan, refused to construe his program in antisaloon terms. The saloon, he believed, provided "poor refuge from an unrighteously imposed toil," but satisfied "an imperative social need" of working people to mingle and make new friends away from their crowded tenements. Rainsford even proposed opening saloons for certain hours on Sunday until the church transformed itself into a "cheap, orderly democratic social centre" to meet those needs. Under his direction, St. George's parish house became "a great religious beehive" where people could nightly play, eat, and drink beer and light wines as well as coffee, tea, and soft drinks.[45] Rainsford's was perhaps the first of all the numerous church efforts to embody the social gospel in a total church program; it was certainly one of the more inclusive and best documented.[46]

Arriving at St. George's in 1883, the thirty-two-year-old Rainsford could look back on a life given to more twists and turns than one of the narrow roads in his native Ireland. A Rainsford ancestor accompanied Oliver Cromwell to Ireland in the mid-seventeenth century, receiving a large estate for his military efforts on behalf of Protestant England. On Rainsford's mother's side, three or four generations of Church of England clergymen served in Irish parishes, and one rose to become bishop of Meath. Rainsford's father was an evangelical Anglican, raising his eight children on a steady diet of Bible study, Calvinist theology, and John Bunyan's *Pilgrim's Progress*. First in Ireland, then for many years in a London parish, the elder Rainsford preached once or twice a week, visited his parishioners, and did little else. His sermons featured frequent exhortations to turn from the devil and be "born again" in order to avoid the fires of hell. He sought "only to evoke personal experience," the son recalled, and "never recognized the opportunity of working in the community."[47] Nothing in the father's thought or pastoral style prepared the son for the social gospel.

Nor did Rainsford's youthful experiences include anything of modern sport. Years later he professed "an almost crazy desire for sport" as a lad growing up in Dundalk, near the mouth of a river on the east coast of Ulster. But that sport was of the field-and-stream variety (the old English meaning of the word), not organized games. A fishing rod was young Rainsford's first memorable gift; at age twelve, he received a gun. For the first fifteen years of his life he frequently fished or hunted rabbits in nearby mountains. In all his many later reminiscences, however, he never once mentioned playing cricket or soccer, or the Irish games of hurling and Gaelic football. Briefly he attended a mediocre boarding school in Shropshire, England, not one of the famed "public" schools where everyone played competitive sport. Finally, as an undergraduate at Cambridge University he put his wiry frame of six feet four inches to rowing for his college, St. John's. Unfortunately, during the very first term he strained his back and failed ever to achieve a varsity level of performance. He faithfully attended the annual Cambridge-Oxford boat race on the Thames near London; but for a man who, in his own words, encouraged athletics "in every way possible" at St. George's, Rainsford had remarkably little athletic experience.[48]

Rather than originating in any native liberalism or athleticism, Rainsford's unique ministry resulted from a series of unusual experiences just prior to his becoming rector of St. George's. First, he served several stints at an evangelical mission in the grimy East End of London. Imitating his father, he preached simple plan-of-salvation sermons, but began to see that dire economic poverty and human physical needs were going unattended by evangelical churches and missions. Although he continued for a while to preach like a simple-minded "Methody," exposure to the East End turned out to be "the turning-point" in his life.[49]

Travel caused yet another kind of turn in Rainsford's thinking. In treks around Europe and especially in a bold venture across the plains and mountains of western Canada, he encountered "many new types and conditions of people" unlike his Irish and English neighbors. Europeans speaking indecipherable languages, Canadians with alien habits, and native

North Americans of strange shades of color all seemed to exhibit an "innate possibility of good" instead of the depravity that Rainsford had always assumed. Ultimately, an optimistic view of human nature would be just as crucial as any grand theological vision in prompting him to entrust people with unorthodox activities and responsibilities.[50] In breaking with his father's Calvinism, Rainsford learned to believe in people, their good intentions and generous capabilities. Sometimes when he got stuck in the composition of a sermon, he left his study and walked the streets, finding his texts in people's faces. Masked or openly expressive, they communicated the fears, hopes, and joys to which he addressed himself. Rainsford needed no sociologist or seminary professor to tell him that the successful minister "must have his finger on the pulse of the community where he is and know how it beats."[51]

The final turn in Rainsford's road to the social gospel came in an upheaval of his theological beliefs. As a young curate in Norwich, England, he first felt tremors of doubt around the subject of infant baptism and then around the Athanasian creed, when he could find neither item in his supposedly inerrant Bible. Those doubts paled, however, in comparison to a crisis that awaited him at St. James Church in Toronto. Arriving there as assistant minister in 1878, he immediately won a devoted following for his conservative views on the atonement, divinely dictated scripture, eternal punishment, and the need for new birth, as well as for his condemnation of dancing, the theater, and other "worldly" amusements. People flocked to hear him preach sermons that would have made his old Calvinist father proud.

In the privacy of his study, however, Rainsford felt "like a crab changing its shell"—"a ticklish business" when public duties required the status quo. Impressed with Darwinian science, he entertained doubts about the Bible as God's sole means of revelation and even about Jesus as the final revelation of God. Surely religious truth was evolutionary even in the Bible itself, from the Pentateuch to the prophets to the New Testament, and was still progressively unfolding. Most of all, Rainsford could no longer stomach the sharp division between "saved" and "unsaved" herds of humanity, the one chosen and guarded by God while "the greater mass rot in ignorance and sin."[52]

His doubts seeped into his sermons, of course, confusing even the most devoted parishioners. "You are pulling down what you so lately built up, undoing what you did," complained one. "Why don't you come out with your old assurance?" asked another. As attendance and monetary contributions fell, Rainsford's rector hinted at dismissal, but decided instead to temporarily relieve his doubt-ridden young assistant of his preaching duties. Slowly Rainsford exchanged his old Calvinist orthodoxy for a new belief in a benevolent, all-embracing God. In his revised version of the gospel, no dramatic conversion experience was necessary to make anyone a child of God. Rather, all people everywhere were God's children; they simply needed to be informed and regularly reminded of their divine birthright.[53]

With the dawning of this realization, "all the church's life and work took new vigour" for Rainsford. Years later he framed the whole traumatic experience in a swimming metaphor. When he was nearly drowning in doubt and confusion, he flailed "like a man struggling in black, stormy waters to keep his own lip above the salt sea. How could such a swimmer save others?" Once he himself was saved by solid answers to his questions, he felt "like a swimmer with the tide under him." In 1883 that tide carried him to St. George's Episcopal church with a vision of "a great free and open liberal church for the people."[54]

At one time, St. George's had been a bustling, fashionable church in the Lower East Side of Manhattan, one of the richest churches in the city. By the early 1880s it still had a few millionaires—including financier J. Pierpont Morgan—on its membership rolls, but it had fallen on bad times. As immigrants (mostly Germans) moved into the Lower East Side in the 1860s and '70s, fashionable folk moved uptown. Faced with a substantial debt, the vestry tried to sell the building to the Roman Catholic Church, but without success. Membership dwindled to a mere twenty families, causing Rainsford's predecessor to resign, utterly discouraged. By 1883 the church had gone two years without a rector.[55]

In a dramatic interview with the vestry in the home of J. P. Morgan, Rainsford agreed to come to St. George's under three conditions. First, for "a church of the people, a truly democratic church," he demanded that the sanctuary be cleared of pews owned by or reserved for affluent members. Second, in order to insure reform on his own terms, he wanted no committees except the vestry, whom he would appoint. Third, he required a discretionary fund of $10,000 each year for three years, separate from his salary. That final demand evoked a collective gasp, then silence from the vestry. Morgan looked slowly around the room and finally fixed on Rainsford with a single word: "Done." As Rainsford recalled years later, J. P. Morgan only respected men like himself, decisive and successful: "men who did things."[56]

Thus began a spectacular twenty-three-year ministry that set the Episcopal Church, renowned for its wealthy, socially conservative heritage, at the forefront of innovative worship, educational, and social-service programs.[57] Lively sermons, choirs, and Sunday-school classes carried on the usual religious business, but better than usual. Seth Low, former mayor of Brooklyn, president of Columbia University, and mayor of New York City, taught a large men's Sunday school class. By 1889 more than 1,000 people partook of early Sunday morning communion; for the late-morning service, the sanctuary regularly filled to capacity, almost 1,600.[58]

Those crowds were not attracted to good preaching and singing, much less to Sunday-school lessons. Most of them showed up on Sunday became they had become involved in some of the dozens of church-related weekday activities. As Rainsford informed one of his members, he wanted St. George's to be "a teaching house and a dancing house; a reading house and a playing house" as well as a preaching and praying house. Over weekly breakfasts, he convinced senior warden J. P. Morgan of his scheme, then proceeded to put together handsome gifts from Morgan and the family of a deceased vestryman to build a five-story parish house at 207 East 16th Street.[59]

Open from eight o'clock in the morning until eleven o'clock at night, the entire third floor of the Parish House was devoted to athletics and leisure activities ranging from gymnastics, wrestling, and basketball to billiards, chess, checkers, and reading. A library contained 500 volumes, but a gymnasium dominated the center of the third floor. A paid staff member, German immigrant Ernest Reinhardt, supervised physical activities. Occasionally he organized "moral and healthful" dances around the men's clubs and boys' clubs, the industrial and sewing classes, the dramatic societies, the Boys' Battalions, and the Girls' Friendly Societies that jockeyed for space in the Parish House. Little wonder that the Parish House was informally dubbed a "palace of delight." Little wonder, too, that by 1891 St. George's Church had some 500 young people, ages fourteen to twenty, actively involved in church programs—more than twice the total number of churchgoers, young and old, at St. George's when Rainsford arrived eight years earlier.[60]

Outdoor activities beckoned in the summer. Another German immigrant staff member, John Reichert, arranged family day outings to Rockaway Beach. With a thick German accent and a lively taste for good beer, the stocky Reichert literally got off the boat in 1883, the same year that

Rainsford arrived at St. George's. As the rector's Man Friday, Reichert's arranging seaside excursions was only one of his many responsibilities. For athletically inclined boys, J. P. Morgan offered something better than a refreshing swim. He loaned a large vacant lot that he owned near the church for use as a sandlot ball field and playground. Dozens of fathers and sons turned out to transform that rough, rocky patch of ground into a reasonably smooth running track and baseball field.[61]

Rainsford and his four assistant clergymen devised a system of rewards to stimulate athletic participation. Annually they gave a medal to the champion swimmer from the Sunday schools and medals to the best all-around athletes from the Men's Club, the Boys' Battalion, and the trade school. Each year the winners' names were engraved on cups representing each group, and placed on view for all to see. The church also gave gold and silver medals for best-around progress made in the gymnasium, and a prize to the church member who scored highest in a points system pertaining to competition against teams representing other churches. By the turn of the century, St. George's sponsored croquet, tennis, and bicycling clubs for both males and females, and cricket, baseball, and basketball teams for the young men of the parish. Baseball and basketball squads competed in a Diocesan Union League and a Protestant Church League.[62]

## For Moral and Religious Training

Nearby Brooklyn churches pioneered in the formation of interdenominational church athletic leagues. In June 1904 a Brooklyn YMCA invited representatives from forty local Protestant churches to organize a Sunday School Athletic League. They agreed to arrange and supervise contests in baseball, basketball, track and field athletics, and bowling; they decided that each participating church should pay an annual fee of $2. They also thrashed out a policy of athletic eligibility. Their athletes would be bona fide amateurs, attend Sunday school for four consecutive weeks before playing, represent only one church in the course of a season, and refrain from competing in any public athletic event on Sunday. For its first major event, the Sunday School Athletic League produced a large indoor track and field meet on a Saturday night in early December 1904. About 6,000 spectators packed into the Fourteenth Regiment Armory at 14th Street and Eighth Avenue, Brooklyn, to watch 700 young men compete in twenty-two events. Neatly dressed in colorful orange and purple uniforms, the Central

Congregational Church won the team trophy. "They had a big delegation on hand," reported the *New York Times,* "and their cry resounded from the iron girders of the roof."[63]

The rafters began to shake for Sunday School Athletic League games all around the Northeast and upper Midwest during the first decade of the new century. Church-sponsored athletic leagues especially flourished in Philadelphia, Rochester, and Detroit. By 1910 more than 200 Chicago churches, too, competed in church league basketball and baseball tournaments. According to a 1916 report, church-sponsored athletic leagues existed in about 140 cities. Well past World War I, church athletic leagues continued to mushroom outside the major cities. In Hagerstown, Maryland, for example, ten churches founded a Sunday School Athletic Association in 1922, in hopes of "securing an increased and more regular attendance" at church. Three years later an organization of the same name and similar intentions began in Wichita, Kansas.[64]

In purely numerical terms, however, the churches that built gyms and promoted recreational programs remained forever in the minority.[65] For every minister like the Baptist preacher in little Chesham, New Hampshire, who demonstrated "the growing liberal tendency in religion" by umpiring baseball games, more were like the Episcopalian rector of the Church of the Ascension in New York City who was reportedly too conservative to believe that bowling alleys, gymnasiums, and billiard tables would do anything more than turn churches into "houses of amusement or clubs of physical contest." Some pastors pragmatically agreed with a group of Philadelphia ministers mentioned in *The Outlook* as being "distinctly conservative in their theological opinions" but warmly supportive of church gyms and athletic programs; but more, it seems, were akin to William Bell Riley, the fundamentalist pastor of the large First Baptist Church of Minneapolis, who denounced churches that added recreational facilities and lighthearted occasions to more serious prayer meetings, Bible study classes, and evangelistic services.[66]

Opposition forced the sponsors of church recreational programs to explain their motives. Most gave the predictable rationale that sport made church more attractive to youths, keeping them off the streets and out of trouble. Yet few apologists depicted their programs in crassly functional terms, as mere bait to catch unwary fish. To "sweeten the gospel" with sport carried intrinsic as well as practical meaning. The Reverend John L. Scudder, for example, happily announced his community program at the

People's Palace in Jersey City as "an attractive and effective refuge from the saloon and kindred haunts of vice." In the same breath, however, he portrayed the People's Palace as a site "designed to pour sunshine into the hearts of thousands who are doomed to lives of poverty and toil, by providing them with a cheerful, commodious and many-sided place of resort, where various forms of culture and entertainment can be obtained at nominal rates."[67]

Defenses of church recreational programs can mostly be found in snippets of sermons, letters, and journalistic essays and interviews, not in more extended book form. Yet three dramatic exceptions to that rule appeared just before the United States went off to war in Europe. Henry A. Atkinson's *The Church and the People's Play* (1915), Richard Henry Edwards's *Christianity and Amusements* (1915), and Herbert Wright Gates's *Recreation and the Church* (1917) all viewed the "play instinct," in Edwards's phrase, as "a profoundly educative and moralizing force" when promoted as an arm of the church's religious purposes.[68]

As Director of Religious Education at the Brick Presbyterian Church in Rochester, New York, Gates especially needed to present an elaborate rationale for church-sponsored recreation. In 1910 Brick Presbyterian constructed a large new building beside the sanctuary, an "Institute" housing a gymnasium, swimming pool, bowling alleys, billiard rooms, club rooms, and a dormitory for eighty men off the streets of downtown Rochester. As one of the half dozen members of the clerical staff, Gates supervised a director of girls' work and a director of boys' work.[69] He saw the function of recreation as something much more than "furnishing amusement and useful occupation to keep boys and girls off the street." Nor did he see church recreation as a mere means of luring children to church, or of providing "superior attractions" in competition with some "more enterprising church." Unfortunately, the name of Herbert Wright Gates has been largely forgotten in the history of the social gospel. His insistence on church recreational and athletic programs furnishing "the best of opportunities for direct as well as indirect moral and religious training" made him a central spokesman for a movement to sweeten the gospel with sport.[70]

For a time, it was a mostly Protestant movement. A liberal faction of priests called for immigrant American Catholics to shape their faith "in view of the needs of the age," but any inclination towards a social gospel was thwarted by an insular, ritualistic, and sentimental religion that has come to be known as "devotional Catholicism." Unlike the highly masculine Jesus in the Protestant version of muscular Christianity, the image of Jesus in devotional Catholicism was that of a suffering servant, a victim akin to the Victorian stereotype of docile, submissive women.[71]

To add irony to insult, the late-nineteenth-century Catholic emphasis on sin and guilt was reminiscent of the old Puritan ethos that had been so detrimental to sport. It was just as well. Like their immigrant flocks, more than half of the Catholic priesthood came from southern or eastern Europe and had no firsthand knowledge of Anglo-American sporting traditions. All the signs at the turn of the century pointed to a continued Protestant monopoly in the use of sport to make the gospel more attractive.

# 5

## WHEN DIXIE TOOK A DIFFERENT STAND

Today the American South, probably more than any other region in the United States, zealously mixes religion and sport. Just over a hundred years ago, however, the religious South had little good to say about sport. Economically and athletically underdeveloped, the South was religiously overheated with numerous churches, doctrinal arguments, and moralistic prohibitions. The liberal social gospel that attached gyms and recreational programs to churches scarcely made a dent in the conservative South. Well into the twentieth century, the South remained largely rural, not urban, and thus lacked the commercial and technological advantages that elsewhere caused modern sport to flourish. Few immigrants made their way south of the Mason-Dixon line. Spared confrontations with strange languages, foreign customs, and alien religious faiths, Southerners went their separate way.

For all their differences, southern whites and blacks alike praised God and—for a time—shut the gates on sporting spectacles. Not until the 1920s did a new gospel of wealth and sectional pride begin giving birth to a new athletic South.

### Home Games

In 1900 the twelve states south of the Potomac and west to the Rio Grande numbered some eighteen million people, about eleven million whites and seven million blacks. More than three-quarters of that population lived in rural areas, twice the percentage of rural folk in the nation at large. Barely touched by industrial and urban growth, southern life rotated largely around seasonal crop cycles, community stores, and rural churches. The churches were overwhelmingly Protestant. With Roman Catholics confined to pockets of Maryland, Kentucky, and Louisiana, a religious census of 1906 indicated a Protestant preference for no fewer than 96.6 percent of all church members in the South. Nine out of ten churchgoers belonged to Baptist or Methodist churches.[1]

Born of earlier revivals that swept the country, southern churches retained a revivalistic fervor. While large immigrant infusions made northern churches increasingly diverse in beliefs and ethical efforts, Southerners held fast to an evangelical mode of thought and behavior. For all their squabbles over doctrinal differences, southern Baptists, Methodists, Disciples of Christ, and Pentecostals fundamentally agreed with more upscale southern Presbyterians and Episcopalians in promoting an orthodox set of beliefs about original sin, the primacy of the Scriptures, and the personal need of conversion. Evangelicals narrowly focused on the salvation of the soul. "The business of the preacher," declared the editor of the Raleigh, North Carolina, *News and Observer* in 1903, "is primarily to call men to repentance." The means to that end, he hastened to add, was "the old-fashioned preaching of the old-fashioned gospel."[2]

A predictable set of social taboos accompanied that old-fashioned gospel. Especially for Methodists, Baptists, and Disciples of Christ, genuine repentance meant giving up "worldly amusements" such as card playing, dancing, circuses, vaudeville, and theaters. Roller-skating never quite made the list of proscribed pleasures, but when skating rinks first appeared in the South's larger towns and cities in the 1870s, several religious weeklies warned that the skating rink could well take its place beside the dance hall as a threat to good Christian morals.[3]

Actually, the evangelical list of suspected pleasures varied according to locale and social class. Backwoods Baptist pulpits forbade "mixed bathing," but coastal boys and girls swam together, Baptist or not. Urban middle-class Methodists played cards and danced, discreetly, as did Episcopalians. For a time, the prohibitions included even the most mildly competitive games. Croquet once came under fire as a distraction for young Disciples of Christ. Reportedly, they could be "often found playing croquet" when they "should be reading the Bible, meditating, conversing about religious matters, praying or attending to some important religious duty."[4]

Few evangelicals thought it important to attend to matters of social and economic justice. Although recent research has modified earlier depictions of a Dixie bereft of any social gospel, southern exemplars of progressive opinion were few and far between—and largely confined to a handful of urban or academic centers. The religious South resisted evolutionary

thought, biblical criticism, and reformist applications of the gospel to social ills. Preoccupation with race took a heavy toll on the minds and hearts
of white Southerners. They necessarily attended to problems of illiteracy
and farm tenancy, but when signs of human woe appeared in tobacco
fields and textile or steel mills at the turn of the century, scarcely could
voices for industrial justice be heard above the din of racial bigotry. At
best, an uneasy alliance existed between a few southern churches and the
social gospel. Fewer still sponsored any kind of church recreational programs like those promoted by progressive churches in the North.[5]

Hostility toward the North strongly influenced the South's reluctance to
mix sport and religion. Both the social gospel and organized sport were,
after all, Yankee inventions. That fact alone disqualified them, for a while,
from any kind of positive reception in the company of good sons and
daughters of the Confederacy. In the wake of the Civil War, Baptist and
Methodist ministers led in crusading for the "Lost Cause"—an emotionally charged attempt to depict the South as a region culturally unique
and superior, though militarily defeated. In a more defensive vein, Southerners feared the intrusion of northern liberal thought, urban corruption,
and immigrants with their alien religion, Roman Catholicism. In turning
thumbs down on all things distinctly northern, Southerners momentarily
rejected many aspects of organized sports. Little southern hospitality was
extended initially to Yankee boxers and their boozing comrades from the
fleshpots of the North, to professional baseball and its "Continental Sunday"
tradition, or to college football programs modeled on the early success of
northern gridiron powers.[6]

Church administrative patterns also figured in the making of North-
South differences. In the North, seminary-trained pastors usually prodded
and coordinated their churches' support of recreation programs. Some led
in that direction because they had athletic experience, others because they
had learned either in seminary or from a neighboring parson that "wholesome recreations" were just as essential as good sermons and Sunday
schools for healthy churches. Most rural and small-town churches in the
South, however, were without full-time pastors who could give thought
and energy to church-related recreation. Of 15,946 Southern Baptist ministers reported in a religious census of 1916, only 2,411 received regular
salaries. The vast majority labored primarily as farmers, barbers, or factory
hands. Typically without seminary training, many served three or four
churches, preaching in each one every fourth week. A minister in the South
is still often referred to merely as "Preacher." Even if they had any interest

in promoting recreation, few turn-of-the-century "preachers" had either the time or the means to do it.[7]

Most, in fact, lacked the inclination. Ultimately the reluctance to give religious blessing to recreational sport in the rural South came not merely from a narrow evangelical creed nor from the untrained, part-time nature of most rural ministries. Rather, it derived from a complex set of tensions between white southern views of manhood and womanhood, between the home and the church, and between the church and the world at large.

Long before the Civil War, outsiders recognized a distinctive style of male behavior in the South. Whether against a backdrop of mountain corn, plantation cotton, Delta marshland, or bayou swamps, southern patricians and plebeians alike seemed addicted to verbal and physical belligerence. In various combinations according to class and region, competitive male activities included swearing, farting, lying, gambling, drinking, whoring, cockfighting, hunting, fistfighting, and arm wrestling. All served as means to establish some sense of personal prowess and social recognition in an intricate status system, or "code of honor," among southern males. Arguably, military defeat in the Civil War intensified the need of Johnny Reb to redeem his honor; and the specter of virile black males, recently emancipated, provoked whites to prove their manhood all the more.[8]

Southern women, fortified by evangelical religion, stood in opposition to that male hubris. Their first line of resistance was the home. Idealized in gospel song and sermon as a foretaste of heaven, the evangelical home became a supposed center of self-controlled virtue and quiet, a counterpoint to self-indulgent male pleasures. "Evangelicals worked hard not to allow into their homes any recreations that seemed to contain masculine forms of excitement or that threatened the idealized purity of women," contends Ted Ownby. Through family prayers, Bible study, and Sunday quiet, "a degree of serious piety touched all features of cultural life in the home," adds Ownby, "making most amusements suspect if not always disagreeable."[9]

As an extension of the home, southern Baptist and Methodist churches became sacred places altogether different from male-dominated sites such as the country store, hills and streams, and ball fields. Southern women ruled the church roost despite the apparent dominance of male pastors and male deacons. Around the turn of the century, women made up almost two-thirds of all evangelical congregations, taught most Sunday school classes, and cooperated with pastors in managing the business as well as the social aspects of church work. Women made their churches in their own domestic, sociable image. They arranged church dinners, all-day sing-ings, and amateur pageants on special occasions like Christmas. Frequent gatherings—Sunday evening as well as morning services, prayer meetings every Wednesday night, and annual revivals—presumably kept the men-folk in church and thus out of trouble.

The building itself came to be called "the house of God" whose every ac-tivity had to contain "a morally edifying purpose untainted by any hint of sinful self-indulgence." That principle amounted to a prohibition of every-thing that resembled gambling. Evangelicals rejected cake bakes, church raffles, and bingo games as inappropriate church endeavors, best left to worldly Roman Catholics. Methodists in New Orleans denounced local Episcopalian sponsorship of a mule race to raise money for church pur-poses. Boisterous, competitive sport also fell under the list of activities for-bidden in "God's house" or on "God's grounds." A gymnasium or even a ball field built on church property in the early years of the twentieth cen-tury would have violated a basic belief of southern evangelicals.[10]

## Far from Heaven

Southerners saw little good in professional sport. Pedestrianism, a kind of endurance foot-race that had been highly popular and commercially pro-moted with cash prizes in Britain, Canada, and the northern United States, received a cold shoulder in the American South. Commenting on its ar-rival in the 1870s, one newspaper editor registered amazement that "us people here in the south" would waste so much time and money "merely to gratify the curiosity of looking at four men walk around a half mile track, for a whole week." In response to a pedestrian race in Savannah, Georgia, in 1879, regional xenophobia and religious moralism linked arms in a de-nunciation of "the introduction and ingrafting of such Northern gambling and demoralizing amusements in southern soil."[11]

Horse racing provoked even more definite rejection from religious quarters. Although innumerable fine horses had been destroyed by the war, the turf revived in the urban centers of Louisville (where the first Kentucky Derby was run in 1876), New Orleans, Memphis, Nashville, Montgomery, and Little Rock. No agricultural state fair was complete, it seems, without a race track. Georgia evangelist Sam Jones, the South's Billy Sunday, thought the turf "the principal attraction" that drew a "de-bauched, disreputable crowd" to the fair. In a time-honored tradition of male fraternity, the turf crowd gambled, imbibed, and bantered with each other in a manner scarcely acceptable in Sunday school. Southern women joined forces with preachers in denouncing horse racing as a danger to hearth, religious faith, and southern virtues. They all amounted to the same thing as far as the evangelist was concerned. By Sam Jones's reckoning, when he railed against horse racing he spoke "for home" and "for God and native land."[12]

Yet agricultural fairs were occasional events whose evils were not to be compared to the moral rot that might result from the creation of a local horse-racing club. The religious community of Birmingham, Alabama, confronted the latter problem in 1894. "Few greater evils could be foisted upon a community than this unmitigated curse," warned the Methodist editor of the *Alabama Christian Advocate* upon hearing that a horse-racing club was coming to town. The turf "operates as a withering blight and moral ulcer," the editor continued, his rhetoric warming to the occasion: "It sends its streams of corruption and poison into every vein and artery of society." Again, the sanctity of the home seemed at stake. Horse racing "invades the sacred precincts of home and pollutes our sons and daughters. It is a reeking carcass around which flock as foul a brood as ever befouled any community." Good Methodists were not good horse people.[13]

Prizefighting also stirred the wrath of God-fearing Southerners. Long confined to England, championship boxing first came to the United States by way of the South when James "Deaf" Burke fought Sam O'Rourke in New Orleans in 1837. Until the final decade of the nineteenth century, boxers fought bare-knuckle "to the finish," until one was unable or unwilling to continue. In 1889 John L. Sullivan and Jake Kilrain endured seventy-five rounds in Richburg, Mississippi, sipping whiskey between rounds. One reporter estimated that Kilrain consumed a quart. Sullivan mixed his whiskey with tea, but vomited it all up in the forty-fourth round. Scarcely could such disgusting behavior be condoned by evangelicals intent on taming the male animal.[14]

Nor could white Southerners smile on a sport that opened the door to black aspirations. The first two famous American boxers, Bill Richmond and Tom Molineaux, were black. According to legend, Molineaux fought his way out of slavery by winning a bout on which his white master had wagered heavily. In 1810 Molineaux went off to England to challenge Britain's Tom Cribb for the heavyweight title. Molineaux barely lost the fight, but remained in London for another losing effort within the year. In the classic mold of the fighter declining fast, he died at thirty-nine years of age, penniless, in Dublin.[15]

Largely unknown or forgotten except in the oral traditions of the South, Tom Molineaux's spirit reappeared late in the nineteenth century in ambitious, heavy-hitting young black fighters who found the ring one of the few places that was never totally closed to men of color. Although many Southerners agreed with the editor of a New Orleans newspaper who thought it "a mistake to match a negro and white man" or "to bring the races together on any terms of equality, even in the prize ring," the male sporting fraternity thought fighting skills more important than color. In 1892 a New Orleans journalist made his readers wince with graphic descriptions of "the ugly half-splashing sound" of "blood-soaked gloves" in a local fight. White readers shuddered all the more because the victor was a young black man who made mincemeat of a white boxer.[16]

Interracial or not, the sheer brutality of the ring could not be tolerated by middle-class religious folk who claimed even the slightest veneer of civilization. Bloody ring spectacles provoked a northern Methodist weekly, the *Christian Advocate*, to alert its readers to "public exhibitions of unspeakable brutality." For the *Christian Advocate*, prizefights represented "a phase of degradation that must necessarily be regarded as a crime against society." Southern evangelicals agreed. Even after the introduction of padded gloves for championship bouts, southern Baptists joined Methodists in regular assaults on "this barbarous and loathsome sport" that seemed "more degrading than dog-fights." Professional boxing was "a brutal and degrading spectacle," declared Nashville's *Baptist and Reflector* in 1894.[17]

Yet for all their colorful denunciations of the nasty business transpiring in the ring, southern religious opposition focused primarily on the gambling, drunken crowd that accompanied the fight game. Just before John L. Sullivan won the heavyweight crown from Paddy Ryan in 1882, Protestant ministers in New Orleans called upon public officials to stop the fight not because of the prospect of a bloody brawl within the ring but rather because of the specter of a "disreputable class of persons from all parts of the country" swarming to the area to leave their "moral stain" on impressionable youths. Irritated by that parochial moralizing, a local journalist happily reported that the train to the site was perfectly peaceful. "No more orderly crowd ever started for a Sunday School picnic. A conference of clergymen couldn't have been more staid."[18]

New Orleans' reputation as a wide-open city seemed to make its evangelical community condemn pugilism all the more, especially during the 1880s and '90s, when the city momentarily became the national center of prizefighting. No different from most states, Louisiana and Mississippi laws forbade prizefights. For a fee, however, officers of the law turned their heads. Several championship belts were won and lost in little towns like Kennerville, Bay St. Louis, Mississippi Bay, and Richburg. All were situated on train lines, affording easy arrival and quick exit. Most important, all were close to New Orleans, where combatants, spectators, and reporters from afar found adequate accommodation and entertainment.

Several male athletic clubs in New Orleans broke the legal deadlock. Around 1890 they began sponsoring "clean and decorous" professional fights with established weight categories, time limits for rounds, qualified referees, and padded gloves in accordance with the reformist Marquess of Queensbury rules; they also promoted amateur boxing programs, helping to give pugilism a more respectable reputation. Leading this movement to "modernize" the fight game, the Olympic Athletic Club built an arena that seated 3,500 spectators and lit it with electricity. For three consecutive nights in early September 1892, the Olympic promoted a spectacular "Carnival of Champions"—a triple-header of featherweight, lightweight, and heavyweight championship bouts. African-American George "Little Chocolate" Dixon was one of the featherweight combatants, but most attention centered on the grand finale that saw "Gentleman Jim" Corbett seize the heavyweight crown from the "Boston Strong Boy," the great John L. Sullivan.[19]

Shortly after that much-ballyhooed spectacle, the center of prizefighting shifted from the Deep South to the West. Yet legal impediments and religious opposition continued to yap at the heels of the fight game. In 1895 Corbett's agreement to defend his title against Australian Bob Fitzsimmons in Dallas, Texas, stirred the local press and churches to lean heavily on the state legislature, the governor, and a federal judge to prevent it. At best, Texas law was ambivalent on the subject of professional boxing. "Texans were not sure how they felt about prizefighting," concludes historian Jeffrey Sammons, who shrewdly chalks up that posture to "the reaction of a state that was somewhere between the Bible Belt and the wide-open West."[20]

Southern evangelicals were also surprisingly ambivalent about baseball. Introduced to the South by Yankee soldiers and by Confederate veterans who learned the game while imprisoned in the North, baseball was a game ideally suited to the South. It required large open fields, warm weather and sunshine, minimal equipment, and a casual, unrushed mentality. The South had it all. Within three years of Appomattox, baseball clubs appeared in Montgomery and Mobile; also in 1868, the Alabama Association of Base Ball Players was established with the membership of five cities. In Thompson, Georgia, in 1877 the colorfully named Up and At Em club outrageously beat the Skunk Em team, 57–27. Organized baseball games appeared at North Carolina state fairs in the 1870s, and in rural Mississippi too. "Baseball is all the go here," wrote a woman from Water Valley, Mississippi, to a distant friend; "they play every day."[21]

Evangelical attitudes toward baseball ranged from the benign to the hostile. The game was fine for children, particularly for youngsters who produced their own rag balls and homemade bats. "Let our boys have these games occasionally as matters of recreation if they want them," suggested the editor of North Carolina's Methodist newspaper, the Raleigh *Christian Advocate*. Baseball was a "fine exercise for school boys who need recreation," chimed in a Methodist physician in Gadsden, Alabama. Vigorous hitting, running, and throwing would healthily stir young blood, expand the lungs, and whet the appetite for food.[22]

For young men approaching adulthood, however, evangelicals sang a different tune. Compared to "coarser sports" like boxing, baseball still seemed "the cleanest sport of the day," but tolerance of children's play turned to preachments against adult idleness. Georgia evangelist Sam Jones thought twenty-one years of age just about the right time "to get hold of" a young man for something more important than chasing a baseball "like a fice [small dog] chasing chickens." Boys should be allowed to play the game for innocent fun, the editor of North Carolina's *Christian Advocate* grudgingly admitted, just before quickly adding that young men—white and colored alike—"ought to be in better employment."[23]

Baseball's slow, leisurely pace aroused old Puritan fears of idleness in many a middle-class religious heart. A Baptist editor of Virginia's *Religious Herald* thought it "a shame that well-developed muscular power should be devoted for a purpose so ignoble. The whole tendency of the amusement is to idleness and vice." That phrase, "idleness and vice," appeared frequently in evangelical denunciations of the diamond. A Baptist in Columbia, Tennessee, dismissed baseball as something worse than a frivolous misuse of time. Rather, it was a "criminal consumption of time" that no genuine Christian could condone. "How can we get further from heaven and God," he wanted to know, "than amid the soaring shouts of a Base Ball contest?"[24]

Evangelicals saved their worst venom for professional baseball. Although the South lacked any major league clubs, the region spawned dozens of professional minor league teams during the two decades prior to 1900. The most important of several new circuits, the Southern League, was begun in 1885. Until well into the twentieth century, it hovered on the brink of financial failure. Part of its problem lay in its abysmal reputation with religious folk, many of whom thought the professional game a concoction brewed in hell for the ruination of Christian homes, churches, and communities.[25]

Like prizefights, early professional baseball in the South labored under a cloud of suspicion. Religious leaders instinctively linked the ballpark to the evils of gambling and strong drink. As if to provide moralists with further ammunition, players regularly engaged in on-the-field brawls and quickly earned the reputation of being drunken louts. An editor of a Baptist journal in Little Rock, Arkansas, denounced professional baseball as an unspeakable evil in which players could "execute more devilry, use more profanity, and make idiots of themselves in more ways" than any other activity imaginable. "Upon the whole," observed an Alabama Methodist, "I conclude that the ideal professional baseball player may lack a great deal of being an ideal man." Not to be outdone by the Baptists and Methodists, a Disciples of Christ spokesman denounced the national pastime as "one of our national curses." He urged good Christian mothers to keep their sons away from baseball in order to prevent fatal fascination.[26]

Worst of all, the professionals played baseball on Sunday. From the outset, the Southern League and the Gulf League (founded in 1886) flew in the face of the Puritan Sabbath, a key tenet of southern folk religion. At a distance, the New York editor of the Methodist *Christian Advocate* denounced the Southern League's promotion of Sunday baseball as "a sin and a shame," warning that "the young fellows composing the 'Southern League' are not going to be allowed to carry on in the South." He was wrong. They did carry on, but under withering fire from evangelicals.[27]

Crusaders against the game looked to Birmingham, Alabama, for an example of how to mobilize moral opinion. Birmingham clergymen regularly preached sermons on, and Sunday school teachers endlessly discussed, the evils of Sunday sport, especially the Sunday games of the local Southern League team, the Birmingham Barons. Denominational weeklies joined the fray, denouncing the police and courts for not enforcing bans against Sunday sport. Baseball crowds on "the holy Sabbath," declared the editor of the *Alabama Christian Advocate*, proceeded to "carouse and bet like bacchanalian heathens." Alarmed that Sunday baseball would lead to the removal of "all moral restraints" in the city, local ministers in 1889 successfully campaigned for the arrest and courtroom conviction of an umpire in charge of a Sunday game. In 1903 the Alabama legislature passed a bill prohibiting Sunday baseball, football, tennis, and golf games in public places.[28]

Elsewhere in the South, Sunday baseball survived only in the larger towns and cities, not in the rural countryside and small towns where evangelical scruples reigned. The issue of Sunday sport played a key role in the favorite southern pastime of looking down on northern irreligious practices. In 1910 a Sunday World Series game between the Philadelphia Athletics and the Chicago Cubs provoked the editor of the *Richmond Virginian* to denounce such "open desecration of the Sabbath" as a first step toward changing the day of rest into "an orgy of sport and gambling." Professional baseball afforded Southerners yet another opportunity of blaming social ills on distant Yankee devils.[29]

## Pieties and Pigskins

Intercollegiate football became a highly controversial issue for southern evangelicals. Later to become football-crazed, the South at the turn of the century echoed a national refrain of hostility toward the gridiron game. College football, it seemed, stood at the head of a flood of athleticism that threatened to swamp academic purposes. Worse still, prior to the game's radical revision (featuring the introduction of the forward pass) in 1906–1910, minimal protective equipment and a juggernaut style of play made football an exceedingly dangerous campus activity.

One of the game's most severe critics, J. M. Buckley, edited a national Methodist weekly, the *Christian Advocate*. Although published in New York City, the *Advocate* was often quoted verbatim in southern Methodist journals. It provided colorful copy. Especially around the annual Yale-Princeton Thanksgiving Day game in New York, it vividly described "barbaric games" on the field and "wild revels, bacchanalian songs, and delirious shouts" among spectators; it outrageously compared football games to prizefights, the Roman Colosseum, medieval tournaments, and Spanish bullfights. In summary, the editor of the *Christian Advocate* knew "nothing to be said in defense of football. It is essentially brutal, and is degrading in its influences."[30]

This negative assessment proved peculiarly attractive to southern evangelicals. To be sure, they did not oppose intramural games—whether football or baseball—for exercise and pleasure. Intercollegiate contests were something else. From the first official football game in the South, when a

Washington and Lee squad lined up in 1877 against the nearby cadets of Virginia Military Institute, a trickle of opposition enlarged to flood proportions by the 1890s. The gridiron game tended to remove campus respect from the head of the scholar to "the quilted, bepadded, disheveled, long-haired, begrimed, scarred football hero" who had done nothing more noble than survive a "savage scrimmage in the mud." Distant games took young men away from campus for extended periods of time, and home games reportedly unleashed a frenzied round of drinking, gambling, and dancing. "No other form of athletics stirs the animal spirit as does football," observed Atlanta's *Wesleyan Christian Advocate.* "There is an excitement about it that carries away both players and spectators."[31]

Whereas the topic of physical injury dominated the more secular northern criticisms of football, the game's animal excitement and "dangerous entanglements" most agitated southern evangelicals. For them, the gridiron represented a throwback to the unbridled masculine subculture that church and home had long worked in tandem to diminish. The game's "horrible brutality" tended to "animalize" its participants at Tuscaloosa and Auburn in a "theater of mud and blood," complained the *Alabama Christian Advocate.*[32]

To Methodist eyes, the scene in Athens, Georgia, similarly bordered on debauchery. Football at the University of Georgia amounted to nothing more than a "revelling, demoralizing, money-making scheme" that threatened "to convert this old historic school into an athletic club," warned the editor of the state's Methodist magazine. The manhood question was most certainly at stake, he added. The university could become a center of "dissipation" or it could "hold the standard of scholarship high, so as to require true manhood to reach after it, and when it is attained, we could feel that we have real men as our sons and not mere prize fighters, or expert ball room managers." Little wonder that Methodists and Baptists stood at the forefront of a crusade to ban intercollegiate football from the campuses of all tax-supported institutions in the South.[33]

Yet the state universities got off easy compared to the indictments of football on the campuses of denominational colleges. Once again the New York organ of Methodist opinion, the *Christian Advocate,* blazed the path by reporting that the gridiron game disrupted academic missions, alienated alumni, and distracted students at Methodist-supported Wesleyan College in Connecticut, at Allegheny College in Pennsylvania, at Carroll College in Wisconsin, and at Northwestern and DePauw universities in Illinois. As one contributor to the *Christian Advocate* framed the case, these

Methodist colleges and universities needed to resist the "passing popular craze" of football because they simply could not promote the gridiron game and remain the "centers of moral force and of religious fervor" they were intended to be.[34]

That proposition was tested with a vengeance in the South. At the turn of the century, more than half of the 26,000 white southern students engaged in higher learning attended some eighty church-related institutions. Southern Baptists sponsored about forty colleges and universities, Methodists twenty, and Presbyterians eighteen. All competed with each other for students and funds. In varying degrees, all stood opposed to the specter of "half atheistic and wholly irreligious" state universities. As the Methodist editor of the *New Orleans Christian Advocate* put it, denominational colleges were places "where the Christian religion is supposed to be taught" and students trained "with prayers and benedictions on their heads and in their hearts, rather than with memories of 'hops' and 'carpet dances' and like abominations."[35]

To many southern Methodists and Baptists in the 1890s, football became the Great Abomination around which all the lesser evils swirled. Would Christian college officials continue to wink at these "barbaric games and bacchanalian revels"? Parents, ministers, and denominational editors wanted to know in order to steer their youths in appropriate directions. Among southern Methodists, Emory College won big and Vanderbilt University finished last in this informal lottery.[36]

Founded by the Georgia Methodist Conference in 1836, Emory until 1919 remained tucked away in the small town of Oxford, miles away from the temptations of Atlanta city life. In addition to a long list of restrictions on student behavior—no liquor, gambling, dancing, theater, horse races, cockfights, firearms, or visits to houses of ill repute—Emory banned intercollegiate baseball and football games from the campus. The stern enforcer of that rule, President Warren A. Candler, became a kind of white knight in the eyes of the antifootball bloc. "Let President Candler stand firm in his determination," urged the editor of the state's Methodist weekly. "The trustees of old Emory will stand by him. Emory College is an institution of learning; it is not an athletic or other sporting club." Candler and his trustees stood firm.[37]

Vanderbilt faced in the opposite direction. True to its original charter (1872) as a southern Methodist institution, Vanderbilt at first attracted mostly Methodist students and faculty, who were required to attend daily chapel and a Sunday afternoon church service for the formation of Chris-

**A muscular Christian student athlete.** While many southern denominational colleges and universities banned football from campus, in 1913 Princeton University erected a life-size bronze statue of "The Christian Student" modeled on a Princeton undergraduate who captained the football team, led the intercollegiate YMCA, and graduated with high academic honors. This idealized figure is appropriately garbed in a football uniform, with an academic gown draped over his shoulder and a stack of books in his hand. (Princeton University Library)

tian character. Yet Commodore Vanderbilt did not establish a million-dollar endowment for a namesake that would rest content with any kind of parochial piety. Priding themselves on being educationally progressive, Vandy officials looked to Harvard, Yale, and Princeton for models of excellence. Athletics soon became an important part of that formula for success.[38]

Although Vanderbilt's first decade coincided with the birth of American football, the campus athletic association, founded in 1886, at first promoted intramural baseball and student track-and-field days, then basketball shortly after the game was invented in 1891. Yet football could not be ignored. In 1894 a Vanderbilt chemistry professor, William Dudley, led in the formation of the Southern Intercollegiate Athletic Association primarily for the governance of gridiron competition among twenty southern colleges and universities. By the mid-1890s Vanderbilt had emerged as a regional football powerhouse. In 1897 Vanderbilt went unbeaten, and from 1901 to 1903 it lost only one game each season. In yet another unbeaten year, Vanderbilt outscored their opponents 452–4.

Success stirred opposition to a fighting pitch. The most severe criticism of Vanderbilt football came from a former member of the faculty, Elijah Embree Hass, who in 1890 became editor of the most influential of all the southern Methodist weeklies, the *Nashville Christian Advocate*. Uncompromisingly puritanical, Hass thought the Vanderbilt campus a hotbed of football frenzy and moral debauchery. Football, he repeatedly insisted, was merely one of many indicators of the "whole inner drift" of the university away from its Methodist moorings. His tirades struck responsive chords all over the South. It was "high time for the church to call a halt" to the "*sporting* departments" in denominational colleges and universities, demanded the editor of the *Alabama Christian Advocate*.[39]

Vanderbilt's trustees had no intention of abolishing football. Instead, they tightened the rules on eligibility and academic requirements, then forbade Sunday travel in order to curtail distant games. If church-related institutions were to call a halt to football, a school other than Vanderbilt would have to lead the way. That task fell onto the shoulders of a little Methodist college in Durham, North Carolina. Two or three decades hence, its name would be changed to Duke University; in the late nineteenth century, it was called Trinity College.

Ever since its affiliation with North Carolina Methodists in 1859, Trinity had struggled to achieve financial stability and denominational acceptance. In that struggle, football in the early 1890s became a lightning rod for many different issues, including a northern educator's attempt to modernize a parochial southern institution. Not the least of the issues, however, had to do with Methodist beliefs and ethical norms at odds with the emerging world of modern sport.

From the first day of his arrival in 1887 as president of Trinity, John Franklin Crowell stirred controversy. A native Pennsylvanian and graduate of Yale, he quickly found that three years' work as principal of a private academy had scarcely prepared him for his tasks at Trinity. He needed to upgrade the faculty, revise the curriculum, enlarge an inadequate library, and raise entrance requirements. Most controversial of all, however, was his decision to move the campus from a remote site in rural Randolph County to the booming tobacco town of Durham, seventy miles or so to the northeast. Opposed at every turn, Crowell especially met resistance to his endorsement of the new game of football as a varsity sport at Trinity.[40]

Crowell's enthusiasm for the gridiron stemmed from his own undergraduate days at Yale. During that era, Yale was the home of coach Walter Camp, the innovative "father of American football," who reshaped English rugby into a rougher, more orderly game. Yale in the 1880s was "incontestably"—as one contemporary put it—"the most athletic institution in America." Although young John Franklin Crowell did not play varsity football, while at Yale he covered all the games as a journalist for campus and New Haven newspapers.[41]

At Trinity he met regularly with the team, frequently extolled football in articles to the local press, and vigorously defended the game in formal reports to the annual assemblies of North Carolina Methodists. Like many other sports proponents, he depicted football as crucial in the building of individual character, student-body morale, and institutional visibility. During his seven-year presidency, he cheered Trinity to several spectacular victories. On Thanksgiving Day 1888, Trinity beat the University of North Carolina, 16–0, at the State Fairgrounds in Raleigh. As Crowell recalled many years later, that feat dispelled the condescending attitude held by Carolina fans toward "the denominational colleges in general and Trinity in particular." On their way to an unofficial southern championship in 1891, the Trinity boys mauled their Baptist small-college counterpart to the south, Furman, by the score of 96–0. Two years later they beat the University of Tennessee almost as badly, 70–0, and claimed the North Carolina state championship as well.

Despite this success, North Carolina's conservative, mostly rural Methodists deemed football dangerous not only to life and limb but also to the morals of the young. Rumors circulated about Trinity's dishonest use of ineligible transfer students and nonacademic walk-ons, foul language and dirty tactics on the field, wild pregame parades and postgame parties, and gambling and drinking orgies on the trains returning home from distant games. North Carolina Methodists were not amused. They stood for propriety and sobriety; Trinity College football seemed to encourage something else.[42]

From the Raleigh office of the *Christian Advocate* came the first attack. The editor, Frank L. Reid, thought football too expensive, too dangerous, too distracting from study, and too conducive to the evils of strong drink, gambling, profanity, and sexual laxity. In brief, football seemed to unleash the *"animal"* side of young men, undoing what centuries of civilization and many decades of devoted evangelical tutelage had managed to accomplish. In a reference common to the era, the *Christian Advocate* informed its readers that football resembled "the blood-curdling games of the [Roman] Colosseum."[43]

Worse still was the opposition that erupted at the annual meeting of the North Carolina Methodist Conference in the late autumn of 1892. Just that summer Trinity had completed its move to Durham, a maneuver that many Methodists in the central and western part of the state bitterly resented. Unable to reverse that measure, they focused on President Crowell's pet project, intercollegiate football, and placed themselves on record condemning it as "a source of evil, and of no little evil" run by and for the Methodists of North Carolina. There was the rub. Like most southern and midwestern denominational colleges of the day, Trinity was heavily subsidized and tightly controlled by sectarian interests. By charter, two-thirds of the school's thirty-six trustees were named at the annual state Methodist conferences. That arrangement guaranteed a strong ministerial presence on a board that was dedicated to the proposition that Trinity College should be a morally safe haven for the children of Carolina's rural and small-town Methodist families.

Their purpose could best be served, they were convinced, by the ouster of President Crowell. Finally, under pressure from the board of trustees, Crowell resigned at the end of the academic year 1894. In naming John Kilgo as his successor, Trinity's trustees attempted to undo some of the "mistakes" they had made seven years earlier. First, they chose a native Southerner, not a Yankee: Kilgo was a South Carolinian. Second, in Kilgo they selected an ordained Methodist minister, unlike Crowell, who had only studied theology for a year at Yale Divinity School and was a member of the Evangelical Christian Church at that. Finally, the trustees chose a man who publicly castigated football as a game "unfit to be played by young men at college, especially at a Christian college."[44]

While Crowell returned north to earn a doctorate degree before launching a successful career in economics, Kilgo allowed a single, long-scheduled game of football in the autumn of 1894: Trinity lost to the University of North Carolina, 28–0. Beginning in 1895, the intercollegiate game was banned from the Trinity campus as "an evil that the best tastes of the public have rebelled against," as Kilgo explained to students. The ban lasted until 1920, a monument to Methodist morality as well as to more general public opinion.

Throughout the South the evangelical press closely followed the Trinity events. In response to the *North Carolina Christian Advocate*'s erroneous report that Trinity students "of their own accord, decided not to play football," Georgia's *Wesleyan Christian Advocate* lauded Trinity's prohibition as "a wholesome manifestation of 'the college spirit.'" Georgia Methodists saw Trinity's repudiation of the "athletic craze" as an omen of good things to come: "This North Carolina incident is a feather showing the way the wind is blowing. There is going to be a blow. This much can be discerned without consulting the weather bureau."[45]

From Durham the wind of reform blew eastward twenty miles to the town of Wake Forest, the home of a little Baptist college of the same name. In 1888 a Wake Forest team had participated in the first intercollegiate football game in the state, beating a University of North Carolina squad on the grounds of the Raleigh State Fair. Like students everywhere, Wake Forest undergraduates loved the excitement, but faculty and trustees feared serious injuries and student rowdiness, which might soil the college's reputation as a Baptist beacon of godliness. Godliness—or authority—prevailed. Following a one-game season in 1895, Wake Forest played no intercollegiate football again until 1908.[46]

In the same year as the Wake Forest ban, trustees acted similarly at Emory and Henry College, a little Methodist school in southwest Virginia. They prohibited students "from engaging in games of football with teams outside the college" until the game was radically reformed to prevent casualties. Apparently that improvement took twenty years. Not until 1915 was football reinstated on the Emory and Henry campus, and then only on a three-year trial basis.[47]

This pattern of prohibition was common throughout the southern network of denominational colleges. In 1889 Furman University and Wofford

College played the first intercollegiate gridiron game in South Carolina, but Wofford officials soon decided that football was not a good thing for young Methodist men. For all the usual reasons, Wofford went without intercollegiate competition from 1897 to 1914. Up the road, at Furman's Baptist campus in Greenville, football hung on until 1903, then disappeared for ten years.[48]

Not all southern church-related colleges went the way of the football ban. In 1897 a statewide gathering of Virginia Baptists denounced "the growing evil of the modern sport of football" and the denomination's periodical, the *Religious Herald,* graphically informed its readers of "that dirtily clad, bare and frowsy headed, rough-and-tumble, shoving, pushing, crushing, pounding, kicking, ground-wallowing, mixed-up mass of players any of whom might come out with broken limbs, or be left on the ground writhing with ruptured vitals." But at Richmond College, a Baptist institution that enrolled about 200 students in 1900, the administration merely winked and alumni demonstrated their enthusiastic support for football. They paid a former University of Virginia player $50 per season to coach the team, and an alumnus picked up the tab for new uniforms. Over the next few years, Richmond faculty occasionally urged "such changes in the game of football as will reduce to a minimum the danger to life and limbs," but reform, not prohibition, was the intent.[49]

In Mississippi, too, Baptist antifootball pronouncements failed to translate into outright prohibition. In 1903 the Jackson editor of Mississippi's Baptist journal castigated football as a "murderous" sport "more brutal than a bull-fight, more reprehensible than a prize-fight, and more deadly than modern warfare." Yet the outfitting of a football team was the first item of business for an underfunded little Baptist school, Mississippi College, when they began competing intercollegiately in 1907. Within four years the team, fifteen players in all, had a full-time coach. In 1914 arrived a new coach who had an apt surname for a conservative Southern Baptist college: Dana X. Bible. A recent graduate of yet another small football-playing Baptist school, Carson-Newman College in rural East Tennessee, Bible stayed at Mississippi College for just three years before moving on to the big time at Louisiana State, Texas A&M, Nebraska, and the University of Texas.[50]

One of Bible's Texas rivals, Baylor University, could proudly claim the most imaginative of all Baptist student responses to the momentary banning of football. In 1906, when Baylor's president and trustees forbade the game on campus, students protested with a mock funeral in the central quadrangle. They eulogized the deceased Mr. Football; they then buried a football, erected a tombstone, and placed flowers on the grave. Within the year the game was restored, but with the warning that if the team did not win more games than in the past, football might be forever banished from the Baylor campus. For Texas Baptists in the early twentieth century, gridiron victory already seemed next to godliness.[51]

## Converting to Sport

On the eve of World War I Methodists, too, began wondering whether sport and religious morality were necessarily destined to remain forever in opposite camps. In 1920 varsity football returned to the campus of Trinity College after an absence of twenty-five years. By then the game had become much less brutal as a result of changes in rules and style of play. More important, Trinity officials found themselves unable to convince military veterans, hardened by the horrors of trench warfare, that a mere athletic contest could be unreasonably dangerous to one's morals or physical health.[52]

World War I did wonders for sport everywhere in the United States. For morale as well as physical training, troops boxed, ran track, and played baseball, football, basketball, and volleyball, often under the direction of YMCA volunteers. Newspapers gave extensive coverage to these activities, extolling sport as an indispensable ally in the struggle against the Hun. Even the seedy old prizefight game got sprinkled with the holy water of patriotism, causing it to enjoy a postwar respectability altogether different from its prior reputation.[53]

The American South especially felt the one-two punch of patriotism and athleticism. Coming on the heels of the Spanish-American War (1898), World War I inspired Southerners to take up arms and attitudes as Americans, not alienated Rebels. Athletics, long held suspect by southern evangelicals, were now transfigured into a good and faithful servant of national interests—and of regional interests too. Primed for popularity, southern sport had only to wait for an economy stimulated by the war and the emergence of a more urban, consumer culture eager to exploit new advertising strategies. It had not long to wait.[54]

By the mid-1920s, a few urban churches began moving away from their earlier rejection of church-sponsored recreational facilities and athletic teams. A national sampling of seventy-seven churches with "recreational features" identified only four in the South, but that number was misleading. Monroe Street Methodist Episcopal Church in Nashville, Tennessee, sponsored athletic clubs in conjunction with a church gymnasium. The Presbyterian Church-by-the-Side-of-the-Road in Greensboro, North Carolina, was even more progressive. It reportedly filled four and a half acres with playgrounds, baseball and softball diamonds, bike paths, and tennis courts, all shared with local high schools and athletic clubs for the good of the community.[55]

For the good of Durham, North Carolina, in 1922 religious, athletic, and business leaders pooled their resources to produce a three-day event called the "North Carolina Olympics." The idea originated with Marmaduke Clark, the energetic physical director of the Durham Young Men's Christian Association. Mixing piety and athleticism in the old YMCA style, "Duke" Clark had for several years coached championship baseball and basketball teams and in early March 1922 successfully produced an indoor track-and-field meet. From that event came plans for some "Olympic Games" that would make Durham "the athletic center of the state of North Carolina."[56]

Unfortunately, rain marred the games, but not before the Pathe News Corporation captured the opening festivities on film. In theaters "throughout the nation as well as the civilized world" (if a Durham journalist can be believed), brief news clips provided just what Durham's city fathers wanted: "big advertisement" and "much notoriety" for the city. Imagining yet another flower in Durham's bonnet, Duke Clark insisted that other states should "follow the stride of North Carolina" in conducting statewide Olympics as a first step toward the selection of athletes to represent the United States in the international Olympic Games.[57]

Churches contributed to the boosterism. The First Presbyterian Church provided housing and food for some of the 500 or so athletes who congregated in Durham from all over the state. Even more remarkable was the warm response of Trinity College Methodists, who turned over their campus athletic facilities for several events. Trinity, on the verge of being renamed Duke University, was whitewashing its longtime ambivalence toward sport. Just a week before the "Olympics," college officials announced plans for a new three-story gymnasium, "the largest and most expensive college gym in the state." For purposes of physical education and intramural sports, it would contain a swimming pool, several handball courts, boxing and wrestling rooms, and a thousand lockers for students. For intercollegiate basketball, the auditorium would hold 2,000 spectators, with seats for 1,300. As the *Charlotte Observer* commented approvingly, this new gym would be "in keeping with the program of expansion of Trinity athletic activities."[58]

Sport expanded dramatically at high schools and colleges throughout the evangelical South in the 1920s. Religion, football, and regional pride linked arms in a world of newfound affluence. The "Friday night lights" of Odessa, Texas, trace their origins to a mid-1920s oil boom that coincided with a football boom. Autumn Saturday editions of the *Odessa News* featured the Texas trinity of black gold (oil), the gridiron, and God. Items about recent strikes in nearby oil fields jostled with reports about the Friday night exploits of the Odessa High Yellowjackets; both competed with church announcements and listings of the next day's sermon titles at local Baptist, Methodist, and Church of Christ churches.[59]

Southern partisans joined in a kind of regional hallelujah chorus when the University of Alabama was invited to compete against the University of Washington in the Rose Bowl of 1926. For a people plagued by memories of military defeat and daily reminders of economic inferiority and alienation from the American cultural mainstream, this event loomed exceedingly large as a symbolic representation of regional prowess. Alabama carried "the reputation of an entire section [of the country]" on its shoulders, noted the sports editor of the Atlanta *Georgian*. While their fans gathered anxiously outside telegraph offices all over the South, the Crimson Tide fell behind, 12–0, in the first half. Then a speedy halfback from Dothan, Alabama, Johnny Mack Brown, led Alabama to an upset victory, 20–19. A future Hollywood cowboy star, Brown was colorfully described by a Birmingham reporter as "slicker than an eel in a sea of stewed okra." Even more appropriately, southern reporters and editors employed the language of Zion to explain the significance of this football victory: it was "a blessed event," even a "miracle."[60]

Whatever the religious metaphors, that distant gridiron contest held little interest for the nine million or so blacks who still lived in the South. Johnny Mack Brown was not brown, much less black, nor did their rural churches or schools familiarize black Southerners with sport. Except for an occasional reference to picnics, sandlot baseball games, and ill-organized track meets adjacent to the local church, little evidence can be found for black participation in the early interplay of southern religion and sport.

Southern black ministers in the rural South were more poorly educated, puritanical, and narrowly focused on a pie-in-the-sky gospel than were their white counterparts. A Fisk University social scientist, Charles S. Johnson, heard a sermon at Mt. Pisgah Church in Johnston County, North

Carolina, in which the preacher proudly refused "to go in for new fangled things" like recreational programs for rural youths. He would cling to "that old time religion" that was good enough for his father, mother, and grandparents. Johnson came away impressed—or, more accurately, depressed—with "the heavy handed domination of the church by the older people and their impatience with the claims of youth for participation."[61]

The black church was "the social center, educational agency, political platform, and heart of the black community" in the South, as Sam Hill explains, but little recreation and even less organized sport figured in that equation, especially not in the rural and small-town South, where most blacks lived during the interwar years.[62]

The South unwittingly booted its best would-be athletes northward in the great black migration of the 1920s. As World War I and anti-immigration laws dried up the flood of European industrial workers, black migrants found work and sent home glowing reports of a land flowing with milk and honey: better jobs, housing, schools, and health care. For a people steeped in biblical imagery, the Great Exodus took on mythological proportions. To escape Egyptian (white Southern) bondage, one had to cross the Jordan River (the Mason-Dixon line). That "religious pilgrimage" contained some of America's finest athletes. Native Alabamans Joe Louis and Jesse Owens dominated their athletic spheres in the 1930s; native Georgian Jackie Robinson demolished the golden calf of racially segregated sport. Long before the South became an athletically dominant region, it contributed mightily, though unintentionally, to the making of modern American sport.[63]

# 6

## GOD AND COUNTRY GAMES

Today, no major sporting event in the United States ever begins without some version of "The Star Spangled Banner." Usually it is sung; sometimes it is played on trumpet or organ. As players on the sidelines mumble the words and struggle with the tune, imaginary bombs burst in air and rockets readily glare over all our Super Bowls, World Series, and NBA championship games. To a generation of Americans who have grown up with televised sport, it seems that "Play ball!" has always been the last line of the National Anthem.

Nothing could be farther from the truth. The alignment of patriotism with sport is essentially an "invented tradition" born in the late nineteenth century when nationalistic holidays, flags, anthems, pledges of allegiance, and parades first flourished throughout the western world. As Europeans coped with two major new nations, Germany and Italy, and as Americans awoke to imperial possibilities in both the Caribbean and the Pacific, people everywhere dusted off old nationalistic traditions and eagerly created new ones. Mass migration made citizenship training an essential feature of schools newly built for mass education. Sport soon became a teammate in the patriotic game.[1]

This new tandem of sport and patriotism joined forces with one of the oldest of human endeavors, religion. Various sporting styles and religious values became entwined in disparate visions of national greatness, in the origins of the modern Olympic Games, and ultimately in the Big Game played out on the muddy fields of World War I. Not by coincidence, the first rendering of the "Star Spangled Banner" at a World Series game occurred in 1918, in honor of American soldiers abroad.

## Learning to Play by the Rules

British historian Eric Hobsbawm observes that some late-nineteenth-century nationalism was "genuine enough" but "was neither as militant nor as single-minded, and certainly not as reactionary, as the flag-waving right would have wanted it to be."[2] For an example of genuine but moderate nationalism, Hobsbawm could well have turned from his usual British, Polish, and Armenian references to immigrant America, where liberal progressives promoted public playgrounds, community centers, youth organizations, school athletic programs, and team sports as patriotic measures to initiate newcomers into the American way of life.

Diverse ethnic and religious traditions among immigrants provoked the great theologian of the social gospel, Walter Rauschenbusch, to come to terms with "the institutions which make for unity." He saw recreation as one of those institutions that fostered community cohesion. "How would it affect the recreational situation if the churches took a constructive rather than a prohibitive attitude toward amusements," asked Rauschenbusch, "and if they promoted the sociability of the community rather than that of church groups?"[3]

Many contemporaries agreed: the purpose of church-sponsored recreation was for the unity and enrichment of the entire community, not merely for the good of the church itself. Recreation was liniment for the world's aching muscles and salve for its wounds, not an adornment for the institution that promoted it. As one writer framed the issue, "the gospel of wholesome play" should be built "into the very sub-culture of community life" for the good of the larger community.[4]

At one level, this principle simply reaffirmed an old Biblical adage that the believer is at best like salt that prevents the world from going to rot. Often unseen, often unrewarded, the salt does its job of preserving the world. And so it was with Christian groups in late-nineteenth-century America. According to one appraisal, the dominant initiative behind some 200 charitable and regulatory groups founded between 1865 and 1900 was "Christian in origin and in spirit" although the impetus came not so much from churches as from Christians acting on reformist principles learned in the home and church. In 1905 the American Institute of Social Service reported that three out of every four social workers in the United States regularly attended some Protestant church, a figure all the more remarkable because Protestants then comprised merely a quarter of the total population.[5]

For an example of religious folk working quietly—that is, religiously unidentified—to save the world through wholesome recreation, one can scarcely do better than consider the saga of Le Roy E. Bowman. Growing up in the cornfields of Illinois, Bowman imbibed "an intense religious faith" in the Baptist tradition, propelling him to college and then to theological studies at the University of Chicago. Soon his interest in sociology swamped his plans for the Baptist ministry, sending him to New York City to engage in community social work. During World War I he served as national personnel director of War Camp Community Service and afterward worked with the Red Cross in coordinating health and relief agencies within the East Harlem Health Center. In 1922 he organized New York City's Recreation Committee, which would direct forty-five citywide recreation agencies. For several years, he served as the secretary-director of the National Community Center Association.[6]

Between 1900 and 1920, community centers mushroomed throughout the United States. Many started as extensions of local churches. Some occupied newly built structures; others were housed in recently closed church buildings. Shortly after the Civil War, Moses Coit Tyler provocatively suggested that two churches in the same small town should join forces and convert one of the buildings into a gym; just before World War I, that proposal turned out to be more reasonable than anyone could have imagined. In 1906 the Christian Meeting House in Randolph, Vermont, united with the local Congregational Society, renovating the old meeting house into a community center that served the athletic, music, dramatic, and social needs of the village. In rural Indiana, a Catholic priest reportedly purchased an abandoned Protestant church for use as a recreation hall open to the entire community. Old barns, brick warehouses, and closed schools as well as churches served community needs in all parts of the country.[7]

The outdoor equivalent of the community center was the playground, and in its construction, too, religiously motivated folk took the lead. As early as 1868 the Old First Church of Boston created a children's playground in a schoolyard near Copley Square. Two decades later, other Boston Protestants constructed "sand gardens" to keep slum children off the streets and provided them with vocational training in summer vacation schools. By 1906 only forty-one American cities sponsored supervised playgrounds, but by the time of the First World War, churches, schools, or city councils provided some sort of playground program in more than five hundred American towns and cities.[8]

As New York City wrested the parks-and-playground lead from Boston, ministers and rabbis spearheaded the charge on behalf of their immigrant congregations. Several clergymen were charter members of the New York Society for Parks and Playgrounds, begun in 1890 as a lobbying group to urge the city council to spend public funds on playgrounds. On the Saturday before Thanksgiving 1891, twenty-seven prominent Jewish rabbis addressed their congregations on the need for community playgrounds; on the very next day, one hundred Protestant and Catholic pastors preached in a similar vein. Although the social clout of the urban church and synagogue was waning, religious bodies could still shape public opinion and, as one contemporary insisted, "not only justify but demand the expenditure of adequate funds for public playgrounds and for their proper equipment and supervision."[9]

Playgrounds promised healthy outdoor play for city youths, but turn-of-the-century apologists more often trumpeted the important function of turning immigrant children into Americans. Playground supervisors encouraged Irish, Italian, and East European newcomers to lay aside their alien ways or to integrate them in cooperative activities. On the playground, potential lawbreakers learned to "play by the rules," like good citizens should. Playground athletic contests provided "large opportunities for social and moral culture," insisted Henry S. Curtis in 1902. Four years later, Curtis and Luther Gulick founded the Playground Association of America.[10]

Team games especially held high promise as makers of law-abiding, patriotic Americans. Playground baseball programs, for example, required self-denial in training as well as cooperative efforts toward victory. Team loyalty inspired players to practice when they had rather go fishing, and to bunt the ball or hit a sacrifice fly when the circumstance demanded it rather than going for the more dramatic home run. "This type of loyalty is the same thing we call good citizenship as applied to the city, that we call patriotism as applied to the country," observed Henry Curtis. "The team game is undoubtedly the best training school for these civic virtues."[11]

The new YMCA game of basketball seemed especially appropriate for the playground. Basketball required vigorous exercise and the development of skill; more important, it rewarded unselfish teamwork. "If a boy can be taught to play the game, so that the team may win, rather than to make star plays himself, he has laid a broad foundation for unselfishness in his other actions," said Curtis. Unlike football and baseball, basketball could be played on a paved inner-city lot. Better still, it could be a great citizen-builder. "A state of mind which prompts a boy to play basket-ball for the success of his team is essentially the same as that which prompts him to strive for the good of his city or country later."[12]

One of the leaders in that movement to use parks and playgrounds for the nation's good was Charles B. Stover, a graduate of Union Theological Seminary. Stover energetically applied his liberal gospel to contemporary social problems. In the mid-1880s he abandoned all intentions to pursue a formal Christian ministry. Instead, he joined the Neighborhood Guild to deal with human distress on New York's Lower East Side. With urban reformers Lillian Wald, Jacob Riis, J. G. Phelps Stokes, and Felix Adler (director of the Ethical Culture Society), Stover in 1898 founded the Outdoor Recreation League. Privately funded, the League built several playgrounds and ultimately convinced the city council to assume full responsibility for them. From 1900 to 1915, New York City spent more than $17 million for parks and playgrounds. Stover, yet another seminarian turned social reformer, became the city's first commissioner of parks.[13]

Schools, too, received churchly nudges toward the inclusion of physical education and athletics in their programs. In 1885 two clergymen figured prominently in the first meeting of the Association for the Advancement of Physical Education, held at Adelphi Academy in Brooklyn, New York. A famous Brooklyn minister, T. DeWitt Talmadge, gave the opening address; the first speaker on the program was the Reverend Edward P. Thwing, who was elected as one of the three vice-presidents of the new organization, which would promote the teaching of physical education in the schools.[14]

What Talmadge and Thwing promised, Luther Gulick delivered. Having decided as a young man that he would not follow the exact route of his missionary parents, Gulick nevertheless carried a missionary spirit to all he did. After several illustrious years at the Springfield YMCA college, he served briefly as principal of Pratt High School in New York City. In 1903 he became head of physical education for the public schools of Greater New York, which included the boroughs of Manhattan, Brooklyn, Queens, the Bronx, and Richmond. He pioneered in providing innovative physical education classes to students, and in 1904 founded the Public Schools Athletic League (PSAL) to keep youths out of mischief after school. As the nation's first athletic league attached to a public school system, PSAL proved to be highly influential in the making of an uniquely American combination: interscholastic sports as an integral part of the public educational system. If schools stepped "beyond the churches in their practice of the philosophy of play," as a contemporary suggested, it was because religiously motivated people helped push schools in that direction.[15] Like community centers and the playground movement, schools taught the virtues of self-control on the one hand and the sentiment of patriotism on the other. For turn-of-the-century immigrants, both these attitudes held out the promise of success as middle-class Americans.

Of all the other agencies through which religious folk worked to shape the world in their own image, the Boy Scouts ranked high as an effective builder of middle-class character. As yet another American adaptation of a British invention, the Boy Scouts offered, in the words of one observer, "fundamental training in manliness, virtue, self-reliance, and efficiency."[16] A hero of the Boer War, British commander Robert S. S. Baden-Powell, founded the Boy Scouts in 1907 as a means to enhance physical health and strength, to diminish class conflict, and to inspire patriotic feelings among British youths. Behind all these purposes lay a "public"-school games ethic that young Baden-Powell imbibed at Charterhouse. There he played goalkeeper for the soccer team and helped organize a competitive rifle squad. Later, as an officer of the Thirteenth Hussars in India, he eagerly played lawn tennis and polo whenever he could "make the chance." As chief commanding officer of British troops under siege in 1899–1900 at Mafeking, South Africa, he organized town cricket games, bicycle races, football games, and polo matches. Fearful that the future of the British Empire might be left in the hands of "wishy-washy slackers without any go or patriotism in them," Baden-Powell instinctively turned to a well-worn athletic exhortation: "Play up! Each man in his place, and play the game!"[17]

Baden-Powell's religious zeal was somewhat less pronounced. The creator of the Boy Scouts was himself something of an agnostic, yet he looked to parsons and Sunday-school teachers as allies in the making of well-disciplined, morally upright, patriotic youths. From the outset, a cornerstone of the Boy Scouts was membership in "some religious denomination" and regular attendance at religious services. No religion or denomination held a monopoly on truth, Baden-Powell believed, but the Scouts' emphasis on a high moral code was "nothing less than applied Christianity." Outdoor hikes and overnight camp-outs supposedly put boys in touch with God through the beauty of nature.[18]

This mixture of athleticism, piety, and patriotism quickly crossed the Atlantic, feeding into the creation of the Boy Scouts of America (BSA) in 1910. At first, the Young Men's Christian Association provided the key affiliation, leadership, and meeting places. Churches quickly followed. In 1913 the Mormons became the first American church officially to adopt the Boy Scouts. Shortly after a papal blessing in 1919, Roman Catholics did the same, but Protestants—Methodists, Presbyterians, Baptists, and Congregationalists, in that order—led in the sponsorship of the Boy Scouts. By 1920 about 80 to 85 percent of the almost 400,000 members of the Boy Scouts of America were affiliated with a church or Sunday school. More than half of all Scout troops were sponsored by churches. "We're going to have Sunday School on Sunday and Scout work through the week," a Methodist boy promised his father as he sought permission to join the Boy Scouts; "and we meet right at the church, and Mr. Simpson, the teacher, is going to be the Scoutmaster." Presumably they sang "Onward Christian Soldiers" with one breath and "America the Beautiful" with the next, just before breaking into a popular new refrain, "Take Me Out to the Ball Game."[19]

## The Goal of National Greatness

In 1899 Thorstein Veblen linked athleticism and religion to a "predatory impulse" that often expressed itself in an aggressive spirit of patriotism. Within the same year, but in much simpler terms, Theodore Roosevelt's memorable speech "The Strenuous Life" captured the physically forceful, nationalistic mood that dominated much of western culture at the turn of the century. Denouncing the "base spirit" of commercial greed as well as "the soft spirit of the cloistered life," Roosevelt called on all Americans to face "the dangers of strife" on the frontiers of nature, in moral and economic reform, and in competitive sport. Only through strenuous struggle, "through hard and dangerous endeavor," insisted Roosevelt, could Americans "ultimately win the goal of true national greatness."[20]

Scarcely did Americans monopolize the mania for "true national greatness" during the three or four decades prior to World War I. After 1870, when the unification of both Germany and Italy caused drastic shifts in political and economic power, xenophobia produced an outburst of rabid nationalism throughout Europe. As Hobsbawm suggests, each nation brought its own distinct traditions and interests to the table. "Nationalism," says Hobsbawm, "became genuinely popular essentially when it was drunk as a cocktail. Its attraction was not just its own flavor, but its combination of some other component or components which, it was hoped, would slake the consumers' spiritual and material thirst." Religion and sport mixed with nationalistic interests made a cocktail that citizens happily swallowed.[21]

Although the specific features of this merger of sport, religion, and nationalism amounted to a late-Victorian "invented tradition," the tendency
lay deeply rooted in European history. Germany's first great physical edu-
cationist, Johann Bernhard Basedow (1723–1790), studied theology and
philosophy at the University of Leipzig. As a schoolmaster, he constructed
a novel program of physical exercises for his pupils. That practice proved
to be highly influential, but Basedow wrote much more on theology than
on any educational or athletic theme. Religion similarly lay at the base of
the German gymnastics movement. The supposed "father" of German
gymnastics, Friedrich Ludwig Jahn (1778–1852), was a son of a north German Lutheran minister. With youthful liberal passion akin to religious
faith, Jahn created gymnastics groups for the purpose of inspiring patriotic
resistance to foreign (Napoleonic) rule in the early years of the nineteenth
century. His motto, "Frisch, frei, frolich, fromm" (bold, free, joyous, and
pious), explicitly yoked religion to sport on behalf of a revolutionary nationalist ideology.[22]

By the end of the nineteenth century, German gymnasts had put their
athleticism and piety to the service of a new kind of nationalism. As proud
inhabitants of a German Empire created by the "blood and iron" tactics of
Otto von Bismarck, they identified with the politically conservative, highly
chauvinistic policies of the Kaiser. By 1898 some 6,400 *Turnvereine* (German gymnastics clubs) flew the Kaiser's new black, white, and red flags;
only 100 clubs stuck with the old national colors. For a new nation like
Germany, gymnastics were a godsend. In a pattern familiar to Denmark
and Sweden, German gymnastics clubs and public performances functioned as a kind of cultural glue, bonding citizens of diverse religious, class,
and regional interests.[23]

For most of central and western Europe, though, gymnastics mirrored
cultural divisions and conflicts. Within Germany itself, rampant anti-Semitism in gymnastics circles produced a backlash. A movement for muscular
Judaism emerged as a minor but important part of the Zionist impulse
that came to the surface in the 1890s, urging Jews to protect themselves by
creating their own territorial state. At the very first Zionist Congress, at
Basel, Switzerland, in 1897, a prominent German neurologist and social
critic, Max Nordau, insisted that "muscular Judaism" held the key to the
future of Jews. "There are no people in the world for whom gymnastics
could have so splendid a result as for us," Nordau later explained. "Gymnastics is destined to fortify us in the body and spirit. It will give us self-
assurance."[24]

For Czech patriots, it gave something more. In Bohemia (now the Czech Republic), a Czech minority within the Austro-Hungarian Empire created groups called Sokols, the Czech word for "falcon." Their lightly veiled purpose was nationalistic: to attach Czech language, literature, and music to paramilitary gymnastics programs. Annual festivals in Prague featured gymnastics displays and mass formations set to patriotic music and speeches. Each participant wore a red shirt and red cap with a feather in it, symbols of unity and a fiery resolve to achieve Czech independence from Austro-Hungarian rule.

In France and Belgium, gymnastics stood at the center of a more complex mixture of religious and patriotic interests. Both French and Belgian national organizations modeled their programs on German gymnastics. Largely supported by their respective governments, they further mimed the Germans in turning their clubs into havens of nationalist rhetoric and military preparedness. In both nations, however, Catholic church-sponsored gymnastics and sport networks emerged—in Belgium in 1892, in France in 1903—to counter liberal antichurch impulses.

Annual festivals brought the faithful together to display their physical prowess and to hear inspirational speeches against a backdrop of flags and the singing of the national anthem. Mother Church embraced the Fatherland. For Belgian and French Catholics alike, Joan of Arc symbolized the piety, bravery, and determination represented in the Catholic gymnastics movement. "Like Joan of Arc at the head of her troops," the president of the Catholic Gymnastics Federation of Belgium announced in 1910, "you will not retreat in the face of any difficulty in order to make sure of the victory of our good cause, and as Joan of Arc once did, you will take as your motto: 'For God and King!'"[25]

Lacking a gymnastics movement, Britain instead had outdoor sports and ball games. For each portion of the United Kingdom—England, Ireland, Scotland, and Wales—different games served distinct nationalistic purposes. Invariably blended with religious ideology, patriotism found its most varied sportive expressions on the Celtic fringes of the British Isles.

In Catholic Ireland, sport became a means of protest against English cultural and political dominance. As Thomas William Croke, the Roman Catholic archbishop of Cashel, voiced the problem, old Irish amusements and athletic games seemed "not only dead and buried but in several locations to be entirely forgotten and unknown," replaced by "mashier habits" resulting from centuries of English rule in Ireland. As part of a larger "Gaelic revival" that emphasized native Irish language, music, literature, and history, this late-nineteenth-century surge of Irish nationalism at-tracted radical Fenians as well as Catholic prelates.[26]

Despite severe political disagreements, Archbishop Croke in 1884 joined forces with a burley, red-bearded old Fenian, Michael Cusack, to create the Gaelic Athletic Association (GAA) for the purpose of resurrecting the an-cient games of Ireland. The GAA fashioned a new game with an ancient name, Gaelic football, which featured imaginative handling, kicking, run-ning with the ball, and scoring. More in tune with its stated purposes, the GAA retrieved the ancient stick-and-ball game of hurling from the trash heap of medieval history.

The "hurley" (stick) took its place alongside the harp as a romantic sym-bol of Irishness and Irish freedom. At tempestuous public meetings of the great nationalist leader, Charles Stewart Parnell, GAA enthusiasts—appro-priately armed with hurley sticks—served as bodyguards. At Parnell's fu-neral in 1891, some 2,000 members of the Irish Republican Brotherhood paraded with black-draped hurley sticks. Several of the martyred leaders of the Easter Rebellion of 1916 were prominent GAA members. So many out-standing hurling athletes were arrested in the wake of the abortive uprising that the final match of the 1916 Wolfe Tone Tournament between counties Kerry and Louth had to be played in a prison camp in Wales.[27]

Lest the religious (Roman Catholic) aspect of this patriotic athleticism be lost from memory, the largest stadium for Gaelic games—Croke Park in Dublin—was named after the original ecclesiastical patron of the Gaelic Athletic Association. Upon issuing the GAA's annual report for 1907–1908, the editor observed that the "ideal Gael" was a zealous, self-reliant athlete who loved "his religion and his country with a deep and restless love."[28] A jigger each of religion, sport, and patriotism made a heady cocktail for re-bellious Irishmen.

In Scotland, too, religion and sport worked in tandem with nationalism. Having adopted the game of "fitba" (football, soccer style) shortly after England's Football Association was formed in 1863, fiercely proud Scots-men liked nothing better than to beat the "auld enemy" at their own game. Victory in the annual international match (begun in 1872) served as salve on the wounds of past military debacles and present economic and political subservience to England. Soccer especially thrived in industrial-ized Glasgow, the second largest city in all of Britain. In 1893 Glasgow's powerful Queen's Park club began construction of a huge new stadium, Hampden Park, that would hold 150,000 spectators. Presbyterian leaders feared this new popular passion. The Saturday evening sporting paper that carried all the football scores seemed, to the presbytery of Dumbarton, "the young man's Bible and sermon."[29]

Catholics as well as Protestants read that football Bible, for ever since the potato famines of the 1840s Irish Catholic immigrants had flooded into Scotland searching for better jobs, health care, and education. As industrial Glasgow proved especially attractive for both Ulster Protestant and Irish Catholic immigrants, soccer clubs emerged to represent each faction. The Rangers, founded in 1872, catered to Protestant players and fans. The Celtic began in 1888 as a means of raising money to feed the Irish Catholic poor in the East End of Glasgow, and of keeping the city's Catholic community focused on Catholic heroes. Fired by sectarian hostilities, a turn-of-the-century Celtic-Rangers match approximated a holy war.[30]

Less violently but no less seriously, Welsh Protestants combined the rugby form of football with chapel sermons and gospel hymns as emblems of Welsh nationality. From the smallest Nonconformist (Methodist, Baptist, Congregationalist, Plymouth Brethren) communities to sprawling industrial towns, religious revivals drew coal miners and mine owners together, and so did amateur rugby. In 1905, when a Welsh team beat an undefeated All Blacks squad from New Zealand at Cardiff Arms Park, the game was ballyhooed for its implications of national prowess. That game "kicked the last great religious revival into touch [off the field]," says one British scholar. "Rugby took its place," says another, "alongside chapel choirs, self-education, and socialist unionism in the new canon of Welshness."[31]

Cricket similarly took a place of honor in the Victorian canon of Englishness. "English cricket," says historian Richard Holt, "came to have a special place in the Anglican heart beside the King James Bible and the Book of Common Prayer." As the ninth edition of the *Encyclopedia Britannica* framed the issue in 1891, cricket was "the national game of Englishmen" because it provided "a combination of intellectual and physical qualities—broad and open shoulders, stout arms and quick legs, with patience, calculation, and promptness of execution."[32] Whatever its personal benefits, the structure of the game brought sport and morality together in a combination most English. Cricket rewarded skill, not raw strength; it demanded courage and patience, not overt aggression or violence. At its highest level, it honored age-old class distinctions by having Gentlemen (amateurs) and Players (professionals) come onto the field through different gates but then play the game with gentlemanly zeal.

Like American baseball, cricket admirably balanced individual and group interests, but cricket in Victorian England took on a hallowed as well as a beloved reputation that baseball never acquired. Curates and parsons played the game alongside mechanics and aristocrats; Anglican sermons frequently called on cricket to illustrate "the Game of Life" with Christ as the great captain of the team. Lord's, the appropriately named home ground of the premier Marylebone Cricket Club, became sacred ground trod with reverence by those who "weighed and pondered and worshipped," as Rudyard Kipling phrased it, "and practiced day by day." Little wonder that England's greatest cricket hero, W. G. Grace, reminded journalists of a favorite old Protestant hymn: Amazing Grace, how sweet the sound of his bat clouting the ball.[33]

Colonial Australians, New Zealanders, South Africans, Indians, and West Indians also worshipped at the cricket altar. By 1900 cricket was the unrivalled British Empire game, affording colonial rivalries as well as emulation of English ways. In that day, before soccer became the global game and before the United States became the world's policeman, cricket was the only game on which the sun never set. God seemed to be an Englishman; to English sporting patriots, He seemed to smile most on a game of cricket.

## Olympic Believers

Of all the turn-of-the-century sports projects doused with the double potion of religious and patriotic passion, the modern Olympic Games head the list. Their founder, French baron Pierre de Coubertin, came of age in the wake of his nation's crushing defeat in the Franco-Prussian war of 1870. He instinctively felt the shame and resentment that coursed through French society in the last quarter of the nineteenth century. As he entered adulthood, France was aggressively competing against German and British imperial interests in Europe, Africa, and the Far East. The politics and literature of that day reeked with preachments about racial pride, national vigor, and physical prowess, and those concerns colored all that Coubertin did on behalf of a renewal of the Olympic Games.[34]

Yet a more religious and philosophical set of assumptions stoked the fire of Coubertin's enthusiasm. He thought of sport as a kind of new religion with its own dogma and rituals, "but especially with religious feeling." Encouraged by his parents to train for the Roman Catholic priesthood, Coubertin spent his early years at daily mass, catechism, and vespers in a French Jesuit school devoted to religious study. The effort misfired when Coubertin became a skeptic, rejecting orthodox creeds. He found refuge from atheism in a humanistic philosophy that was then fashionable, the "religion of humanity" espoused by a fellow Frenchman, Auguste Comte. On behalf of that liberal faith, Coubertin poured huge sums of money and energy toward the creation of the modern Olympics as a means of achieving a "ceaselessly reborn humanity." Often and loudly he preached his new gospel of sport. "Have faith in it," Coubertin wrote to a friend; "pour out your strength for it; make its hope your own."[35]

Although a doctrinal renegade, Coubertin remained wedded to religious terms and sensibilities. He saw athletes as "new adepts," disciples of the new "muscular religion." He thought of spectators and coaches as "the laity of sport" and the International Olympic Committee as "a college of disinterested priests." In his construction of Olympic festivals, Coubertin employed rites and ceremonies reminiscent of the liturgical traditions of his Catholic youth: holy processions, oaths, hymns, invocations, myths, sacred sites, statues, wreaths, and crowns. Like worshippers of old, Olympic spectators were exposed to a plethora of colorful sights and sounds that would, by repetition, achieve the status of ritual.[36]

Yet when Coubertin referred to modern Olympism as "a pilgrimage to the past," he primarily had pre-Christian Greece, not medieval Europe, in mind. Predictably, his study of the Greek classics revealed a "human religion" or "cult of humanity" radically different from modern French Catholicism. Hellenism, he believed, provided "a great novelty in the mental outlook of all peoples and times": an emphasis on temporal happiness and achievement rather than "the idea of recompense and happiness beyond the tomb and the fear of punishment for him who has offended the gods." This idealized Hellenism meant, for Coubertin, a balanced "bilateral cult of the things of the body and the things of the mind," the philosophical basis of his zealous support of athleticism.[37]

Although he never tired of comparing his renewed Olympism with the ancient Greek Olympics, Coubertin occasionally slipped into admiration of old preclassical fertility rites. In a piecemeal, unscholarly fashion, his thought reflected the new anthropological studies of his day. He was conversant with French and German versions of the great English anthropologist James George Frazier, whose *Totemism* (1887) and multivolume classic *The Golden Bough* (1880–1915) attempted to make sense of ancient religious beliefs and systems of worship that revolved around seasonal rituals dramatizing life-and-death issues.

Coubertin insisted that the modern Olympic games should be celebrated every four years "in a rhythm of astronomic rigidity, because they constitute the quarterly celebration of human springtime in honor of the constant renewal of mankind." Little wonder that Pope Pius X was at first suspicious of the "pagan-seeming" character of modern Olympism. Not until 1906, when French, Belgian, and Italian gymnasts provided a private exhibition at the Vatican, did the Pope give his blessings to Coubertin's creation. Most modern scholars conclude, though, that Coubertin possessed little "in the way of genuine piety." His "peculiar religiosity," it seems, should not be mistaken for Christianity.[38]

For the most part, Coubertin merely used the ancients as a kind of backdrop or standard of reference for what he wanted the modern Olympics to be. In seeking social acceptance of Olympic athleticism as a serious, culturally significant enterprise, he insisted that ancient sport was the "central idea" or "essential principle" of modern athletics: "a religion, a cult, an impassioned soaring which is capable of going from play to heroism." In his very last public pronouncement, a recorded message broadcast at the opening ceremonies of the Berlin games in 1936, Coubertin reiterated the "religious sense" that lay at the heart of Olympism past and present. Though changed by time and circumstance, a religious spirit remained "in essence the same as that which led the young Greeks, zealous for victory through the strength of their muscles, to the foot of the altar of Zeus."[39]

The essence of ancient and modern Olympism differed, however, at one fundamental point. According to Coubertin, patriotism was the modern equivalent of what the ancients called the gods. Around little Olympia, "the capital of ancient sport," he sensed a spirit of "patriotic piety" hovering, "impregnating its atmosphere and investing its monuments" with sacred meaning. Now, in "this secularized century," the one thing that could rekindle the flame and adequately honor a victorious athlete was the national flag, the prime symbol of modern patriotism. Coubertin framed the issue in that final recorded speech for Berlin in 1936: "The contestants of the ancient world formed their bodies in the gymnasium just as the sculptor formed statues in his workshop, and both in doing so did honor to the gods. The modern athlete likewise does honor to his country, to his race, to his flag."[40]

Blasphemy by all the usual standards of religious belief, this deification of the nation-state and its symbols marks Pierre de Coubertin as a distinctly modern, thoroughly secularized person. At worst, he sounds like a fascist. To be sure, he was a fervent French patriot. Yet Coubertin made a distinction between patriotism and nationalism. He extolled patriotism as the love of one's own country and the unselfish desire to serve her; he rejected the militaristic nationalism that provoked citizens to hate other countries and seek to do them harm.[41]

For all his aristocratic, royalist heritage, Coubertin was a liberal democrat and an internationalist. Like older nineteenth-century European liberals, he loathed war, thinking it an irrational throwback to primitive barbarism. Other liberals attempted to replace war with negotiations and unfettered economic competition (free trade); Coubertin thought that international athletic competition would do the trick. In his optimistic vision, quadrennial Olympic gatherings would foster international understanding, tolerance, and peace. Patriotism, he insisted, was a good thing so long as it was muted in "peaceful and chivalrous contests" that would transform nationalism into "the best of internationalisms."[42]

Despite much evidence to the contrary, this cheerful hope has stood at the center of Olympic rhetoric for much of the twentieth century. So has Coubertin's preachments on sportsmanship. "The important thing in the Olympic Games is not winning but taking part," Coubertin often declared in various combinations of phrases. "The essential thing is not conquering but fighting well." Even this little homily had religious roots. Coubertin apparently took it directly from a sermon delivered by an American Episcopal bishop, the Right Reverend Ethelbert Talbot. Ironically, this classic Olympic principle originated as a clergyman's protest against the nationalism that was all too obvious in the early modern Olympic Games.

Talbot, the Bishop of Central Pennsylvania, served as a guest preacher at St. Paul's Cathedral in mid-July 1908, on the Sunday following the first week of the London Olympics. With athletes and Olympic officials present as guests of honor, Talbot lauded "the great Olympic Games" for bringing robust youths together from all parts of the world. Yet he saw a worm in the apple. Athletes seemed to be competing not only for the sake of sport, but for the sake of their countries. He could well have cited several awkward, patriotically charged moments in the first week of the London games, beginning with the American team's thinking their flag so dishonored by English officials that they stubbornly refused to dip the Stars and Stripes to the King of England in the opening ceremonies. During the second week of the games, patriotic tempers flared again over controversies in the marathon and the 400-meter race.

The remedy, said Bishop Talbot, lay in the principles that "the Games themselves are better than the race and the prize" and "though only one may wear the laurel wreath, all may share the equal joy of the contest." In conclusion, Talbot wanted to encourage "the exhilarating—I might also say soul-saving—interest that comes in active and fair and clean athletic sports." Coubertin heard it all, and was impressed. Over the next several years, he publicly lauded Bishop Talbot's views as "the foundation of a clear and sound philosophy" of Olympism: "The importance of these Olympiads is not so much to win as to take part."[43]

Blessed by official Christendom, the quasi-religious aspects of the Olympic movement exercised mystic attraction for strong personalities who had given up conventional religion. One true believer, Carl Diem, the German organizer of the 1936 Olympics, happily thought the solemnity and exuberance of the Berlin games "equal to a church festivity." The powerful president of the International Olympic Committee, Avery Brundage, depicted modern Olympism as "a twentieth century religion, a religion with universal appeal which incorporates all the basic values of other religions, a modern, exciting, virile, dynamic religion, attractive to the youth."[44] Himself not a religious man in any orthodox sense of the term, Brundage once mentioned his "conversion, along with many others, to Coubertin's religion." He certainly followed in the footsteps of the French baron in propounding a creed of fair play, good sportsmanship, and amateur athletics. As biographer Allen Guttmann shrewdly phrases it, Brundage voiced his beliefs as frequently and as earnestly "as other clerics speak of the Immaculate Conception and the Virgin Birth."[45]

## Over There

The Young Men's Christian Association also draped the flag around sport and religion in the early years of the twentieth century. The YMCA functioned both more vigorously and more subtly than did modern Olympism: more vigorously because it was inspired by an evangelical, missionary creed; more subtly because much of its patriotism flourished under the guise of humanitarian principles, Christian compassion, and wartime necessity.

The YMCA leader should be "a sort of physical evangelist—to go up and down the land looking after gymnasiums to see that they are run properly and to preach to the physical directors the value of exercises," suggested an Association journal in 1894. Seven years later a Jubilee Convention in Boston exuded, in the words of one report, "a great confidence in the future of the YMCA and a deep sense of mission."[46] That evangelical zeal not only propelled the YMCA into both the inner cities and the rural boondocks of North America, but also to far-flung corners of the world. To

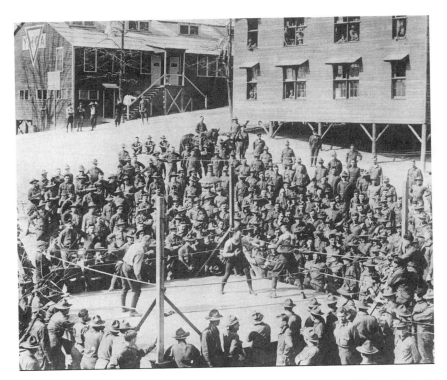

**The YMCA at war.** Sponsored largely by the YMCA, sports programs provided physical exercise and pleasant diversion for American doughboys in World War I. Here a large gathering of soldiers watches a boxing match at an army training camp; a YMCA emblem oversees an informal three-on-three game of outdoor basketball at Camp Gordon, near Atlanta, Georgia; and a baseball game heats up behind the front lines in France. (From the Kautz Family Archives, YMCA of the USA.)

South America, to the Orient, to the Philippines, to India, and even to tsarist Russia, YMCA missionaries carried the gospel of salvation and healthy games. But they were hardly the first to do so. For several decades prior to the YMCA's missionary activity, Victorian Englishmen planted their public-school games ethic in the alien soil of Africa, India, and all the other places controlled by British soldiers and imperial administrators. Compared to the British imperialists, American YMCA missionaries established a more informal, but similarly purposeful, empire of American values, technology, and sport.[47]

The YMCA focused on China, a vast nation of some 400 million people at the beginning of the twentieth century. Since the mid-nineteenth century, China's traditional religions had been in decline, their demise hastened by mission schools and churches founded by English and American denominational missionaries. China's ruling elite, the old mandarin class and its Manchu dynasty, was also on its last leg. Viewing Western technology and commercial expertise as beacons to a brighter future, native reformers welcomed missionaries more for their material benefits than for their religious message. YMCA missionaries provided both. In a pragmatic, activist style already perfected in the United States, they added athletic games to the American mix of the gospel, goods, and gadgetry.[48]

The coming of the First World War prompted the YMCA to play out more recognizable patriotic games. Canadians led the way. At the outbreak of war in August 1914, the Canadian YMCA (recently reorganized as a national entity, separate from the United States) offered its services to the Canadian government as part of the Commonwealth nations' support of Britain. At training camps, on troop ships, and along the Western front, YMCA personnel made sure that Allied troops were adequately supplied with canteen items, reading material, spiritual and moral advice, and recreational gear.[49]

Canada's camp recreational programs came under the direction of Fred J. Smith, a stocky, bespectacled man who regularly taught Bible classes in Presbyterian churches while fulfilling his YMCA duties. Given the rank of major in the Canadian army, Smith in 1917 was placed in charge of all YMCA work in England and France. In the last year of the war, he directed no fewer than eighty-four YMCA centers in Britain alone. England's King George V honored Smith with the Order of the British Empire medal for his distinguished service on behalf of the war effort.[50]

On the path blazed by Canadians, the American YMCA followed. As one of seven groups affiliated with the Commission on Training Camp Activities (CTCA), a new federal agency created by President Woodrow Wilson just a few days after the United States entered the War in April 1917, the YMCA placed an athletic director in charge of recreational and athletic programs at every American military base. Their program included calisthenics and less structured recreational activities as well as competitive football, baseball, basketball, volleyball, boxing matches, and track and field meets.[51]

Something more than mere sportive diversion was at stake. The "science of boxing," for example, was thought to be "intimately related to the business of bayonet-fighting." For all their differences, throwing a baseball seemed analogous to tossing a grenade at the enemy: the one supposedly trained soldiers for the other. In order to become comfortable with the use of gas masks, troops wore them while playing baseball games. For soldiers destined for combat in the trenches, training camp athleticism would presumably "be the means of saving their lives."[52]

Moral purposes, too, stood tall. As antidotes to the saloons and whorehouses that enticed servicemen, athletic participation marched hand in hand with chaperoned dances, talent shows, movies, religious services, and indoctrination in social hygiene. The fear of troop "debauchery" was great, especially after disastrous bouts with alcoholism and venereal disease suffered by U.S. troops stationed along the Mexican border in 1916. Without antibiotics to combat sexually transmitted diseases, moral suasion and counterattractions seemed essential. As Secretary of War Newton D. Baker explained at the outset of hostilities, innovative training camp measures would be conducted "along the line of healthy and wholesome and stimulating and strengthening substitutes as counterweights to temptation."[53]

Military chaplains lauded the YMCA's provision of athletic activities, especially the Sunday afternoon games that were regularly scheduled after morning religious services. Enjoying a day of rest from their military training, idle soldiers grew restless; worse still, they grew thirsty. In France on July 4, 1918 (a Sunday), a huge athletic program inspired one chaplain to note in his diary that the program "was designed to cover the whole day and evening in order to give Satan no chance at filling idle soldiers with noxious liquors."[54]

For this moralistic, patriotic crusade, the YMCA recruited not only its best local physical directors but also notable college coaches and former athletes to serve as Y athletic directors. Coaches from Yale, Princeton, Brown, and Bowdoin volunteered, as did several Olympic medalists. Max J. Exner, a Springfield College athlete who had recently returned home from a missionary stint in China, headed the Social Hygiene Division. Another Springfield College man, James H. McCurdy, momentarily laid aside his research and administrative chores to direct the Division of Health Hygiene and Athletics in France. One of his assistants was none other than James Naismith, the inventor of basketball. On leave from his faculty position at the University of Kansas to give health and morality lectures to servicemen in France, Naismith happily saw basketball games being played on American bases all over Europe.[55]

Games under the auspices of the YMCA were also played in prisoner-of-war camps. Fully two years before his fellow countrymen went "over there," American John R. Mott, secretary of foreign work in the International Committee, negotiated a scheme of reciprocity that allowed American Y officials to provide personal amenities and recreational equipment for Allied prisoners in German and Austrian camps in return for similar privileges extended to Axis prisoners in Britain and North America.[56]

By the end of the war, some seven hundred physical directors of the American YMCA had been assigned to military camps overseas, mostly in France. Scarcely were they spared the dangers of war. Ten were killed in action, largely from artillery bombardment near the front lines. Another 154 were wounded in action, and 111 died of various other causes while in the service. So extraordinary was their work that the War Department awarded 180 special citations for meritorious devotion to duty.[57]

This wartime promotion of sport on behalf of God and country was an activity destined to be repeated often in the course of the war-filled twentieth century, as witnessed by the many Hollywood films that feature lively softball and volleyball games in the South Pacific, Asian, and European war zones during both World War II and the Korean conflict. More subtly, the coming of the Cold War and its xenophobic successor, the latter-day fear of terrorism, have given a patriotic edge to all our sport spectacles. Lest we forget, these God and country games began long ago in circumstances altogether different from the present.

# 7

## FOR GOD, THE GIPPER, AND THE GREEN

A huge mosaic of Jesus and his disciples adorns the front façade of the Hesburgh Library on the campus of the University of Notre Dame. Shortly after the construction of the mosaic in 1964, some undergraduates observed that Jesus' arms were stretched heavenward, as if he were signaling a touchdown. Imaginative youths dispensed with the official title of the work, the "Word of Life" mural, and instead tabbed the figure "Touchdown Jesus." The nickname stuck. After all, he is appropriately positioned to overlook the football stadium, whose 80,000 occupants have been known to implore the heavens for a victory for the Fighting Irish.

Although he was late in coming to campus, Touchdown Jesus is a majestic reminder of Notre Dame's central importance in the American saga of sport and religion, and of Roman Catholics' contribution to the story. To be sure, long before Notre Dame's emergence in the 1920s, individual Catholic athletes made impressive marks on the sporting landscape. America's first superstar, John L. Sullivan, intended to be a priest prior to embarking on a prizefighting career that culminated in the heavyweight crown, 1882–1892. While the Great John L basked in public adulation, another Irish Catholic, Mike "King" Kelly of "Slide, Kelly, slide" fame, captained the Boston Red Sox. But neither man made much of his Catholic affiliation. Numerous Catholic colleges and universities originated in the nineteenth century just as sport was being organized. Georgetown (founded in 1789), Villanova, Boston College, Holy Cross, Duquesne, Marquette, and Santa Clara all fielded baseball and football squads for intercollegiate competition, but without much success or acclaim.

Notre Dame football first gained national attention in the 1920s, the so-called golden age of American sport. As people turned to automobiles, radio, jazz, talking movies, and airplanes, mediocre presidents Warren G.

**Touchdown Jesus.** A relative newcomer (1964) to the Notre Dame campus, the "Touchdown Jesus" mural on the face of the Hesburgh Library can be seen from the football stadium, joining the echo of excellence that derives from the Rockne era of the 1920s, when the Fighting Irish emerged as a major player in American athletic culture. (From Getty Images.)

Harding, Calvin Coolidge, and Herbert Hoover relinquished the limelight to athletic heroes. Names such as Babe Ruth, Jack Dempsey, Red Grange, Bill Tilden, and Bobby Jones grabbed the headlines. College football flourished as a major spectator sport. The construction of numerous new stadiums (most called "Memorial Stadium" in honor of soldiers killed in World

War I) provoked journalist John R. Tunis to depict the gridiron game as something more than a mere diversion for undergraduates. "It is at present a religion," wrote Tunis; "sometimes it seems to be almost our national religion." Willard Sperry, the dean of Harvard's divinity school, agreed. Enthusiasm for football seemed to be "the only true religious spirit to be discerned" on the college campus.[1]

## Echoes across the Country

Of all its Protestant and Catholic guises, this new campus religion found fullest expression at a remote little Catholic men's college on the outskirts of a modest industrial center, South Bend, Indiana, some ninety miles east of Chicago. Founded in 1842 by inspired but pragmatic men of faith, Notre Dame retained a complex mixture of idealism and realism as it evolved from a parochial midwestern college into a modern university. By the end of the First World War, its priest-heavy faculty still emphasized moral and philosophical pedagogy over research. Predominantly Roman Catholic and Irish, German, Polish, Italian, and Czech in ethnic origin, the all-male undergraduate population numbered about a thousand in 1918.[2]

Reflecting its immigrant, working-class foundations, Notre Dame was an exceedingly poor institution. Prior to 1920 it had no endowment whatsoever until a professor of sociology was released from his teaching duties to direct an endowment campaign. He couched his initial exhortation in athletic terms. "Notre Dame is entering one of the biggest games of its career," he told a group of undergraduates, "and to win that game will require all the fighting spirit characteristic of Notre Dame teams." The football captain spoke at the same rally, urging student contributions to an endowment fund. Then coach Knute Rockne summoned students to "get back of the movement and boost." Sounding as if he were delivering yet another of his famous pregame pep talks, Rockne promised that "if better athletic teams will help, you will find next year's captain Eddie Anderson and his boys hitting the line next fall with an echo that will be heard across the country."[3]

Scarcely was sport a new campus activity. In the wake of the American Civil War, Notre Dame undergraduates eagerly took to baseball, rowing, track, and football. By 1870 dormitories and clubs competed fiercely for intramural honors; by 1890 the entire student body cheered on their athletic teams in intercollegiate contests. At the turn of the century, baseball remained the favorite varsity sport, as it was for Irish-Americans everywhere. Yet football was coming on strong. From 1906 to 1912 Notre

Dame lost only three of fifty-two varsity games. By the First World War, the Blue and Gold was widely recognized as a major midwestern power. Contrary to popular lore, Knute Rockne and his boys merely enlarged and refined firmly established sports programs. Scarcely did they create them ex nihilo.[4]

Bigotry provided some of the spur. Neither Irish nor central and southern European Catholics "need apply" for decent jobs, social clubs, or high political office in early twentieth-century America. Excluded from the tangible fruit of Eden, Catholic boys turned all the more to sports as a means of achievement and self-esteem. The prizefight ring and the baseball diamond beckoned first, followed shortly by football at church-sponsored colleges and universities. At one level, Catholic college football served "a socioreligious purpose," as a recent Notre Dame graduate put it, "demonstrating the upward mobility of a significant American minority." At another level, social barriers made football doubly important.[5]

In the 1920s Protestant prejudice and Catholic football zeal combined to prevent Notre Dame from becoming a member of the Western Conference (later renamed the Big Ten). Administrators at the University of Michigan, eager to establish the Western Conference as a model union of academic and athletic excellence, led the way in believing the worst rumors about inferior Catholic education and unscrupulous athletic practices. Thinking themselves excluded "on the grounds of religion," Notre Dame men harbored long-term hostilities toward Michigan. Three years after formal rejection by the Western Conference, Rockne wrote to a friend castigating Michigan head coach Fielding Yost as "a hill-billy from Tennessee and hence very narrow on religion." On one count, at least, Rockne was misinformed: Yost was a native of West Virginia, not Tennessee.[6]

At any rate, religious bigotry could be found much closer to home. Protestant fundamentalism and the Ku Klux Klan thrived in the 1920s, especially in Indiana. Both crusaded on behalf of traditional Protestant beliefs and practices in the face of vast cultural change brought on by technological and population growth. In a nastier vein, under the banner "one hundred per cent Americanism" the Klan spewed venom against Catholics, Jews, blacks, and other minorities who were knocking at the door of the American dream. As few blacks and fewer Jews lived in Indiana, Catholics bore the brunt of the bitterness. Nearly one-third of the population in central and northern Indiana, the area surrounding South Bend, belonged to the Ku Klux Klan. Catholic students at Notre Dame understandably felt under siege.[7]

They responded angrily in mid-May 1924, when the Klan held a week-long convention in South Bend, complete with hooded marches down the main street. Ignoring President Walsh's temporary ban of off-campus activities, students roughed up several Klansmen. Two nights later they emptied the dorms when informed that Klansmen had seized an undergraduate and were beating him to death near the courthouse. As hundreds of students confronted armed policemen, President Walsh interceded to restore order. For several days his mailbox was stuffed and campus phones buzzed with anonymous threats. Student patrols guarded the campus each night against Klan violence.[8]

In old Western terms, the Notre Dame community was forced to "circle the wagons" against their Klan foes. Under duress, they unified; physically threatened, they flexed their muscles. Their patriotism called into question by Hoosier rednecks and white-collar politicians alike, they excelled at the All-American game of football. Knute Rockne was Notre Dame's answer to the Ku Klux Klan. "Notre Dame football is a new crusade: it kills prejudice," declared campus chaplain Father John F. O'Hara just a few months after the rumble in 1924. Two years later an Indiana native observed that Notre Dame's football team was the one Catholic institution immune to the bigotry "that frowns upon the Pope and his other works."[9]

Klansmen and Notre Dame boosters especially clashed in the city of Chicago. By 1920 Chicago was the home of about a million Roman Catholics, three-quarters of whom were foreign-born immigrants. The Klan found no shortage of Protestant patriots eager to stem the alien tide. By contrast, support for Notre Dame became permanently fixed, and in the 1920s Notre Dame essentially became Catholic Chicago's team of choice. Their competitors were few. Local Catholic colleges played football poorly or not at all. Loyola fielded weak teams that remained virtually invisible in the press; DePaul's gridiron program was so mediocre that its 1930 squad, deemed "one of the best in the history of the school," opened its season against tiny Buena Vista College from Storm Lake, Iowa.[10]

Nor did professional teams pose any challenge. Although the Chicago Bears were founded in 1922, professional football was scarcely any more successful than barnstorming basketball professionals. All the while, Chicago's major league baseball teams offered little popular appeal. For years the "Black Sox" reeled from the scandal following the World Series fix of 1919; the Cubs languished in their losing ways. Little wonder that Chicago sportswriters devoted much column space to nearby Notre Dame. Little wonder too that Chicago's Roman Catholic diocesan weekly, *The New*

*World*, virtually built a sports page around Notre Dame news and personalities. Beginning in 1920, annual Chicago gatherings of the Notre Dame alumni association were regularly announced in the sports section of *The New World*.[11]

Beyond its Catholic core of support, the new city of Chicago (largely rebuilt since a disastrous fire in 1871) doted on Notre Dame as a symbol of midwestern interests opposed to eastern elites. For a city whose reputation was tainted with gangsterism, close association with a highly visible religious institution was a civic booster's dream. Chicago avidly supported games in South Bend as well as occasional contests in Chicago and Evanston. In 1927 the city provided the largest football crowd ever assembled, more than 120,000 people at Soldier Field, to watch the Fighting Irish host the University of Southern California. Two years later, while a new stadium was being built on the campus at South Bend, Notre Dame played all its home games before sellout crowds at Soldier Field.[12]

Thus Chicago—especially the city's Catholic community—gave Notre Dame important material and emotional support. One of the city's greatest gifts to Notre Dame, however, was the great Rockne himself.

## Catholic Connections

Norwegian by birth, Kenneth Rockne at age five emigrated with his family to the United States, settling in the Logan Square neighborhood of northwest Chicago. Years later, Rockne recalled the "new, spacious city, with its endless corner lots and tolerant police" as "a great place for a boy to grow up in." He grew up playing sandlot football and baseball, and he excelled in schoolboy track. A high school dropout, he beat around at several odd jobs, then saved money for college by working for three years in the U.S. postal service. In 1910 he matriculated at Notre Dame, whose student body then numbered a mere four hundred young men. Although he stood only five feet, eight inches tall and weighed 165 pounds, for three years Rockne starred as an end on gridiron teams that never lost a game. As captain in his senior year, he led the team to a 35–13 victory over Army by teaming with quarterback Gus Dorais in an innovative use of the new forward pass.[13]

After graduation in 1914, Rockne stayed on at Notre Dame as an assistant to football coach Jesse Harper, then took over the head coaching job when Harper retired in 1918. For the next thirteen years the Rock combined a kind of Puritan work ethic with an evangelical charisma in pushing Notre Dame to the limits of success and national renown. His composite coaching record of 105–12–5 included six national championships, five undefeated seasons, a Rose Bowl victory, and twenty All-Americans.

Rockne was scarcely an innocent, idealistic coach of zealous fight-talk. His success derived from "no legends of mystifying systems or magical wizardry," as one of his friends insisted: Rockne was simply "the greatest tutor of football logic" and precision. He recruited aggressively, worked long hours, and employed up-to-date training techniques. He perfected an offensive system that he inherited, shrewdly adding new wrinkles to both offensive and defensive schemes. He built schedules to Notre Dame's advantage, creating the need and overseeing the construction of a new stadium. With awesome efficiency, he managed pregame preparations and game-day activities. Most of all, he was a pragmatic, tough-minded promoter of Notre Dame's reputation and his own economic interests. He shamelessly manipulated the press and hustled appearance fees and endorsements.[14]

A national network of Notre Dame and larger Catholic connections served Rockne well in these endeavors, especially in his relation to the press. He himself set the terms by regularly seeking out the best undergraduate journalism major as his personal press assistant during the football season. Rockne personally gave the instructions and supplied information, then edited press releases before they went out. He insisted that midwestern newspaper editors accept articles about Notre Dame only from his press assistant, not from any freelance journalist.[15]

In Rockne's first student worker, Archibald ("Arch") Ward, religion, sport, and Notre Dame connections cohered in a peculiarly intimate fashion. Born of Roman Catholic parents near Joliet, Indiana, Ward grew up in northern Iowa, where he served as an altar boy before going to a Catholic boarding school in Dubuque. Priests attempted to recruit him for the priesthood, but sport claimed his attention. Too small, slow, and weak sighted to compete athletically, Ward wrote up sport for the school paper. Then for two years he attended Dubuque College, where Gus Dorais, Rockne's old teammate, happened to be the head football coach. In 1918 Rockne invited Dorais back to South Bend to coach the Notre Dame backfield. Dorais in turn convinced Arch Ward to accompany him to South Bend, there to finish his degree while serving as Rockne's personal publicity assistant.[16]

Ward seized the opportunity. For the seasons of 1919 and 1920 he artfully honed his "gee whiz" style of sportswriting by embellishing the gospel according to Knute. He well knew that Rockne was his meal ticket into big-time sports journalism. After Notre Dame, Ward served a five-year stint as the sports editor of the *Morning Star* in Rockford, Illinois, then moved on to the sports room of the *Chicago Tribune.* During thirty years with the *Tribune,* he helped found the Golden Gloves tournament, the major league baseball all-star game, an annual all-star football matchup of college graduates and professional champions, and the All-American Football Conference.[17]

First as a reporter, later as the *Tribune's* sports editor, Ward capitalized on his personal acquaintance with Rockne. During the football season, he often scooped the opposition with information fresh from Rockne's desk. During Rockne's off-season travel for public appearances, banquet speeches, and recruitment, the coach frequently changed trains in Chicago and as often as not popped into Ward's office at the *Tribune.* Ward's colleagues were duly impressed and his readers informed of Notre Dame's doings. Not by coincidence, the *Chicago Tribune* virtually became a cheerleader for the Fighting Irish.[18]

Of Rockne's six student assistants, only one failed to carry the Notre Dame banner into some sports reportage or publicity role. Ward's successor, Francis Wallace, officially managed the news for the Fighting Irish from 1921 to 1923 and later unofficially did the same in several books and a lifetime of sportswriting and sports news management at the *New York Daily News.* George Strickler, the young man who arranged and distributed the famous photograph of the Four Horsemen in 1924, followed Arch Ward to the *Chicago Tribune* and later became publicity director of the National Football League. Another of Rockne's boys, Joe Pertritz, handled publicity for the short-lived All-American Football Conference.[19]

Several players also carried the ethos of the Rockne era into newspaper work. We know much about the many athletes who diffused the Rockne system as coaches throughout the United States; we know less about the such former players as novelist and sportswriter Chet Grant and newspaper publishers Joe Brandy and Danny Coughlin. We know even less about the Notre Dame graduates of the 1920s who never played football but nevertheless joined the proud company of sportswriting alums. Tennis captain Bill Fay graduated to the sports room of the *Chicago Tribune* beside Arch Ward and George Strickler; nonathlete W. F. Fox became a notable sportswriter for the *Indianapolis News.*[20]

Most impressive of all was a young redheaded graduate of 1927 from a Roman Catholic family in Green Bay, Wisconsin, named Walter Wellesley

Smith. No athlete, he wrote for campus newspapers and in his senior year edited *The Dome*. Always a proud Notre Dame man, he became sports editor of the *New York Herald Tribune* and later of the *New York Times*. His readers knew him as Red Smith. For sportswriters, he had a simple rule: "Use the mother tongue with respect, and don't gush." Throughout the many years that he stood at the pinnacle of his craft, he refrained from gushing about Notre Dame. Yet not even Red Smith broke the code enunciated by Francis Wallace: that none of these Notre Dame sportswriting graduates could ever be "accused of giving his alma mater the worst of it."[21]

Although Knute Rockne did not live to see the emergence of Red Smith as one of New York's premier sportswriters, he fully recognized the crucial role of the New York press in the making of a national reputation for Notre Dame. "New York is the heart of the matter," he confided to Arch Ward. "That's the big time. When they start noticing us there, everybody else will fall in line." Making that happen required a broad base of support from Notre Dame alumni and more general Roman Catholic press connections, not just a few well-placed sportswriters. To Notre Dame's great advantage, alumnus Hugh O'Donnell served as business manager of the *New York Times,* and high-ranking executives at the *New York Telegram* and the *New York Evening Mail* also had strong Catholic affiliations.[22]

A second-generation Notre Dame man, Joe Byrne, Jr., led the charge to enhance the visibility of the Fighting Irish in New York City. A highly successful businessman, Byrne was a self-styled "Eastern representative, University of Notre Dame." In 1923 he negotiated the moving of the Army game from the Polo Grounds (because the Giants were in the World Series) to Ebbets Field in Brooklyn, and even signed the contract on behalf of his alma mater. Whenever the team visited the New York area, he bought theater tickets and arranged lodging and food accommodations, then distributed game tickets to local Notre Dame alumni. He corresponded frequently with Rockne and was in the locker room when Rockne delivered his famous "Win one for the Gipper" speech. In 1928 Byrne made all the arrangements and accompanied an exhausted Rockne on a trip to Europe for the Amsterdam summer Olympics. Inordinately proud to be a Notre Dame alum, Joe Byrne did everything possible to promote the Blue and Gold.[23]

He especially proved his devotion in 1924, when he financed a scheme devised by fellow alumnus Hugh O'Donnell of the *New York Times*. O'Donnell arranged for a *Times* journalist to be assigned solely to Notre Dame as a kind of publicity agent whose daily articles on players and coaches would be eagerly bought up by New York's sports editors. At Rockne's suggestion, Byrne paid the reporter handsomely for his extra work on behalf of the Fighting Irish. Never again could any Notre Dame coach feel slighted by the New York press.[24]

## A Mystic Blend

Attentive though he was to practical details, Rockne knew full well that men do not live by bread alone. Nor do football programs thrive on mere managerial efficiency. They require intangible strengths and inspirations. At Rockne's fingertips was a religious heritage of vast mythic and ritualistic resources and priests eager to call down thunder from the sky for the creation of gridiron prowess. Rockne wisely and regularly tapped those religious possibilities. As one of his contemporaries put it, "Never in history was there such a mystic blending of religion and sport. Rockne reveled in it."[25]

He was joined, if not led, in his revelry by a Notre Dame chaplain, Father John Francis O'Hara, who happily sprinkled holy water on the gridiron. Destined to become the president of Notre Dame in the 1930s, O'Hara spent several years of his youth in South America, where his father held U.S. consulates in Uruguay and Brazil. O'Hara was therefore more familiar with soccer than with American football; but as a Notre Dame undergraduate and then (after 1917) as a member of the faculty, he shifted his sporting allegiance. For the gridiron game he displayed all the cheerful, uncritical zeal common to the new convert.[26]

Football, O'Hara believed, held many benefits for both participants and spectators. It filled idle moments, thus removing fleshly temptations for cloistered young men. In a vision remarkably similar to that of Protestant muscular Christians, Father O'Hara insisted that football taught physical and mental discipline and required "courage, initiative, generosity, equanimity, dependability, alertness [and] frankness." Stepping beyond Rockne's bromide that "outside the church, the best thing we've got is good, clean football," Father O'Hara genuinely believed that Catholic-based Notre Dame football "stimulates faith."[27]

On behalf of the Faith, Father O'Hara initiated daily early morning communion on campus and made it into a popular event by getting athletes to attend. "When students saw some of the football huskies, like Ray Eichenlaub, going simply and quietly to the altar rail," recalled a student participant, "they followed without much persuasion." Actually Eichenlaub, a "thunderous" 210-pound fullback from the 1912–14 teams, made less of an impression than did John Smith, a smallish guard from the mid-1920s era. When Smith first received communion as a freshman in 1924, he stood only five feet, six inches tall and weighed less than 160 pounds. Yet to Father O'Hara he identified himself as a candidate for the position of left guard on the football team. For the next four years he regularly attended morning Mass, often assisting Father O'Hara in the service. By his third year, Smith was a varsity stalwart, having picked up the nickname "Clipper" Smith. Captain of the team during his final year, he won mythic fame by repeatedly stopping the bull-like rushes of a large All-American fullback for the University of Minnesota, Bronko Nagurski. To Father O'Hara's great delight, Smith himself achieved All-American status that year.[28]

Whatever his contribution to the success of Clipper Smith, Father O'Hara was largely responsible for the creation of two Notre Dame rituals that persist to the present. First, he arranged and publicized ceremonious communion services on the eve of games. This practice began in 1927, when O'Hara accompanied the team on a train to West Point, New York, for the annual contest with Army. By prior arrangement the train stopped in Albany, where the entire squad took limousines to Farrell Institute for communion at a replica of the Grotto of Our Lady of Lourdes. Also by prior arrangement, local reporters put the story on the wire service, beginning a team tradition of highly publicized religious rituals. The Albany stopover immediately established Notre Dame as a Catholic alternative to the Protestant "Praying Colonels" of Centre College, a little sectarian college in Kentucky that had displayed its prayerful posture to the world just a year earlier.[29]

The comparison was not lost on mainstream America, and certainly not on Protestant ministers looking for religious or moral lessons to be drawn from the sports page. Several years later an Irish romp over the University of Southern California inspired a popular California radio minister, Robert Shuler, to reflect upon the divergent religious moorings of the two schools. Shuler thought USC a former "great Methodist university" whose student newspaper now seemed content to devote "half its space to jokes about gin and women." Notre Dame, on the other hand, "has for years been known as the team that prays." Not one to miss a modern parable, Shuler hinted at gridiron success for Protestant colleges and universities if they would take religion "as seriously as our Catholic schools take the teaching of Roman Catholicism."[30]

If Protestants took notice, American Catholics took pleasure in the spectacle of burly Notre Dame men kneeling in prayer before knocking off their opponents. In 1930 a Philadelphia attorney wrote to the president of the University expressing amazement that his three sons rose at 6:00 A.M. on a Saturday morning to take an eight-mile trolley ride to St. Luke's Church, where "the archangel of the laity, Mr. Rockne, and his squad" were taking communion. "The example of manly, matter-of-fact devotion to the Blessed Sacrament manifested by the Notre Dame squad and its coach impressed my boys so strongly that it is impossible to exaggerate its effect," he stated. Himself a graduate of the University of Pennsylvania, the correspondent gladly gave Notre Dame its due: "Your men have done, unconsciously, more to back up parental example and suggestion than anybody else could possibly do." It was "hard, indeed, under such circumstance, not to root for Notre Dame even if one is a University of Pennsylvania man."[31]

In 1923 Father O'Hara invented yet another team tradition that linked athleticism to religious piety. Once again the occasion was an Army game, this time in Brooklyn. Word reached Father O'Hara that West Point officials had asked a popular musical comedy actress, Elsie Janis, to perform the ceremonial kickoff. O'Hara replied that if Elsie Janis kicked off for Army, Joan of Arc would kick off for Notre Dame. He proceeded to give each member of the team a Joan of Arc medal, suitably blessed, to wear on a chain around the neck during the game. For the next ten years O'Hara regularly distributed saints' medals before ball games. His successors have continued the practice right up to the present. As a contemporary from the 1920s put it, the gesture imbued Notre Dame athletes "with the spirit of crusaders."[32]

Press notices emphasized Protestant as well as Catholic participation in the Notre Dame ceremonies. By special dispensation, Protestant players joined in the communion ritual; Protestants also eagerly took the pregame medal blessed by Father O'Hara, as good-luck charms if nothing else. For the sake of team unity, Rockne, a Norwegian Lutheran from birth, also participated, and in 1925 converted to Roman Catholicism. Needless to say, his conversion inspired extravagant notice in the Catholic press. Explanatory yarns circulated freely. Some credited Rockne's Catholic wife, Bonnie, with nudging him toward the true faith. Others cited pressure from players who informed Rockne that his becoming Catholic "would mean more to every last man on the squad, and in the university, than anything else that any of them could think of."[33]

Rockne's own explanation displayed a certain charm mixed with candor. To a group of 1,000 men at a Catholic laymen's retreat, he admitted that he first attended game-day communion services "for the sake of appearances, if nothing else," but soon came to see "what a powerful ally their religion was to those boys in their work on the football field." Then, added Rockne, he "really began to see the light." He came "to know what I was missing in my life, and, later on, I had the great pleasure of being able to join my boys at the Communion rail." True to form, the practical use of religion as a "powerful ally" on the football field and the poetic impulse to "see the light" blended together in the complex person of Knute Rockne.[34]

## Living and Dying for Notre Dame

For all the liveliness of the Rockne era, death hovered in the wings. During Rockne's first season as head coach, 1918, a lethal influenza epidemic swept the nation. Some 200 cases and nine deaths on campus caused several football games to be cancelled. "The influenza was almost the death of all human joy," wrote the president to a friend.[35] The spectre of death lay behind the most famous nickname of the era: the "Four Horsemen," the invention of an imaginative sportswriter, Grantland Rice. Against the backdrop of "a blue-gray October sky," gushed Rice at the Notre Dame–Army game in 1924, "the Four Horsemen rode again." A native Tennessean, Grantland Rice knew his Bible. From the New Testament book of Revelations he drew his "Four Horsemen of the Apocalypse" reference, then turned it on its head. "In dramatic lore they are known as Famine, Pestilence, Destruction, and Death. These are only aliases. Their real names are Stuhldreher, Miller, Crowley and Layden." Presumably, the original Four Horsemen wore black for their ancient ritual of doom. Now they were garbed in blue and gold. In the liturgy of Our Lady, young legs and strong hearts replaced Death and his destructive cohorts. Apocalypse became apotheosis.[36]

In the real world, however, Rockne himself almost died of phlebitis (blood clots in the legs) in the autumn of 1929. He refrained from most road trips, but against doctors' orders coached home games from a bed or wheelchair on the sidelines. During his rousing pregame speeches, doctors anxiously measured Rockne's pulse, fearing that a blood clot would dislodge and cause a stroke or heart attack. Rumors had physicians giving Rockne only three years to live. While the shadow of death hung over his own doorway, he received word that an old teammate, Rupe Mills, had died tragically in an auto accident. Unable to "shake off the effect of poor Rupe's death," Rockne confronted the painful truth "that we can't tell when the same thing is going to come to any of us."[37]

It came too soon, wrapping two dramatic, highly publicized deaths around the Rockne era. In 1920 Notre Dame's All-American halfback, George Gipp, succumbed to pneumonia; in 1931 the forty-three-year-old Rockne died in a Kansas plane crash. Both these deaths, sudden and unexpected, sent shock waves across the American Catholic community and throughout the sports-focused public at large. Both deaths seemed doubly senseless because each victim stood at the peak of his powers. As Gipp battled his fatal fever, he was not only named to Walter Camp's All-American team but also received a lucrative offer to play professional baseball with the Chicago Cubs. Rockne crashed from the pinnacle of eighteen straight victories and two consecutive national championships.

Amidst all the eulogies, both these deaths resonated with meanings that outstripped the lives of the deceased. Rather than negating the achievements of the fallen, the deaths of these two heroes meant something to the living and for the future. Ever since the Enlightenment, death had become an occasion for the teaching of public, communal virtues. What people had done for the civic good increasingly mattered more than unverifiable assertions of eternal bliss or damnation. Nineteenth-century nationalism had extended these public, communal themes, making patriotic death a special kind of tribal commodity. In a tradition that extends right up to this morning's newscast, the fallen soldier especially carries a heavy freight of meaning for young manhood, for national consciousness, and for the larger community of nations.[38]

The cult of the fallen athlete mirrors the cult of the fallen soldier. George Gipp died just two years after the end of World War I, when Notre Dame ceremoniously mourned the wartime loss of forty-six "fallen sons," and just over a year after the highly publicized fatal plane crash of Princeton's Hobey Baker, a young man who romantically combined good looks, athletic stardom, military heroism, and an untimely, tragic end. Part of the poignancy in all these cases, of course, was the demise of *young* men whose promise would never be fulfilled. The drum bangs slowly for the grave that swallows up both the personal dreams and the social promise of youth.[39] For Notre Dame in the 1920s, George Gipp's death transformed an athletically gifted but morally and academically deficient young man into a veritable saint. "O Lady! You have taken of our best / To make a playmate for the Seraphim," wrote the editor of the campus paper, *The Dome*. "There on the wide sweet campus of the blest, / Be good to him."[40]

Whatever the Blessed Virgin did with the Gipper, history was exceedingly good to him. Rockne himself triggered the process of canonization with a halftime yarn in 1928. As Notre Dame struggled once again against an Army team, Rockne "recalled" Gipp's dying words: "Some time, Rock, when the team's up against it; when things are wrong and the breaks are beating the boys—tell them to go in there with all they've got and win just one for the Gipper. I don't know where I'll be then, Rock. But I'll know about it, and I'll be happy." In the final chapter of his *Autobiography,* Rockne embellished the Gipp legend, which was largely his own creation. In 1940 Warner Brothers and Ronald Reagan further airbrushed the offending parts for the film *Knute Rockne—All American* and concocted a scene with Gipp on his deathbed embracing the Catholic faith.[41]

In life is death, warned the preachers of old; in death is life, and new life at that, dreamed the ancient martyrs. Young George Gipp enjoyed a kind of resurrection. His mortal self took on immortality. Once a high school dropout, a pool shark, an inveterate gambler, a tipsy womanizer, and an expelled collegian, he became a living embodiment of the unbeaten, unbeatable spirit of Notre Dame. The motto coined by Knute Rockne and immortalized by Ronald Reagan, "Win one for the Gipper," represented both a whitewash of nonheroic elements from the past and the hoisting of an inspirational flag for generations to come.

In contrast to the prolonged process of canonization that turned George Gipp into a football saint, mythmakers set to work immediately on the Rockne legend. A former president of Notre Dame, Father John W. Cavanaugh, eulogized Rockne as a man comparable to the great Abe Lincoln, struck down at "the peak of his powers." Then Father Cavanaugh delivered an uncanny prediction: "Rockne's fame and influence may ultimately grow into a myth of epic proportions because tragedy struck him in the strength and splendor of his noonday."[42]

Rockne died in springtime, and by the end of the year his autobiography, collections of speeches and coaching hints, and no fewer than seven biographical potboilers could be found in bookstores. Instant biography inevitably meant hagiography: largely sentimental, anecdotal, and worshipful. As Michael Steele generously summarizes the issue, "Without a living Rockne to fill the hero's role on a daily basis, it became necessary to create an idealized Rockne to match the need of the myth."[43]

The first need was to confirm Rockne as a faithful, God-fearing Catholic to the end. Although his body was mangled beyond immediate recognition, the word circulated widely that he plummeted to earth clutching a rosary. The coroner, by coincidence a Notre Dame alumnus, never mentioned a rosary, nor did any eyewitness. But fact was beside the point. "When you saw Eternity through those clouds over Kansas," Rockne's literary agent imaginatively announced in a radio tribute several days after the crash, "you reached for your Holy Rosary. And when kindly hands lifted you from the ground, the Rosary of Notre Dame—the Rosary of Our Lady—was lying at your fingertips." A broken rosary in the Rock's hands, or lying near his body, quickly became a staple item in the Rockne legend.[44]

Not only did the deceased hero need to be a man of earnest faith. He also had to be a dutiful servant of Notre Dame to the end. That part of the laundering required some heavy detergent. The earliest accounts of Rockne's motive for taking the ill-fated flight to California casually mentioned his interest in pursuing a lucrative role in a Hollywood film about football, but that candor soon disappeared. It was replaced by yarns about Rockne embarking on a recruiting tour of the West Coast, eager to sign the best boys the Notre Dame reputation could buy. In the film *Knute Rockne,* the hero was responding out of the sheer goodness of his heart to some Notre Dame "fellows" who needed him in California. In truth, Rockne, having ignored President O'Donnell's complaint that he was spending too much time away from campus, flew off to negotiate a contract with Universal Pictures for a film adapted from a Broadway play, *Good News,* in which he would play the part of a football coach. Universal had offered him $50,000 for the job, an astronomical sum in the midst of the depression in 1931. Universal scored big on two counts. They kept their fee and exploited the occasion by changing the name of the film to *The Spirit of Notre Dame.*[45]

Notre Dame, too, cashed in on Rockne. In life, he had clashed frequently with faculty and administrators on issues ranging from athletic eligibility and too many road games to his lucrative off-campus interests. In death, those disputes were buried from view. James Armstrong, the editor of the alumni magazine, said more than he intended when he observed that the living Rockne had been "mortal, subject to death, subject to error, as are we all." For the deceased Rockne, however, time was "no longer an element." The Great One was now "unlimited by time and space, bonds that troubled his restless life." Physically absent, Rockne could "now be molded into that particular form which each of us may prefer."[46]

People preferred a kind of idealized saint, it seems. With religious faith and devotional practices on the wane, they framed their adulation of Coach Rockne in religious terms. The *New York World Telegram* depicted him as a "miracle man" who functioned as a "high priest of the American gridiron"; the *New York Times* saw him as "sort of a god." In various other accounts, Rockne was a "fallen idol" whose "godlike influence" continued to inspire "unshaken faith"; he was an archangel, a shaman, a "devout crusader," and an evangelist all rolled into one. Scarcely can one imagine such unqualified praise couched in that kind of religious language today. Certainly no mere football coach has ever again received such accolades, not even in the Deep South, where religion and sport have passionately embraced each other.[47]

The transfigured Rockne stands at the center of a Notre Dame mystique that continues to thrive. No easy believer, New York journalist Paul Gallico alluded to this mystique as a "mysterious intangible" that transcended won-lost records and institutional propaganda. Chicago sportswriter Ralph Cannon was similarly impressed when he visited the South Bend campus in 1946 and observed a "mystic touch" shared by athletes and nonathletes alike. "They play with a sense of responsibility to a grand tradition, to the great ones who remain only in the intangible atmosphere around them." Rockne thrived in that atmosphere and enhanced it.[48]

The essence of Rockne's appeal was best embedded in a yarn (a "touching invention," as the *New Republic* put it) circulated by the Associated Press in 1931. After Rockne's body arrived at the funeral home in South Bend, a shabbily dressed young boy reportedly began to cry as he gazed through the window. "Aw, don't cry," urged his playmate. "I know; but wasn't he one great guy!" replied the boy, as he wiped away his tears. "Why, he used to speak even to me."[49]

Rockne was revered because he did indeed speak to boys like that, and to the needs of many people in the 1920s. He and his Notre Dame enterprise spoke especially to Irish and Polish immigrants and to Roman Catholics of all ethnic origins who sought respect in their adopted land. He also spoke to midwesterners who were eager to drive the nail in the coffin of eastern athletic and cultural dominance. Most of all, he spoke to mainstream Americans who anxiously coped with change. For people newly immersed in a consumer culture, and for people baffled by more new technologies, codes of behavior, and ways of thinking than their parents could have imagined, Knute Rockne represented a highly successful blend of tradition and innovation.

He served something more than the "compensatory cultural function" that historian Ben Rader assigns to athletic heroes of the 1920s. "They assisted the public in compensating for the passing of the traditional dream of success, the erosion of Victorian values, and feelings of individual powerlessness," says Rader. "As the society became more complicated and systematized and as success had to be won increasingly in bureaucracies, the need for heroes who leaped to fame and fortune outside the rules of the system grew."[50] Rockne surely leaped to fame and fortune, often by following rules of success that he himself created. His attraction, however, lay in his successful negotiation of some of the tensions common to people in the 1920s, and in his accommodation of new with old ways of thought and behavior. Like him, people seized the new and quirky, but pined for the quaint.

Rockne eagerly embraced all the latest technologies. Anecdotes about his extensive use of radio, cinema, telephone, automobile, and airplane come readily to mind. He effectively exploited each one for his own personal and institutional purposes. In a world that was increasingly mechanized and bureaucratized, he bestrode America's most scientifically structured game. For good measure, he emphasized speed and finesse rather than brute force, and perfected a finely tuned offensive system of mass mechanization called the Notre Dame box-shift. Quickly recognizing the celebrity value of sport in a nation mushrooming with massive new steel-ribbed arenas, he displayed a sure grasp of both the psychology and the techniques of modern advertising. In step with the modern mania for statistics and records as measures of success, he compiled the best won-lost record in the history of major college football.[51]

Yet Father O'Donnell, the president of Notre Dame at the time of Rockne's death, perceptively eulogized the Rock as a man who "made use of all the proper machinery and legitimate methods of modern activity to be essentially not modern at all." Like so many Americans of his generation, Rockne's feet were firmly planted in modern material culture, but his heart longed for the "normalcy" of an earlier age. As his contemporaries entertained misgivings, if not severe doubts, about their religious moorings, he confidently barged forward—first as an unreflective Lutheran, then as a Catholic convert. Never outspoken on religious matters, he nevertheless stood as a beacon pointing Catholic Americans to the same sort of refuge that fundamentalism offered Protestants: a simple, solid faith in an age of doubt, an anchor in a time of storm. Moreover, in an anti-Puritan age of leisure, Rockne remained wedded to the Puritan work ethic. He was a throwback to an earlier, less complicated era.[52]

He especially urged a renewal of tough, masculine virtues that explorers, pioneers, and soldiers supposedly exhibited in days of old. Temperamentally suited to the all-male student body at Notre Dame, Rockne considered himself a "man-builder" in mortal combat against the "effeminization" of American life. He dismissed the "effeminizing trends" of all national and local attempts to curtail the growth of his football program. At best, he patronized women; at worst, he ridiculed them and all the males engaged in activities stereotyped as feminine. For young men tempted to take up the fox trot, tea parties, prom dances, knitting needles, and the like, he recommended the antidote of "good, clean football" for the inculcation of "rough, but manly" ways.[53]

If Rockne's "severely masculine" message seems an exaggeration of the earlier muscular Christian views of men such as Thomas Wentworth Higginson and Theodore Roosevelt, the reason is not hard to find. Compared to the trickle of doubt felt by Higginson and Roosevelt about traditional male roles, Rockne and his generation suffered a deluge of anxiety. Urban growth, World War I, and consumerism conspired to bring women to the fore. Flappers and feminists stood in the vanguard of a vast social movement that threatened to bring about a fundamental change in gender relations. Men like Knute Rockne stood their ground, then took the offensive. Unlike the earlier Higginson, they had a rough and popular college sport, football, that was wholly reserved for tough males. Unlike Roosevelt, they could easily get away with indiscriminate, venomous use of words like "sissy," "girls," and "ladies."

Rockne got his way because his was a winning way. In its earlier Protestant guise, muscular Christianity assumed that sports built strong, admirable character—strong enough even to lose a game rather than break the rules. Rockne, however, thought it "the Sunday school's place to take care of those things." Too much emphasis on "this character stuff" produced soft, mushy, effeminate youths. "We've got to make it tougher for them," the Rock insisted, "and put them into a football game where obstacles are met and must be overcome." In brief, Knute Rockne believed in God, football, and manliness, not necessarily in that order. "Play tough, play fair, play to win," went his creed: "Don't beef if you lose, but don't lose."[54]

Rockne's Fighting Irish seldom lost.

# 8

## SUNDAY GAMES

As a new baseball season got underway in May 1915, Sunday newspapers carried detailed accounts of the sinking of a passenger steamship, the *Lusitania,* by a German submarine off the coast of Ireland. Destined to be instrumental in the turning of American sympathies against the Axis powers, these Sunday reports had little competition from announcements of professional baseball games because in most places old Puritan prohibitions against Sunday sport remained embedded in law and public opinion. Just twenty-six years later, however, when the Japanese attacked Pearl Harbor in the early Sunday morning of December 7, 1941, many Americans on the East coast first heard the news in the late afternoon as they filed out of stadiums at the end of National Football League games. By then, every big-league city enjoyed Sunday baseball as well as professional football games. Between World War I and World War II, the nation underwent a massive readjustment of behavior regarding Sunday sport.

This change was deeply rooted in nineteenth-century industrial growth, new technologies, and larger, more diverse urban centers of population. In sharp contrast to puritanical Protestants, Catholic and Lutheran immigrants brought more tolerant, "Continental Sunday" ideas to the United States. If most Catholics and Lutherans had their way, Sunday afternoon games and other leisure activities would be allowed once morning prayers, sermons, and communions were finished. Jewish immigrants, of course, had no investment at all in the Victorian Christian Sabbath, because Jews celebrated their Sabbath on Saturday.

Sunday sport rode into town on the shoulders of early Victorian movements to make urban practicalities such as Sunday train travel, mail deliveries, and newspapers both legal and socially acceptable. Sunday athletic events arrived on the heels of turn-of-the-century reforms to open up shops, libraries, museums, theaters, movie houses, and taverns for Sunday business. Within the Protestant camp, the Sunday question provoked fierce debate in the 1920s. In the wake of that controversy, colorful new stained glass windows in the nation's largest cathedral bore witness to the church's acceptance of Sunday sport.

## Early to Rise

Defenders of the Puritan Sabbath considered bicycling, the great middle-class sporting rage of the 1890s, an activity especially laden with peril. By the turn of the century, just before the automobile became the vehicle of choice for travel and pleasure, some ten million Americans owned bicycles. Cycling put young men and women on equal terms, transporting them into the countryside free from adult scrutiny. It also caused a dramatic change in women's attire. Female cyclists shortened their dresses more "than the laws of morality and decency permit," complained a Chicago policemen to a sympathetic Methodist minister.[1]

Worse still for the guardians of tradition, the bicycle allowed easy escape from the service of worship and all the restraints of proper Sunday behavior. "The thousands of young men and women joining the host of desecrators, betrayed by the allurements of a Sunday wheeling, is alarming," wailed the editors of a Methodist periodical, the *Christian Advocate*. As a devout leader of the YMCA framed the issue, the bicycle rather than the saloon was "the great enemy of a proper observance of the Sabbath." Not only were cyclists easy to caricature in print and cartoon; for a time, they were the favorite targets of sermonizers.[2]

Sunday golfers quickly joined cyclists in the line of fire. In 1887 Americans, eager to imitate Scottish golf, constructed rough courses in Foxburg, Pennsylvania, and Yonkers, New York; by 1900 more than 1,000 clubs existed in the United States. From the outset, golfers took lightly the old assumption that Sunday should be reserved for religious services and quiet, homebound pleasures. "Both bicycling and the other new game—new so far as America is concerned—of golf, are having a marked effect on the popular method of passing the Sabbath," observed a journalist in 1896. "People who do not allow wheeling in their families on Sunday are now regarded as strict Sabbatarians, and while the same cannot be said perhaps of golf, still numbers devote themselves to it of a Sunday afternoon who would not think of playing tennis or baseball on that day."[3]

Sunday afternoon golf was one thing, and bad enough; Sunday morning tee time was something else, and increasingly common around the beginning of the twentieth century. Gospel ministers regularly railed against the well-heeled "leisure class" that rose at break of day to violate the Sabbath on country-club links. More liberal clergymen, however, saw golf as the "very topmost crest" of the wave of new opportunities for health and pleasure. The Reverend S. D. McConnell, Episcopalian rector of Holy Trinity Church, Brooklyn, depicted golf devotees as "the priests and priestesses of a new cult." Himself an avowed enthusiast, Father McConnell wanted his golf and his godliness too. "Might it not be well for the golfer to stop at church and say his prayers of a Sunday morning on his way to the links?" the rector asked in all seriousness. The golfer could leave his clubs in the vestibule, under the watchful eye of the church sexton. Presumably on a somewhat less serious note, McConnell hoped "the spirit of the holy place" would steady the golfer so that he would "go out a better man, will find fuller satisfaction in his game, will treat his caddie with more consideration, and will count his strokes more carefully."[4]

Public playgrounds, too, became a highly charged focus of the Sunday question. Unlike golf and cycling, playgrounds catered primarily to youths, not adults; they appealed largely to poorer inhabitants of the inner city, not to youngsters in the affluent suburbs. Playgrounds were designed to provide healthy, wholesome activities for ethnic and working-class youths—to keep them off the back streets, away from the gangs. Scarcely could one hope for good health if the hospital closed one day a week, so how could one justify closing an inner-city playground on Sunday? In 1910 the president of the Playground Association, Joseph Lee, put this question to delegates at the fourth annual conference of the Association. Sunday was the very day that neighborhood gangs usually gathered to roll dice and plan their mischief, insisted Lee. Sunday play, he concluded, should not be merely permitted; it should be encouraged. Seeking to slay one old Puritan dragon with another, Lee recommended Sunday play as an antidote to idleness. On a more modern note, he urged that playgrounds be open on Sunday to encourage "the turning of the vital force into refreshing channels."[5]

Reformers knew that the question of Sunday playgrounds would be answered locally, not nationally. Each town and city determined its own policy according to its own traditions, values, and interests. Scranton, Pennsylvania, for example, required three years of religious negotiations and political maneuvering before a central "play center" was opened on Sunday afternoon, 13 July 1919. Fully supervised, the playground stayed open for five hours, between the times of morning and evening Protestant worship. Reports made much of the large size and working-class character of the crowd that turned out for that first Sunday. Scattered among the youths were adults who had worked all week. Except for Sunday, they could not take advantage of the playground facilities. Just two weeks after Scranton's breakthrough, Pittsburgh opened its playgrounds for the first time on Sunday.[6]

Many of the campaigners for Sunday playgrounds and amateur sport bitterly resisted Sunday professional sport. One playground enthusiast abhorred a Sunday of "rigid solemnity and inactivity" bereft of "wholesome recreation," but still saw no place for the "boisterous play" of professional baseball players. Liberal clergyman Lyman Abbott wanted few restrictions on Sunday except some protection of the working man's right to a day of rest. Yet Abbott, too, would happily retain the bans against "the paid ball game, with its gate receipts, its great crowd, its inevitable disturbance of the [Sabbath] day's quiet."[7]

The opposition notwithstanding, several decades before professional football or basketball became important features of the American athletic landscape, baseball forged a niche for Sunday sport—but not by any grand design. The National League, founded in 1876 as the first of two "major" leagues, initially refrained from Sunday play. For reasons of respectability, National League clubs also agreed to sell no beer and to allow no gambling at their ballparks. An early rival, the American Association, explicitly tried to attract working-class spectators by selling beer at games and by allowing each club to set its own policy on Sunday games. When the Association folded in 1891, four clubs survived by being incorporated into the National League. A few continued to play on Sundays; most, constricted by state and local blue laws, did not.[8]

Minor league as well as major league clubs imaginatively devised ways to get around the law. Some made their Sunday contests "amateur" affairs by charging no admission, then made up the loss by jacking up the price of food, drink, and scorecards. Others took a page from the old prizefight promoter's book and moved momentarily to a remote venue. Rhode Island's Providence Grays regularly moved down Narragansett Bay to host their Sunday games at Rocky Point, New England's best-known amusement resort. Cincinnati occasionally shifted its Sunday games to Covington, Kentucky, just across the state line. Detroit played on Sunday at Burns Park, outside the city limits, where the police were lenient. Some clubs simply bribed local law-enforcement officers.[9]

A subtle variation on the bribery theme occurred in a Pennsylvania minor league town. During the team's first year of operation, club owners gave out season tickets to every clergyman in town and regularly noticed them in attendance at the ballpark. Just before the second season of play, club owners asked the ministers if they wanted their tickets renewed. Most did, and their requests were honored. Shortly thereafter, when the team began playing on Sunday, not a murmur of protest could be heard from the local ministerial association. Without pressure from the churches, the police made no move to suppress the games—especially since every policeman, too, had free season tickets. All the while, the clergymen preached and the policemen acted against a local cinema's effort to open for business on Sunday.[10]

Some minor league teams had an easier time of it than did major league clubs. In small towns, the distinction between professional and semiprofessional ballplayers was blurred; likely as not, the local owner of the club wielded considerable political influence, causing policemen and judges to wink at infractions. So Sunday games were played in Toledo, but not Cleveland; in Wilkes-Barre and Scranton, not Philadelphia or Pittsburgh. The upstate New York minor league towns of Albany, Troy, Syracuse, Schenectady, and Utica enjoyed Sunday games "by local consent," but no big league Sunday baseball could be found in New York City or Brooklyn. Fans in nearby New Jersey also cheered at minor league games on Sundays, and small towns in both New Jersey and Long Island occasionally hosted New York and Brooklyn major league clubs for Sunday contests.[11]

Surrounded by successful violations of the blue laws, the Brooklyn Dodgers tested local prohibitions with several Sunday games in 1904–1906. Rather than pay entrance fees, spectators "donated" money to a box or paid fifty to seventy-five cents for scorecards. Authorities arrested a few players, but sympathetic policemen and judges kept fines at a minimum. Still, opponents of Sunday sport put sufficient pressure on the police to prevent further breakage of the law. As major league baseball entered the twentieth century, the future of games on Sunday was far from assured.[12]

## Losing Ground

The question of Sunday ball games was related to a more general decline of the Puritan, or Victorian, Sabbath. As a Methodist minister in Hudson, Massachusetts, lamented in 1900, city governments and institutions of higher education had lately begun to treat Sunday like any other day of the week. Civic officials directed the repair of municipal streets, buildings, and bridges on Sunday in order to avoid workday traffic. Colleges no longer required Sunday chapel attendance; professors made heavy assignments to be prepared over the weekend; and on Sundays college football teams frequently traveled home by train from distant games. On campus, collegians turned to a new machine, the automobile, for Sunday afternoon and evening pleasures that were simply unavailable to their forebears. Quick and easy sightseeing treks, roadside restaurants, and commercial amusement parks sucked the lifeblood out of the Victorian Sabbath.[13]

Yet the Sunday question had distinct regional nuances. Roughly it divided on East-West terms, with the South more similar to the East than the West. The earliest major league Sunday baseball was played in midwestern cities including Chicago, Cincinnati, St. Louis, and Louisville, not eastern Boston, New York, or Philadelphia. The states of Maine, Pennsylvania, Tennessee, Arkansas, and Kansas had the most severe laws against Sunday commercial and recreational activities. Heavy Quaker and Presbyterian influence made Pennsylvania the most stringent state by far; and rural conservatism made Kansas an exception to the East-West division. On the Sunday question, Texas departed from its usual similarity to the South: by 1900 every major Texas city allowed Sunday baseball. In sharp contrast to eastern and southern ways, the statute books of the far western states of California, Oregon, Arizona, and Montana had virtually no prohibition on Sunday activity.[14]

New Orleans was pretty much a southern world of its own. "Sunday in New Orleans loses the quiet stillness which hallows the day in New England," observed an Episcopalian priest, Henry Whipple, prior to the Civil War. "Here it is a day of leisure, not of rest." A New Orleans Sunday, Whipple added, was "a day of toil, not in business, but in pleasure seeking." So it was in 1844; so it remained into the twentieth century, far different from the rest of the South and East. More representative of southern religious opinion was a colorful alarm issued in 1884 by a conference of Tennessee Methodists. Sunday sport, they warned, was "an entering wedge designed by infidels and skeptics to destroy the influence of the Christian religion, and an open door for the exercise of the unrestrained passions of the human heart." For supporting evidence from afar, Tennessee Methodists could well have consulted their Minnesota brethren, who rattled around in empty churches. "With the attraction of Sunday baseball, theaters, saloons, and excursions to the lakes," complained one Minnesota Methodist in 1895, "the churches are somewhat lonesome."[15]

Moralists first framed the Sunday problem in urban, not rural, terms.

Even while city churches continued to thrive, the congestion and complexity of urban life severely eroded the idea of Sunday as a sacred day. Businesses brought in supplies and shipped out goods on Sunday. Industrial bosses found it more profitable to break the law and pay a fine rather than shut down machines for one day a week. As urban anonymity freed people from the watchful eye of parson or priest and from parents and neighbors, Sunday became a leisurely day of diverse options. "Where is the city in which the Sabbath day is not losing ground?" asked Samuel Lane Loomis in 1887. To the great mass of city people, Sunday seemed "no more than a holiday" conveniently available once a week "for labor meetings, for excursions, for saloons, beer-gardens, base-ball games, and carousels."[16]

The city of Milwaukee in the rural state of Wisconsin dramatically illustrated the urban essence of the movement to do away with strict Sabbath practices. Everywhere else in the state, farmers and small-town residents kept a quiet, physically inactive, and (for some) worshipful lid on Sunday. Outrageously different, Milwaukee promoted professional baseball, auto races, horse races, theaters, vaudeville, and motion picture houses on Sunday. The Milwaukee scene lent credence to a Pennsylvania lawmaker's contention that the battle for Sunday was largely fought out between the "city slicker" and the "country rube."[17]

It was most certainly a battle between native-born and foreign-born Americans, and Milwaukee was a prime example. German immigrants ruled the Milwaukee roost; their "Continental Sunday" traditions ruled the weekend. The Continental Sunday, so named by English critics, derived from a tradition rooted in pre-Reformation Europe, with Christians viewing Sunday as a day of spiritual and physical refreshment. Prior to the Puritans, afternoon games, dances, and feasts followed morning prayers and sacraments. Especially popular in Catholic and Lutheran countries, this scheme was bitterly opposed by John Calvin and his followers. Finally, some four centuries after the Protestant Reformation, the Puritan gloss began to be removed from the Lord's Day in the United States.[18]

European immigrants forced the issue. As Polish, Lithuanian, and Italian immigrants dominated the coal-mining towns in the Pennsylvania anthracite district, it was no coincidence that Sunday minor league baseball flourished there long before it was accepted in Philadelphia and Pittsburgh. In the four western states with no Sunday prohibitions in 1925, one of every four citizens was foreign born. Within the eight states that had the weakest blue laws, some 14 percent of the population were born abroad; in the eighteen states retaining the strictest Sunday laws, no less than 92 percent of the population were native born. Rural pockets of conservative New England and the South figured heavily in that equation, of course. From both regions, native-born conservatives frequently blamed the Sunday problem on the "foreign population among us" and "the wider dissemination of European sentiments."[19]

Yet social class weighed more heavily than ethnic origin in one's acceptance or rejection of blue laws. As a rule, comfortable middle-class Americans had the greatest interest in defending the traditional Sunday. They could afford to play or watch sports on some other day, in some place other than public sites. "The rich man has his golf and croquet or anything he wants to play at his country club," explained a Pennsylvania legislator in 1913, as he submitted "a poor man's bill" to abolish the state's age-old blue laws. In Philadelphia's affluent Germantown section, private croquet grounds and lawn tennis courts could be seen everywhere one turned, but there was "no place in Philadelphia for the poor man to enjoy himself legally on Sunday," lamented the legislator.[20]

Nor would there have been any Sunday place for working-class folk on a popular lake near Worcester, Massachusetts—if Worcester's leading Protestant ministers and wealthy parishioners had their way. In response to their heavy-handed attempt to close a commercialized lakeside site, one local citizen wrote to the *Worcester Evening Gazette* questioning "the right of one class of people to dictate to another class the manner in which they shall worship God or spend the Sabbath." People of ample means could ride out on weekdays to enjoy the country air and scenery, but "all the good people of Worcester are not thus favored." In a far less subtle measure designed to control Sunday activities along class lines, until 1928 an old Connecticut law banned Sunday concerts unless the music was "symphonic or classical."[21]

This crusade for the retention of the traditional Sabbath was decidedly a Protestant—not Catholic—concern. Early in the nineteenth century, a Protestant student at Georgetown University reported to a distant friend that Catholic officials and students at Georgetown entertained the strange notion that it was "no harm to play Ball, Draughts or play the Fiddle and dance of a Sunday." Nearly a century later, a Catholic priest in Scranton, Pennsylvania, announced that he saw "no harm" in Sunday baseball. He proceeded to castigate the "modern Pharisees" (Protestants) who prevented ball games on Sunday, thus destroying "the only opportunity hundreds have for recreation during the summer." Cincinnati's Roman Catholic diocesan newsletter, the *Catholic Watchman*, lauded Sunday baseball as "both a measure of health and morals."[22]

Another Catholic diocesan paper, Chicago's *New World*, vividly reflected the chasm that divided Catholics and Protestants on the issue of Sunday sport. The *New World* casually reported the outcome of games on the previous Sunday and announced forthcoming Sunday contests, especially those involving Catholic teams in the Chicago area. In the early months of 1930 basketball teams in the Bohemian Catholic Association regularly competed on Sunday afternoons and evenings. On the last Sunday in March the Holy Name, Cicero, team squeezed past the St. Cyril Rangers, 30–29, in a semifinal tournament game; the Sokols beat St. Procopins for the championship, 12–7.[23]

Sunday games involving local Catholic colleges and schools received frequent notice in the *New World*. On a Sunday afternoon in August 1930, intracity gridiron rivals DePaul and Loyola competed at Soldier Field for local Catholic bragging rights. Two months later two Catholic high schools, Mt. Carmel and De LaSalle, played a benefit game for the Mercy Nuns, again on Sunday afternoon at Soldier Field. These events stirred liberal Protestants to admiration. "Here is where the Roman Church reveals its common sense and its cleverness," commented Caspar Whitney, "for not only do its priests tolerate harmless Sunday diversion, but they encourage their people to it after attendance at church in the morning." It was most certainly a far cry from the behavior of most Protestants.[24]

## Athletes against Sunday Sport

Methodist, Baptist, and Presbyterian ministers stood at the head of congregations largely composed of middle-aged, middle-class religious folk. All prayed for a Sunday filled with worship, not athletic competition. Yet some athletes, too, internalized the message they had received from their parents, their churches, and the communities of their youth. Whatever the source of their convictions, several highly visible athletes came to the Sabbatarian fore during the first quarter of the twentieth century. Momentarily reversing roles, they cheered on the crowd that clamored for the retention of a sacred Sunday, absent of sport.

In global terms, the most notable athlete to oppose Sunday sport was Olympic sprinter Eric Liddell, hero of the film *Chariots of Fire*. Liddell was born of Scottish Congregational Church missionaries in China at the turn of the century. Schooled in London and at the University of Edinburgh, he emerged as an outstanding rugby player and track athlete, then used his sporting fame as an attraction for evangelistic crusades throughout the United Kingdom. At the Paris Olympics of 1924, however, Liddell's religious principles clashed with his athletic ambition. When informed that he was scheduled to run the opening heat of the 100 meters on Sunday, he quietly refused. Everything from his home and his larger Scottish culture told him that Sunday was exclusively for God, not sport. While his nemesis, Harold Abrahams, won preliminary heats on Sunday morning, Liddell preached at the Scots Kirk on the other side of Paris.

His virtue was rewarded. Later in the week Liddell won a bronze medal in the 200 meters, then stunned everyone with a gold-winning world record time of 47.6 seconds in the 400 meters. He became something of a national hero in Scotland. For a year or so he frequently appeared as the guest of honor at sports events and as a featured speaker at religious gatherings all over Scotland, England, and Ireland. In July 1925, precisely a year after the Paris Olympics, Liddell booked passage for China, returning as a missionary to the land of his birth.[25]

Only one American of that era similarly combined athletic achievement and ministerial zeal in opposition to Sunday sport. Actually, this American's loud, brash evangelistic style would have made the polished, mild-mannered Liddell wince with embarrassment. Appropriately enough, his name was Billy Sunday.

William Ashley Sunday, a "rube" from the cornfields of Iowa, signed as a pitcher with the Chicago White Stockings in 1883. Switched to the outfield, he proved to be a weak hitter whose .248 lifetime batting average kept him often on the bench; good fielding and a swift, daring style of baserunning kept him on the roster. Someone called him a "famous sprinter with a sabbatical name." For five years Sunday played for Chicago; then he moved on to compete for three more years with Pittsburgh and Philadelphia.[26]

Just before leaving Chicago, Sunday underwent a life-changing religious conversion. One evening, as he and several teammates burst out of a saloon, they met a gospel troupe playing instruments and singing hymns reminiscent of Sunday's Iowa childhood. Emotionally moved, Sunday accepted an invitation to a nearby rescue mission and soon repented of his evil ways. In good evangelical style, he stopped swearing, drinking, gambling, and attending the theater. More awkward was his decision to play no more baseball on Sunday. Instead, on those days he gave inspirational talks at the YMCA in whatever town his team happened to be. Finally, at age twenty-eight, Sunday hung up his baseball gear in exchange for full-time religious work with the YMCA.[27]

He quickly became a colorful, magnetic preacher, and around the turn of the century was conducting highly successful crusades throughout the

Midwest. "Sunday was a fast man on the base lines," observed a contemporary, "but he was a faster talker and faster worker in the pulpit." His sermons, filled with warnings about sin and destruction, were laced with baseball yarns, jargon, and metaphors. He urged listeners to a "ninth-inning rally" for Christ and country, frequently flung an imaginary "fastball at the devil," and lamented sinners "dying on second or third base." Critics thought him vulgar. "I don't use much highfalutin language," Sunday admitted. "I learned long ago to put the cookies and jam on the lowest shelf."[28]

Athletic antics accompanied the homilies. Until middle age caught up with him, Sunday was broad shouldered and slender waisted—"a vigorous man with a bulldog face, a pug nose, bright piercing eyes, athletic in appearance," according to a visitor from abroad. He bounced around the podium like a "restless gymnast," reported one journalist; he frequently rolled up his sleeves and punched "an uppercut on the devil's chin," reported another. A favorite stunt seems to have been sprinting from one side of the stage to the other, then "sliding home" as an illustration of salvation.[29]

Billy Sunday reached the apex of his appeal in the decade 1910–1920, just when the question of Sunday baseball was becoming most urgent. Actually, he was far more concerned about the evils of strong drink than he was about Sunday sport. "I'm trying to make America so dry that a man must be primed before he can spit," he often quipped. Yet he was also "against Sabbath desecration under all circumstances" and thought baseball "overstepped itself" in scheduling Sunday games. He read the daily sports page, umpired some games, and attended others when he could. But never on Sunday. "One day a week is not too much to give up to higher things," he insisted. "Most of us need more. This giving up cannot be done on baseball bleachers of a Sunday afternoon."[30]

Even less could it be done on the field, or so thought several major league players in the early twentieth century. Frank "Home Run" Baker, a hard-hitting, steady-fielding third baseman for seven years with the Philadelphia Athletics, then for another seven with the New York Yankees, was momentarily suspended in 1917 for refusing to play on Sunday. Similarly inclined was Branch Rickey, an athlete whose greatest fame was to come later in the administration of major league baseball. Destined to build the St. Louis Cardinals' farm system and to spearhead the racial reintegration of baseball by signing Jackie Robinson to a Brooklyn Dodgers contract, Rickey enjoyed a brief, mediocre career as a catcher for the Cincinnati Reds, St. Louis Browns, and New York Highlanders. The Reds released him when he refused to play on Sunday; the Browns and Highlanders tolerated his Sabbatarian quirk until his arm went bad.[31]

His scruples against Sunday play came from pious Methodist moorings in rural southern Ohio. Rickey grew up having his boyhood misdemeanors punished by having to kneel beside his mother while she sought divine forgiveness for her failure to raise him properly. Emotionally hooked, he vowed to be a "good boy": honest, never swearing, regularly in church, and never playing ball on Sunday. He kept at least one of those promises. Even after his playing days were finished, he always had a "Sunday manager" take over his baseball duties on the Lord's Day. To his critics, he seemed "peculiar"; some said he was self-righteous and hypocritical. Shortly after he became manager of the St. Louis Browns in 1913, *The Sporting News* issued a colorful piece of doggerel:

> Branch Rickey is a funny cuss,
>    Though cussin he forbids,
> His rules have started quite a fuss
>    Among his Brownie kids.
> When Sunday comes he leaves his team
>    Completely in the lurch.
> And Jimmy Austin rules supreme
>    While Branch hikes off to church.[32]

Carl Mays, an irritable son of a Kentucky Methodist minister, also left his team in the lurch when he hiked off to church on Sunday. During a major league career that stretched over fifteen years, Mays compiled a 208–126 record. A premier "submarine" (low side-arm) pitcher, five times he won at least twenty games a season. He played for four different major league teams, but with each club his contract excused him from Sunday play. Whatever the combination of paternal influence and principled piety that inspired that clause, the temperamental Mays frequently alienated baseball owners, managers, players, and fans. Ironically, he is best remembered for killing Cleveland shortstop Ray Chapman with a pitch to the head in 1920. Despite his refusal to play Sunday baseball, Carl Mays was no candidate for Protestant sainthood.[33]

Christy Mathewson was. Born of a solid middle-class Baptist family in the little mining town of Factoryville, Pennsylvania, the blond, blue-eyed, six-foot-two Mathewson seems to have stepped right out of a Frank Merriwell novel. He learned baseball on a Factoryville YMCA team. Unlike most professional ballplayers of that era, he attended college. Although he did not finish his degree, for three years he was a campus hero in football and basketball as well as baseball at Bucknell College. From 1899 to 1916, he stood tall—like a New York Giant should—as the finest major league pitcher of the pre–World War I era. A master of the "fadeaway" (screwball) pitch, he compiled a lifetime record of 373–188, with 80 shutouts and an earned run average of 2.13 per game.[34]

Yet Mathewson achieved much more than mere statistical success. He was an all-American boy, a walking advertisement for muscular Christianity. Although he quietly dabbled in most of the minor sins of the flesh (smoking, chewing, drinking beer, playing poker, and swearing), his image was squeaky clean. He represented sportsmanship, fair play, and respectability. Surrounded by men like the mean-spirited Ty Cobb and the beer-bellied Honus Wagner, Mathewson stuck out like a beacon of virtue and grace. He "became something of a paragon," says baseball historian Charles Alexander, "really the first professional athlete to function as a role model for America's youth."[35]

To the great mass of Protestants for whom religion was still important, Mathewson's refusal to play on Sunday enlarged his heroic status. His resolve largely came from a heritage of sober-minded Scottish Calvinism. According to Mathewson family lore, their Presbyterian allegiance switched to Baptist in seventeenth-century Rhode Island. It all amounted to the same sort of stern, no-nonsense behavior. For practical as well as religious reasons, his parents hoped that young Chris would become a Baptist minister. He could thus serve God and be spared the arduous life of the miner. Not only did Mathewson refuse to go that route; he doubly disappointed the family by announcing that he would be playing professional baseball instead. Distressed, his mother finally agreed that he could play for money only if he would promise never to play on Sunday.[36]

For the first half of his career, Mathewson steadfastly kept that promise. In practical terms it mattered little, for Sunday baseball was still illegal in New York City—and Chicago, Cincinnati, and St. Louis were the only Giants opponents who played Sunday games. Yet these teams reportedly exploited the situation by piling up Sunday double-headers, provoking Mathewson in 1908 to offer his services to relieve the arm-weary Giants pitching staff. After that, Mathewson's resolve against Sunday baseball gradually eroded. New York City provided him "a wider horizon" of thought and behavior, he explained. To the end of his career, he wanted Sundays free of baseball so that players could have one day for themselves.

He came to believe, however, that there was "much to be said in favor of al-lowing the laboring man his only opportunity to go to a baseball game on Sunday."[37]

Having recently retired from active play, Mathewson was managing the Cincinnati Reds when the United States entered World War I in 1917. His old Giants manager and friend, John McGraw, convinced him that a Sunday game would be the ideal tonic for American servicemen and work-ers, so Mathewson agreed to a Reds-Giants "benefit game" on August 19 at the Polo Grounds in defiance of New York City's blue laws. After the game the Sabbath Society brought suit against both managers, who were sum-moned to a police court. Magistrate Francis X. McQuade, who later be-came part owner and treasurer of the Giants, not only dismissed the case; he praised Mathewson and McGraw for their patriotic efforts on behalf of America's warriors and war workers.[38]

## When the Walls Came Tumbling Down

World War I left the blue laws in shambles. The war changed people and their personal values; it disrupted families and family patterns, com-munities and community traditions. Compared to the dangers of war, Sunday sport seemed innocuous. Scarcely were all the dangers confined to frontline trenches—as James Naismith, the inventor of basketball, discov-ered while serving as a chaplain of the First Kansas Regiment. As the troops trained on the Texas-Mexico border, Naismith became distressed over some "camp followers"—prostitutes—in a nearby town. Although he had been raised in a strict Scottish Presbyterian home where Sundays were hallowed by churchgoing, Bible study, and quiet conversation, this imme-diate problem required a fresh approach to the Sabbath. "Sunday is treated differently here," Naismith wrote home to his wife. "It is impossible to keep the men confined to their tents. So I want them to take part in athletics." Better to have athletics on Sundays than to discover sexually transmitted disease on Monday.[39]

At a more public level, the war effort required round-the-clock military training and factory labor, effectively making Sunday like every other day of the week. Sunday also became the day of choice for military parades, fund-raising concerts, and benefit athletic contests—activities that would have been thought indecorous for Sundays except for the patriotic mean-ing assigned them in wartime. For the cities of Detroit, Cleveland, and Washington, practical and ceremonial needs coalesced to nudge local officials toward the opening up of Sundays for activities other than religious services. At the war's end, exactly half of all the major league baseball teams could play in their home parks on Sundays without fear of legal recrimination.[40]

New York City in 1919 joined a parade of cities welcoming Sunday major league baseball. The change came by way of a local option bill to permit professional sporting events on Sunday afternoons between 2:00 and 6:00 P.M. Senator James J. Walker introduced the bill in the state legislature; new Democratic governor Al Smith signed it into law. Smith, a Catholic, was a longtime opponent of blue laws. Walker later became New York City's mayor, campaigning under the slogan that he brought Sunday baseball to the city. Sunday games certainly proved to be popular. As masses of working people could now attend ball games for the first time, huge crowds turned out on Sunday afternoons to watch the Giants, Yankees, and Brooklyn Dodgers. Arguably, Sunday games made possible the mass popularity of Babe Ruth in the 1920s.[41]

As fundamentalists clung to strict Sabbath views and moderate evangelicals proceeded cautiously, other Protestants came around to new ways of thinking. For reasons derived from their own histories, Lutherans, Episcopalians, and Unitarians cast liberal eyes upon the Sunday question. Moreover, old social gospel liberals could be found scattered throughout most evangelical denominations. Though some balked at the idea of commercialized entertainment and professional sport, they happily handed over Sunday—or to be more precise, Sunday afternoon—to healthful leisure and recreational activities.

A war of words occurred early in 1926, when clergymen rallied round their respective Sunday flags. An Episcopalian bishop, William Thomas Manning, initiated the debate with a controversial address on December 30, 1925, to delegates at a National Collegiate Athletic Association (NCAA) gathering at the Astor Hotel in New York City. Manning, the Bishop of New York, extolled "clean, wholesome, well-regulated sport" as religion's ally in the making of "true manhood and true womanhood." Wholesome sport was "so good a thing that it may have its place on any day," including Sunday, said Bishop Manning. "I believe that a well-played game of polo or of football or of any other game is, in its own place and in its own way, just as pleasing to God as a beautiful service of worship in a cathedral, and what we want is both of these things in our lives in right and true proportion."[42]

As the Montreal *Gazette* observed from a distance, this religious embrace of athleticism was nothing new. Over the past three-quarters of a century, English, American, and Canadian advocacy of "muscular Christianity" had become commonplace. Still, the *Gazette* lauded Manning for "going out to meet the devotees of sport." Other commentators mentioned the authoritative signal conveyed by virtue of Bishop Manning's elevated position. Few people, however, thought it newsworthy that religion and sport might be friends rather than enemies. That fight was long finished.[43]

The Sabbath conflict still raged. Manning wanted to "make it unmistakably clear" that there was nothing inherently wrong in playing tennis, golf, or polo on Sunday, "provided that we do not let this take the place of our proper religious duties." Consistent as this view might have been with age-old Anglican and Catholic practices, it posed "a distinct challenge to the Sabbatarians of the evangelical denominations," observed the editor of the Brooklyn *Eagle;* "one might almost call it a challenge to Main Street in general."[44]

Main Street rose to the challenge. As the daily press reported Bishop Manning's speech all over the United States, Manning found himself bombarded with hundreds of letters. Some supported his views about Sunday sport; others seethed with hostility. Numerous editorials divided along traditional evangelical and nonevangelical lines, as did a group of ministers contacted by the editors of the *Literary Digest.* The Reverend J. Frank Norris, a Baptist fundamentalist in Fort Worth, Texas, headed the list of Manning's most severe critics. "It is impossible to believe that Jesus would endorse sports on the holy day of His resurrection," declared Norris. He associated Sunday sport with a recent increase in marital infidelity and divorce and with an apparent decrease in church attendance. It all spelled "the doom of American civilization," warned Norris.[45]

Admirers declared Bishop Manning "clearly right" in principle, then proceeded to debate the details. Several noted his upper-class bias in mentioning only the country club sports of polo, golf, and tennis. Manning had also referred to college football, but that too was still a privileged, "elite" game in the 1920s, when few Americans pursued any sort of education beyond high school. Yet even college football was already going the way of commercialized sport on Saturdays, the very kind of thing that Bishop Manning himself resisted for Sundays. Never once did Manning mention professional baseball, the dominant game that was then winning its struggle for the right to play on Sunday.

Some of the most liberal clergymen joined Bishop Manning in making a sharp distinction between healthful outdoor recreation and professional ball games on Sunday. Commercialized baseball, they believed, was part of the gaudy entertainment industry of amusement parks, dance halls, and motion-picture theaters. Moreover, professional ball games forced players to function as workers on the Sabbath and required a support staff to take tickets, sell food and drink, and groom the playing field. At best, the religious opposition to Sunday professional sport was rooted in the belief that workers should have at least one day of the week free of labor. At worst, it reflected a severe class bias against crude players and noisy, unruly spectators who supposedly spoiled the quiet dignity of a proper Sunday. In 1926 a public-safety official in Pittsburgh banned Sunday baseball and football games, but refrained from interfering with Sunday play at public golf and tennis clubs.[46]

Critics pointed out the inconsistency. "The Sunday question will be full of hypocrisy as long as we try to tell one man he can indulge in the kind of recreation he enjoys and another man that he can't enjoy himself of a Sunday afternoon the way he likes," observed the editors of the Newark, New Jersey, *News*. "The one who wants to be out-of-doors watching a well-played game of baseball or football by professional teams will not be patient when told he can't do that, but he can go over to another field and watch some unpaid amateurs play or go to church and hear a concert by some paid musicians." Consistency, concluded the *News*, made "ducks and drakes of current ways of observing the Sabbath."[47]

Those ways were rapidly changing. In November 1928 Massachusetts voters decided by a decisive majority to grant local options on Sunday sport between 2:00 and 6:00 P.M., with the proviso that no professional game be played within 1,000 feet of a church. Two months later the Boston City Council added several clauses to regulate "athletic outdoor sports or games on the Lord's Day," then voted the measure into law. In the spring of 1929 the Boston Braves threw out the first ball for Sunday play; not until 1932 did Red Sox fans begin making their way to Fenway Park on Sunday afternoon.[48]

The economic depression of the early 1930s accelerated the dismantling of the blue laws. Hard times meant unemployment, which in turn dried up tax funds. State legislators and city councils soon began looking to Sunday amusements as a means of raising tax dollars. The Depression also emptied the coffers of organizations such as the Lord's Day Alliance and the Sabbath Day Observance Committee, whose earlier propaganda and lobbying efforts had helped keep the blue laws intact. Finally, the Democratic Party's victory at the polls in 1932 replaced older Republican Protestants with politicians more ethnically diverse and thus more sympathetic to the prospect of a Continental Sunday for the United States.[49]

The opening up of Sunday proceeded apace. In 1932 the city of Baltimore, exercising a local option, voted overwhelmingly to permit "sports and amusements" on Sunday afternoons. Within the next year the mayor of Atlanta devised a hook slide around a Georgia state law that allowed Sunday amusements only for charitable purposes. When the Atlanta Crackers took the field on a bright Sunday afternoon in the spring of 1934, a portion of their profits went to charity. Dotted in the 1930s with progressively permissive Sundays in Atlanta, Richmond, Nashville, and Birmingham as well as New Orleans, Mobile, and Memphis, the South set its sights toward a commercialized future of Sunday shopping malls.[50]

The South may have been the last region to accept Sunday ball games, movies, and the like, but Philadelphia and Pittsburgh were the last major league baseball cities to resist Sunday play. Upholding a set of blue laws that dated from 1794, the Pennsylvania Supreme Court in 1927 decided that professional baseball was purely a "business" for owners and "worldly employment" for players; it partook in no way of "the nature of holiness" protected by law. For Sunday professional baseball to be allowed, the law would have to be changed. Toward that end, no fewer than five bills were introduced in the Pennsylvania legislature in 1929, but all failed.[51]

Economic hard times did the trick. In 1933 Connie Mack, manager of the Philadelphia Athletics, complained that he could no longer meet his payroll without Sunday games; politicians envisaged 10 percent of all Sunday game receipts going toward unemployment relief. A local option bill passed both houses of the Pennsylvania legislature, and in April 1933 the governor signed it after "long, anxious, and prayerful consideration." In November, local referenda asked cities and towns simply if they wanted baseball and football games between the hours of 2:00 and 6:00 P.M. on Sundays. Most Pennsylvania cities did; many small towns and rural communities did not.[52]

Ironically, this measure, which had largely been pushed by major league baseball interests, first benefited Pennsylvania's two new franchises in the National Football League. On November 12, 1933, just a week after the referendum, some 20,000 fans watched the Philadelphia Eagles battle the Chicago Bears to a 3–3 draw in Philadelphia; across the state, 12,000 spectators endured a 32–0 loss by the Pittsburgh Steelers (then called the Pirates) to Brooklyn. Not until the season of 1934 did the baseball Athletics,

Phillies, and Pirates play Sunday games, opening the last door to major league baseball on the Christian Sabbath.[53]

## Stained Glass Sportsmen

As rural and small-town churches came to terms with sports on Sunday, a remarkable story transpired in the nation's dominant urban center, New York City. At the center of this drama stood William Thomas Manning, the Episcopal Bishop of New York who had stood tall in the crusade to open up parks, playgrounds, and ballparks to Sunday play. While engaged in that effort, Manning was overseeing the completion of the Cathedral of St. John the Divine at Morningside Heights on the upper west side of Manhattan. At that time, St. John's was the largest religious structure in the United States, the third largest in the world. Manning and his architects decided that the bays off the side aisles of the nave should be dedicated to notable human endeavors, such as education, the arts, law, medicine, the press, and labor. Each bay would serve as an open chapel with unique stained glass windows designed to honor the group's activities. To the surprise of even his closest friends and admirers, Bishop Manning proposed a sports bay window for the first chapel off the left aisle of the cathedral.

The idea reportedly came from the bishop's daughter, Elizabeth. In 1924 she attended the Paris Olympics (the scene of Eric Liddell's performance that later inspired *Chariots of Fire*), and returned home impressed with the wholesome attitudes and friendships engendered by athletic competition. Bishop Manning needed a mere nudge, not an extended argument. In 1925 he announced his intention to add a sports bay to the design of St. John the Divine. It would be a "visible and beautiful symbol to tell all who enter," he reckoned, "not only that the Church does not frown on sport but that the Church sympathizes with it, encourages it and rejoices in it."[54]

First, though, the Church debated it. Within a week of Manning's announcement, he received more than a hundred letters supporting or opposing his proposal. Some wanted more information; others requested copies of the design and photographs of the work once it got underway. Predictably, the president of the Madison Square Garden Association congratulated the bishop on his breadth of vision; from the opposite corner, Charles C. Marshall, a lawyer and outspoken conservative within the diocese, registered stern complaint. He feared that this acknowledgment of athletes might leave the impression that sport stood "coequal with the religion of Christ in the latter's redemptive and regenerative work." A sports

bay, Marshall warned, would obscure the Gospel amidst "the general welter of sport, pleasure, and materialism on Manhattan Island."[55]

No doubt other churchmen shared that fear, but few voiced it. Instead,
several Episcopalians highly placed in New York sports circles lavished
both verbal and financial support on the project. Eminent sportswriter
Grantland Rice insisted that sport and religion were "much alike" in their
concern for fair play, clean living, and high ideals, and that America's
"golden age" of sport "should be represented in the world's greatest Cathedral." Even more imposing was the enthusiastic support of retired Briga-
dier General Charles H. Sherrill. As a track athlete at Yale in the 1880s,
Sherrill reportedly invented the crouched start for sprints. Now a bristle-
mustached member of the American Olympic Committee, he served as
vice-chair of the sports bay fund-raising committee.[56]

The committee collected money mostly through direct solicitations to
wealthy sports-minded individuals and groups, and by staging athletic
contests and exhibitions. The events included a "Cathedral Horse Show" at
the Westchester Biltmore Country Club, a golf tournament sponsored by
the Oakland Golf Club at Bayside on Long Island, YMCA swim meets
throughout New York City, and a "monster track meet" at Yankee Stadium. On behalf of the sports bay, Madison Square Garden hosted boxing
matches, ice hockey games, and bicycle races, as well as an attempt at a
world record by famous Finnish long-distance runner Paavo Nurmi. At
one of several ice hockey benefit games, between periods Bishop Manning
walked to center ice to appeal for contributions to the sports bay.[57]

Numerous sports associations came through handsomely, pledging to
bear the cost of various parts of the sports bay. The U.S. Lawn Tennis Association paid for an upper stained-glass window in honor of Robert D.
Wrenn, an old singles and doubles champion from the 1890s. Yet another
star of old, Hobie Baker, inspired St. Paul's School and Princeton University gifts toward a window in honor of the Public School Athletic League.
The Intercollegiate Amateur Athletic Association promised to pay for the
construction of the chapel's floor, and the National Collegiate Athletic Association contributed $500 toward the altar.[58]

The great Depression of the 1930s made this project all the more difficult, and its success all the more noteworthy. By 1935 federal and local
government relief programs had constructed athletic stadiums, swimming
pools, community centers, summer camp sites, and city parks at public expense. As government, schools, and industries assumed responsibility for
public welfare, churches and other "character building agencies" of the

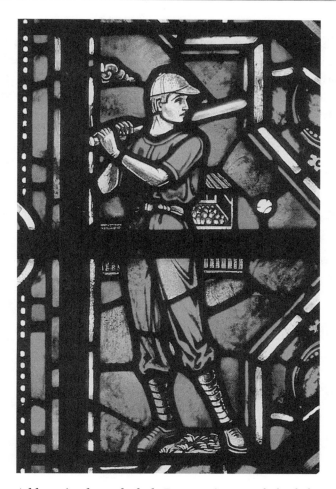

**Athletes in the cathedral.** For a unique symbol of the church's acceptance of sport in the 1920s, the Episcopalian Bishop of New York, William Thomas Manning, commissioned a sports bay window in the Cathedral Church of St. John the Divine on Morningside Heights. Finished shortly after World War II, the window honors dozens of different athletic endeavors. (From Archives of the Episcopal Diocese of New York at the Cathedral of St. John the Divine.)

day struggled to pay their light bills. The sports bay was a monument to private enterprise and paternalistic benevolence in an era that saw Protestant churches lose their grip on the sponsorship of sport.[59]

Although it was one of the first bays to be designated for the Cathedral of St. John the Divine, the sports bay was the last to be completed. When

Bishop Manning retired in 1947, stained glass had not yet been added to the chapel's clerestory windows, nor were various memorials yet inscribed on the granite. Today the sports bay, finally finished, stands as an imaginative and colorful reminder of an earlier Protestant era that confidently linked religion and sport in the quest for the common good—even on Sunday.[60]

# 9

## PLAYING ON THE FRINGE

In the 1920s and 1930s religious links to sport in the United States grew clearer and broader. Protestants and Catholics continued to stake claims on the American soul, frequently endorsing sport for sectarian purposes. At the same time other, smaller groups came to the marriage of religion and sport. Ideologically and geographically distant from each other, Mormons in largely rural Utah and immigrant Jews in East coast urban ghettoes eagerly took to sport.

By traditional Christian standards, members of the Church of Jesus Christ of Latter-day Saints, popularly known as Mormons, were strange. They supplemented the Bible with the Book of Mormon, a compilation of heroic tales and moral mandates purportedly given by the angel Moroni to Church founder Joseph Smith. Strangest of all, Mormons practiced and adamantly defended polygamy until late in the nineteenth century. From their very inception in the 1830s, however, Mormons endorsed wholesome recreation as a means of teaching moral values. Joseph Smith and his successor, Brigham Young, took a page from muscular Christianity in blending masculinity and religious principles. Muscular Mormonism served pioneers well as they trekked from upper New York state to Illinois and Missouri on their way to Utah. It served them all the more as they sought to create a Zion in the Rocky Mountains.

The Jews took a much longer route to America. By the 1870s some 250,000 Jewish immigrants had arrived in the United States, flooding in from central and eastern Europe with baggage that included strange customs, an alien language (Yiddish), and religious holidays ill coordinated with the American calendar. By the 1920s, some two million Jews had immigrated to the United States, almost a million of them to New York City. Although they came with scant exposure to any kind of organized sport, they quickly learned that prizefights and ball games were godsends, tickets into the American mainstream.

## Zion at Play

Mormon pioneers enthusiastically took to competitive sport as well as physical exercise programs, but their early years in Utah featured little debate about the propriety of sport. Stern prohibitions against pork, alcoholic drink, and premarital sex shaped Mormon behavior. Until late in the nineteenth century, the rights and wrongs of polygamy dominated their discussions.

By the early twentieth century, however, Mormons began creating a "recreation ideology" that linked religious principles to athletic practices. By the 1920s, an athletic director and a traveling secretary oversaw all recreational and sports programs sponsored by Latter-day Saints churches in Utah. Workshops, pamphlets, and summer institutes spread the Mormon gospel of sport throughout the state. Whatever their assumptions about the intrinsic value of sport, Mormons consistently saw it as a practical way to entice youths to be better Mormons. Under the auspices of the Young Men's and Young Ladies' Mutual Improvement Associations, missionaries went from town to town upholding "the fundamental ideals and standards of the Church" through local volunteers and supervised recreational programs in some 900 community centers.[1]

Built in 1910 just a block east of Temple Square in Salt Lake City, the Deseret Gym stood as a model Mormon endeavor. Compared to other gyms of the day, it was huge: 150 feet long, 90 feet wide, three stories high, "the largest and best equipped institution in the intermountain district." Its array of physical, cultural, and athletic activities put its prime competitor, the YMCA, in the shade. In addition to the usual reading rooms, game rooms, and fitness and athletic facilities, the Deseret regularly offered band and orchestra concerts, dances, and music lessons to Mormon youths.[2]

Competitive sport flourished, beginning with track meets, or "field days," like the three-day meet held in 1910 in Holden, Utah. About 100 athletes competed in footraces, high jumps, pole vaults, ball games, and wrestling matches, with each day's activities followed by refreshments, movies, and chaperoned dances in the evening. At American Fork, a little town north of Holden, a Mormon official reported a "large and enthusiastic" crowd of spectators at a similar athletic festival two months later.[3]

Within the following year, Brigham Young University produced a colossal "field day" that attracted Mormon athletes and families from all over

Utah. The program featured track-and-field competition, young women's "posture parades," and a tennis tournament. Its success prompted BYU officials to make this sports festival an annual event. By 1940 it was attracting some 3,000 athletic participants and several thousand spectators each year. It was "one of the most colorful events on the state's athletic calendar," according to one sportswriter. "Reaching as it does into so many homes in this vast intermountain empire," he added, this athletic festival offered "a striking display of modern youth in body-building activities."[4]

Clearly, modern sport had great appeal to the Latter-day Saints. More immediately, the annual sports festival underscored the importance of Brigham Young University for the inculcation and expansion of Mormon piety. The university had begun in 1876 as a parochial academy in Provo, some fifty miles south of Salt Lake City, for the integration of Biblical and Mormon doctrine with literary and scientific studies. As founder Brigham Young himself explained, here was an institution where the children of Latter-day Saints could "receive a good education unmixed with the pernicious, atheistic influences that are found in so many of the higher schools of the country."[5]

Athletics were not deemed one of those "pernicious influences" to be avoided. By the time the academy officially became Brigham Young University in 1903, varsity baseball, basketball, and track-and-field teams regularly competed against off-campus squads. Football was another matter. As elsewhere, the gridiron game was a highly controversial presence on campus. Latter-day Saints officials deplored the drinking, profanity, and raucous cheers that accompanied football games. Rough, noisy behavior at a Christmas Day game in 1897 damaged "the religious tone that should always characterize every Latter-day Saint school of learning," insisted the general superintendent of the Church Sunday School Union.[6]

In a pattern common to turn-of-century colleges and universities all over the United States, the sheer physical danger of the gridiron game put Brigham Young football on trial more decisively than moralistic scruples could ever do. Wearing few pads and no helmets, players mauled and mangled each other amidst mass power plays without a forward pass to open up the game. In the late 1890s a player in Salt Lake City died of football injuries, prompting the Board of Education (trustees) to ban the game from the Provo campus. Enacted in 1900, the ban stayed in effect until 1919. While the forward pass was being invented in the years surrounding World War I, Brigham Young students toiled without the campus presence of an autumn athletic spectacle.[7]

In the 1920s they found other spectator pleasures. First, the university joined the new Rocky Mountain Conference and promptly won conference titles in swimming, track, and wrestling. In 1924 the Brigham Young basketball team beat the University of Colorado, 32–25, for the conference championship. In 1928–1929 the team achieved national prominence with a 20–10 record, and four years later produced its first basketball All-American, Elwood Romney. Football, meanwhile, struggled to recover, an ordeal made all the more difficult by the absence of football programs in most of Utah's small farm communities. Nonetheless, in 1922 BYU students began contributing to a football stadium fund, and in 1928 their dream was fulfilled. In 1929 the BYU grid squad registered its first winning record: five wins and three losses.[8]

Yet neither Brigham Young University nor football dominates the early story of sport among Mormons. Sport first flourished as a community activity, not as a campus enterprise; basketball, not football or baseball, received the most attention. Basketball leagues had formed in Salt Lake City as early as 1908, and basketball in the 1920s replaced not only cultural programs, such as music, but also other recreational activities among Utah's youth. Despite the onset of economic woes in the Depression, an all-church basketball tournament in 1931 drew some 8,000 spectators from all over the state to Salt Lake City.[9]

Before the automobile and the bus made travel easy, team treks up the valley or over the mountain became events savored in local lore. One of those memorable moments occurred in mid-March 1923, when a basketball team from little Alma and Malta was scheduled to play Grouse Creek. On the morning of the game, a blizzard swept down the valley, forcing the boys and their coaches to set out on foot without benefit of horse and wagon. Midway to their destination, they stopped at a Mormon home, where the wife fed them a warming meal. The husband then loaded them into a four-horse bobsled, only to have his horses give out halfway up the mountain. By walking in each other's footsteps in the snow, the boys and their leaders arrived in Grouse Creek barely in time for the game.

They played in the basement of the Grouse Creek chapel. The room was lit by new electric lights, but the ceiling was ridiculously low: just a couple of feet above the rims of the baskets. The teams played two games, with home-court advantage easily winning both. Yet the difficulty of both travel and play seemed merely to enhance the athletic experience for Mormon youths. "Along the mountains of Malta and in the gymnasium at Grouse Creek," concludes historian Richard Kimball, "Mormon males were made."[10]

## Catholic Shiners

If gymnasium sport made good Mormons in the mountains of Utah, it also made good Catholics on the Depression-era streets of American cities. Formally begun in Chicago in 1930, the Catholic Youth Organization (CYO) built on earlier Big Brother programs (assistance for juvenile delinquents on probation), Boy Scout troops, and Church-sponsored athletic leagues. The first director of the CYO was a handsome, athletic-looking young assistant pastor of Our Lady Help of Christians parish, Father Raphael Ashenden. Chicago's archdiocesan paper, New World, credited Ashenden's "brilliant leadership" for the initial "tremendous success" of the CYO. Unfortunately, Ashenden was killed by a speeding automobile on an icy Chicago street in February 1931, less than a year after he launched the CYO.[11]

The Catholic archbishop of Chicago, George Cardinal Mundelein, warmly supported the CYO, but the bulk of the administrative work, and the credit for making the CYO a highly effective, visible arm of the Catholic Church, fell to Bishop Bernard J. Sheil. A native Chicagoan from a middle-class Irish-American home, Sheil was weaned on sport. He dabbled in boxing and fencing, but baseball was his favorite game. The hero of his youth was the major league good-guy pitcher, Christy Mathewson. Young Sheil himself tossed a reasonably good curve ball for his Catholic boarding school and college, St. Viator's. For two of his college summers, he pitched semiprofessionally for the Logan Squares and reportedly received offers from several major league clubs.[12]

Instead of becoming a professional ballplayer, Sheil turned to the seminary, then served three years as a prison chaplain at the Cook County jail. Years later, Sheil frequently recalled that his jail experience was an important factor in his enthusiasm for the CYO. He escorted dozens of men, some of them teenagers, to the gallows; he counseled young men ruined by urban filth, low aspirations, and lack of guidance. The CYO, for Sheil, represented a bold march into the slums to provide for Catholic youths "the firm moorings of religion upon which they could restore their faith, recreation through which they could develop their bodies, and education in which they could expand their knowledge and understanding of life."[13]

Taking its first step toward giving Catholic children "wholesome occupation," and to "keep them off those breeding places of crime, the streets" (as the New World put it), the Chicago CYO officially took the Boy Scouts under its wing. Thus were two monsters killed with one slingshot. Catholic

fears that the Boy Scouts were too solidly associated with Protestantism were put to rest; and accusations of Catholics being unassimilated immigrants were refuted by the Church's explicit sponsorship of a popular youth organization that was based on teachings of civic responsibility and pride of American citizenship.[14]

Shortly after committing itself to the Boy Scouts, the CYO announced an ambitious program of vacation schools in neighborhood churches, particularly in Al Capone's bloody Twentieth Ward and in "the ant-heap of misery in the Negro South Side." In contrast to the sectarian, male interests embodied in the Catholic Boy Scouts, the CYO vacation schools welcomed all urban youths regardless of gender or religious affiliation. Vacation schools were open to "little boys and girls of every race and creed," announced the politically liberal Bishop Sheil. "Whether they are Catholic, Protestants, Jews or Colored, they are welcome to the free education and supervision which the Catholic Youth Organization provides."[15]

Primarily, though, the CYO provided competitive sports programs. From the outset, softball games, swim meets, bowling tournaments, and basketball leagues appeared on the agenda. Boxing tournaments, track meets, and even golf matches soon followed; and in November 1933, six teams began competing every Monday night in a CYO ice hockey league at the Chicago Coliseum. The CYO initially used neighborhood gyms, pools, bowling alleys, and playing fields throughout the city. When the CYO Softball League was begun, one observer commented that "vacant lots all over Chicago were cleared of tin cans and bottles by the boys themselves."[16]

Despite the economic severities of the Depression, in June 1932 Bishop Sheil opened the doors to a huge new CYO center at 31 East Congress Street. It provided a few rooms for educational and religious instruction, but mainly featured gyms, handball courts, and game rooms. In the basement and on the third and fourth floors were no fewer than fifty-two bowling alleys that catered to more than 1,000 bowling teams. Overseeing

---

**Catholic Youth Organization.** The Catholic answer to the YMCA, the CYO originated in Chicago in 1930. Nuns tended playgrounds in Catholic neighborhoods (above) and priests supervised competitive inner-city sports programs, especially basketball and boxing tournaments. Below, the legendary founder and ardent patron of the CYO, Bishop Bernard J. Shiel, poses with some pugilistic hopefuls. (From the Archdiocese of Chicago's Joseph Cardinal Bernardin Archives and Records Center.)

this plethora of athletic activity was a full-time athletic director, Jack Elder, a Notre Dame gridiron star from the glory days of Knute Rockne.[17]

Of all the sports sponsored by the CYO, basketball and boxing mattered most. Despite its Protestant origins as a YMCA game, the popularity of basketball came as no surprise: Chicago was a hotbed for hoops. As early as 1895, the city hosted tournaments for both girls and boys. Beginning in 1918 Amos Alonzo Stagg, the athletic director at the University of Chicago, promoted interscholastic basketball tournaments every year between Christmas and New Year's Day, attracting the best high school teams from all over the state of Illinois. In 1923 Loyola University began an annual National Catholic Basketball Tournament. On the eve of the founding of the CYO, some thirty Chicago squads represented virtually "every section of the city" in that all-Catholic event. No fewer than 140 teams registered for the initial CYO boys' and girls' basketball tournaments in the spring of 1931; just a year later, some 2,200 players competed on 182 teams. On the way to the 1933 tournaments, one wag predicted "enough basket shooting in the CYO to satisfy the hysterical tendencies of all cage fiends in Chicago."[18]

Chicago also had its boxing fiends, inspiring another focus for the CYO. As the nation embraced prizefighting in the wake of World War I, the city actively welcomed both professional and amateur championship bouts. At Soldier Field in 1927, 105,000 spectators cheered a rematch of heavyweights Jack Dempsey and Gene Tunney. That fight put Chicago on the boxing map when Dempsey lost after an infamous "long count" provoked by his refusal to go to a neutral corner after a knockdown. At the amateur level, Chicagoans eagerly supported an annual charity boxing program begun in 1923 under the sponsorship of the *Chicago Tribune;* in 1929 the *Tribune* and the *New York Times* cooperatively produced the first Golden Gloves tournament.[19]

Yet mere popularity was insufficient reason for putting the Catholic Church's stamp of approval on the fight game. As Bishop Sheil explained, boxing was a moral endeavor, a perfect antidote to urban youth gangs and violent crime. A well-regulated program was a potential savior for slum youths who grew up literally fighting for survival. Moreover, CYO boxing tournaments would replace gangster heroes such as Al Capone and Machine-Gun Jack McGurn with local boxing heroes. "We'll knock the hoodlum off the pedestal out there," insisted Sheil. "And we'll put another neighborhood boy in his place. He'll be dressed in CYO boxing shorts and a pair of leather mitts. He may have a shiner and a bloody nose, but he'll also have a Championship medal."[20]

A candidate for a CYO shiner and bloody nose had to be over sixteen years of age, a "duly baptized" Catholic, and an amateur. He was also required to maintain passing grades in school, avoid vulgar language, and publicly pledge himself to good sportsmanship, devotion to God and Church, and love of country. Once the young man cleared those hurdles, he trained under the watchful eye of a former professional lightweight champion, Packey McFarland, the director of the CYO's boxing program. Over the years, McFarland obtained the hands-on assistance of other retired professionals such as Benny Leonard and Tony Zale.[21]

In the inaugural year of the CYO boxing tournament (1931), 1,600 young men signed on in one of eight weight divisions. For preliminary bouts, the diocese was divided into four sections, each of which was in turn subdivided into four districts. A parish priest oversaw the arrangements and publicity within each district. Support of friends and families insured good turnouts, even for opening round fights. On October 30, some 2,000 people paid to see preliminary bouts in the gym of DePaul University. On November 20, ushers attired in tuxedos welcomed a Monday-night crowd of 1,100 at St. Agnes Church parish house.[22]

For the finals on December 4, 1931, more than 18,000 spectators packed the newly built Chicago Stadium. They enjoyed a ceremonious blend of traditional Catholic ritual and modern political pageantry. Fifteen minutes before the fights began, 1,000 Catholic Boy Scouts lined the aisles from the dressing rooms to the ring. Finalists paraded proudly to the brightly lit ring, followed by Bishop Sheil. Cheers shook the rafters for several minutes, then the bishop raised his arms, called for silence, and thanked everyone—especially God—for a successful tournament. Finally, Sheil led a lively recitation of the CYO Pledge of Sportsmanship:

> I promise upon my honor to be loyal to my God, to my Country, and to my Church; to be faithful and true to my obligations as a Christian, a man, and a citizen. I pledge myself to live a clean, honest, and upright life—to avoid profane, obscene, and vulgar language, and to induce others to avoid it. I bind myself to promote, by word and example, clean, wholesome, and manly sport; I will strive earnestly to be a man of whom my Church and my Country may be justly proud.[23]

Winners received gold medals reportedly sculpted at Vatican City in Rome. Better still, they won four-year college scholarships, but were more immediately dazzled by the new suits, shirts, ties, hats, shoes, and topcoats they were given for an early January trip to Los Angeles on a chartered railway car, where they were scheduled to square off against a team of amateur boxers. In subsequent years, Chicago's CYO champions annually alternated trips to Hawaii and Panama with visits from West Coast, South American, and Irish boxing teams. Opponents on several of these jaunts included Army and Navy personnel, but in the 1930s the Chicago CYO squad never lost a single exhibition tourney. As another sure sign of success, three CYO boxers represented the United States at the Berlin Olympics in 1936.[24]

Yet the CYO was a child of hard times and zealous clerical patronage, and the removal of those factors would entail drastic change in the character of the organization. Economic recovery and the coming of World War II ended the Depression; the death of Cardinal Mundelein in 1939 meant the loss of support for the CYO at the highest administrative level. Bishop Sheil, meanwhile, turned his energies toward support of organized labor and community social services. He distinguished himself as a liberal opponent of anti-Semitism in American life, and also opposed the anticommunist crusade of Senator Joe McCarthy.[25]

In 1954 Sheil resigned as bishop and head of the CYO. His successor, Edward J. Kelley, lacked enthusiasm for athletic programs as a primary means of keeping inner-city Catholic youths from crime. He immediately called a halt to the controversial boxing tournament and closed the downtown athletic center. Basketball and outdoor recreational and camp programs survived as CYO emphases throughout the country, but by the late 1950s the Chicago base of the Catholic Youth Organization was a mere shadow of its former self.[26]

## Jewels of the Ghetto

As Catholics joined Protestants in making an ally of sport in twentieth-century America, Jews also took to the ring, the court, and fields of play.[27] American Jews competed on early gymnastics, baseball, and track squads. Founded in Baltimore in 1854, the Young Men's Hebrew Association (YMHA) encouraged physical fitness, recreation, and moral spirituality in a vein similar to the Protestant YMCA and the later Catholic CYO. By 1900 about a hundred YMHA centers claimed some 20,000 members.[28]

Early Jewish athletic enthusiasts were mostly second-generation German-Americans whose interest in sport reflected their thoroughly urbanized, Americanized style of life. By 1900, however, they were being outnumbered by Yiddish-speaking Jewish immigrants from the cultural backwaters of eastern Europe, where organized sport was unknown. From the early 1880s to the outbreak of World War I, two million Jews from Russia, Poland, and Rumania passed through Ellis Island to find refuge in the United States. Almost half of them settled in New York City, especially in the densely crowded tenements of the Lower East Side.

Jewish parents, eager to become Americans but fearful of Christian ways, chafed at the prospect of their sons choosing a gym over the synagogue and the sports page over the Torah. By all accounts, many Jewish immigrant families struggled with the athletic question in a fashion similar to the cantor and his son arguing over alien American music in the first motion-picture talkie, *The Jazz Singer* (1927). Yet some Jewish immigrant parents, nudged by older German-American Jews as well as Anglo-American reformers, embraced sport as a way for their children to become fully American. Through sport, youths could overcome the stereotype of Jews as physically weak newcomers to America more devoted to Old World religious and intellectual pursuits than to New World competition. Between 1900 and 1920, the Young Men's Hebrew Association, Jewish community centers, settlement houses, and labor organizations differed little from public playgrounds and schools in providing a wide range of athletic options for Jewish youths.[29]

During the interwar years, Jews competed athletically not only in their local communities but also at the highest levels of all the major sports in the United States. They especially excelled at boxing and basketball, two unlikely venues for Jewish achievement. Prizefighting, long banned because of its dehumanizing brutality and corrupt clientele, seemed to violate Jewish intellectual values and cultural traditions. Hoops, too, carried unsavory associations, but of a different sort. Basketball was a game made in, by, and for the YMCA, a distinctly Protestant institution.

For the attraction of both sports to Jews, immediate practicalities outweighed historical impediments. Previous prizefighters were working class, needy, and hungry, likely as not just off the immigrant boat. Irishmen filled that bill for much of the nineteenth century; East European Jews and Italians took over during the first half of the twentieth. Especially for New York City's Lower East Side residents, ghetto realities meant conflict with other ethnic youths on the way to school, in street games, and at playgrounds and swimming pools. As Benny Leonard recalled his East Village childhood near Eighth Street and Second Avenue, he and his friends faced daily challenges from "Irish 'Micks,' Italian 'Wops,' and the hoodlums of a dozen different races."[30]

In most Jewish reminiscences, Irish youths loomed as the great enemy, the worst of the anti-Semitic taunters. The Jews killed Christ, went the bigot's line, so Irish Catholics could happily take revenge on the "Jew bastards." By all accounts, a Jewish boy suffered sheer hell any time he had to trek through, or even near, an Irish neighborhood. He quickly learned to fight. Fists and fast footwork allowed a boy to defend his manhood and carve out a measure of self-esteem. As a result, by the late 1920s Jewish fighters had replaced the Irish as the dominant ethnicity of titleholders in the eight professional weight divisions. From 1920 to 1939, Jewish boxers held no fewer than eighteen titles.

One of the earliest, and arguably the greatest, Jewish prizefighter was lightweight Benny Leonard. Like many of his contemporaries, he fought at first against his parents' wishes, changing his name from Leiner to Leonard in order to keep his pugilistic efforts a secret from his parents. Only a good paycheck brought his father around. Many good paychecks awaited. In a professional career that spanned thirteen years, Leonard lost only 4 of 210 bouts. From 1917 to 1925, he reigned as undefeated lightweight champion.

Unfortunately, the stock market crash of 1929 wiped out the considerable wealth Leonard had amassed from the ring, vaudeville, and real estate. In financial straits, he returned in 1932 for one last hurrah against a new champion, Jimmy McLarnin. The thirty-six-year-old Leonard started furiously, but ran out of steam. McLarnin knocked him out in the sixth round, a demise all the more painful because it happened at the hands of an Irish-American. Yet the heroic reputation of "The Great Bennah" survived that defeat. Half a century later, novelist Budd Schulberg recalled the heady days of the 1920s when Benny Leonard climbed nimbly into the ring "sporting the six-pointed Jewish star on his fighting trunks," raising Jewish hopes of "sweet revenge for all the bloody noses, split lips, and mocking laughter at pale little Jewish boys who had run the neighborhood gauntlet."[31]

What Benny Leonard was to the 1920s, Barney Ross was to the 1930s. Their similarities were uncanny. Like Leonard, Ross was born in New York City's Lower East Side. His family moved to Chicago when he was two years of age, but Ross, like Leonard, had to contend with his parents' severe disapproval of the fight game. Also like Leonard, he changed his name—from Rasofsky to Ross—to conceal his unacceptable activity. Of similar size, he fought in the lightweight division; like Leonard, he held the lightweight crown for a time (1933–1935); but he held the welterweight title to boot (1934, 1935–1938).[32] In fact, Ross held the crown in three different divisions, beginning in 1929 with the amateur featherweight Golden

Gloves championship. In 1933 he took the professional lightweight title from Tony Canzoneri, and two years later moved up a weight class by
defeating Benny Leonard's old nemesis, welterweight champion Jimmy
McLarnin. When he finished his career by being soundly defeated by black
challenger Henry Armstrong in 1938, Ross could look back on a career record of 74 victories in 82 bouts. Then, in a feat unavailable to Benny Leonard, Ross became a widely acclaimed war hero, winning the Silver Star for
his courageous action with the Marines at Guadalcanal.[33]

Yet too much emphasis on Barney Ross, Benny Leonard, and a few other
highly visible world champions blurs the fact that boxing, for Jews, forever
remained primarily a ghetto affair. Jewish boxers known only to family and
neighbors filled the cards of local club fights. Before television, in the
interwar years, those clubs thrived. But whether his fights occurred in,
near, or outside the ghetto, the old neighborhood was the fighter's base
of support. Lightweight Ruby Goldstein thought his "social club" to be
Sandberg's candy store on the Lower East Side. "Placards announcing my
fights were hung in the windows of the store. Pictures were on the walls.
Tickets for my fights were hung there. After every fight it was jammed with
'members' waiting to see me." Never a champion, Goldstein nevertheless
proudly wore the nickname "Jewel of the Ghetto."[34]

Scarcely was New York's Lower East Side the only ghetto to produce
tough Jews. San Francisco's turn-of-the-century Jewish quarters produced
battlers Joe Choynski and Abe Attell. Chicago's West Side claimed featherweight Jackie ("just American for Jacob") Fields, lightweight contender
Ray Miller, and heavyweight Kingfish Levinsky as well as Barney Ross. Jews
in South Philadelphia cheered local light heavyweight champion Battling
Levinsky, and in 1926 a Cleveland Jewish newspaper lauded hometown
pugilists Henry Goldberg, George Levine, and Sammy Aaronson as confirmation of "the prowess of the Jew in athletics."[35]

Jews in boxing were not confined to the contestants themselves. Jewish
managers, trainers, promoters, referees, and sportswriters put boxing on
the American sports map during the interwar era. By the 1930s, more than
twenty Jewish managers handled the affairs of prominent boxers. Of the
many successful trainers, Heinie Blaustein, Israel "Charley" Goldman, and
Ray Arcel stood tallest. Blaustein and Goldman each trained five world
champions; Arcel trained no fewer than twenty-one. At least another two
dozen Jews promoted fights throughout the country. Mike Jacobs led the
list but aroused severe opposition from American Jews when he brought
German heavyweight Max Schmeling to New York to battle Joe Louis in

1936 and again in 1938. The rematch drew 70,000 fans to Yankee Stadium, a million-dollar gate for Jacobs.[36]

For the more general promotion of the fight game, journalist Nat Fleischer was supremely important. He excelled at both refereeing and sportswriting, and in 1922 began publication of *The Ring,* a highly influential periodical. *The Ring*'s controversial edge, historical tidbits, lively reportage, accurate records, and authoritative monthly rankings of fighters quickly made it "the Bible of boxing." Owned, managed, and edited by Nat Fleischer, *The Ring* was a Jewish Bible for the Jewish interwar world of boxing.[37]

## Sporting the Jewish Star

Basketball, too, was sometimes dubbed "the Jewish game" in the 1920s and '30s. Arguably, basketball topped boxing as an important sport for immigrant communities because it involved more people and rewarded something more than pugnacity and survivor skills. As Nat Krinsky, a Brooklyn high school gym teacher, phrased it in 1923, the basketball court was an ideal place to develop "the qualities of courage, respect for authority, cooperation, unselfishness, and a desire to play cleanly and in a sportsmanlike manner."[38]

From the outset, basketball was a city game. Requiring little space or special equipment, it was especially suited to the crowded inner-city streets and playgrounds of poor immigrant communities. Basketball and the American Jew were born of the same womb and of the same era. One of the first Jewish stars, Barney Sedran—a "Mighty Mite" whose five feet, four inches and 115 pounds make him the smallest member of the Basketball Hall of Fame—was born in 1891, the same year that James Naismith invented basketball. Just five years later, Nat Holman, destined to be the greatest of all Jewish basketball figures, was born in New York City. Thus, American Jews and hoops grew up together. The one helped Americanize the other.

For the first third of the twentieth century, Jewish teams and leagues thrived. As early as 1902, a Jewish Basketball League represented YMHAs, community centers, settlement houses, and synagogues on the South Side of Philadelphia. Winter Tuesday nights meant festive basketball doubleheaders, followed by a dance. The basketball-and-dance scene was a family affair, an occasion for young men and women to socialize with their own ethnic and religious kind. In places other than Philadelphia, Jewish games and dances were usually held on Friday nights—a reasonable time for working people at the end of the week but a terrible imposition on Orthodox Jews, for whom the Sabbath began at sundown on Friday.[39]

This community pattern—filled with pleasure, tinged with religious misgivings—repeated itself in Jewish enclaves all along the eastern seaboard. But whatever its conflict with orthodoxy, community basketball allowed Jews to maintain their tradition of helping the needy and contributing generously to good causes. In Brooklyn a Jewish team created a Matzoh Fund from the proceeds of a basketball game to help "the needy of Brownsville during Passover." Several teams annually used basketball revenues to send children to summer camp; still others contributed to the Jewish Relief Fund or to various other Jewish charities.

Charitable or not, Jewish teams drew good crowds because they played good basketball. The all-Jewish Atlas Club, founded in New Haven in 1906, went undefeated over a 24-game schedule in 1919–1920, and in 1922 trounced Yale University, 42–22, in an exhibition contest that drew nearly 3,000 spectators. By the 1930s the Dux Club, formed in 1925 in the Brownsville section of Brooklyn, was taking on New York University, the City College of New York, and various professional barnstorming teams such as the New York Jewels, the Jersey City Reds, and the Chicago Studebakers.

Professional and semiprofessional clubs proliferated in the 1920s. At the head of the Jewish pack were the Cleveland Rosenblums, named after their prime sponsor, a local businessman; and the Nonpareils of Brooklyn. Neither could outshine the greatest of the all-Jewish squads, the SPHAs. Just after their old community league folded in 1925, the South Philadelphia Hebrew Association (SPHA) became a highly successful semiprofessional team that played all comers. Even after a name change to the South Philadelphia Hebrew All-Stars, the SPHAs proudly retained, and proclaimed, their Jewish roots. They embroidered their shirts with the six-pointed Mogen David and Hebrew letters for SPHA; they barnstormed as "the Wandering Jews" or "Philadelphia Hebrews," nicknames only slightly less provocative than the "Fighting Rabbis" of the Talmud Torah Athletic Club in Minneapolis.[40]

Of all the basketball players and coaches whose names resonated within the communities of Jewish youth, five-foot-eleven-inch forward Nat Holman was probably the best known. Having learned the game in the usual hoop haunts of the Lower East Side, in 1917 he began a sixteen-year professional career as a deft playmaker, set-shot artist, and defensive whiz on a dozen or so teams ranging from Bridgeport, Albany, and Scranton to

Syracuse and Chicago. He starred for three different clubs in New York City, including several years with the barnstorming Original Celtics. Complementing the extraordinary talent of Joe Lapchick, Dutch Dehnert, and Johnny Beckman, Holman was the only Jew ever to wear the Celtics shamrock.[41]

Holman's most impressive feat was an off-court juggling act: balancing a high-level playing career with a weighty coaching commitment. In 1919 he began a thirty-eight-year career as head coach of the City College of New York (CCNY) Beavers. However distant his barnstorming games, Holman regularly took overnight trains back to the city for CCNY practice sessions and games. As his playing career wound down in the early 1930s, he added yet another duty, as athletic director at the Ninety-second Street YMHA. Appropriately, he once played for a New York team called the Whirlwinds.

Holman's CCNY teams were overwhelmingly Jewish, in large measure because CCNY was an immigrant's dream. Financed solely by taxes, the college charged small fees but no tuition until well after World War II. For Lower East Side Jews who could commute from home, it was a magnet: higher education that was cheap and reasonably near. Basketball scholarships were not even necessary. In the 1930s more than 90 percent of all the CCNY basketball Beavers were Jewish. Nat Holman coached some 518 players during his thirty-eight years there; no fewer than 428, about 83 percent, were Jews.[42]

Jews also dominated the interwar basketball rosters of two other New York City schools. St. John's University, a Jesuit Catholic institution, naturally attracted Irish and Italian students. Yet when the Redmen posted a 68–4 mark from 1928 to 1931 and finished 21–1 in 1930–1931, their lineups were laced with Jewish names such as Max Posnack, Allie Shuckman, Max Kinsbrunner, and "Rip" Gerson. Jewish athletes also rang the bells for New York University (NYU). In 1934, Willie Rubenstein, Sid Gross, and Irwin "King Kong" Klein led NYU to an undefeated 16–0 season. For the following year, Len Maidman and Milt Shulman filled out the starting lineup with Jews. They achieved an 18–1 season and won the national championship.

These New York basketball Jews were all men, of course. Not until 1924 was the NYU women's basketball team granted full varsity status. Yet even there NYU had a Jewish presence in captain and star forward Claire Strassman. Basketball was highly attractive to women as well as men, and Jewish women were no exception. Within a year of James Naismith's invention, a Jewish immigrant from Lithuania, Senda Berenson, adapted the game for women at Smith College. At Chicago's Hull House, Polish immigrant Hilda Polacheck enthusiastically played basketball in the 1890s. In Chicago, which contained the third largest Jewish population of all the world's cities, the Jewish People's Institute proudly cheered its women's basketball squad to three citywide championships in the early 1920s. Despite the double-dose prohibition of Orthodox Judaism and American Victorianism, Jewish women exercised and competed across the spectrum of American sport.[43]

Nor did Jewish males limit their athleticism to basketball and boxing. Between 1920 and 1940, Jews could be found in virtually every segment of American sport. A lack of sufficient playground space inspired the invention of the street game of stickball, a simplified imitation of baseball. A mere broom handle and rubber ball or stuffed sock put Jewish boys in touch with the National Game, the supposed essence of American sport. Almost every summer evening, radios in open apartment windows on the Lower East Side blared a Yankees, Dodgers, or Giants game. For Jewish boys, fantasies of major league careers flourished.[44]

Few of those dreams materialized. In the 1930s, the decade of the heaviest Jewish presence in major league baseball, only nine or ten Jewish players made it each year. Though not numerous, several were highly visible. Infielder Charles Solomon "Buddy" Myer, for example, compiled an impressive .303 batting average over a seventeen-year career (1925–1941), all but two years as a Washington Senator. He played in two All-Star games, and in 1935 hit for .349 to win the American League batting crown. Unfortunately, Myer is remembered best for an ugly incident in 1933 when, at second base for the Senators, he angrily retaliated with kicks and punches against a New York Yankees opponent who roughly tried to break up a double play. As a riot ensued, Lower East Side listeners of the game might well have felt their loyalties divided between a fellow Jew and their hometown Yankees.[45]

Despite Myer's extraordinary year at the plate in 1935, another Jewish star, Hank Greenberg, won the balloting for American League player of the year. A big right-handed hitting first baseman for the Detroit Tigers, Greenberg was indisputably the premier Jewish ballplayer of his day, and perhaps of all time. During a thirteen-year career that was interrupted by four years of military service in World War II, he hit 331 home runs, compiled a batting average of .313, and led the Tigers to four World Series.

Born of Rumanian immigrants who met after arriving in the United States, Greenberg grew up in a kosher home, observed the high holidays, and attended a Hebrew school in his Jewish neighborhood in the Bronx. In 1934 he refused to play baseball on Yom Kippur, the holiest of Jewish holidays, and received widespread positive publicity from that gesture. Yet Greenberg chose not to continue in his parents' path of religious piety. As he grew older, he ceased observing the holidays, synagogue rituals, and dietary habits of his ancestors.[46]

Nevertheless, for Jews and Gentiles alike, Greenberg was the most popular of all Jewish standard-bearers in the most popular of all American sports. His giant physique (six feet, four inches in an era that saw the average major leaguer stand only five feet eleven) and sterling moments on the field helped mute the anti-Semitic rantings of two Detroit contemporaries, Henry Ford and Father Charles Coughlin. In 1938—a year that began with Hitler's annexation of Austria and ended with *Kristallnacht*—Greenberg hit fifty-eight home runs, just two short of Babe Ruth's record. As his European ancestors confronted the threat of annihilation, Hank Greenberg projected an image of the Jew as victor, not victim.[47]

Jews also competed vigorously on the gridiron. In a physically violent game long dominated by muscular Christians eager to prove their manhood, Jews had some of their own proving to do. In 1920 Harvard fullback Arnold Horween became the first Jew to be selected to an All-American team; he captained the Crimson to victory in the Rose Bowl. By 1927 more than 500 lesser-known Jewish athletes were playing college football all over the United States, but the interwar Big Three were backs Benny Friedman of the University of Michigan, Marshall Goldberg of the University of Pittsburgh, and Sid Luckman of Columbia University. All three played professionally after college. Two of them landed in Chicago, Goldberg playing for the Cardinals and Luckman for the Bears. Under the tutelage of innovative coach George Halas, Luckman became the first famous T-formation quarterback. From 1940 to 1946, he led the Bears to four National Football League championships.[48]

Just as the horrid details of Hitler's murder of six million European Jews were coming to light and just as Israel was being created as an independent Jewish state, a notable cluster of Jewish-American athletes stepped out of the spotlight. Sid Luckman retired in 1947, the same year that Hank Greenberg hung up his baseball spikes in exchange for an administrative assignment; Marshall Goldberg followed them "out to pasture" in 1948. Never again would so many big-name Jewish athletes grace American fields of play.

## When David Departed the Field

After 1950, the Los Angeles Dodgers' brilliant Sandy Koufax, three-time Duke All-American Art Heyman, Olympic swimming champion Mark Spitz, and basketball whiz Nancy Lieberman were the exceptions, not the rule. By the 1980s an average of only two Jews played major league baseball each year, compared to the ten per year who competed in the much smaller baseball world of Hank Greenberg.[49]

One of the major causes of this sharp decline in the number of Jews in American sports lies in the social and economic success that Jewish immigrant parents wanted for their children. Second- and third-generation Jews moved from the ghetto to the suburbs, from the streets to college, from blue-collar labor to the professions. The old local communities that supported boxing cards, basketball games-and-dances, and ethnic heroes in big-time baseball and football disappeared. Success diminished the hunger for fame and fortune that puts fire in the athlete's belly. Like the Irish in nineteenth-century America and African-Americans in the second half of the twentieth century, Jews for a time competed athletically as if their lives depended on the outcome—which they did. But by the 1950s, Jews had outgrown that hunger; American blacks and Hispanics inherited it. In addition, the creation of Israel had reduced the American Jews' need for tough athletic heroes. Once Israel was established in 1948 as an independent Jewish state, American Jews could admire able, articulate statesmen and strong Israeli soldiers committed to Jewish survival. No longer did they need to fawn over Jewish boxers or basketball, football, and baseball players. The decline of top-level Jewish athletes, however, did not occur simply because of the sociological and political changes that affected American Jews. Conscious decisions were made by Jewish families and institutions who decided that the expense and distraction outweighed the value of sport. The story of Brandeis University's brief flirtation with football illustrates the point.

Founded in 1948 in Waltham, Massachusetts, Brandeis billed itself as the first Jewish but nonsectarian institution of higher learning. From the beginning, neither faculty nor student had to subscribe to any particular religion. Three campus chapels—Protestant, Catholic, and Jewish—symbolized the Brandeis liberal ideal. Yet the college was most definitely Jewish in inspiration and tone. Born just three years after the Holocaust and in the same year that the independent state of Israel was formed, the university took its name from Louis D. Brandeis, the nation's first Jewish member of the Supreme Court. For their first president, college trustees sought the eminent Jewish scientist, Albert Einstein. When he refused, they turned to Abram Sachar, a prominent historian whose *History of the Jews* (1930) displayed Zionist zeal. Brandeis quickly became a kind of mecca for Jewish students.[50]

Familiar with irrational outbursts of anti-Semitism, Brandeis's founders feared a backlash against this concentration of Jewish intellectuals. Age-old stereotypes depicted Jews as physically weak bookworms prone to victimization. For some Americans, the disaster recently suffered at the hands of European Nazis simply confirmed the stereotype. Consequently, Brandeis's early leaders envisaged their new university as a place of well-rounded, physically fit youths in the usual mode of American colleges and universities.[51] Strong physical education, intramural, and intercollegiate athletic programs would best serve that purpose, they agreed. Early visitors to the Brandeis campus saw an athletic center built before an adequate library or physical science laboratories got off the drawing board. The school's prime benefactor, Abraham Shapiro, had come to the United States from Lithuania by way of South Africa and had amassed a fortune as a shoe manufacturer in nearby Worcester. "He wanted the athletic center," President Sachar later recalled, "and he wanted it not only for its functional service [physical fitness] but because it would carry the message to the general public that Brandeis was a normal, wholesome American institution."[52]

For similar reasons, President Sachar also wanted intercollegiate athletics at Brandeis. Early in his academic career, Sachar had taught history at the University of Illinois, when the "Fighting Illini" regularly fielded championship football teams. In one of Sachar's classes sat All-American halfback Harold "Red" Grange, a "competent" student who presumably could have made better than the obligatory C if he had not spent so much time on the practice field. Instead, Grange prepared himself to dazzle the crowd each Saturday afternoon. Youthful Professor Sachar might well have sat among the 67,000 spectators in 1924 when his most famous student dedicated the new Memorial Stadium with some 500 yards running and passing against the University of Michigan. Whether present that day or not, Sachar was no stranger to intercollegiate sport. Knowing some of its benefits as well as its liabilities, he envisaged "modestly organized" athletic teams at Brandeis, with schedules confined "to the smaller schools where intercollegiate athletics did not dominate."[53]

Sachar tapped one of Red Grange's old foes from the mid-1920s, Benny

Friedman, to head the athletic program at Brandeis. A two-time All-American quarterback at the University of Michigan, the five-foot, eight-inch Friedman made All-Pro for four of the seven years he played professionally in the National Football League. In 1928 he led the NFL in both rushing and passing for touchdowns. Then, for twenty years or so, he coached at Yale and the City College of New York. He was intelligent, articulate, and energetic. Moreover, he was Jewish, with name recognition in both Jewish and Gentile circles. "Benny, you owe this to us," insisted President Sachar, in his attempt to woo Friedman to Brandeis. "This is the first school founded by our people. Everything we do has got to have quality. When we bring in a coach like Benny Friedman, it's like bringing in a Lenny Bernstein to head up our school of music."[54]

Sachar lived to regret that sales pitch, for Friedman set Brandeis on an athletic course that was far more ambitious than the university's philosophy and funds could sustain. Basketball, soccer, tennis, golf, fencing, and baseball teams soon represented Brandeis in intercollegiate contests; but the new athletic director, true to his experience, promoted football most of all. As the self-appointed head coach, Friedman fielded a freshman squad that opened the 1950 season with a victory over Harvard's freshmen, 3–0. Subsequent varsity success included a 5–2–1 season in 1952 and a 6–1 record in 1957, when Brandeis shut out New Hampshire and Northeastern and mauled Massachusetts, 47–7.

David frequently took on Goliath. Brandeis had a mere 200 male undergraduates enrolled in 1950, and ten years later numbered fewer than 600 males within a student body of 1,200. Still, the Judges (their athletic nickname) regularly lined up against Boston University, Northeastern, Massachusetts, New Hampshire, and Temple, whose athletic histories and number of students dwarfed Brandeis. For a brief moment, however, the gridiron game thrived at Brandeis. Large crowds ringed the field for home games. General financial support and the number of athletic scholarships grew dramatically. Although no separate athletic dormitory ever existed, a training table catered to athletes—with kosher food provided for those who wanted it. Friedman traveled afar during the off-season, extolling the university and its athletic program in passionate speeches to civic groups and synagogues. Apparently, he dreamed that Brandeis would become a major football power, "the Jewish Notre Dame of college football," as one player recalled.[55]

Some members of the Brandeis community thought Friedman's dream preposterous. It was one thing to support low-cost varsity teams in basketball, soccer, and fencing; it was another to throw financial resources at an expensive enterprise such as football with no assurance that Brandeis could ever compete successfully beyond the small-college level. Had not dozens of American colleges and universities dropped football in the early 1950s? For them, as for Brandeis critics of the gridiron game, it had come to be a luxury they could not afford.[56]

Yet a substantial number of Brandeis faculty and students considered the practical, dollars-and-cents argument against football an evasion of the central issue. They insisted that the hoopla surrounding football student-athletes and Saturday spectacles distracted students from the academic mission of the college. Others lamented the fact that football games were Saturday afternoon events, in violation of the Sabbath. Still others expressed discomfort at Benny Friedman's dynamic, persuasive style, which made him a highly popular speaker in synagogues and alumni gatherings around the country. However much Friedman might "sell" Brandeis, ultimately he was raising funds for an expanded athletic program.

As the football question divided trustees, alumni, faculty, and student opinion, President Sachar began cutting funds for athletic scholarships and varsity operating expenses. Consequently, the Judges, who had lost only one game in 1957, won not a single football game in 1959. Varsity basketball, too, suffered from the fallout. During the 1959–1960 season, the basketball squad won only two of its twenty games, a drastic downward turn from an 18–4 record two years earlier. Yet varsity basketball survived, a low-cost item so long as the team competed with schools mostly in the Boston vicinity. Brandeis football failed to outlive the decade. In the fall of 1960, Benny Friedman stood aside as Brandeis students competed in an intramural flag-football program.

Embittered, Friedman resigned as athletic director in 1963, drawing down the curtains on a bold experiment that yoked religion and sport for the supposed good of a new academic institution. In deciding that its unique ethnic, intellectual, and religious interests would best be served apart from big-time athletics, Brandeis set itself in opposition to most Protestant and Catholic institutions in the United States.

# 10

## MAKING A PITCH FOR JESUS

As Jews, Mormons, Catholics, and moderate Protestants embraced sport during the first half of the twentieth century, evangelical Protestants refused to join the love-fest. On the extreme right wing of the evangelical spectrum, fundamentalists especially resisted change. Fundamentalist beliefs in Biblical inerrancy, a decisive spiritual rebirth, and the urgency of winning converts before the imminent return of Christ produced a defensive posture that largely left these believers estranged from most aspects of modern culture, including sport.[1]

Between the end of World War II and the winding down of the Vietnam War, however, evangelicals—including fundamentalists—reversed their attitudes toward sport. By 1976, *Sports Illustrated* writer Frank Deford was designating this recent mixture of sport and religion as "Sportianity": an energetic, theologically conservative movement that used sport as a means of witnessing for Christ. Emphasizing the conversion ("born again") experience, Sportians endorsed Jesus "much as they would a new sneaker or a graphite-shafted driver," observed Deford. Commercial assumptions, tactics, and rhetoric had never been wholly absent from previous versions of Christian muscularity, but their pervasive presence gave Sportianity a distinctive flavor.[2]

This aggressive, proselytizing mode of behavior derives from a religious revival that seized the United States in the wake of World War II. It is a mentality, and a movement, most associated with evangelist Billy Graham. It first thrived in the Cold War era of the 1950s, when Americans added sport to religious faith and patriotism to create an idealized American "way of life" as an antidote to "godless Communism." Shaken but not destroyed by the turbulent youth rebellion of the 1960s, the evangelical version of this union has settled into a kind of familiar, easily recognizable barrage of pious gestures and phrases, all designed as a sales pitch for Jesus.

## The Birth of Born-Again Sport

Like the postwar religious revival of which it was a part, Sportianity was born of the vast social and ideological change that began shortly after the Second World War. The religious revival actually began during the war. Wartime fears prompted Americans to reconstruct some of the religious belief that had waned during the boom and bust interwar years. Perhaps there are no atheists in foxholes, as the saying goes; certainly few could be found in homes anxious for the safety of fathers and sons in distant foxholes.[3]

Clergymen called on the nation to turn to God as a Mighty Fortress against the foe. Reduced to fundamental issues of life and death, many Americans responded favorably to conservative ministers and evangelists who were discarding the argumentative, anti-intellectual style that had hampered their fundamentalist predecessors. A National Association of Evangelicals, founded in 1942, promoted conservative theology by the innovative use of radio, film, and modern advertising techniques. Appropriately, one of the most visible wartime evangelicals, Jack Wyrtzen, was a former insurance salesman. From New York City, his weekly "Word of Life" radio shows beamed throughout the United States and Canada. Similarly evangelical, the Youth for Christ movement, begun in 1943, aimed to convert college and high school youths. By D-day, in 1944, some 20,000 teenagers regularly attended Saturday night religious rallies at Madison Square Garden.[4]

Evangelistic "fishers of men" baited their hook with sports stars. Distance runner Gil Dodds, the 1943 winner of the James E. Sullivan Award for the nation's outstanding amateur athlete, proved especially attractive. In distances ranging from 1,000 yards to a mile, Dodds dominated NCAA and AAU events for most of the war years. He twice set world indoor mile records. Over a two-year stretch, he won thirty-nine consecutive races, and all the while regularly appeared in Youth for Christ gatherings throughout the Midwest. On Memorial Day 1945 he helped draw 65,000 people to a youth rally at Soldier Field, Chicago. He wore his track uniform, ran a mile against the clock, then gave a brief inspirational address while still dripping with sweat. "Running is only a hobby," Dodds told his rapt audience. "My mission is teaching the gospel of Jesus Christ."[5]

Dodds learned that conservative, fervent gospel from his father, a Church of the Brethren minister in rural Nebraska; he honed it at the Gordon School of Theology and Missions in Boston. Over the next forty years, Dodds would pursue his gospel mission through active evangelism, coaching track at Wheaton College in Illinois and serving as a high school guidance counselor in nearby Napierville. In the beginning (around the end of World War II), however, he set the style that numerous high-profile athletes would emulate for years to come: using his athletic visibility to call attention to Christ, giving credit to the Lord for helping him to win, and adding a scripture reference after his name when signing autographs. Responding to the latter habit, one fan mistakenly interpreted "Gil Dodds Phil. 4:13" ("I can do all things through Christ who strengthens me") as a reference to Dodds's recently having run a 4:13 mile in Philadelphia.[6]

A zealous, puritanical young Southerner, Billy Graham, served beside Gil Dodds on the small staff of the Youth for Christ organization. Himself a lover of sport (baseball in his youth, golf as an adult), Graham quickly caught on to the benefits of using the testimonies of sports figures to call attention to the gospel. To several of his early revivals, he invited Dodds to display his athleticism and tell about his devotion to Christ. In 1947, at an outdoor crusade in Charlotte, North Carolina, Dodds and a local miler raced around the track as a kind of warm-up for the religious service. A large crowd, enticed by this highly advertised but unorthodox linkage of sport and religion, quietly watched the race, then joined in religious song as the service began. Grady Wilson, an associate of Graham's, was baffled at first. He thought it "awfully silly" to promote all that "streakin' around and around" as a ploy to sell the gospel. Yet Wilson himself quickly underwent a conversion to the selling power of sport. When "an incredible number of young people" responded to Billy Graham's invitation that night, Wilson became convinced that God could use "just about anything," even athletics, to further His cause.[7]

Affluence most surely furthered the cause. After nearly two decades of depression and war, the nation turned to material pleasures long denied. Between 1947 and 1960, the average income of American workers increased as much as it had for the entire previous half century. Fueled in part by the benefits of the GI Bill, new businesses, houses, automobiles, television sets, refrigerators, washing machines, and other modern conveniences proliferated. By 1960 suburbs were flourishing, a national network of highways was in place, and the United States had a greater percentage of its citizens enrolled in colleges and universities than any other nation in the history of the planet. During the postwar era, one in every four Americans changed home addresses each year.[8]

Religion provided an anchor, a familiar voice and customary values amidst the Babel of social and economic mobility. Church afforded a personal touch in the face of impersonal economic change. Rather than sitting in judgment on the dominant culture, churches learned quickly to take advantage of the consumerist mentality of the day. To paraphrase one wag, people bought food during the week, leisure and excitement on Saturday, and peace of mind on Sunday. Between 1945 and 1960, churches were marching in a commercial parade that saw an increase of some 400 percent in the money spent for advertising.[9]

Revivalists proved to be peculiarly effective in the 1950s. They not only offered an old-time religion that satisfied the need for stability in a time of great movement and change; they also artfully packaged and sold their product in the American marketplace. The Billy Graham Evangelistic Association, incorporated in 1950, efficiently yoked a conservative theology with ultramodern organizational and business tactics. Cooperating with local churches, Graham's team planned their evangelistic campaigns to the most minute detail. Perhaps they left matters in the hands of the Holy Spirit, but not to chance. They perfected the art of advertising through the mass media of television, radio, cinema, and paperback books. At their public gatherings, they used popular music, cheerful banter, and heartfelt testimonies from show-biz and sports celebrities.[10]

Billy Graham crusades regularly featured sport terminology, personalities, and sites. Graham's group always referred to itself as a "team." In good ball game and business fashion, they kept score of every convert and then publicized the numbers "won to Christ." They especially publicized the conversions of well-known athletes, and some not so well known. In Graham's first major revival effort, at Los Angeles in 1949, Louis Zamperini, a long distance runner in the Berlin Olympics of 1936, walked the aisle seeking Christ. On the very next night, the converted Zamperini appeared on the platform beside Graham, urging others to accept Jesus. For reasons other than mere space, Graham selected sports venues like Yankee Stadium, Madison Square Garden, Wembley Stadium in London, Boston Garden, and the Los Angeles Coliseum for his early campaigns.[11]

In addition to affluence and its stepchild, consumerism, a kind of fearful anxiety lay behind the postwar religious revival. The mushroom clouds of Hiroshima and Nagasaki hung heavily over the world as the United States and the Soviet Union engaged in postwar "cold war" confrontation. Each superpower possessed nuclear means of global destruction; each, in different ways, mobilized citizen opinion against the other. In the United States, Wisconsin senator Joseph McCarthy briefly but vigorously led an anticommunist crusade on behalf of "the American way of life." As the Russians and their Communist-bloc allies extolled atheism, Americans reaffirmed faith in God as a patriotic badge of identity. A good churchgoer was a good American, it seemed. In 1950 some 55 percent of all Americans were affiliated with some church or synagogue; by 1960 formal religious affiliation peaked at 69 percent.[12]

Sport as well as religion danced to a political, anticommunist tune. The best example could be found in the postwar Olympic Games. Long excluded from the Olympics, the Soviet Union was finally allowed to compete at Helsinki in 1952. Reports in American Protestant and Catholic periodicals suggested widespread religious interest in the outcome of the games. Even the liberal *Christian Century* became flustered when the Russians challenged the United States in point totals. A Communist-bloc nation, Hungary, placed third. Yet another, Czechoslovakia, produced the individual star of the Helsinki Olympics, long-distance runner Emil Zatopek, whose three gold-medal performances included the marathon. Although a Catholic weekly happily observed that the Helsinki games failed to degenerate into "a side show of the cold war," religious as well as political concerns kept Americans focused on the 1952 Olympics.[13]

One of the most lauded of all American athletes at Helsinki was an ordained Protestant minister, pole vaulter Bob Richards. Having won a bronze medal in the 1948 London games, in 1951 Richards received the James E. Sullivan Memorial Trophy as the athlete of the year. At Helsinki he set Olympic records in winning the gold, and he did so again at Melbourne in 1956. People called him "the Vaulting Vicar" and "the Reverend" but detected no holier-than-thou posturing on his part. He bantered freely with friends and foes alike, even with the Russians in the few words he and they knew of each other's language. The *Saturday Evening Post* featured him as a "big-talking, pole-vaulting parson."[14]

Shortly after his athletic career ended in 1957, Bob Richards shelved his plans to become an active gospel minister. Yet he stayed in the mainstream of the new kind of muscular Christianity that barged to the fore in the 1950s. His style was distinctly evangelical, his theology conservative. Like Gil Dodds, Bob Richards was a member of the fundamentalist Church of the Brethren. He hitched his religious wagon to the consumerist star. For some fifteen years, he was the official "Wheaties Man," selling a clean image and breakfast cereals for General Mills. Hitting the advertisement trail just when television could be found in most American homes, Richards became a household name. He turned from gospel precepts to material goals, successfully marketing himself on the lecture circuit as "America's master of motivation and positive thinking." In the gospel according to Bob Richards, Billy Graham's lion and Norman Vincent Peale's lamb lay down together.[15]

## Evangelical Ventures for Victory

The evangelical impulse to use sport to win converts to Christianity took specific shape through several new organizations in the 1950s and '60s, preaching a simple gospel that was light on intellectual substance and strong on emotional appeal. Although theologically narrow, evangelicals cast their nets widely across sectarian boundaries. Intentionally non-denominational, they seldom even mentioned specific church affiliation. They nominally accepted women and older adults, but primarily attracted young adult males.

The inaugural group, Sports Ambassadors, was born of missionary, anticommunist zeal in the early 1950s. As newly independent African and Asian states emerged, religious as well as political leaders found sport to be an effective means to keep Western thumbs in third-world pies. Government-sponsored agencies eagerly sent Olympic champions Jesse Owens to India and Mal Whitfield to Kenya in the 1950s, extolling the American way of life. Religious missionaries, too, carried the banner of Americanism in one hand and Christianity in the other. While the Korean War raged (1950–1953), an American Youth for Christ evangelist, Dick Hillis, went to nearby Formosa (Taiwan) to win converts among the refugees who had fled from mainland Communist China. Hillis envisaged sport as an ally in his missionary effort. Taking his cue from a Youth for Christ basketball team that had recently played and preached in Europe, in 1952 Hillis requested a similar enterprise for Formosa: exhibition contests against the best native squads, with evangelistic meetings before and after each game. Don Odle, of Taylor University in Indiana, coached the team; Don Schaeffer, an accomplished player at Wheaton College, starred on the court. Calling themselves the "Venture for Victory" team, they played for eight weeks in Formosa. Reportedly, they won an armload of basketball games, friends for America, and souls for Christ.[16]

As a result of that experience, Hillis decided that the Youth for Christ

**The evangelical kind.** At a Fellowship of Christian Athletes gathering in the mid-1960s, University of Alabama coach Paul "Bear" Bryant and his star quarterback, Steve Sloan, meet a handsome young Billy Graham, the fount of much of the postwar evangelical impulse that now permeates sport. (FCA photo)

movement should not be confined to North America. He resigned from Youth for Christ to create an independent organization, Orient Crusades, for similar purposes with different audiences in Formosa, Okinawa, Hong Kong, and the Philippines. The name soon changed to Overseas Crusades, and Odle and Schaeffer constructed another basketball team to head a subsidiary sport evangelism arm. Calling their new group the Sports Ambassadors, they defined it as "a ministry of Overseas Crusades that utilizes international sports for evangelism and that equips Christian coaches and athletes for effective growth and service for Christ."[17]

Back in the American heartland, the Fellowship of Christian Athletes was formed in the early 1950s. Destined to become the largest and most influential of all the religious athletes' organizations, it was the brainchild of an Oklahoman, Don McClanen. While playing football at Oklahoma A&M and later coaching high school football, McClanen observed that high school students idolized athletes. He began to ponder the possibility of using that hero worship as a means of promoting Christian faith and values. Beginning at the local level, he identified prominent athletes who were known to be Christian, then persuaded them to "bear testimony" at schools, athletic events, and religious youth rallies throughout Oklahoma.[18]

For some seven years McClanen sought a larger, national scope for his idea. He finally hit the jackpot when he aroused the enthusiasm of major league baseball magnate Branch Rickey. According to Fellowship of Christian Athlete lore, McClanen sold his car in order to pay for a plane ticket to visit Rickey in Pittsburgh. Whatever the means of transport, the visit was well timed. Having recently left the front office of the Brooklyn Dodgers for the vice-presidency of the Pittsburgh Pirates, the stern Rickey was reeling from several recent encounters with liberal clergymen, whose pale convictions he abhorred. By contrast, McClanen's proposal seemed "a new and worthy approach to Christian teaching and living." Rickey eagerly volunteered material as well as moral assistance to the cause. He invited several prominent Pittsburgh businessmen to a luncheon at which McClanen announced his plans for a national organization. The group pledged $25,000, and on November 12, 1954, the Fellowship of Christian Athletes (FCA) was officially launched from an office in Norman, Oklahoma.[19]

With McClanen serving as full-time executive director, in 1956 the FCA moved its headquarters to Kansas City. In the summer of the same year, it convened its first annual conference near Estes Park, Colorado. Branch Rickey gave the keynote address. He lauded the FCA for being no "namby-pamby thing"; rather, it was "a cooperative grouping of athletes to embrace and have others embrace Jesus as the Christ." For "inspiration and perspiration," some 256 athletes and coaches attended the four-day gathering. They wrapped Bible study, gospel addresses, songs, prayers, and meditative conversations around athletic exhibitions and competitive events. Olympic champion Bob Richards arrived on the next-to-last evening to display his pole vaulting expertise. By the illumination of car lights, he performed on a rocky field in a drizzling rain.[20]

Several big-name athletes joined Rickey and Richards in supporting the fledgling FCA. Football stars Doak Walker, Donn Moomaw, Otto Graham, and "Deacon" Dan Towler stood beside major league baseball players Robin Roberts, Carl Erskine, George Kell, Vernon Law, and Al Dark in the FCA's earliest efforts to nudge youths toward Christ and Christian morality. In that day before greater church-state sensitivities, FCA members from college and professional teams often addressed high school assemblies.

In the 1960s, as the nation divided over complex issues of civil rights, the Vietnam War, and new lifestyles, the simple gospel espoused by virile, well-scrubbed coaches and athletes had great appeal for many Americans, especially in the conservative South, Southwest, and Midwest. FCA summer sports camps, regional conferences, and local "huddles" (prayer and Bible study groups) flourished. Superstars like NFL quarterbacks Bill Wade and Fran Tarkenton, football coaches Paul Dietzel, Frank Broyles, and Tom Landry, baseball notables Bobby Richardson and Brooks Robinson, basketball stars Bob Pettit and Bill Bradley, and Olympic weight lifter Paul Anderson provided glittering antidotes to black-power salutes and the rebellious style of "Broadway Joe" Namath. Corporations like Kresge and Lilly Endowment came through with foundation funds for sites and programs, and in October 1970 President Richard Nixon got on the bandwagon by inviting FCA members to conduct a White House worship service.[21]

At the outset, white males dominated the FCA. In the mid-1970s, however, local huddles and national conferences opened their doors to women, and the central office hired a women's program director. They could afford it. In 1976 the FCA's annual budget was $2.2 million; by 1990 it reached some $20 million, boasted a staff of 500, and claimed a membership of 500,000. Today the modern three-story FCA headquarters and chapel, overlooking Royals Stadium in Kansas City, stand for a grand tradition of artfully blended American athleticism, religious zeal, and big business.

The last of the big three formal unions of conservative religion and commercial sport, Athletes in Action (AIA), was founded in 1966 by a former All-American and professional football player, Dave Hannah. Like Sports Ambassadors, AIA derived from the evangelical Campus Crusade for Christ; like the Fellowship of Christian Athletes, it sought "to use the ready-made platform of sports to share the adventure and excitement of following Christ." Athletes in Action specifically mimed the FCA in organizing sports clinics, summer camps, prayer breakfasts, and speeches to high schoolers. Its distinction, however, lay in its sponsorship of traveling athletic squads. AIA track, gymnastics, and weight-lifting teams competed and preached, but the organization's specialties were wrestling and basketball. In 1975 the AIA's wrestling and basketball squads won Amateur Athletic Union national championships.[22]

As all their matches were on the road, Athletes in Action took on the reputation of a kind of barnstorming gospel troupe in smelly socks and jock straps. At the halftime of their basketball games, while their opponents went off to the locker room, AIA players put on red, white, and blue sweatsuits and mingled among the fans, handing out gospel tracts and team photographs. Then two or three of the more articulate players gave testimonies punctuated with verses of scripture, all focused on the benefits of accepting and serving Christ. As the opponents came back on the floor for the second half of the game, fans were asked to fill out cards to indicate if they had received Christ during the evening, or if they wanted further information. After each game, AIA players personally distributed copies of the New Testament to both officials and opposing players, then hung around to speak informally with spectators about their faith.[23]

Although Athletes in Action and the Fellowship of Christian Athletes were cut from the same evangelical cloth, AIA differed in its public emphasis on basketball rather than football or baseball. In part because of this basketball focus, AIA involved more African-Americans and women than did the FCA; globally its reputation soared as the hoop game enjoyed a worldwide increase in popularity. In Canada the AIA was by far the stronger of the two representatives of Sportianity.[24]

Several new evangelical organizations emerged in the 1970s. Professional Athletes Outreach, founded in 1971 in Issaquah, Washington, offered Christian leadership training programs; during the off-season it sponsored conferences for professional athletes and their families. Sports Outreach America, directed by former UCLA basketball player Ralph Drollinger, emphasized private "Christian counseling" of coaches and athletes, and in a more public ministry produced inspirational videos of sports champions testifying to the importance of Christ in their lives. Sports World Ministry, headed by Ira Eshleman in Tennessee, rivaled the missionary purpose of Sports Ambassadors.[25]

Yet for all their differences, religious sports organizations agreed on the fundamental need to have Christ represented in locker rooms and for athletes to exploit their celebrity status in order to "share" the gospel with the world. And all agreed on a commercial model for the spread of the gospel. As John Erickson put it shortly after he became head of the Fellowship of Christian Athletes in 1973, "If athletes can endorse products, why can't they endorse a way of life? Athletes and coaches, be it right or wrong, have a platform in this country. Athletes have power, a voice. So, simply, how can we best use this for something constructive in the faith life?"[26]

## Locker Room Religion

A sure sign of Sportianity's public acceptance occurred on New Year's Day 1971, when Billy Graham became the first clergyman ever to serve as grand marshal of the Rose Parade. On the reviewing stand beside him stood

Donn Moomaw, a former All-American linebacker at UCLA who was now a Presbyterian minister in Los Angeles and a zealous member of the Fellowship of Christian Athletes. Americans everywhere gazed on the televised spectacle of Graham and Moomaw taking their reserved seats that afternoon to watch the Rose Bowl game. Well could Dallas Cowboy coach Tom Landry say shortly afterwards, "The star of athletic influence [for Christianity] is shining brightly now."[27]

Behind this public coalescence of evangelical religion and sport lay a quiet revolution in the locker room behavior of professional sports teams. Prior to the 1970s, baseball, football, basketball, and hockey inner sanctums all harbored off-color oaths and jokes, crude pranks, and loud boasts about the previous night's drinking bouts and sexual conquests. Jim Bouton's best-selling *Ball Four* (1970) is a window to that earthy world. Abstainers became the butt of clubhouse humor. New York Yankees manager Casey Stengel always got a laugh when he called straight-arrow second baseman Bobby Richardson and shortstop Tony Kubek his "milkshake twins." More in tune with the times were Yankee free spirits Billy Martin and Mickey Mantle, whose drunken forays and clubhouse vulgarity became legendary.[28]

Scarcely were the Yankees unique. In 1961, a Catholic priest was shamed into leaving the Boston Red Sox clubhouse at Fenway Park when the air filled with off-color stories and jokes. "In the old days, there was a lot of drinking and carrying on," recalled Red Sox third baseman Rico Petrocelli in 1978, when a fear of negative publicity had aligned with puritanical evangelicalism to diminish the raucous atmosphere of days past.[29]

The change began with professional football teams. Warriors in imminent danger of injury, if not death, find it difficult to remain religiously indifferent. Moreover, many professional football players came from the religious South and Southwest. Playing in northern Chicago, Detroit, and New York, they felt like strangers in Babylon. For them to turn to evangelical religion was to reaffirm their regional roots.

An All-American lineman and zealous youth evangelist from Baylor University, Bill Glass was the first-draft choice of the Detroit Lions in 1957. Instead, he followed a Baylor assistant coach to the Canadian Football League, where he played for a year; at season's end, he enrolled parttime in a theological seminary. Shortly after his arrival in Detroit in 1958, he recognized a fundamental impediment to any professional football player's interest in religion. With most NFL games scheduled on Sunday afternoon, pregame meals and team meetings conflicted with the usual

Sunday-morning hour of Protestant worship. The answer to the problem, Glass decided, was to hold devotional services prior to the pregame meal.[30]

By most seminarian standards, Bill Glass was just another Texas fundamentalist. In truth, he was as much of a pragmatic salesman as he was an evangelical ideologue. "When I speak to a team before a game," he noted years later, "I find that I'm talking a Christian line, but I'm also talking motivation." He knew that football players weren't interested in spiritual or theological niceties, so he refrained from preaching a churchy sermon. Talking most about how an athlete could get himself "ready for a game," Glass preached "the Christian power of positive thinking."[31]

So did Tom Landry of the Dallas Cowboys. Landry grew up a Methodist in small-town Texas, and in the mid-1950s joined the classy, respectably moderate Highland Park Methodist Church in Dallas. In the spring of 1959, however, he underwent a "born again" conversion to evangelical Christianity. Soon he affiliated with the Fellowship of Christian Athletes and became a regular speaker on their Estes Park summer program. In 1966 Billy Graham asked Landry to "share his testimony" at Graham's San Antonio evangelistic crusade—the first of many appearances by Landry in support of Billy Graham's efforts.[32] Just a year after his religious conversion, Landry accepted the head coaching job of the new NFL Dallas Cowboys. From the outset, he established a ritual of telling the story of his religious pilgrimage each summer to incoming rookies; at team meetings he frequently quoted Bible verses. Tom Landry's oft-stated priorities were God, family, and football. Leaving nothing to chance, he appointed players to arrange programs and invite outside speakers for short devotional services before the Cowboys' Sunday road games. These events were nondenominational and voluntary. So were weekly evening gatherings of Cowboys and their wives for Bible study, encouraged by Landry as a means of building family and spiritual values.[33]

Unlikely as it may seem, the no-nonsense, hard-driving coach of the Green Bay Packers, Vince Lombardi, also added to the NFL's religious mix. Lombardi echoed Landry in his insistence that players should keep focused on the three important things in life: their religion, their families, and the Green Bay Packers, "in that order." Lombardi "means just what he says," commented his offensive guard, Jerry Kramer, "but sometimes I think he gets his order confused." Lombardi, a devout Roman Catholic, daily attended early morning mass. He had the Packers say the Lord's Prayer before and after all their games. When someone reminded him that early Sunday afternoon football contests made it impossible for Protestant players to attend church, Lombardi encouraged informal, nondenominational services in the team's hotel before breakfast on game day.[34]

Begun in 1966, these devotional sessions were led by two Southerners, quarterback Bart Starr, an Alabama graduate, and receiver Carroll Dale, a Virginian. Some twenty players, almost half the squad, usually attended. The program, twenty minutes long, featured readings from scripture, a couple of prayers, and a brief discussion or inspirational address. The homily, given by one of the players or a local minister, lawyer, or doctor known for his piety as well as athletic enthusiasm, was usually a lightly veiled exhortation to practice courage and teamwork.[35]

These meditative moments were heavily charged with the urgencies of the upcoming game. On the morning of a big game against the Detroit Lions and their defensive goliath, Alex Karras, Jerry Kramer made sure his roommate woke him in time for the devotional service. Feeling the need for "a little extra insurance," Kramer figured "a few prayers certainly wouldn't hurt me any against Karras." After Carroll Dale read the Bible that morning, Bart Starr gave a little sermon on the theme that if a man doesn't strive mightily to do the best he can with the ability God has given him, he is cheating God. "The theme of the sermon, of course," concluded Kramer, "came from the Book of Vincent [Lombardi], and Bart did a very nice job."[36]

Others were quietly doing similar jobs of promoting pregame chapel services throughout the National Football League. By 1970, with the notable exception of the Oakland Raiders, every NFL club promoted some kind of devotional activity on game day. Club-appointed chaplains came on apace in the 1970s. Father John Duggan, a witty Irish Catholic chaplain for the Pittsburgh Steelers, best caught the humor of the occasion. "I'm praying out my option," he commented just before retiring to his native Ireland.[37]

Like the NFL, major league baseball stepped piecemeal into the chapel business. Early in the 1960s, Bobby Richardson, Tony Kubek, and announcer Red Barber led Sunday devotionals for the New York Yankees. A handful of players met for twenty minutes or so in a hotel room or banquet room for prayers, a brief homily, and discussion. Sometime in the 1960s the venue changed from the hotel to a weight room or locker room at the ball park itself. As late as 1972, however, only two major league teams, the Minnesota Twins and the Chicago Cubs, regularly held religious services before Sunday games away from home.[38]

The decisive change came at the hands of a Detroit sportswriter and for-

**Rock 'em, sock 'em football for Jesus.** An earlier version of this cartoon, a humorous but perceptive reminder of the pervasive presence of evangelical zeal in college sport, appeared on the cover of *Christianity Today* (7 November 1975). (With thanks to the cartoonist, John L. Lawing.)

mer president of the Baseball Writers Association of America, Watson Spoelstra. A heavy drinker and self-professed "hell-raiser," Spoelstra stumbled onto conversion as a result of a family trauma: his eighteen-year-old daughter's collapse in 1957 with a mysterious brain hemorrhage. Spoelstra, an Episcopalian, made a deal with God: if God would heal his daughter, he would reform his ways. She recovered, and he quit drinking. He also started reading the Bible and soon joined a church that espoused evangelical doctrines. He linked up with Detroit Lion Bill Glass's evangelistic efforts, frequently telling his story of conversion before Glass preached.[39]

Religion became an obsession with Spoelstra—in prayer and Bible study, in conversation with old friends, and even in the press box. Having once read that a great musical composer always thanked God for inspiration before putting any musical notes on paper, Spoelstra decided to do the same for sportswriting. Before starting his daily story for the *Detroit News*, he wrote the acronyms INOG, PBTG, and TYL at the top of the page: "In the name of God," "Praise be to God," and Thank You, Lord." After twenty-nine years at the *News*, he retired in 1973 and approached baseball commissioner Bowie Kuhn with a plan to meet baseball players' need for pregame worship on Sundays.[40]

Having picked up the idea from his close association with Bill Glass's locker room ministry, Spoelstra envisaged "Baseball Chapel" as an organization that would coordinate chapel services within each team's clubhouse. Team representatives ("chapel leaders") would be identified, physical details of place and time arranged, speakers scheduled, and the whole program publicized. With the help of local volunteers, Spoelstra offered to do it. Commissioner Kuhn liked the idea and provided some funds to get it started. During its first year, Baseball Chapel found active support on twelve teams; by 1975 all twenty-four major league clubs were participating.[41]

Locker room religion initially raised alarm in several quarters. The Protestant character of the born-again movement aroused apprehension among Catholic players, and still more anxiety among Jewish and Muslim athletes. Players feared proselytizing efforts from fanatical teammates, and some self-professed Christian athletes felt pressure from evangelical mates to be more outspoken in their faith. Coaches and managers abhorred the prospect of a team divided between "carousers and born-againers." Some feared that the assurance of divine favor might make their warriors passive, sapped of the aggressive urges essential for high-level competition. For some reason, baseball managers expressed this concern more often than did football coaches. In the 1970s Earl Weaver of the Baltimore Orioles and Dick Williams of the California Angels competed fiercely against each other, but they agreed on one thing. Both preferred their athletes practicing more and praying less. Weaver once insisted that Pat Kelly, one of his born-again players, curtail Bible study in the Orioles' locker room. "Skip," Kelly asked, "don't you want me to walk with the Lord?" Weaver replied, "Kel, I'd rather you walk with the bases loaded." In Weaver's view, outspoken locker room religion was an unwelcome distraction.[42]

These anxieties came to the surface in 1978, when San Francisco Giants pitcher Bob Knepper gave up a game-winning home run and reportedly brushed it off as "God's will." Knepper denied having made the statement to a reporter, but major league management, players, and media everywhere rushed to debate the issue. "I've seen guys who used to be very intense and are now very placid. You wonder if guys think things are pre-destined," commented Giants player Darrell Evans, one of the founders of the team's chapel group. Others rushed to Knepper's defense, insisting that if Jesus Christ were around today he would happily throw the brush-back pitch when necessary and slide hard into second base to break up the double play. "God does not expect us to be goody-two-shoes," declared relief pitcher Gary Lavelle, who wore his evangelical badge for all to see. For a decade or so the Giants lived with the derisive nickname "God Squad"—until similar charges and countercharges rattled the clubhouse walls of the Minnesota Twins in 1989, causing a celebrated breach in the friendship of old drinking buddies Kent Hrbek and Gary Gaetti.[43]

Clubhouse tensions notwithstanding, Baseball Chapel quickly made its way into the minors. Arguably, minor leaguers needed the evangelical gospel even more than did major league players. Younger players, many of whom were away from home for the first time, turned to alcohol, drugs, and random sex to combat loneliness. Worse still, every minor leaguer played under the pressure of knowing that pitifully few of them (a mere 4 percent) ever made the majors.[44] In 1979 Rip Kirby of Knoxville, Tennessee, began coordinating a chapel program in the minors. Without sufficient indoor space at the ball park, more often than not the "chapel" was a remote corner in the stands or on the field just outside the right-field foul line. Within five years, Kirby claimed to have 140 pastors and laymen volunteering to lead nondenominational services for players in 150 cities, spread out over sixteen minor leagues. In 1982, when Watson Spoelstra turned over the helm of Baseball Chapel to former Yankee Bobby Richardson, the *Sporting News* observed that "Baseball Chapel is now a staple in the majors and minors. Hundreds of players attend each Sunday and Bible-study groups are flourishing."[45]

Beyond professional football and baseball, locker room chapels and Bible study groups now seem to be flourishing throughout the sports world. A Professional Tour Chapel caters to golfers who seek something more than the nineteenth hole. An International Fellowship of Christian Iron Men provides evangelical ministry for bodybuilders, and the Christian Surfing Association does the same for the beach crowd. Ice hockey professionals and their wives can attend annual religious retreats sponsored by Hockey Ministries International, headquartered in Kirkland, Canada. In 1991 the last of the major team sports to step in line, professional basketball, began offering religious lectures and workshops for NBA players, wives, and chaplains. By 1996 more than 100 sports ministries existed in the United States.[46]

Several such ministries thrived amid the roar of high-powered engines on the NASCAR circuit. Founded in 1948, the National Association for Stock Car Auto Racing (NASCAR) expanded rapidly from dirt-track to cement- or asphalt-surface races and from a regional to a national passion sponsored by major auto, beer, and retail-store corporations. For a huge fee, NASCAR named its prime schedule, the Winston Cup series, for a R. J. Reynolds Tobacco product. In the 1980s a new cable sports channel, ESPN, began regular telecasts that now total thirty-nine major races per year. As a multi-billion-dollar business that attracts six million live spectators each year, NASCAR is undoubtedly the fastest-growing sport in the United States.[47]

It is also the sport most receptive to evangelical religion. NASCAR originated deep in the heart of the Bible Belt, a region whose grass roots are traditionally both pious and crude. Today's major speedways in Florida, North Carolina, South Carolina, and Alabama recall the unique southern origins of a sport that prides itself on the legendary exploits of Appalachian moonshine-runners. According to NASCAR lore, imaginative mountain boys stripped down their cars, souped up their engines, and refined their driving techniques in order to evade the authorities. During the Depression, they took those modified cars and hell-bent-for-leather attitudes into competition with each other on country roads and fields, then onto enclosed dirt tracks. Native enthusiasts proudly cling to these blue-collar roots, referring to their sport as "redneck racin'." As a popular T-shirt proclaims, "Badass boys drive badass toys." Badass boys eat fried chicken and drink whiskey or beer, not wine and cheese. In an obvious jibe at more pretentious ways, "Happy Hour" is the afternoon prior to each big race when drivers give their cars a final fast spin around the track, trying to detect last-minute motor and steering flaws.[48]

Careful preparations or not, stock car racing is an exceedingly dangerous activity. As dozens of cars jostle for position at speeds approaching 200 miles per hour while careening around a track enclosed with cement walls, each race threatens disaster. NASCAR history is strewn with monstrous, fatal accidents. Within nine months in 2000, three drivers on the Winston Cup series died. One of those crashes took the life of nineteen-year-old Kyle Petty, a third-generation member of one of NASCAR's most visible family of drivers. Just a few months later, in 2001 highly successful veteran

Dale Earnhardt died instantly when he smashed head-on into the wall on the final lap of the Daytona 500. "Earnhardt was considered invincible, a god. But it turned out he was only human," lamented the editors of a NASCAR book of records. "In this sport," as one of its chroniclers noted, "if you sneeze at the wrong time, you meet your Maker."[49]

That danger combines with southern folk culture to subject NASCAR to a flood of evangelical piety. Races are scheduled for virtually every weekend, but never on Easter Sunday. Religious tracts, pamphlets, and signs are common sights at the speedway. Most cars are covered with advertisements for their sponsors; some advertise Jesus. Although Dale Earnhardt was known as a rough-hewn fellow with a devil-may-care swagger, he taped scripture verses on his dashboard. Just before each major race, a chaplain conducts a brief nondenominational worship service for drivers, crews, and their families. The attire is informal: blue jeans and jerseys with baseball caps, jumpsuits colorfully covered with corporate logos. Likely as not, the music is a familiar Baptist or Methodist hymn, or a country-and-western rendition of pop gospel accompanied by guitar. In fashionable running shoes, the chaplain concludes with a prayer: "You are an awesome God. Please protect us not only in the race today, but in the race of life."[50]

An organization called Motor Racing Outreach supervises these religious activities. Founded in 1988, Motor Racing Outreach by 2005 employed a full-time director and five chaplains and had an annual budget of $2 million. A chaplain regularly appears at each of the thirty-nine races on the grueling Winston Cup circuit, leading Bible studies with drivers and crews, counseling families (especially when tragedy strikes), and even organizing youth events and child-care facilities. Just before the race begins, the chaplain or a local pastor always gives an invocation. Sometimes, prayers to God turn into mini-sermons. At the speedway in Bristol, Tennessee, a chaplain from Motor Racing Outreach once urged his audience "to be thankful to God for this track, this race—and our great sponsors."[51]

## Expecting Miracles

As religious activities became commonplace in professional sports, evangelical colleges and universities eagerly turned to intercollegiate athletics. Two of these institutions of higher learning virtually included sport in their founding charters. Oral Roberts University, begun in 1963 by televangelist faith healer Oral Roberts, and Liberty University, founded in 1971 by fundamentalist preacher and future Moral Majority leader Jerry Falwell, envisaged strong sports programs as means of instant credibility, Christian witness, and financial support.

Long before he dreamed of creating a university, Oral Roberts "heard the call" to a faith-healing ministry against a backdrop of sport. At age sixteen, while playing varsity high school basketball in Atoka, Oklahoma, he collapsed and was diagnosed with tuberculosis. As he recuperated at home, he promised God that he would preach the gospel. Soon afterward he was taken to a revival meeting, where he heard God promise to heal him and send him as an instrument of "healing power" in the world. Roberts's first ministerial attempt, a faith-healing mission church in Tulsa, proved spectacularly successful. From a local television slot he moved to a national network program. The creation of Oral Roberts University (ORU) in Tulsa put a stamp of respectable rationality on an empire commonly thought to be characterized by chicanery and emotionalism.[52]

True to his preoccupation with bodily health, Roberts thought campus athletics important for purposes of physical fitness. But if his mind was on the body, his heart was on the pocketbook. He saw athletics as a meal ticket to institutional viability. As always, he framed his rationale in terms of Christian influence. Athletics offered "one of the greatest opportunities for a Christian witness, without which millions of people might never be reached," he insisted. "If we can display a strong witness on the floor or field, take the good with the bad, the victories with the defeats, and keep a dynamic Christian attitude, it's got to have a positive effect on people's lives for Christ."[53]

Roberts might have chosen the most popular college game of the 1960s, football, but the state university Sooners stood as the unrivaled kings of the gridiron in Oklahoma. Moreover, football seemed too expensive a sport for a small new college. Given Roberts's personal experience and unbridled enthusiasm for the game, basketball was the way for ORU to go. "Nearly every man in America reads the sports pages, and a Christian school cannot ignore these people," he believed. "If we can field a basketball team that can compete successfully with NCAA colleges, and [if] we can conduct ourselves in a sportsmanlike way, that's a fine thing."[54]

In pursuit of that dream, Roberts in 1969 lured coach Ken Trickey from Middle Tennessee State University to install a "runnin' and gunnin'" fast-break offense. Trickey brought several players with him, but he found it difficult to recruit blue-chip athletes to ORU. Campus rules forbade drinking, smoking, swearing, and dancing. Every student had to take religion courses and attend chapel twice a week. All males were required to wear ties on campus; under threat of expulsion, they were forbidden in women's dormitories. A curfew was strictly enforced. The ORU campus atmosphere scarcely appealed to any prospect who was more interested in playing basketball than in obeying the stern code of evangelical moralism.

Yet ORU offered some compensations. Set on a glitzy new $50 million campus, a separate, more lenient athletic dormitory got around some campus problems by hiding athletes' moral indiscretions away from the main student body. Basketball stars, some from extremely poor homes, mysteriously found the money to drive shiny new cars; players' wives appeared on the college payroll. The president himself kept a personal hand on the athletic effort. Punctuating his conversations with basketball allusions (putting a zone press on evil, running a pick and roll against the devil), Roberts attended most home games and excitedly clapped his hands when the pep band struck up "Let the Sunshine In."[55]

Recruits could hardly help being impressed with the ORU Mabee Center, an $11 million arena that held some 10,000 spectators in comfortable, theater-style seats. Emblazoned on the floor and in signs on the rafters was the campus motto, "Expect a Miracle." Coach Trickey produced one, it seems. Although little ORU numbered just over a thousand students, within five years they sent their Titans twice to the NIT (National Invitational Tournament) and once to the NCAA playoffs. Admittedly loading his schedule with inferior opponents, in 1971–1972 Trickey ran-and-gunned his squad to a 25–1 record, an invitation to the NIT, and the selection of high-scoring guard Richard Fuqua to an All-American team.[56]

The bubble burst in 1974, just after little Oral Roberts University beat mighty Louisville at the Mabee Center in the Final Sixteen of the NCAA tournament. Unfortunately, Coach Trickey celebrated the victory at a Tulsa bar. On his way home he was arrested by Tulsa police on charges of drunken driving. A shrewd lawyer got the charges, fees, and fines reduced, and a sentence suspended. On the following weekend the Titans faced the Kansas Jayhawks in the NCAA quarterfinals before a packed house at the Mabee Center. Probably only a victory would have saved the coach's job. The Titans narrowly lost, 93–90; within the week, Trickey resigned under pressure.[57]

After Trickey's departure, ORU's basketball program took a nosedive into mediocrity and scandal. During the thirteen years from 1974 to 1987, no fewer than four head coaches came and went. Negative rumors and bad publicity plagued the Titans. For the 1980–1981 season the NCAA placed the team on probation for recruiting violations and inflated summer salaries for athletes. In 1986 reports surfaced about a raucous party for recruits at a local Sheraton, paid for by the school. Close on the heels of those allegations came further charges of players receiving free airline tickets, having access to school cars, and using coaches' credit cards to run up telephone bills totaling some $50,000. Years earlier a writer for *Sports Illustrated* described the Oral Roberts University campus as "a cross between the Houston Space Center and a Bible Belt Xanadu." Xanadu, it seems, had become a zoo.[58]

Strange animals were scarcely confined to the athletic dorms. In the spring of 1987 Oral Roberts himself became something of a national joke. Fearful that his university was about to drown in a sea of red ink, he locked himself in the school's prayer tower and warned that unless the faithful came up with $8 million by April 1, God would "call [him] home." Enough money poured in to save God the bother. It also gave Roberts the means to recall Ken Trickey in an attempt to restore the Titans to their short-lived glory of old.

Renewed success in Division I basketball proved to be impossible. During the second season after his return, Trickey's team won only eight of twenty-eight games. Like sacrificial lambs, the Titans were mauled by giants Georgetown, Oklahoma, Texas, and Memphis State. Those debacles, plus rumors of yet more NCAA investigations, prompted ORU to demote itself to a smaller college affiliation, the National Association of Intercollegiate Athletics (NAIA). A 36–6 season in 1989–1990 sent hopes for a national championship (albeit an NAIA crown) soaring once again. Until that miracle happens, an older, more sober Oral Roberts can only reminisce, as he did with a *Sports Illustrated* journalist in 1990, about the way basketball "brought our university to the attention of the nation" in the 1970s.[59]

## Fanning the Flame

What basketball did for Oral Roberts University, football did for a small midwestern college affiliated with a faith-healing denomination, the Assembly of God. In 1977 Evangel College in Springfield, Missouri, fielded its first football team, the Crusaders. Under the supervision of head coach Denny Duron, a gospel minister and former star quarterback at Louisiana Tech, Evangel's gridiron exploits could be viewed each week in a sixty-minute "game highlights" show carried by 200 regional cable television stations. Inspirational commentary by Coach Duron and his players accompanied films of the games. The *Saturday Evening Post* dubbed this mixture of pigskin, piety, and prime-time showmanship "a kind of minor miracle."[60]

Miraculous as it might have been, the program needed a touch of realism. Evangel ambitiously scheduled its team to play too many large state universities, such as Northern Iowa and Arkansas State, only to get mauled week after week. As the losses mounted, the market for weekly televised highlights dried up. Moreover, the video productions required more technical expertise and financial support than little Evangel could muster. By the mid-1980s, Denny Duron had resigned and gone back into full-time church ministry. The Crusaders, chastened, joined the small-college Heart of America Conference. Now on a more level playing field, they enjoyed an undefeated season in 1988 and made it into the NAIA playoffs virtually every year in the 1990s.

Whereas both Oral Roberts University and Evangel College learned to be content with something less than the top rung of the athletic ladder, Jerry Falwell's Liberty University continues to seek "strength for the journey" (the title of Falwell's autobiography) to the top. In 1971 the Baptist minister launched Lynchburg Baptist College as an affiliate of Thomas Road Baptist Church, in an abandoned high school in Lynchburg, Virginia. By 1985, when the institution was renamed Liberty University, the student body numbered about 6,000.[61] From the outset, Falwell projected an ambitious athletic program. In his vision for a first-rate evangelical center of higher education, he saw sport "as much a part of it as English and biology." Sport builds character and discipline, he insisted, in terms little different from a century-long mantra of muscular Christianity. More to the immediate point, as Falwell told a journalist in 1989, sport "helps a school build an identity around which students and alumni can join hands."[62]

In the beginning, however, Falwell's institution was more like a religious seminary than a college. The earnest atmosphere of conservative Lynchburg Baptist College suffered no interruptions from a whack of bat on ball or a clank of basketball on metal rim. Strict rules held sway. The school mandated coats and ties for men, with hair trimmed at least an inch above the collar. Women wore dresses, not slacks, until 4:30 P.M. each day. Alcohol, tobacco, and drugs were strictly forbidden. So were "godless" television and rock music, movies away from campus, and even uncensored films on campus. No men were allowed in women's dorms, and vice versa, of course. First-year and second-year students could only double-date. They were required to attend chapel three days a week in addition to Tuesday late-night dorm devotions and Sunday morning worship. It all seemed perfectly normal for a "spiritual boot camp" that Falwell himself termed "sort of the West Point of evangelicalism."[63]

Not for long would sport be absent from Lynchburg. Even more than his theological and social conservatism, Falwell's enthusiasm for sport came right out of his own experience. As a Lynchburg youth, he played fullback and captained the Brookville High School football squad. At eighteen years of age, he tried out for the St. Louis Cardinals baseball organization. Later he played basketball at Baptist Bible College in Springfield, Missouri. Largely because of Falwell's personal patronage, little Lynchburg Baptist College started football in 1973 with a 3–3 record against nearby junior colleges and prep schools.[64]

For years Falwell had invited prominent athletic figures to give their testimonies for Christ at the Thomas Road church. Bobby Richardson, second baseman of the New York Yankees; coach Tom Landry of the Dallas Cowboys; and NFL stars Terry Bradshaw, Carroll Dale, and Raymond Berry all made the trek to Lynchburg. In 1974 another big-league Christian, Al Worthington, invited himself for something more than a visit. For twelve years or so in the 1950s and '60s, Worthington had pitched for several major league clubs. After a conversion experience at a Billy Graham crusade in San Francisco in the summer of 1958, he earned a reputation as "some sort of cuckoo" because of his fundamentalist religious principles. Retired as a player, he coached pitchers for the Minnesota Twins until he happened to hear Falwell on the radio talking about his Christian school. He contacted Falwell immediately. A new Christian college, Worthington insisted, should have a good Christian baseball coach. Jerry Falwell needed no convincing.[65]

At Lynchburg, Worthington found a baseball program with no field, no dressing-room facilities, and little equipment. The team practiced and played at a little Colt League park whose surface was so rough that the former big leaguer often had to rig up a janitor's broom on the rear end of his car to groom the infield. The car's trunk served as a storage bin for the team's bats, balls, and catcher's equipment. Worthington rose to the challenge, and by the early 1980s his Liberty Flames (a nickname derived from the school motto, "Knowledge Aflame") were playing in the NAIA finals. Three of the Flames, Sid Bream, Randy Tomlin, and Lee Guetterman, went on to play in the major leagues. During this time, Worthington became the school's athletic director, overseeing a program that was undergoing dramatic expansion. In 1987 he turned over the baseball program to former

Yankee Bobby Richardson, who had recently won Coach of the Year honors for leading Coastal Carolina College (South Carolina) to the Big South Conference championship.[66]

Within a year of Richardson's arrival, Liberty's football program also landed a big-name coach. In March 1988, Sam Rutigliano, former coach of the Cleveland Browns (1978–1984) and NBC sportscaster, spoke at the campus. He told of his religious conversion many years earlier, when his drowsiness at the wheel of his car caused an accident that killed his four-year-old daughter. Grief and guilt drove him to God; through Christ he found forgiveness and emotional support. Since that day in the early 1960s, Rutigliano informed his Liberty audience, he had been an active member of the Fellowship of Christian Athletes through almost twenty different jobs in the coaching profession.[67]

Now Falwell wanted Rutigliano to join the Liberty effort, to take the football program to a "higher level," Division I-AA. Despite a budget crisis that required a 25 percent cut for the athletic department, Falwell's ambitions soared. He frequently promised journalists, alumni, and students that the football team would soon be playing Notre Dame and Brigham Young, the highly visible powerhouses that represented excellence for Catholics and Mormons. Liberty University was becoming that sort of beacon for fundamentalists, Falwell insisted. Not an emotional faith-healer like Oral Roberts, Falwell nevertheless expected miracles.[68]

Rutigliano, Falwell felt, could help make it happen. For him, Liberty offered a return to a coaching career that he had missed more than he thought he would, and a commitment to a religious, moral community whose values he shared. At Liberty Rutigliano would have none of the discipline problems that plagued most college coaches. Moreover, he was reminded, Liberty's admissions requirements would make for easier recruiting. Athlete or not, an applicant merely had to present a high school diploma, evidence of being born again (usually a letter from a pastor), and a willingness to abide by the school's stern dress and behavior code. Plans for a spacious new weight room and a new 12,000-seat, artificial-turf stadium made the offer irresistible for Rutigliano.[69]

Unfortunately, his arrival required a cash settlement for previous head coach Morgan Hout, whose eight wins and three losses in his final season (1988) gave him one of the best records imaginable for a dismissed football coach. For the next eleven years, Rutigliano guided several Liberty grads into the National Football League, but he scarcely turned Liberty into a football power. He retired after the 1999 season with a moderately successful record of 67 wins and 53 losses.

While the notoriously expensive sport of football gobbled up about one-third of Liberty's athletic budget, by the 1990s the university was sponsoring sixteen intercollegiate sports, ten for men and six for women. Baseball, women's volleyball, and both men's and women's basketball teams fared well in the Big South Conference, making their way into postseason NCAA tournaments. In 1994 the men's hoops squad went 18–11, beating a North Carolina Baptist college, Campbell, for the Big South trophy. Beginning in 1997, for five consecutive years the women's basketball team won its way into the first round of the NCAA regional championships.[70]

Just before the Flames took the court against the Tarheels in 1994 in the first round of the NCAA tournament, *New York Times* sportswriter George Vecsey observed that Reverend Falwell's "big dreams" for Liberty athletics were "starting to come true."[71] For basketball, yes, but not for Falwell's original passion, football. Coach Rutigliano's successor, Ken Karcher, lost more than twice as many games as he won. Finishing the 2005 season with ten losses in an underwhelming I-AA Big South Conference, Karcher and two other varsity coaches were fired, and the athletic director resigned.

Liberty's athletic program exemplified all the strengths and weaknesses of the evangelical vision of muscular Christianity. Like Oral Roberts University and many smaller evangelical colleges, Liberty University welcomed the public attention that came from sports. Athletics put new, struggling institutions on the map. Liberty athletes used hard-won podiums to share their witness with the world. They emblazoned gospel scriptural references on towels, shoes, and headgear and zealously used postgame moments of sociability with opponents to make personal pitches on behalf of Christ.

Unfortunately, this approach frequently comes across as a mere sales pitch. As authors Tony Ladd and James Mathisen explain, the entrepreneurial personality type has "always been valued more than others" in evangelical circles.[72] Most athletes and other celebrities sell soap and cell phones; evangelicals sell Jesus. They use sports as a means to the end of religious conversion. Gone, in the evangelical equation, are older concerns about the relation of sports to physical health or the moral lessons to be gained from athletic competition. For all their focus on the athletic arena, evangelicals have yet to produce anything approximating a theology of sport.

# 11

## ATHLETES FOR ALLAH

In sharp contrast to evangelical Christian athletes' lack of a theological rationale for anything other than winning converts, Muslims enter the athletic arena armed with principles and rules. Islam's prime assumption is akin to the old muscular Christian idea of "a sound mind in a sound body": to be physically and morally strong and to practice the means of strength. More severe than the Judaeo-Christian deity, Allah is a jealous god who sanctions no activity that interferes with a believer's religious duties. These duties include five daily prayers, strict fasting during the daylight hours of the holy month of Ramadan, food and drink restrictions (no pork or alcohol), and premarital as well as extramarital sexual abstinence. Like the Puritans of old, Muslims abhor sport's association with gambling, foul language, and drunkenness. Modern sports, particularly modern American sports, correlate unevenly with Islamic beliefs and codes of behavior.

Americans knew none of this in 1956 when a little book entitled *The Call of the Minaret* documented the appeal of Islam to nearly a billion people in numerous newly independent African, Middle Eastern, and Asian states.[1]

Americans were too busy to bother. Preoccupied with an anti-Communist crusade, the accumulation of consumer comforts, and a plethora of new sporting events, in the 1950s they largely ignored a domestic splinter group, the Nation of Islam, that was emerging in the metropolitan centers of Detroit, Chicago, Miami, and New York City. Founded in Detroit in the early 1930s with a distinctly American flavor, the Nation of Islam emphasized African-American racial identity and pride. Black Americans should feel pride, not shame, insisted "Prophet" Elijah Muhammad. Blacks needed to separate themselves from whites, not integrate; they would best

**Religion, sport, and racial dignity.** When Jackie Robinson broke the color barrier in professional baseball, he created a model—racial pride that led to integration rather than separation—counter to the Black Muslim quest for racial dignity. Here Robinson, with basketball in hand, and Dodgers catcher Roy Campanella instruct youths at the Harlem YMCA circa 1950. (From the Kautz Family Archives, YMCA of the USA.)

dispense with their slaveowner's name in favor of a new, Muslim name. Nation of Islam believers soon came to be known as Black Muslims. Racially separatist, they would play a prominent role in the integration of sport and religion.

## Black Muslims and Sport

The earliest athletic converts to the Nation of Islam were to be found in prizefight circles. Walter Youngblood migrated from Louisiana to Harlem, worked at odd jobs, and lived for years on the streets of New York. In 1953 he joined the Nation of Islam, changed his name to Wali Muhammad, and began working as an assistant to welterweight boxing champion Sugar Ray Robinson. Three years later, Booker Johnson, an assistant to light-heavyweight champion Archie Moore, also joined the Nation of Islam. Thus began the collusion of two spheres from the margins of respectability, boxing and Islam.

For a time, the loudest and most articulate voice for Islam was a native Nebraskan. His name, Malcolm Little, was changed to Malcolm X after his conversion in prison, where he was serving time for burglary. Released in 1952, Malcolm spent the next decade insisting to his "black brothers and sisters of all religious beliefs or of no religious beliefs" that they were bound together by the color of their skin and by a common heritage of oppression at the hands of "so-called Christians" who worshiped "the same white Christian God." Malcolm X preached a new gospel: "a special religion for the black man." He carefully explained, "It's called Islam. Let me spell it for you, I-s-l-a-m! Islam!"[2]

Ironically, the ideals of orthodox Islam made Malcolm X uneasy with the behavior of Nation of Islam leaders. He found himself increasingly unable to ignore allegations of Elijah Muhammad's sexual misconduct and financial corruption. Worse still, when Malcolm X made his obligatory pilgrimage to Mecca in 1964, he confronted a fundamental flaw in the Nation of Islam's castigation of all white people as "devils." For eleven days he lived with and prayed beside fellow Muslims from all over the world, some of whom had "the bluest of blue" eyes, "the blondest of blond" hair, and "the whitest of white" skin. "The true Islam has shown me," he announced, "that a blanket indictment of all white people is as wrong as when whites make blanket indictments against blacks." In 1965, Malcolm X was brutally slain during a rally on behalf of the Organization of Afro-American Unity, a newly established rival to the Nation of Islam. Three men, including two Black Muslims, were sentenced to life in prison for the murder. Up to, and even after, Elijah Muhammad's own death (of natural causes) in 1975, he was rumored to have ordered the assassination.[3]

Meanwhile, the Nation of Islam welcomed its first major convert from the athletic arena, a light-footed, quick-fisted, fast-talking young boxer by the name of Cassius Marcellus Clay. Having attended black Baptist and Methodist churches in his hometown of Louisville, Kentucky, Clay grew up in a home that was adamantly Protestant. "I'm a Methodist and I'll be a Methodist till the day I die!" declared his father. The Clay family's Christianity, observed one reporter, was "an absolute, admitting of no possibility of error" with "no time for sects or other religious points of view."[4] Young

Cassius Clay never heard about the Nation of Islam until he went off to a Golden Gloves tournament in Chicago. He was seventeen years of age, on the verge of winning a gold medal in the light-heavyweight division at the Rome Olympics (1960). Within the following year, as he trained for a professional fight in Miami, he attended a Nation of Islam meeting and responded warmly to their emphasis on racial pride and separatism.[5]

Clay was an easy convert. The standards demanded by the Nation of Islam merely confirmed the discipline required of an ambitious young fighter: no tobacco, liquor, drugs, or sexual experimentation. From his father, a great admirer of Marcus Garvey, the young warrior had already been indoctrinated in racial self-respect. For the next three years, though, he kept a low profile, fearful that any controversial posture might thwart his aspirations for the heavyweight crown.[6]

After he won the championship with a sixth-round technical knockout of Sonny Liston in 1964, Cassius Clay felt free to speak. At a press conference shortly after the bout, he announced his conversion. "I believe in Allah, and in peace," he informed a roomful of journalists. "I was baptized when I was twelve, but I didn't know what I was doing. I'm not a Christian anymore." Pressed on the point, he explained, "I ain't no Christian. I can't be, when I see all the colored people fighting for forced integration getting blowed up. They get hit by stones and chewed by dogs. . . . I don't want to be blown up. I don't want to be washed down sewers. I just want to be happy with my own kind."[7]

His conversion from Christianity to Islam seemed not to bother journalists nearly so much as did his decision to change his name. Cassius Clay was his slaveowner's name, he insisted. His new name, assigned by Elijah Muhammad, would be Muhammad Ali. Sportswriters balked. Confronted with a brash young black fighter who was confrontational on the issue of race, they adopted a dismissive attitude toward the Nation of Islam. New York journalist Jimmy Cannon denounced Ali as "a weapon of wickedness," a pawn in the hands of "a sect that deforms the beautiful purpose of religion."[8]

Prior to his conversion, the colorful Ali often referred to himself as "the greatest"; now he more frequently gave "all praise to Allah." Always feisty, he had found a different agenda. "A rooster crows only when it sees the light. Put him in the dark and he'll never crow," Ali explained to one interviewer. "I have seen the light and I'm crowing." He crowed all the way to the mosque.[9]

Yet Ali never adopted the Nation of Islam's hatred of all whites. Too many whites—his trainer, his lawyer, and the Louisville businessmen who paid his bills early in his boxing career—were important to him. Nor did he consider the essence of his newfound faith radically different from the core teachings of his youth. Following a pilgrimage to Mecca in 1964, he recalled his mother imparting to him "all she knew about God" and the need to deal kindly and truthfully with people. "I've changed my religion and some of my beliefs since then," he said, "but her God is still my God; I just call him by a different name."[10]

To most Americans, Ali's religion was a mystery at best. As issues over civil rights and the Vietnam War became increasingly divisive, Black Muslims seemed more political than religious—more radical and racist than reverential. Worst of all, Black Muslim complaints about the racial dimensions of American capitalism and imperialism made Muslims appear anti-American. In 1967 Muhammad Ali confirmed all those negative assumptions when he refused induction into the United States Army. His explanation became a signpost to the antiwar fervor of the 1960s: "I ain't got nothing against them Viet Cong."[11]

To the disgust of his critics, Ali claimed to be motivated by religious principles. Shortly after the draft-board spectacle, a dozen big-name black athletes gathered in Cleveland to register support of Ali's right to refuse military service. Racial solidarity was at stake, of course. Yet Boston Celtics star player and coach Bill Russell came away impressed with the firm religious basis of Ali's action. "I envy Muhammad Ali," announced Russell. "He has something I have never been able to attain and something very few people I know possess. He has an absolute and sincere faith."[12]

His faith notwithstanding, Ali within the next few years reeled from one professional and personal crisis to another. Immediately stripped of his heavyweight crown, he was sentenced to a five-year prison term. In 1970 the Supreme Court reversed the conviction, freeing him to return to the ring. Amidst classic battles with Joe Frazier and George Foreman, twice in the 1970s Ali regained, then lost, the title. After humiliating defeats to Larry Holmes and Trevor Berbick, he retired in 1981, just three years before being diagnosed with Parkinson's disease.

By then his religion, too, had undergone drastic changes. His mentor, Elijah Muhammad, died in 1975, ending a forty-one-year reign as head of the Nation of Islam. Elijah's son, Wallace D. Muhammad, changed the name of the movement to the World Community of Al-Islam in the West. More importantly, he called for an end to the idea of black superiority and separation from white America and urged Nation of Islam believers to adopt orthodox Islamic practices.[13]

Ali adapted quickly to these new directives. In the process, he evolved from an angry rebel to a patriotic, conservative American—destined to be honored as the person selected to light the flame on the Olympic altar at the 1996 Atlanta Summer Olympic Games. As he aged, he devoted himself less to divisive issues of race and more to matters of the spirit. On a return flight home from a ten-day visit to Indonesia in the early 1990s, biographer Thomas Hauser sat across the aisle from Ali and his wife, Lonnie. As the cabin lights dimmed, Hauser dropped off to sleep. Some time later, he awoke to a dark cabin except for one light over Ali's seat. There sat Ali, wide awake, reading the Koran. "And in that moment, bathed in light," noted Hauser, "he looked stronger and more at peace with himself than any person I've ever known."[14]

## Game-Winning Conversions

Muhammad Ali was not the only high-profile black athlete who turned to Islam for inner peace amid the chaos of the 1960s. Basketball giant Lew Alcindor and football whiz Bobby Moore did likewise, but from the outset both rejected the Nation of Islam for a more traditional form of Islam. Soon the world would know these two athletes by their converted names, Kareem Abdul-Jabbar and Ahmad Rashad.

Alcindor came to Islam from a strong Catholic heritage. Serving as a tall, gangly altar boy in his New York City parish church, he moved comfortably in the company of priests and nuns at two Catholic private schools, St. Jude's and Power Memorial Academy. Literally and figuratively a big man on campus, he led Power Memorial to seventy-one consecutive victories and broke New York City schoolboy records with 2,067 points and 2,002 rebounds. As he grew physically taller and athletically more skilled, however, the serious-minded Alcindor became disenchanted with authoritarian priests, the confession box, and Trinitarian conceptions of God that seemed vaguely connected to Biblical compilations of fiction and mythology. By the middle of his senior year at Power Memorial, he felt "totally fed up" with Catholicism. "Alienated from what I had believed and ignorant of the alternatives," he later recalled, "I found myself hungry at the core."[15]

To satisfy that hunger, Alcindor briefly considered the Nation of Islam. As a high schooler, he read the Black Muslim newspaper, *Muhammad Speaks,* and was initially attracted to the group's emphasis on black pride, black power, and black courage. Finally, though, he concluded that the Black Muslims' racial views were identical to white racism's "continual negative power that feeds on itself" to everyone's detriment. Alcindor's refusal to embrace the Nation of Islam withstood even the highly visible commitment of one of his athletic heroes, Muhammad Ali.[16]

A nonathlete, Malcolm X, exerted an altogether different, more profound, influence. During his sophomore year at UCLA, Alcindor read Alex Haley's *The Autobiography of Malcolm X* and afterward lauded it as the most important book he ever read. All Alcindor felt, Malcolm said loudly and clearly. "His life was like a primer for me," Alcindor recalled in his own autobiography; "his growth from nigger to man developed as if he could be the race in microcosm." Especially impressive was Malcolm's discovery of himself through religion. As Alcincor read the story, Malcolm moved from "the distortions of the Black Muslims" to "the more compelling images of Islam," precisely the route that Alcindor decided to take.[17]

By his sophomore year, Alcindor was struggling to balance his inner personal quest with external pressures to perform athletically. Now almost a full seven feet, two inches tall, he was well on his way to becoming one of basketball's all-time greats. For each of his three years of college eligibility, he won first-team All-American honors. Leading UCLA to consecutive NCAA championships in 1967, 1968, and 1969, he averaged 26.4 points per game, for a total of 2,325 points. Yet his athletic achievement did not quench the religious fire burning within. As a history major, Alcindor studied Chinese, Indian, African, and Afro-American history, concentrating on comparative religion; he read widely in Buddhism, Taoism, Hinduism, Zen, and existentialism. None held his attention. Zen was too subtle, Hinduism appeared confusingly polytheistic, and existentialism seemed emotionally cold.[18]

Islam provided the warmth and clarity—not to mention the racial identification—that Alcindor needed. During the summer of 1968, he returned home to New York City, located a mosque near his parents' apartment, and there plunged into an intensive month-long study of the Koran. Working with a transliteration from Arabic into English, he committed large passages to memory. Finally, he formally announced his conversion to Islam: his belief *(shahada)* "that there is no god but Allah and that Muhammad is His messenger."[19]

Several months earlier, Alcindor had begun wearing a large, colorful African robe of red, orange, and yellow stripes. Now he made the more controversial gesture of changing his name—no small thing for a college student at home for the summer with strong-willed, devoutly Catholic parents. A Muslim mentor provided the encouragement. Lewis Ferdinand Alcindor's new Muslim name, Kareem Abdul-Jabbar, essentially meant "generous servant of God, powerful in spirit."[20]

That strong spirit was tested by the alien climate of Milwaukee, Wisconsin, where Abdul-Jabbar landed as a result of the NBA draft of 1969. A big-city boy set in a conservative midwestern town, he was also something of a Puritan thrown into a beer-drinking culture foreign to both his experience and his religious beliefs. "Surrounded by hostile forces, as I felt myself to be," he later recalled, "I needed someone to believe in." Between visits to friends in Chicago and long-distance phone consultations with a Muslim mentor in Harlem, Abdul-Jabbar filled vacant wintry evenings by regularly praying to Allah and studying the Koran. His mentor, Hamaas Abdul-Khaalis, carefully defined Islam as a religion altogether different from the more racially motivated Nation of Islam. A true believer, he insisted, accepted the dogma but also obeyed the practices specified in the Koran. Purity, patience, compassion, and toleration headed the virtues espoused by Abdul-Khaalis.[21]

In the summer of 1973, Abdul-Jabbar visited Islamic communities in Libya, Saudi Arabia, Iran, Afghanistan, Thailand, and Malaysia, and observed that their religion was inclusive and accommodating, not exclusive. Wherever Islam was the dominant culture, it embraced casual believers as well as devout enthusiasts. Abdul-Jabbar himself began to take his religion more casually. He would continue to pray, read the Koran, and celebrate Ramadan, but less rigorously than he did as a new convert.[22]

His professional athletic career ended in 1989, after twenty splendid years in the NBA. He walked away with six championship rings (one with the Milwaukee Bucks, five with the Los Angeles Lakers), six Most Valuable Player awards, and nineteen All-Star Game appearances. Along with an armload of NBA records for baskets made and time played, he scored a total of 38,387 points and averaged 24.6 points per game.

What did Abdul-Jabbar's religion have to do with these extraordinary achievements? Everything, if he is to be believed. During his final season, 1988–1989, he kept a diary, and once commented that he had survived twenty seasons of tough NBA play because of his Islamic dietary principles (no pork, no alcohol). As the Lakers neared the 1989 play-offs, Abdul-Jabbar observed that with the Islamic holy month of Ramadan approaching, he wanted to read the entire Koran as he had done the year before. "I thought the daily reading was going to be difficult, maybe even distracting," he noted, "but it turned out to be of great help to me in preparing my mind for play-off competition." A large part of Islam's appeal for Abdul-Jabbar lay in its regimented mentality, which he felt complemented athletic discipline.[23]

Ahmad Rashad, too, turned to Islam for confirmation of personal (especially racial and athletic) values. Like Abdul-Jabbar, Rashad was an African-American for whom religion carried all sorts of historical and racial freight. Also like Abdul-Jabbar, Rashad saw Allah, the Koran, and Ramadan rituals as correctives to a home-defined religion that he found increasingly unsatisfactory as he matured.

Far removed from the big-city Catholicism of the Alcindor family in New York City, Bobby Moore (the future Ahmad Rashad) was born on November 19, 1949, in Tacoma, Washington. He grew up in a home saturated with a fire-and-brimstone mentality derived from a fundamentalist Pentecostal Holiness church. Until he entered high school, he was required to attend church virtually all day every Sunday, a prayer meeting at least one night a week, and a two-week annual summer revival.

Had the young Lew Alcindor lived in the neighborhood, Moore would have envied him, as he did his Catholic friends whose parents required church attendance for only "one measly hour on Sunday morning." The Pentecostal church allowed no sports—not even board games or radio—on Sunday. These Sabbatarian strictures ebbed over into a more general suspicion of almost all athletic activity. Once young Bobby Moore and his friends were caught running competitive races just outside their church, which prompted one of the faithful to predict that Moore would "never amount to anything" because he was "out there chasing that ball all day like a dog chasing a bone."[24]

Moore's church emphasized exorcism, speaking in tongues, and miracle healing, the usual staples of pentecostalism. Frequently, Moore himself was the subject of miracle efforts, for until his teenage years he suffered a skin disease that doctors could neither diagnose nor cure. Irritated by the pain and embarrassed with unsightly abrasions and bumps on his joints, he spent much of his time alone. As he later recalled, his malady forced him to turn inward, "to look beyond appearances, to seek beauty within things." Despite the rigid mandates of his fundamentalist church, Moore in his formative years learned to dwell on personal standards of spirituality rather than on rules of public behavior.[25]

By the time he reached high school, Moore's skin disease had mysteriously disappeared. Athletic stardom beckoned against a backdrop of troubling events. Moore's senior year in high school (1967–1968) saw the Tet offensive in Vietnam, the assassinations of Martin Luther King and Robert Kennedy, the publication of Eldridge Cleaver's *Soul on Ice*, and the controversial black-power demonstration of John Carlos and Tommie Smith during the awards ceremony at the Mexico City Olympics. In conservative

Tacoma, Moore grew an Afro, openly identifying with angry black youths. He wore that symbol of protest off to the University of Oregon, where he played both basketball and football on an athletic scholarship. As a running back, he set more than a dozen school records, and in his senior year was selected on several All-American teams. In 1972 he was taken by the St. Louis Cardinals in the first round of the NFL draft. A fast, strongly built six feet, two inch, 200-pounder, Moore was converted to wide receiver.[26]

Another kind of conversion was also under way. Throughout college, Moore had struggled to make sense of his fundamentalist heritage, his racial experience, and the attractions of Islam as they were variously represented by two highly visible athletes, Muhammad Ali and Kareem Abdul-Jabbar. Slowly he came to find that his religious beliefs were "put into the right words and given full expression in Islam." Unfortunately, he never elaborated on this tantalizingly spare "explanation" in his 1988 autobiography.[27]

Moore seems to have opted for traditional Islam, not the Nation of Islam. Abdul-Jabbar put him in touch with a Muslim mentor, Rashad Khalifa, in St. Louis. By the beginning of his second season with the Cardinals, Moore was firm in his decision. To signify his conversion to Islam, he would officially change his name to Ahmad Rashad, "Admirable one led to truth." Conservative St. Louis resisted the gesture. During the first preseason exhibition game, Rashad's every move was greeted by a chorus of boos.[28]

The catcalls died out as Islamic names became more common in athletic lineups, and as Rashad himself emerged as a premier wide receiver in the NFL. After brief stints with the Cardinals and the Buffalo Bills, he spent the bulk of his eleven-year career with the Minnesota Vikings. Exceptionally gifted, he caught forty-four touchdown passes and played in four Pro Bowls; exceptionally tough, he started every Vikings game except one from 1976 to 1982. Once he retired as a Vike, Ashad turned to the mike: working on-camera as a poised, articulate television sportscaster.

## Called to Stand Tall

Unlike Rashad, Abdul-Jabbar, and Ali, NBA basketball star Hakeem Olajuwan had no need to convert to Islam. He grew up with it in his native Nigeria in West Africa, a region that has been heavily Islamic for centuries. A mosque stood in the center of Olajuwan's Lagos neighborhood. Daily sights, smells, and sounds reminded him of his Muslim heritage. Every Friday morning he walked to school hearing the Koran rhythmically chanted in Arabic, blaring from the radios of Hausa guards in front of private homes. On Friday afternoons he left school, beckoned by a loud, haunting call to prayer at the mosque. Both of his parents were devout Muslims. More traditional than modern, they regularly read the Koran, strictly celebrated Ramadan, and saved the money necessary to make pilgrimages to Mecca. Within their Yoruba tribe, the father was known as Hajji (Pilgrimage) Salam Olajuwon, the mother as Hajja Abike. For young Hakeem and his friends, religion seemed to be a habit reserved for older folk.[29]

Olajuwon arrived in the United States in 1980, on an athletic scholarship at the University of Houston, and left behind many of his old African ways. In America he dressed, talked, and behaved differently. For a while, he happily dispensed with the religion of his elders. Campus acclaim expanded to All-American fame and translated into a first-round selection by the Houston Rockets. By the late 1980s he was both financially and psychologically insulated from his African past. All that changed, however, when he discovered a mosque just around the corner from the Summit, where the Rockets played their home games. As he entered the mosque, he felt himself overcome with emotion, memory, and nostalgia. "I felt goose bumps all over my body," he later wrote. "Everything I had known growing up came back to me in that instant: the feeling of my knees on the floor of the mosque, the sound of the words of Allah as they washed over me. I remembered walking to school on Friday mornings and having the Call on every radio, as if I was being shepherded. It was the most beautiful sound I had ever heard."[30]

Drawn to the substance of his youth, Olajuwon returned often to the mosque after basketball practice, to study and pray. There he found a mentor, a Muslim immigrant by the name of Hasan, from Saudi Arabia. For three years Hasan helped Olajuwon understand Islam in all its philosophical and ethical nuances. By the early 1990s, Olajuwon was "soaking up the faith" by praying and reading the Koran at home and in airplanes and hotel rooms before and after games.

A pilgrimage to Mecca was the next logical step, and in the summer of 1991 Olajuwon and Hasan made the trip together. The plane from the United States to Jedda, Saudi Arabia, was filled with pilgrims. Prior to landing, the six foot, nine inch Olajuwon crammed himself into a tiny restroom to exchange his western shirt and slacks for a cotton wrap. Blistering heat and a cacophony of African, French, and English dialects greeted him at Ka'abah, the center of Mecca, where the Prophet Muhammad was born. Amid the heat and crowds, prayerful meditation set everything right. "Understanding came over me like a cool wave," Olajuwon later recalled. At Mecca he stood among some three million Muslims, attentive brothers and sisters of the Faith loving each other "not for personal gain, not for money, not for physical attraction or faithful admiration; they love their brothers and sisters simply because they are all servants of God."[31]

Like Ali and Abdul-Jabbar, Hakeem Olajuwon returned home totally convinced of the Muslim way of life. Eager to put his faith into practice, he determined to use his talent not just to win ball games and accumulate material wealth, but rather "to do good and to encourage others, for the pleasure of Allah." Islam, he believed, would reinforce his work ethic and strengthen him against the temptation to abuse his body with drugs. Anticipating the inevitable decline of his athletic prowess, Olajuwon wanted "to be remembered as a great person; not the greatest player in the world but a person who was honest and gracious and honorable, a man who did his best, a good Muslim."[32]

His athletic best left little to be desired. In 1993–1994 he won the NBA's Most Valuable Player and Defensive Player of the Year awards. In the 1994 championship series, he led the Rockets in a seven-game defeat of the New York Knicks for the NBA crown and took home the series' MVP trophy. In 1995 the Rockets—having obtained Olajuwon's old college teammate, Clyde Drexler—won their second consecutive NBA title by sweeping the Orlando Magic, four games to none.

Prior to the 1995 play-offs, Olajuwon's religion contributed to his being sidelined for two weeks. He was taking anti-inflammatory pills for a leg bruise, and during the month-long fast at Ramadan he ingested an insufficient amount of water and food, which resulted in a disastrously low blood count. Fortunately, Olajuwon recovered from his anemia in time for the play-offs.

Another NBA player did not recover so easily from a course of action he took in accordance with his Muslim beliefs. In March 1996, Mahmoud Abdul-Rauf of the Denver Nuggets became embroiled in a controversy resulting from his refusal to stand at attention during the pregame playing of the National Anthem. To NBA officials, he was breaking a league rule that required players, coaches, and trainers to assume "a dignified posture" during the American and Canadian anthems; to some American patriots, he was arrogantly showing disrespect for the flag and all that it represented.

For Abdul-Rauf, whose original name was Chris Jackson, the truth was not so simple as that. Until he reached high school in his hometown of Gulfport, Mississippi, young Jackson was frequently shunned and easily dismissed, for he had a peculiar habit of twitching, jerking, and rolling his eyes, whooping uncontrollably, and compulsively touching things. Extended conversations with him were nearly impossible, interrupted as they were with whoops, repeated phrases, and nonsensical "uh-huhs" from Jackson. Finally, at age seventeen he was diagnosed with Tourette's syndrome, a genetic imbalance of chemicals in the brain.[33]

Medicated with Prozac and Prolixin, Jackson miraculously made his way successfully over the academic hurdles of high school and two years of college. Extraordinary basketball skills worked to his advantage, prompting special attention from teachers and academic advisors. Their efforts paid big dividends on the court. At Gulfport High he twice won the Mississippi Player of the Year award. In his very first year at Louisiana State University, he led the Southeastern Conference in scoring; his 55 points in one game set an NCAA record for freshmen.

Yet his transition to the professional ranks was not easy. Drafted in the third round by the Denver Nuggets in 1990, Jackson was advised to "bulk up" for the pros. He came into training camp some twenty pounds overweight, slow and sluggish. Worse still, no professional basketball team (as best we know) had ever been expected to cope with the disruptive peculiarities of a teammate afflicted with Tourette's syndrome. On team flights or buses, any Nugget sitting next to Jackson ran the risk of being unintentionally elbowed or swatted. In team meetings the coach, Paul Westhead, thought Jackson's unpredictable "uh-huhs" and "whoops" distracting at best, if not willfully sarcastic. Jackson rode the bench for much of his first year in the NBA.

Alienated, Jackson turned inward and in 1991 embraced Islam as an antidote to despair. For this son of the Deep South, born of a momentary fling between a black hospital cafeteria worker and a white man, the color factor was crucial. For a young man whose physical ailment could not be easily controlled, Islam's orderly instructions, rituals, and prohibitions provided a welcome framework. In 1991 Jackson adopted the name Mahmoud Abdul-Rauf, meaning "praiseworthy, merciful, and kind." Two years later he made it legal, even changing his driver's license. By then he had also climbed out of his athletic hole. With a new coach, a body more physically fit, and teammates accustomed to his nervous tics, he lit up the scoreboard. His average of almost 20 points a game led the Nuggets in scoring.

Then came the political equivalent of one of Abdul-Rauf's sudden "whoops." At the start of the 1995–1996 season, he stayed in the locker room during the National Anthem, coming onto the floor only after the song and flag ceremonies were finished. After several repetitions of that pregame behavior, sportswriters began grilling Abdul-Rauf on the reasons for it. To one inquirer, he carelessly muttered that the American flag was "a symbol of oppression" that no faithful Muslim should honor; to another he explained that flags and national anthems represented a kind of nationalistic idolatry forbidden by Islam. A few sportswriters observed that this gesture seemed a throwback to the demonstrations of radicalized black athletes in the late 1960s and early 1970s. Yet for several months no formal action was taken, not even a reprimand. Early in 1996, NBA officials registered their concerns privately to Abdul-Rauf, but secret negotiations failed to resolve the problem. Finally, on March 12, 1996, the NBA informed Abdul-Rauf that he would be suspended without pay until he mended his ways.

Why did the NBA wait so long to act? Why did it wait until then to come down on Abdul-Rauf? *New York Times* columnist Robert Lipsyte smelled a rat. "Had a sponsor secretly complained?" he asked. "Perhaps," he conjectured, only slightly tongue-in-cheek, "it was the nation of Nike, or the planet of Reebok, alarmed at a lack of respect for sovereign states." Whatever the answer, Lipsyte's irony was the exception, not the rule, among the responses to Abdul-Rauf's principled act.[34]

Eager to shield Islam from criticism, the American Muslim Council in Washington, D.C., issued a memorandum asserting that Abdul-Rauf was motivated by "very personal reasons that do not have to do with Islamic beliefs." A Harvard professor of Islamic studies agreed, adding that Abdul-Rauf was simply "adopting some of the ideas of Islam" within "a black nationalist framework." Predictably conservative, those comments were at least thoughtful. Others castigated Abdul-Rauf for rejecting the American flag while taking the money, comfort, and freedoms that the flag stood for. "Is he an American?" rhetorically asked former Boston Celtics star and coach Tommy Heinsohn. "Is he taking all those greenbacks with George Washington's face on them?"[35]

For a one-game suspension, Abdul-Rauf gave up nearly $32,000. He and the NBA then reached a compromise. He agreed to stand politely but silently pray to Allah during the National Anthem. When he returned to the Nuggets lineup for a Friday night game against the Bulls in Chicago, fans cheered loudly throughout the playing of the National Anthem and then booed Abdul-Rauf almost as loudly upon his entering the game midway through the first quarter.[36]

During his brief suspension, Abdul-Rauf insisted to reporters that his religious beliefs were "more important than anything," even basketball. "If I have to give up basketball, I will."[37] It never came to that, but at the end of the season, the Nuggets traded Abdul-Rauf to the Sacramento Kings. After two reasonably good years in Sacramento, he went off for a season to Turkey, a more friendly venue for the exercise of his Islamic faith.

## Holy Wars

The night after Chicago fans gave Mahmoud Abdul-Rauf a raucous, nasty return to the Denver Nuggets lineup in mid-March 1996, heavyweight boxers Mike Tyson and Frank Bruno squared off under the lights of the MGM Grand in Las Vegas. Bruno, the British holder of the World Boxing Council crown, never had a prayer. Tyson did, literally. First he won, then he prayed. When the referee stopped the fight in the third round, Tyson fell to his knees right in the center of the ring, praying and bowing three times to Allah. As Black Muslim minister Louis Farrakhan prominently positioned himself for postfight television interviews that never came, Tyson thanked Allah for the victory.[38]

Tyson's road to fortune and faith had snaked through a rocky, barren wasteland. Like many prizefighters, he carried scars of poverty, crime, and violence from his childhood. Growing up on welfare in the dangerous, drug-infested Bedford-Stuyvesant and Brownsville sections of Brooklyn, Tyson quickly learned the craft of pickpocketing and purse snatching, then moved on to armed robbery. By twelve years of age, he was regularly being arrested and thrown into juvenile detention centers. At the Spofford Center in the Bronx, he met Muhammad Ali, who urged the boys to stay on the right side of the law. For Tyson, the seed fell on hardened soil. In 1979 the thirteen-year-old hoodlum was sent to a reform school in upstate New York.[39]

There he learned to box and soon came under the tutelage of a veteran professional manager, Cus D'Amato. Impressed with Tyson's raw power, D'Amato worked with Tyson on weekends, then assumed custody in order to obtain Tyson's release from reform school. Just six years later, Tyson became the youngest heavyweight champion in history. He was a mere twenty years of age when he won the World Boxing Council title on November 2, 1986, with a second-round knockout of Trevor Berbick. By the autumn of 1987 Tyson also wore the crowns of the World Boxing Association (WBA) and the International Boxing Federation (IBF).

From that pinnacle, Tyson found himself on a roller-coaster. For a moment, he soared into the heavens, where the streets are literally paved with gold. His vast income included a $20 million purse in 1988 for a successful title defense against Michael Spinks. In a short-lived marriage to actress Robin Givens, he paid more than $4 million cash for a mansion in Bernardsville, New Jersey. Pretentiously named Kenilworth (after a famous Elizabethan estate in England), it was a stone castle built in 1897 in the Victorian Gothic style. Despite the prospect of costly renovations, "it was the house that Mike Tyson wanted," says a biographer: "the house of his dreams."[40]

Yet Tyson the dreamer remained a son of the urban jungle where physical aggression, not refinement, was the rule. Reports of reckless driving, physical and verbal assaults on both women and men, scuffles with reporters, public vulgarity, and wife abuse regularly surfaced. Distracted, in February 1990 Tyson went off to Tokyo to defend his title against Buster Douglas, an obscure opponent. Douglas knocked him out in the tenth round. Worse still, in July 1991 Tyson was charged with raping a Rhode Island beauty queen, Desiree Washington, in Indianapolis, Indiana. Ironically, a local Baptist minister, the Reverend Charles Williams, had invited Tyson to come to Indianapolis to help publicize the beauty pageant.

Found guilty, Tyson was sentenced to six years in a medium-security prison several miles west of Indianapolis. Heavily populated with African-Americans, the prison was a hotbed of Islamic study, discussion, and worship. A local junior high school teacher, Muhammad Siddeeq, became Tyson's "spiritual advisor" in the ways of Islam. Betty Shabazz, widow of the slain Malcolm X, visited Tyson to discuss his educational program and religious studies and to pray with him. Shabazz's visit launched Tyson on an impressive binge of readings in history, biography, political philosophy, and poetry. When Maya Angelou later visited, she was astounded at how conversant he was with her poetry.[41]

Other visitors included Jesse Jackson, filmmaker Spike Lee, professional basketball stars Shaquille O'Neal and Hakeem Olajuwon, and singers Whitney Houston and James Brown. All had words of encouragement and advice for Tyson. Former light-heavyweight champion Eddie Mustafa Muhammad went on a special mission. Himself a native of the same Brownsville neighborhood that had produced Tyson, Eddie (formerly known as Eddie Gregory) went "as a Muslim, to see if Mike truly had discovered Islam." As he later told British writer Donald McRae, he thought Tyson was "on the path to finding himself . . . on the path of righteousness." By the spring of 1993, rumors circulated to the effect that Tyson had converted to Islam and was changing his name to Malik Abdul Aziz. His lawyer, Alan Dershowitz, denied both parts of the rumor.[42]

Although he chose not to change his name, Tyson did become a Muslim. Islam's rituals apparently nurtured Tyson's inner life and prompted him to reflect on matters of the soul. As journalist Jonah Brand explained, one of Islam's prime concepts was that of *jihad,* or holy war. Usually interpreted as a physical battle against the enemies of Allah, *jihad* also has a more personal, spiritual meaning: a lifelong struggle to turn oneself into a better person. Shortly after his conversion, Tyson informed a reporter that being a Muslim was "probably not going to make me an angel in heaven, but it's going to make me a better person."[43] Raised as a Roman Catholic, in 1988 he had been baptized a Baptist by the Reverend Jesse Jackson. Promoter Don King arranged for photographers to make a media event of that incident, but Tyson's "conversion" to the Baptists was no conversion at all, Tyson confided in prison to journalist Pete Hamill. "As soon as I got baptized, I got one of the girls in the choir and went to a hotel room or my place or something." Presumably, Allah would inspire him to act differently. To his credit, Tyson did not latch onto Islam for any pie-in-the-sky promise of an afterlife. "When you die, nothing matters but the dash," he told Hamill. "On your tombstone, it says 1933–2025, or something like that. The only thing that matters is the dash. That dash is your life. How you live is your life. And were you happy the way you lived it."[44]

Having served three years of his six-year sentence, Tyson was released from prison in the spring of 1995 to a media blitz that focused primarily on his newfound faith. Tyson dressed properly for the occasion. A white Muslim *kufi* (prayer cap) topped off a spiffy black collarless jacket and an open white shirt. Merely a quarter of a century after Muhammad Ali's controversial religious change, now a conversion to Islam made for good public relations.

Don King orchestrated the event. King, a boxing promoter and hustler extraordinaire, hoped to get a big piece of the Tyson pie. Shortly after sunrise on the day of Tyson's release, King brought several bodyguards with him to greet Tyson at the prison gate. Surrounded by photographers and reporters, they piled into a shiny black limousine for a drive to the site of Tyson's choosing. Would it be to a nearby mosque, or would it be to the airport for a hasty flight to Tyson's new estate in Southington, Ohio, near Cleveland? For Don King and his cronies, a decision in favor of the mosque could only mean that Tyson was demonstrating his independence of King's control. "No mosque, no mosque," one of King's aides was heard to mutter, in an obvious reference to Roberto Duran's infamous line "No mas, no mas," ending his fight against Sugar Ray Leonard several years earlier.[45]

The mosque won out, at least for the moment. As Tyson disembarked from the limousine, a fan waved a sign, "May Allah Bless Mike Tyson." Inside, Tyson beamed at the presence of Muhammad Ali and Eddie Mustafa Muhammad. As King and his entourage took seats at the back of the mosque, Tyson knelt in the front row. Muhammad Siddeeq offered prayers in Arabic. Afterward, the party moved downstairs for a brief "prayer breakfast." By 7:30 A.M. the event was finished, and Tyson—still accompanied by Don King and his crew—sped off to the Indianapolis International Airport for a chartered flight to Cleveland. According to one report, King made a monumental gaffe by stocking his limousine with Dom Perignon and Tyson's Southington refrigerator with beef, lamb, goat, pork, rabbit, and seafood. For Muslims, alcohol, pork, and shellfish are strictly forbidden. In truth, this entire mosque visitation was out of the ordinary. Muslim prayers are normally said at sunrise, noon, and three other set times spaced throughout the day. Obviously, Mike Tyson was a special case.[46]

Shortly after his release from prison, some sixty black ministers in Harlem attempted to restore Tyson's special reputation within the black community. As the Reverend Al Sharpton and Nation of Islam minister Conrad Muhammad led the effort, the Reverend Wyatt Tee Walker, pastor of Harlem's Canaan Baptist Church, headed a "blue ribbon panel" that would distribute a million dollars pledged by Tyson and Don King to the needy of Harlem. In stifling 95-degree heat on June 20, 1995, a large crowd gathered at the Apollo Theater with banners, prayers, and speeches, welcoming their "prodigal son" who was returning home after his "riotous living."

A smaller but still vocal crowd stood across the street from the Apollo, demonstrating against this restoration of a fallen hero. Women made up the bulk of an organization called African Americans Against Violence, who insisted—as *Newsday* columnist Sheryl McCarthy put it—that "redemption presupposes remorse." Tyson had never even admitted his rape of Desiree Washington, much less shown remorse. Nor had he ever publicly acknowledged his well-documented history of fondling, groping, and battering black women. "In trying to resuscitate Iron Mike's rep," declared an angry black female reporter for the *Village Voice*, "Sharpton's welcoming committee spin doctors have reminded us that some of Harlem's own would still rather sacrifice a woman than lose a male role model."[47]

Yet countless interviews promised a new self-awareness, even a touch of humility, stemming from Tyson's new religious commitment. "I'm a very private Muslim. I feel at peace with it," Tyson told an *Esquire* reporter in 1996. "I go to the prayer rug every day." He especially enjoyed the rituals surrounding the holy month of Ramadan: "No food from sunup to sundown, then just enough for dinner, no pigging out. I love it. Look forward to it. I feel like a different man. It's a high, makes you feel a little light-headed."[48]

Unfortunately, Tyson did not confine his light-headedness to moments of religious devotion. After his release from prison, he repeatedly made a public spectacle of himself. Two minor auto collisions triggered assaults on motorists, sending Tyson back to jail for three and a half months. In the ring, he was even more erratic. A 1996 bout with Orlin Norris was ruled no contest when Tyson kept punching after the bell, rendering Norris unable to continue beyond the first round. Less than a year later, in another match, Tyson bit off half of Evander Holyfield's ear. While boxing officials pondered an appropriate punishment, journalists created shameless puns such as "heavyweight chomp," "teething ring," and "ear today, gone tomorrow."

Even sedate Scotland got a dose of the Tyson circus. At Glasgow in June 2000, the referee awarded Tyson a technical knockout over Lou Savarese in the first round, but Tyson continued swinging and knocking Savarese down. In the bedlam, the referee got bowled over, leaving Tyson with precious few fans in Britain. Britain's Muslim immigrants, already on the margins of British society, suffered some twinges of embarrassment over Tyson's endorsement of Islam.[49]

Back home in the States, Tyson's Muslim faith provoked his two-time conqueror, Evander Holyfield, to frame their encounters as holy wars. An outspoken born-again Christian, Holyfield was scarcely in the business of merely providing hype in order to sell tickets to his fights. He relished the symbolic victory of his Jehovah-God over the Muslim god, Allah. "I give the glory to God!" he announced after his first defeat of Tyson, an eleven-round technical knockout. "I live by the spirit of God. You can't choose against God! My God is the only true God!"[50]

Apparently this rant came from a sincere soul, if not a clear mind. "A lot of people think I'm not real when I say I believe in God," Holyfield told a British interviewer. "But I believe every word God says. And God says,

'I would never give you more than you can't [sic] handle.'" Fractured prose notwithstanding, Holyfield has handled difficulties such as a relatively small frame for a heavyweight, a heart problem, and several defeats on his way to the top. His faith—in God and in himself (often seeming to be one and the same)—saw him through. Preparing for all his big bouts, he sweated, punched, and skipped rope to the sound of church hymns and Christian rock playing in the background. Before and after each gym session, he regularly prayed with his trainers and sparring partners. For the first Tyson fight, he wore a purple robe into the ring with "Philippians 4:13" emblazoned on the back. Holyfield genuinely believed he could do "all things" through the strength of Christ. "There is no way I cannot win," he told a reporter for *U.S. News and World Report* shortly before the second Tyson fight. "I believe in God, so I will surely beat Tyson."[51]

An older born-again heavyweight, George Foreman, also viewed the world in stark terms, Christians versus Muslims. Soundly beaten by Muhammad Ali in the famous "rumble in the jungle" of Zaire in 1974, three years later Foreman converted to Christianity, became a Baptist minister in Houston, Texas, and years afterward made a spectacular comeback in the ring. Asked in the late 1980s to comment on Ali's conversion to Islam, Foreman dismissed it as an incident that was more a social awakening than a religious experience. "It was something that he needed at the time. The whole country needed it. Young people in particular were tired of walking around with a feeling of inferiority, and some of them were awakened socially by the call of the Muslims." Admitting that Ali later came to a faith that was more authentically religious, Foreman viewed his own conversion as "truly religious." His life had been set on the right path, he believed, by a "deep pull from God," not a social movement or racial consciousness. True to his evangelical tradition, for years Foreman attempted to turn Ali to Jesus, away from Allah, but Ali refused to budge. Foreman finally realized that he should stop trying to put his beliefs on his old foe, now a friend. "If Jesus wants to convert Muhammad Ali," Foreman concluded, "Jesus will do it."[52]

## A Dedicated Game Plan

The names of Muhammad Ali, Kareem Abdul-Jabbar, Hakeem Olajuwon, and Mike Tyson occupy prominent places in the recent history of American sport. All enjoyed extraordinary athletic careers; all made huge sums of money from professional competition. Yet they scarcely represent the whole of the Muslim experience in the United States. Lest these elite cases be considered the totality of the complex interaction of American Muslims with sport, a high school football scene in Dearborn, Michigan, invites attention. Dearborn is a western suburb of Detroit, in southeast Michigan. The region contains more than a quarter of a million people of ethnic Arab descent, the second largest Muslim community outside the Middle East.

These immigrants—some from Africa and Asia, most from the Middle East—have transformed Dearborn's social fabric, especially in the public schools. Over the past twenty or thirty years, ethnic Arab children have come to compose about 90 percent of the town's elementary schools. As of 2005, Muslims counted for one-third of Dearborn High School's student population; Muslims at nearby Fordson High School numbered some 70 percent of the students. Controversy inevitably surfaced at these schools regarding such issues as student dress codes (especially the girls' head scarf, the *hijab*), the serving of pork (forbidden by Islamic law) in school cafeterias, the Ramadan food drive (whether it was given equal time with the Key Club in morning intercom announcements), and the separation of gym classes by gender (a fundamental principle for most Muslim parents).

Muslims especially made their presence felt in Dearborn's high school football programs. For the Fordson High School Tractors, Muslims occupied all but two gridiron lockers in 2003. Two years later, no fewer than twenty-five Muslims played for the Dearborn High School Pioneers. Fordson's quarterback, Salah Abazeed, and tailback, Ali Hosaak, led Fordson to the championship play-offs. Fullback Hassan Cheaib, linebacker Amir Rustom, nose guard Mohammad Kassab, and defensive back Khalil Dabaja did the same for the Pioneers. Coaches had to guard carefully against culturally insensitive gestures. They could not organize pizza parties that featured pepperoni pizza, because pepperoni was pork. For barbecue cookouts, *halal* (kosher) meat had to be served. Prior to each game a player led his teammates in *al-Fateeha*, a Muslim prayer invoking Allah's protection against spiritual as well as physical injury. Dearborn players and coaches alike seem to have mastered what a *New York Times* reporter calls "the rhythms of the twin rituals of Islam and the gridiron."[53]

One issue, however, threatened to upset the rhythm. Most of Islam's holy month, Ramadan, fell in October, just when schoolboy teams faced their most important games. As Fordson and Dearborn High cast their eyes on the play-offs, the Muslim code required a month-long regimen of fasting—no food and no liquid of any kind—from sunrise to sunset. Muslim players awoke before daybreak for a predawn breakfast, *shahoor*, then attended classes all day without any food or drink. At afternoon practice, they resisted the temptation to take a water break, and on Friday nights they began their games on empty stomachs until full darkness allowed them to drink and snack on the sidelines.

Some grumbled; a few no doubt slipped a sip of water. Most adhered to the rules of their faith but devised tactics to make sugary drinks, sandwiches, crackers, and candy bars available on the sidelines just as soon as the sun set. One player had his cheerleading sweetheart store a snack under her coat; another hid a tuna-fish sandwich in his locker to be devoured at halftime. Several came up with practical as well as religious explanations for fasting. Ramadan instilled discipline and "a sense of inner strength," making you "a better man," thought Fordson's tailback, Ali Hosaak. These virtues translated into being a better athlete. "You know you've been faithful. And that makes you much tougher out on the field," Dearborn High's seventeen-year-old fullback told a reporter. "You have to have a crazy mentality out on the field, and after fasting all day, you feel like a warrior."

The ritual of Ramadan also made these players feel like a team. As the Fordson quarterback told an interviewer, fasting wasn't actually "that bad, you know. We know what our priorities are. We set them straight and in a way it helps us as a team. It disciplines us and it helps us through adversity." The Fordson coach, Jeff Stergalas, found a way to make the apparent incongruity of Ramadan work to the team's advantage. He scheduled daily practices late in the afternoon, and by the time the team came indoors and showered, darkness had called a halt to the day's required fast. Food, provided by school funds and parental assistance, awaited the players. Before they went off to the weight room or film session, non-Muslims joined Muslims in eating and drinking together.

For much of the previous half-century, Muslim athletes had been controversial participants in American sports. Often their presence had proved divisive for sporting events and for American society at large. To these Dearborn football players, however, the practice of their Islamic faith meant something more than an alien irritant. It came to mean friendship and mutual trust, a sense of cohesion that is central to the making of a strong team.

# 12

## TEAMMATES AND SOUL MATES

For all the drama surrounding a championship boxing bout or top-flight tennis match, team sports most vividly mirror the various delights and difficulties of the human experience. Like a church, a synagogue, or a mosque, an athletic team is more than the sum of its parts. Its fortunes rise or fall on the performance of individual players, but by definition the team's core reality transcends the individual athlete. A team is communal; its members are necessarily cooperative. At best, teammates like each other and respect the others' physical skills, intelligence, and courage. People of faith, accustomed to institutionalized mythologies and rituals that celebrate communal virtues, might well sense a certain kinship with athletic teams.

Two stories related here weave religious significance into extraordinary team efforts. The first illustrates a favorite sporting theme: a Cinderella team overcoming deficient resources to take home all the honors. In this case, Cinderella was a Catholic women's college that remained self-consciously Catholic, especially when clad in basketball shorts and sneakers. The second drama also pertains to basketball meshing with a traditional religion. The religion in this case is Zen Buddhism as understood and appropriated by a widely acclaimed coach whose religious pilgrimage falls outside the experience of mainstream America.

Within the past quarter of a century, the mainstream has taken a sharp turn to the right. The religious right, originally a Protestant fundamentalist movement, finds ideological comrades among evangelical Christians of all stripes, and among non-Christians as well. Evangelical religion and sport reinforce each other. The one sustains the other. They are more than teammates; they are soul mates.

## Immaculate Perceptions

In 1972 the "Mighty Macs" of Immaculata College won the first national women's basketball championship. For good measure, they also won the championship in 1973 and again in 1974. Despite having no athletic scholarships, no recruiting budget, and a mere pittance to pay their coach, by the end of 1975 they had played the historic first game of women's basketball at Madison Square Garden and had been featured in the first women's game on live television. Heady stuff, this, for a small, all-women's Catholic school set in cow pastures and cornfields thirty miles west of Philadelphia.[1]

The Macs came mostly from Philadelphia's large working-class Catholic community, whose parochial school system enrolled nearly 40 percent of the city's youth. As conservative (mostly Irish) priests and nuns dispensed the gospel of patriarchy, Catholic girls felt the pinch. They were expected to marry, produce children, and raise them in the Catholic faith. Scarcely could anyone have predicted a championship basketball squad coming out of that situation. Circumstances conspired, however, to produce a lively women's basketball culture in Catholic Philadelphia. Single-sex schools allowed young women to find their own athletic niche, free from male competition for facilities and funds. Field hockey, not football or baseball, flourished in early autumn and spring; basketball dominated the girls' athletic calendar for the rest of the school year. Girls competed against boys in backyards, on inner-city playgrounds, and in neighborhood Catholic Youth Organization (CYO) gyms. Not by coincidence, Immaculata's president from 1954 to 1972, Sister Mary of Lourdes, proudly enjoyed her reputation for having been an outstanding athlete.

For many Philadelphia Catholics, basketball was a family ritual. Several generations faithfully attended games at the city's three Catholic colleges for men, St. Joseph's, Villanova, and LaSalle. Beginning in the 1940s, Catholic families packed Convention Hall for Friday night girls' doubleheaders featuring the best parochial school teams in the city. This pattern of family support carried over to Immaculata. Parents and siblings made the short drive from Philadelphia for home games. Attentive fathers carried signs and led cheers. One father, a hardware store owner in Philadelphia, supplied metal buckets to be used as noisemakers. Another father remained home but stayed awake after evening games waiting for a phone call with information about how the team did and how many points his daughter scored.

Like an extended family, Immaculata faculty, staff, and students enthusiastically supported their basketball team. President Sister Mary often dropped in to watch the Macs practice and usually shot a few goals before she left. At home games, nuns and priests, easily recognizable in their black and white garb, cheered on the team. For big games away from the home court, nuns rented buses to transport faculty and student fans. As Julie Byrne sensitively paints this picture, these Catholic women were not merely consecrating a secular activity with religious devotion. Instead, players and fans alike "assumed basketball was already sacred, if played by Catholics who understood their whole lives as an ongoing offering to God." One Immaculata player concluded simply that her "entire experience" convinced her "that the Catholic Church supported and promoted women's basketball."[2]

Within the same year that the Mighty Macs won their first national crown, the Title IX ruling reshaped the future of college sports for women. Prohibiting the customary disparities in federal funds spent for women compared to men, Title IX resulted in the creation of numerous new basketball programs with athletic scholarships, recruitment budgets, better coaches, and upgraded facilities for women athletes. Whereas just over 200 college women's basketball teams competed for the crown in 1972, no fewer than 900 took the floor in 1980. Large state universities, heavily dependent on public funding, benefited enormously; small private colleges like Immaculata were the losers.

By the 1980s, the glory years of 1972–1974 had faded from memory, though the Immaculata family of faculty, students, parents, and a few friends still turned out to watch the Macs compete. The crowd still went quiet just before the tip-off as the team and the coach huddled at courtside to pray:

> O God of Players, hear our prayer,
> to play this game, and play it fair.

The Mighty Macs played it fair, and they played it well.


## Zen and the Art of Teamwork

Within a totally different tradition, Protestant fundamentalism, Phil Jackson also learned to pray and play basketball. Jackson's parents were both ordained Pentecostal ministers who puritanically banned all the usual vices from their North Dakota home. In high school sports, Jackson found refuge from religious strictures. A spectacular senior year in basketball won him an athletic scholarship to the University of North Dakota, where a future NBA coach, Bill Fitch, groomed him for two years of All-American honors and a second-round selection by the New York Knicks in the NBA draft.[3]

Off the court, Jackson ran headlong into the counterculture of the 1960s. First at college, then in New York City, he encountered the restless, rebellious spirit of the age. As he later recalled, his devout childhood seemed to have left him with "an emptiness, a yearning to reconnect with the deeper mysteries of life."[4] By the mid-1970s, Jackson was into all the experiments common to the new-age search for personal identity and spirituality: pot-smoking, astrology, yoga, vegetarianism, and mysticism. Native American religion beckoned. In the summer of 1973, just a few months after a highly publicized Lakota Sioux protest at Wounded Knee, Jackson worked with Knicks teammates Bill Bradley and Willis Reed in the first of six annual basketball clinics at the Pine Ridge Reservation in South Dakota. For Jackson, the Lakota belief in the interconnectedness of all life and "deep reverence for the mysteries of life" served as a mirror for his own spiritual quest. The words of a Sioux seer especially impressed him: "We are the earth people on a spiritual journey to the stars. Our quest, our earth walk, is to look within, to know who we are, to see that we are connected to all things, that there is no separation, only in the mind."[5]

Jackson's immediate "earth walk" was more literally a run around NBA basketball courts, largely in a backup role for the New York Knickerbockers. In 1970, Willis Reed, Dave Debusschere, Bill Bradley, and Walt Frazier led the Knicks to the NBA crown; three years later, the addition of Earl "the Pearl" Monroe enabled them to repeat as champions. For most of the first championship season, Jackson lay sidelined with back surgery. He healed sufficiently to stick with the Knicks into the late 1970s as an unspectacular but dependable forward.

Jackson's spiritual quest took him far from his fundamentalist roots. Deliverance came by way of total confusion. A messy divorce and remarriage complicated the issues as Jackson grappled seriously with theological misgivings. At one moment, he still thought Christ his "personal savior" in usual evangelical terms; in the next breath, he was convinced that Christ was subordinate to God, that St. Paul smothered Jesus' spiritual message with intellectual baggage, and that the entire Christian conception of God was erroneous. Jackson's highly personal faith was as eccentric as it was eclectic. By the mid-1970s he was most inclined to believe "that God might very well be some kind of Aristotelian energy force."[6]

A Muslim acquaintance made a pitch for Islam, but Islam held little appeal for Jackson. It was too theocentric, dogmatic, and rules laden, much like the Christianity that he was laying aside. To Zen Buddhism, however, Jackson responded differently. He had first come to know it through his older brother, Joe, when both were in college. Joe's description of Zen, derived from one of his professors at the University of Texas, sent Phil spinning with questions. "How could you have a religion that didn't involve belief in God—or at least the personalized idea of God I was familiar with? What did Zen practitioners do?" Joe's explanation that Zen Buddhists "simply tried to clear their minds and be in the present" baffled Phil all the more. As he recalled years later, "To someone raised in a Pentecostal household—where attention was focused more on the hereafter than the here and now—this was a mind-boggling concept."[7]

By the mid-1970s, Jackson was thoroughly wearied with questions about heaven and hell, sin and redemption, guilt and shame. Zen's emphasis on clearing the mind of memories and associations extraneous to the moment allowed him to let go of those elements in his past that no longer worked for him and to open himself to new possibilities without feeling that he was "committing a major sacrilege against God and family."[8] Jackson was not even sure if Buddhism was an authentic religion. Perhaps it was merely a "non-theistic philosophy," but it did not matter. Zen required concentration, an immersion in the immediate experience that allowed one to respond spontaneously to whatever was taking place. This philosophy served Jackson well as a player; it served him even more effectively as a coach. Finishing with the Knicks in 1978, he briefly played and served as an assistant coach with the New Jersey Nets. Through the 1980s he worked first as a television commentator, then as a coach for the Albany Patroons of the minor-league Continental Basketball Association. With the Patroons, he won a league title and a CBA Coach of the Year Award, but for several years had to supplement his meager salary by coaching in a Puerto Rican summer league.

In 1989, Jackson became head coach of the Chicago Bulls, a team dominated by the incomparable Michael Jordan. For the past several years, Jordan had led the league in scoring, but the Bulls had never won an NBA championship. Prior to Jackson's arrival, Jordan's dominance worked to the detriment of the team. Players tended to feed Jordan the ball, then stand back and watch his adroit, uncanny maneuvers to the basket. He scored frequently, but not enough to win consistently without more coordination between him and his teammates. The need, as Jackson saw it, was to plug the Bulls into "the power of *oneness* instead of the power of one man." This achievement would be "essentially a spiritual act" related to Jackson's own spiritual quest. "The day I took over the Bulls," he wrote several years later, "I vowed to create an environment based on the principles of selflessness and compassion I'd learned as a Christian in my parents' home; sitting on a cushion practicing Zen; and studying the teachings of the Lakota Sioux." More precisely, he believed that "the only way to win consistently was to give everybody—from the stars to the number 12 player on the bench—a vital role on the team, and inspire them to be acutely aware of what was happening, even when the spotlight was on someone else."[9]

Eclectic as ever, Jackson wrapped Lakota Sioux symbols around Zen Buddhist concepts. He especially warmed to the Lakota Sioux's belief in the sanctity of the tribe. A basketball team is a tribe, "a society, a club," he frequently told his players. "The point is to win respect, to help one another," metaphorically to fight and die for one another. As visible signs of this belief, Jackson decorated the Chicago Bulls team room with a painting of the great Sioux warrior Crazy Horse, and with totems such as a tobacco pouch attached to a wooden arrow, symbolic of prayer; a bear claw necklace, which supposedly grants power and wisdom to its viewer; the middle feather of an owl, representing balance and harmony; and photographs of a white buffalo calf, the sacred Sioux embodiment of prosperity and good fortune.[10]

Not surprisingly, some players thought Jackson a bit weird, especially when he walked around the locker room before games, burning sticks of sage or beating a tom-tom, or introducing transcendental meditation and the music of the Grateful Dead. Players quickly learned, however, that this freakiness had a purpose. As journalist David Shields shrewdly observed, Jackson was "a freaky control freak." He firmly believed in structure balanced with freedom. Directing by indirection, he rigorously organized practices, but kept them loose. He introduced a highly patterned offense, but kept it flexible.[11]

Jackson's offensive scheme, "the Triangle," departed from the usual pattern of set plays and players frequently challenging each other one on one. Largely designed and taught by Jackson's assistant, Tex Winter, the Triangle emphasized coordinated, instinctive movement to open spaces and creative reactions to opportunities caused by defensive lapses. Jackson thought of it as a Bach or Mozart concert with all the instruments blended together, vastly different from an improvised, individualistic jazz event. He frequently compared the Triangle to five fingers working cooperatively on a single hand. He saw it as an embodiment of his spiritual principles: "a vehicle for integrating mind and body, sport and spirit, in a practical down-to-earth form. It was awareness in action." It was Zen in expensive sneakers.[12]

And it was highly successful. Not only did the Triangle offense allow Michael Jordan to stay on his scoring rampage; it also contributed to the Chicago Bulls' emergence as the NBA's dominant team in the 1990s. Their championship season of 1990–1991 was the first in the club's twenty-five-year history. By the decade's end, they had claimed six NBA titles, one with Jordan momentarily absent as he tried his hand at professional baseball.

The most dramatic moment occurred in 1994, in the final minute of a play-off game. As the team gathered for a time-out, the clock indicated time for only one more shot. Little could anyone foresee a team disaster that would call Phil Jackson's preachments on teamwork into question, requiring him to summon all his Sioux and Zen sources of strength. With Jordan in retirement, Scotty Pippen had become the Bulls' unofficial leader, their go-to guy when the game was on the line. But now Jackson designated another player, Toni Kukoc, to take the crucial shot. His pride severely wounded, Pippen refused to go back on the floor. Kukoc missed the shot, sending the team slumping into the dressing room, shaken by Pippen's petulance. Jackson's gospel of tribal cohesion had been violated. Now he had to address the issue. "What was broken was sacred," he began, instinctively using religious terminology. "What has happened has hurt us. Now, you—you have to work this out." With that said, he left the matter in the hands of the team. To their credit, and his, they worked it out on their way to another championship.[13]

A more formidable gathering of egos awaited Jackson in Los Angeles, where he arrived in 1999 to coach the Lakers. Despite the remarkable talents of giant center Shaquille O'Neal and teenage prodigy Kobe Bryant, for the past several years the Lakers had not gotten past the second round of the NBA play-offs. Ervin "Magic" Johnson, who had once served briefly as interim coach, had thrown up his hands in despair. "Me, me, me! Nobody cared about anything else," he lamented. Shortly before Johnson arrived, Kobe Bryant and coach Kurt Rambis engaged in a face-to-face shouting match during a time-out. Clearly, the Lakers needed something more than a coach. They needed a miracle-worker who would pry them loose from their self-centered ways.[14]

Yet Jackson claimed to be "no savior" for the Lakers. Shortly after arriving in Los Angeles, he announced in characteristic religious terms, "They have to be the savior of themselves." Bryant would have to hog the ball less and pass it off more; Shaq needed to improve his foul shots in order to punish opponents who frequently fouled him in the waning minutes of most games. The entire team had to avoid mental lapses on the court as well as the distractions of postgame parties. "Phil came in here and told this team to grow up and stop being little boys," observed forward John Salley, brought by Jackson from the championship Bulls. "Be men and play the game the way it's supposed to be played. It's that simple."[15]

Of course, it's not really that simple; but Jackson's conjoining of age-old Judaeo-Christian values with new-age beliefs and rituals proved an effective combination in the high-octane world of professional basketball. At the outset of the twenty-first century, he added three more NBA championship rings to his collection—not bad for a small-town boy whose early religious commitments got swamped, then redirected, by athletic imperatives.[16]

## Soul Mates

For a full, largely uncritical embrace of religion and sport, one must turn to the born-again camp of evangelical Christians, whose conservative assumptions are increasingly prominent across the board of religious opinion. Evangelicals and athletes metaphorically recite similar liturgies, sing hymns in a common cadence, and drink from a single communion cup.

Both hold a simple, clear-cut vision of reality that divides the world into winners and losers. For the born-again Christian, one either believes in Christ or rejects Christ; one is saved or lost, bound for heaven or doomed to hell. Evangelical theology allows no place for purgatory, much less for a liberal middle ground of uncertainty. "It is a dramatic, stark, even simple faith," says Chicago theologian Martin Marty. "There is little toleration for ambiguity, just like in sports. You win or you lose. The ball bounces one way or the other. Classical Judaism, Catholicism, and Protestantism make room for doubt: not evangelical Christianity."[17]

The born-again athlete is twice blessed with definite rules, boundaries, and measures of success. His gospel focuses on a "plan of salvation" in a few well-defined steps. He is encouraged to exert a childlike trust in an infallible Bible, a simple code of ethics, and a mandate to witness for Christ. Then he takes the field and steps to the plate knowing he has three strikes, not four; four balls, not five; three outs per inning, and nine innings per game. "Psychologically," says sportswriter Leonard Koppett, "sports offer an island of stability in a confusing, shifting cosmos." So does evangelical Christianity.[18]

Evangelical Christianity offers an "island of stability" especially for athletes under pressure to perform. A fundamental problem for professional athletes is "being in a profession where you live on a scoreboard," observed a recent chaplain for the Boston Celtics. "How do you deal with the pressure?" he asked rhetorically. "I tell them not only is God real, but He loves you for who you are, not for what you did." In the evangelical equation, acceptance of this divine, unconditional love wins one a secure future (God's favor now, heaven hereafter) regardless of physical injury, diminishing athletic skills, fickle fans, or arbitrary management.[19]

Evangelical Christianity bridges the gap that some athletes feel between public achievement and personal contentment. Quarterback Jim Harbaugh, for example, heard plenty of cheers in his climb from high school stardom to the University of Michigan, then into the professional ranks—only to have his sense of self-worth shrink with each enlargement of his public image. "I should have been happy," says Harbaugh. "I had everything I wanted, but I still knew something was missing." Fame and fortune were not enough. God, through Christ, made the difference.[20]

For basketball star David Robinson, too, athletic achievement did not bring satisfaction. All-American honors at the Naval Academy and the NBA Rookie of the Year Award left Robinson hungry for something more. "I wasn't happy," he says. "Here I had everything I ever wanted—I had graduated from a good school, had a good family behind me, was doing things I never dreamed I'd do—and I wasn't happy at all." From his team chaplain, Robinson received a Bible—"a manual for life"—and instructions on how to "find the Lord." In Christ he found an emotional anchor, a spiritual wholeness, and a purpose he had never known.[21]

If these and other religiously inclined athletes are to be believed, faith gives them quiet confidence for their athletic efforts. Instead of sapping the competitive juices, intense religious faith frees some athletes to compete fiercely without fear of failure. Orel Hershiser, star pitcher for the Los Angeles Dodgers in the 1980s, thought himself "more aggressive, more of a risk-taker and a harder worker" after he became a Christian. Why? "Because everything in my future is taken care of, I can risk everything or anything in a game of baseball. I don't have to worry about throwing the 3–2 curveball in a pressure situation, because if I get hit or if I get him out, the world's still going to be okay in my life. There's no pressure."[22]

Modern athletes often mention the need to "keep focused." For evangelicals, Christ is the great focusmeister. "There's a lot of tension in what I do," said born-again former relief pitcher Tim Burke. "To be an effective reliever, you've got to have great focus. I was worried about things I had no control over. But when I became a Christian, I found I could leave my worries and anxieties with Him." Similarly conducive to focus was the semireligious formula espoused by professional wrestler Terry Bollea, more commonly known as Hulk Hogan. Before parading his tanned, heavily muscled body into the ring, he reminded himself of his "Four Demandments": "Train, say your prayers, eat your vitamins, and believe in yourself." Hulk Hogan did it all, including the prayers. "A lot of people say it's bull," he told a reporter in 1991, "but it's done a lot for me."[23]

Hulk Hogan's formula is a reminder that piety and sport share a tendency toward ritual and that athletes thrive on it. However personal its meaning, most ritual is public. The basketball player crosses himself as he approaches the foul line, the baseball player as he steps into the batter's box. Teams say the Lord's Prayer before the big game; afterward, the star thanks the Lord for victory. Yet some rituals are quiet and intensely personal. On his way to the plate, baseball player Gary Gaetti made a mantra of Philippians 4:13: "I can do all things through Christ, who strengthens me." Several years ago Portland Trail Blazer center Mychal Thompson learned from his Baptist pastor to get into a rhythm of shooting free throws by saying "God the Father" while bouncing the ball the first time, "God the Son" on the second bounce, and "God the Holy Ghost" with the third. "Praise the Lord," Thompson regularly said while finally putting up his foul shot. (Unfortunately, his ritual did little to improve his abysmal success rate of 61 percent from the foul line.)[24]

No clear line separates religion from superstition in modern sport. Little different from their ancient counterparts, today's athletes are notoriously superstitious. Until his recent retirement, Olympic hurdler Edwin Moses always did three hours of stretches in the same order, at the same pace, before each track meet; third baseman Wade Boggs, first with the Red Sox then with the Yankees and finally with the Tampa Bay Devil Rays, always ate chicken cooked a certain way before each game. Baseball players carefully avoid stepping on the foul line; ice hockey players play pregame head games with hockey sticks. In hope of victory, players wear the same smelly socks and coaches the same soiled ties that saw them win previous games.

Searching for any advantage they can find, superstitious athletes readily turn to God, the chaplain, prayer, or whatever might help. "If I felt I needed three hits, I would go to chapel," a somewhat embarrassed Pittsburgh outfielder, Andy Van Slyke, admitted after his religious conversion. As the New York Giants' Bill Currier put it years ago, even the most disbelieving athlete was not going to be "hostile to the chaplain" before a big game.[25]

Most athletes deny praying for victory. Sometimes, though, the urge to win at all costs wins out in private supplications; occasionally it appears in public for all to see. In mid-January 1991, New York Giants placekicker Matt Bahr lined up a decisive forty-two-yard field goal try with four seconds left against the San Francisco Forty-Niners. A good kick would put the Giants into the Super Bowl. In full view of a nationwide television audience, seven Giants players knelt along the sidelines, praying for success. Bahr came through on a leg and a prayer. Two weeks later, the Giants found themselves on the other side of the prayer table. As time ran out at the end of the Super Bowl game against the Buffalo Bills, Bills kicker Scott Norwood came on the field to attempt a game-winning forty-seven-yard kick. Again the Giants' prayer squad knelt to hold hands and pray, but this time for their opponent to miss the field goal. He did just that, causing theologians and sports fans everywhere to wonder if the Lord held a grudge against Norwood and the Buffalo Bills.[26]

More bizarre still were the postgame explanations for Buffalo's Black Sunday. Bills defensive back Mark Kelso admitted that he, too, was praying, but for Norwood to kick the ball accurately. He hastened to add, though, that if God had wanted the Bills to win, the kick would have gone through the uprights. "But for some reason, He didn't want us to win," said Kelso. On the other side of the field, Giants coach Bill Parcells informed a journalist that on that particular day, God was virtually a New York Giants twelfth man. "I realized a long time ago that God is playing some of these games," said Parcells, "and He was on our side today."[27]

God "on our side": a sentiment as old as Homer, who claimed it for athletes as well as warriors in ancient Greece. In its modern guise, it has served to explain feats as varied as Reggie Jackson's World Series home runs, Isiah Thomas's game-winning basket, Lou Holtz's by-the-skin-of-the-teeth victories for Notre Dame, a Florida Gators NCAA football national championship, heavyweight champion Evander Holyfield's prowess, and Betsy King's birdies. Rare, even worthy of mention, is the athlete who does not now drag the Almighty into the victory circle. Several years ago a writer for *Sports Illustrated* cited German tennis champion Boris Becker as a unique athlete, one who had not yet burned out from stress and fame; nor had Becker yet begun "to credit religion with putting the top-spin on his lob."[28]

Some athletes are less prone to credit God with specific victories, but still look to religion as a means of overcoming alcohol and drug addictions common to high-profile celebrities. NFL stars Chris Carter and Deion Sanders joined major league baseball players Paul Molitor and Darryl Strawberry at the head of an impressive list of born-again athletes in the 1980s and '90s whose faith helped them kick destructive habits. Strawberry's testimony is the most dramatic, and most problematic, of all. With several different teams this large, multitalented man rode the roller coaster of great success, abysmal failure, physical maladies, and addictions. In 1991 he came to religious faith shortly after signing a five-year, $20.3 million contract with the Los Angeles Dodgers. "All this here, baseball and prestigious things, and money and houses and cars, these things are irrelevant," he told a reporter. "They are meaningless to me. I have Jesus now, and I know what I have after that. I have eternal life." He publicly promised to give 10 percent of his hefty income to his church.[29] By the end of the 1990s, however, Strawberry was finished with baseball, and baseball with him. Having squandered his extraordinary athletic talent, he had little to show for the $30 million he had made with the Mets, Dodgers, Giants, and Yankees. His legendary big bat stood silent, sidelined by cocaine and alcohol addictions, arrests and probation violations, income tax evasions, charges of wife abuse, and failure to pay child support. "I never had a problem hitting," he told a reporter. "I had a problem living."[30]

Strawberry's ups and downs suggest some similarities between born-again religion and high-level sport. Both require total commitment of body and mind; both hook true believers into obsessive behavior. "You see," as pitcher Jim Bouton phrased it many years ago, "you spend a good piece of your life gripping a baseball and in the end it turns out that it was the other way around all the time." In many cases, the born-again athlete is gripped by—addicted to—a competitive view of life on the one hand and an evangelical view of Christ on the other. Little wonder that an old New York Mets fan cynically dismissed Darryl Strawberry's religious conversion: "He's been a rookie; he's been a druggie. Now he's just addicted to God."[31]

In the end, the most important connection between born-again religion and modern sport is forged by the consumer culture of which both are part. Both have a product to sell; both eagerly advertise and dispense their

wares. Sports promoters call it good business; evangelicals call it "witnessing" and "sharing." "It's my responsibility to God to tell people where the
talent came from and who should get the glory and why I feel a certain way
in a certain situation," says Orel Hershiser. Years ago an Alabama Baptist
preacher said it best as he towed a portable chapel from Gadsden to the
Talladega 500 auto race. "I'm going to promote God," the good reverend
explained, "just like the other guys promote STP."[32]

This eagerness to make a public, demonstrative sales pitch for Jesus is a
first cousin, if not a twin brother, of the tendency of athletes to call attention to themselves by preening, gesturing, and taunting opponents. Drop-
ping to a knee or pointing skyward after a touchdown, in full view of the
television camera, presumably gives God the glory. In fact, it calls attention
to oneself. Ultimately, the Thee Squad and the Me Generation play the
same game. They are soul mates.

# 13

## GODS AND GAMES TODAY

The long arc of modern sport's interaction with religion can best be viewed as a dance in which the terms of engagement have changed over time. At first, both parties clung to opposite ends of the floor, each uncertain of the other's motives. Mutual friends finally introduced them to each other. Timid conversation ensued, flirtation followed, and over the years each party learned to take pleasure and reap material gain from the other. Within the past half-century or so, a formal, old style of ballroom dancing has given way to a lively, improvised rhythm in which partners alternately touch, disengage, and then passionately embrace while moving to the latest music. The dancers have grown in number to include Muslims and Zen Buddhists as well as Protestant, Catholic, and Jewish participants.

Amid these changes, two basic beliefs espoused by the earliest muscular Christians have become muted, if not mangled beyond recognition. Charles Kingsley, Thomas Wentworth Higginson, and their reformist friends insisted that church folk should welcome sport as a friend in the struggle for healthy limbs and lungs. In addition, these early apologists saw sport as a builder of strong character, a moral agent on behalf of values long espoused by churches and synagogues. For millions of Americans, these two assumptions quickly coalesced to form a single item of civic faith: that competitive sport is physically and morally good for human beings.

At first, this belief enjoyed spectacular growth. As urban congestion, disease, and frayed nerves in the wake of the Civil War made sport's promise of health increasingly attractive, fears of moral decline, political corruption, and alien immigrants spurred religious folk to seek moral assistance beyond the usual confines of church dogma. On one street corner they found a new YMCA or YMHA; just down the street a public park and playground beckoned; around the corner a minister of the social gospel nudged his parishioners to promote sport as an indispensable ally in the crusade against bad habits and bad health.

Although World War I proved to be detrimental to both habits and health, it was a boon to American sport. Religious faith linked up with sporting fervor in the patriotic effort. Ever afterward, and especially on the international Olympic stage when American athletes confronted representatives of fascist and communist states, the American credo would be decidedly Trinitarian: faith in the Nation, faith in God, and faith in Sports.

Shortly after the Great War, a worm appeared in the apple. For the World Series of 1919, gamblers bribed eight members of the Chicago White Sox to throw the series to the Cincinnati Reds. Gamblers thus played loosely with "the faith of fifty million fans," observed one of F. Scott Fitzgerald's characters in *The Great Gatsby* (1925). In truth, the players and club owners were the culprits. Superstar "Shoeless" Joe Jackson received the brunt of the nasty publicity for his failings. As one journalist told the story, Jackson left the courtroom to be met by a youngster's plea: "Say it ain't so, Joe." Say it ain't so, that you violated our trust, betraying us for filthy lucre. Say it ain't so, that you flagrantly broke the rules. Say it ain't so, that sport—our National Pastime, at that—failed to make you honest and trustworthy.[1]

"Say it ain't so, Joe." This quixotic denial echoed through subsequent decades as the character-building ideals of sport clashed with the stark reality of the athlete's vulnerability to human frailty. The year 1951 was a banner year for disappointment born of tarnished idealism. As young Americans died in Korea resisting communist aggression, Americans at home confronted a more immediate challenge to some cherished beliefs. Within a few months after dozens of college basketball players were indicted for shaving points, sixty varsity athletes at West Point—including an All-American quarterback and son of Army football coach Red Blaik—were expelled for cheating on academic exams. Athletes and would-be military officers supposedly represented the nation's highest virtues of honor and honesty, but they had failed the test of character.

This fall from grace was all the more painful in the early 1950s because Americans still clung to the old muscular Christian belief that sports built character. Except for the journalists who exposed the Black Sox fiasco, sportswriters prior to World War II held themselves to a "gee whiz" standard that amounted to little more than cheerleading. By the early 1950s, uncritical popular opinion found scholarly support in academic attempts to frame American history and contemporary life as "exceptional," different from and probably better than most other societies. Sport figured heavily in that rosy view. In 1951, sociologists David Riesman and Reuel Denney depicted college football as a uniquely American embodiment of healthy competition and democratic values; in 1954, historian Jacques Barzun lauded the blend of individualism and team spirit in baseball, and concluded with the oft-quoted line that "whoever wants to know the heart and mind of America had better learn baseball."[2]

Scandals notwithstanding, events in the 1950s seemed to lend credence to these assertions of faith. More impressive than Bobby Thomson's "shot heard round the world" (the game-winning home run that won the National League pennant for the New York Giants in 1951), major league baseball confronted racial bigots with the sterling talent of Giants outfielder Willie Mays, who ably continued the process of racial integration begun earlier with Jackie Robinson. Meanwhile, college football put out the welcome mat for two regions long confined to the margins of American life. In 1951 the Tennessee Volunteers mastered Robert Neyland's old single-wing offense to win the national championship; shortly thereafter, Bud Wilkinson's new split-T offense made the Oklahoma Sooners the dominant gridiron power of the decade. Wilkinson's strategy was innovative, his principles traditional. Although his program twice fell under the NCAA hammer for recruiting violations, Wilkinson frequently expressed his faith in God, the nation, and the wholesome, positive influence that big-time sport could make on the nation's youth. In the early 1960s, he rode that tandem to the While House, to serve as President John F. Kennedy's national advisor on physical fitness.

Like so many other aspects of American life, this tripod of religious faith, patriotic fervor, and athletic enthusiasm came apart in the 1960s. Civil rights marches and antiwar demonstrations competed with sporting events for prime media coverage. For many Americans, sport provided a reprieve from gender, racial, and political negotiations: a throwback to earlier, simpler days. Football especially flourished in the turbulent sixties. As the world threatened to spin out of control on marijuana, experimental sex, and civil disobedience, championship coaches such as Woody Hayes of Ohio State, Paul "Bear" Bryant of Alabama, and Vince Lombardi of the Green Bay Packers extolled the hard work and self-discipline that make a championship gridiron power.

For Americans fearful of Vietnam becoming the nation's first military loss, sport held out a win-at-all-cost mentality. Bear Bryant urged Alabama parents to teach their sons "to work, to sacrifice, to fight" for the honor of playing for the Crimson Tide. Football, he insisted, taught young men to refuse ever to quit in the face of difficult odds. "I've laid it on the line to a lot of boys," Bryant recalled in his autobiography. "I've grabbed 'em, kicked 'em, and embarrassed them in front of the squad. I've got down in the dirt with them, and if they didn't give as well as they took I'd tell them they were insults to their upbringing, and I've cleaned out their lockers for them and piled their clothes out in the hall, thinking I'd make them prove what they had in their veins, blood or spit, one way or the other, and praying they would come through."[3]

Although the choice of "blood or spit, one way or the other" was not quite the option that the first muscular moralists had in mind, it served Bear Bryant well in carving out a highly successful coaching career. Within a month of his final game on the Alabama sidelines, Bryant in 1983 took this curious mixture of athletic boosterism, shameless intimidation, and homespun piety to the grave. We are not likely to see a resurrection of his blood-or-spit kind.

Instead, we are now inundated with vivid refutations of the belief that sport builds character. Pete Rose hustled all the way home, on and off the field, but finished in a pathetic, bumbling denial of gambling misdemeanors. O. J. Simpson, sweet "Juice" with the finest stride and arguably the most impressive rushing records ever to grace college and professional football, ended his public career on an exceedingly sour note. Television viewers remember him best from the evening news, moving in his white SUV down a Los Angeles motorway with the police on his tail, then enduring a long, dismal court trial, accused of killing his wife and her friend. Less publicized but no less unfortunate, basketball star Lenny Bias died of a cocaine overdose on the eve of signing a multimillion-dollar contract with the Boston Celtics. The list goes on and on: athletes learning to play by the rules only to break them on drugs, sweetheart and spouse abuse, gambling, and bank fraud.[4]

Like a football on a basketball court, contradictory images abound, bouncing around in the most unlikely places. At Duke University, athletes garbed in neat, conservative blue-and-white uniforms represent their expensive, high-quality institution, an Ivy-like presence in the South. In the center of the campus, a huge gothic chapel recalls a Methodist moral tradition that once banned the "pernicious" game of football. In the spirit of this well-kept place, basketball coach Mike Krzyzewski runs a squeaky-clean program, carefully playing by the rules. But Duke's lacrosse team, it seems, played by different rules. Having learned macho, arrogant behav-

ior at expensive eastern prep schools, the players on Duke's men's lacrosse team perfected the fine art of disgusting rowdiness: excessive under-
age drinking, lewd public gestures, and raucous parties. Planning a party
to celebrate a successful start to the 2006 season, lacrosse team captains
rented a private house near the campus, then hired two exotic dancers
from a local escort service. As both dancers were African-American students from nearby North Carolina Central University and all except one of
the lacrosse players were white, the age-old issue of racial conflict raised its
ugly head. Shortly after the party, one of the girls accused three Duke players of assault and rape. Within the month, the lacrosse coach had resigned
under pressure, and teams of lawyers were lining up evidence for both
sides.

Whether the athletes were guilty or innocent of the charges, their coarse
attitudes and indulgent behavior resounded loudly throughout the world
of sports. Sensitive to a plethora of moral and legal (not to mention public
relations) issues, Duke officials wondered aloud if their university was being undermined by "a culture of crassness at the expense of a culture of
character."[5]

Somewhere between these polar opposites—crassness on the one hand,
character on the other—modern sport seeks to recover its soul. Crassly
commercial and pervasive, sport today struggles to prove that it is anything
more than a dreamland with occasional nightmares, that it exists for any
purpose other than hawking merchandise, that it offers something more
than pampered, decadent role models for American youths. Sport, in brief,
has lost the moral compass that for more than a century taught Americans
to honor boundaries, play by the rules, and work together for a common
good.[6]

The widespread use of steroids forces all these issues to the fore. Not
long ago, only weight lifters bulked up artificially. Most could be found
in the Olympics, as likely as not from some communist country's state-
run sports factory. In the 1970s, East German women swimmers found
the chemical means momentarily to dominate their sport. More recently,
Western athletes quietly took up the steroids game. Pumped up, track athletes ran faster—until a urine sample caused Canadian sprinter Ben Johnson to be stripped of his 1988 Olympic gold medal. While most other governing bodies hesitantly made rules banning steroids, a few football players
became larger and more aggressive, and some baseball players hit the ball
harder and farther than ever before.

A trail of suspicion that ran through the mighty home-run blasts of

**Say it ain't so, Barry.** As Barry Bonds threatened to break Babe Ruth's record of 714 home runs in the summer of 2006, he pointed both index fingers heavenward after each mighty clout. By his account, he was giving God the credit for his talent; but to many baseball fans these religious gestures were merely part of a cover-up for Bonds's refusal to deal honestly with the rumors and accusations surrounding performance-enhancing drugs. (AP photo / Ben Margot)

Mark McGwire, Jose Canseco, and Jason Giambi ended in 2006 on the doorstep of Barry Bonds. Except in his home park in San Francisco, a chorus of boos greeted Bonds every time he stepped to the plate to put his massive, substance-enhanced body to the task of breaking Babe Ruth's hallowed home run records. In Philadelphia, when he jogged to his position in left field to start the game, fans unfurled a large banner that read, "Ruth did it on hot dogs and beer." Scrawled on a T-shirt was a simple message: "Giant Cheater," a pun on the nickname of Bonds's team, the San Francisco Giants.

Adding insult to corruption, Bonds piously offered to forgive and to pray for all the journalists who wrote "nasty things" about him. For public consumption, he claimed to be giving credit to God when he raised his eyes and pointed both hands skyward as he crossed home plate after each mighty swat. When asked by reporters to explain his dramatic enlargement of body and late-career surge of power, Bonds evasively replied, "There are some things I don't understand right now. Call God. Ask him."[7]

We need not bother the Almighty on this one. The use of anabolic steroids for the improvement of athletic performance is both illegal and immoral. It also violates the very first motive (stated in the mid-nineteenth century) for bringing sport and religion together: the concern for better health. No sane person can make a convincing argument for athletic performance-enhancing chemicals adding to the physical quality of life. Cheating for the sake of extra quickness and power, athletes suffer a loss of hair, shrunken testicles, raised cholesterol levels, and sharp mood swings. They also risk liver damage, an enlarged heart, and other long-term health risks yet to be identified.

Is it possible these days to find any positive expressions of moral athleticism spawned by the marriage of religion and sport? Only rarely can we find them in professional and college locker rooms, where male testosterone and profit motives coalesce to feed a win-at-all-cost mentality. As women athletes mime the male norms, and as youths mime their elders, they simply replicate the problem. My nomination for a star exception is a coach, not an athlete; a woman, not a man; a poorly paid high school coach, not an overpaid professional. Except to her family, friends, and colleagues, she is virtually unknown, not a celebrity. Her name is Linda Head Flanagan, and she coaches track at an elite high school for girls in a high-pressure New Jersey suburb.

Ambitious, intrusive parents and exclusive teenage cliques within the team grate all the more when coach Flanagan remembers that while she is on the job, her own three children are at home with a babysitter. So why does she do it? Why does she keep coming back for more? She responds with the standard sports rationale: "to develop discipline and courage—a reservoir of strength to draw on throughout life."

But Flanagan's riches are in her specifics. "I come back," she explains, "to watch my rising star—a girl who is beautiful yet untouched by vanity—achieve beyond everyone's hopes. I come back to remind the overachiever that she is more than just a runner. I come back to signal the middle-of-the-packers that just doing this hard thing every day will bring immeasurable personal rewards." Despite the low pay and difficult moments from both parents and athletes, writes Flanagan, "I want to be here to tell the wounded fighter who suffered terrible personal loss and who treats every race like a test of courage that she will be OK. I want to assure the striver— the gentle soul who always goes out too fast, so eager is she to excel—that trying hard is the way to live, cool cliques be damned. And I'm here to show my own kids that sharing your talents with others is valuable, even when it's not easy."[8]

In declaring this impressive credo, coach Flanagan never once mentions God, Jehovah, or Allah, nor does she bring Jesus into the picture. Yet she represents the healthiest, most wholesome features of a religious effort that began almost two centuries ago to bring God and sports together.

**NOTES**
**ACKNOWLEDGMENTS**
**INDEX**

# NOTES

## Introduction

1. Robert J. Higgs and Michael C. Braswell, *An Unholy Alliance: The Sacred and Modern Sports* (Macon, GA: Mercer University Press, 2004), 1, 12.

2. Gary Smith, "Blood Relations," *Sports Illustrated,* April 17, 2006), 54–62.

3. Thorstein Veblen, *The Theory of the Leisure Class: An Economic Study of Institutions* (New York: New American Library, 1953, orig. pub. 1899), 195–197.

4. For a definition of "modern" sport, see Allen Guttmann, *From Ritual to Record: The Nature of Modern Sports* (New York: Columbia University Press, 1978).

5. Norbert Elias, *The Civilizing Process,* 2 vols. (Oxford: Blackwell, 1978).

6. Joseph L. Price, "The Super Bowl as a Religious Ritual," *Christian Century* 101, no. 6 (22 Feb. 1984): 190–191.

7. On Faith Nights, see Reid Chernier, "If You Billed It around Faith, They Will Surely Come," *USA Today,* 21 July 2005; and Warren St. John, "Sports, Songs, and Salvation on Faith Night at the Stadium," *New York Times,* 2 June 2006.

## 1. Old Gods and Games

1. For the origins of sport, see Johan Huizinga, *Homo Ludens: A Study of the Play Element in Culture* (Boston: Beacon, 1950); Allen Guttmann, *From Ritual to Record: The Nature of Modern Sports* (New York: Columbia University Press, 1978); and R. Brasch, *How Did Sports Begin? A Look at the Origins of Man at Play* (New York: McKay, 1970).

2. Theodore Stern, *The Rubber-Ball Game of the Americas* (New York: Augustin, 1949), is a useful older account written prior to many important archaeological discoveries. Fifteen essays in *The Mesoamerican Ballgame,* ed. Vernon L. Scarborough and David R. Wilcox (Tucson: University of Arizona Press, 1991), represent the best of the more recent scholarship.

3. For a more elaborate rendition of the twins' myth, see Karl Taube, *Aztec and*

*Maya Myths* (Austin: University of Texas Press, 1993), 59–60; see also Susan B. Gillespie, "Ballgames and Boundaries," in Scarborough and Wilcox, eds., *Mesoamerican Ballgame*, 320–324.

4. Morris Edward Opler, "The Jacarilla Apache Ceremonial Relay Race," *American Anthropologist* 46 (January–March 1944): 75–97; Allen Guttmann, *A Whole New Ball Game: An Interpretation of American Sports* (Chapel Hill: University of North Carolina Press, 1988), 21.

5. Thomas Vennum, Jr., *American Indian Lacrosse: Little Brother of War* (Washington, DC: Smithsonian Institution Press, 1994).

6. Stewart Culin, *Games of the North American Indians* (New York: Dover, 1975), 574–586; James Mooney, "The Cherokee Ball Play," *American Anthropologist* 3 (1890): 105–132.

7. Culin, *Games of the North American Indians*, 586–587.

8. See William J. Baker, "Traditional Sports, Africa," in *Encyclopedia of World Sport: From Ancient Times to the Present,* ed. David Levinson and Karen Christiansen, 3 vols. (Santa Barbara, CA: ABC-CLIO, 1996), 3:1062–1067; and Sigrid Paul, "The Wrestling Tradition and Its Social Functions," *in Sport in Africa: Essays in Social History,* ed. William J. Baker and James A. Mangan (New York: Africana, 1987), 23–46.

9. Homer, *The Iliad,* trans. Robert Fitzgerald (Garden City, NY: Anchor Press/Doubleday, 1974), 559.

10. See E. Norman Gardiner, *Athletics of the Ancient World* (Oxford: Clarendon, 1930); and H. A. Harris, *Sport in Greece and Rome* (London: Thames and Hudson, 1972).

11. For the Greek Olympics, see Ludwig Drees, *Olympia: Gods, Artists, and Athletes,* trans. Gerald Onn (New York: Praeger, 1968), and M. I. Finley and H. W. Pleket, *The Olympic Games: The First Thousand Years* (London: Chatto and Windus, 1976).

12. *Pindar's Victory Songs,* trans. Frank J. Nisetich (Baltimore: Johns Hopkins University Press, 1980).

13. For the Roman spectacles, see Auguet Roland, *Cruelty and Civilization: The Roman Games* (New York: Humanities, 1972); Alan Cameron, *Circus Factions: Blues and Greens at Rome and Byzantium* (Oxford: Clarendon, 1976); and Keith Hopkins, "Murderous Games," *History Today* 33 (June 1983): 16–22.

14. Richard Franklin DeVoe, "The Christians and the Games: The Relationship between Christianity and the Roman Games from the First through the Fifth Centuries, A.D." (Ph.D. diss., Texas Tech University, 1987).

15. Tertullian, *Apologeticus* and *De Spectaculis,* trans. G. R. Glover (London: Heinemann, 1931), 230–301.

16. Ibid., 295.

17. See Robert W. Henderson, *Ball, Bat, and Bishop: The Origins of Ball Games* (New York: Rockport, 1947).

18. See Thomas S. Hendricks, *Disputed Pleasures: Sport and Society in Preindustrial England* (Westport, CT: Greenwood Press, 1991), 13–68.

19. See Derek Birley, *Sport and the Making of Britain* (Manchester: Manchester University Press, 1993), 26–47.

20. For Scaino, see *The Oxford Companion to Sports and Games,* ed. John Arlott (London: Oxford University Press, 1975), 827–828.

21. Quoted in Deobold B. van Dalen and Bruce L. Bennett, *A World History of Physical Education: Cultural, Philosophical, Comparative* (Englewood Cliffs, NJ: Prentice Hall, 1971), 145.

22. For English Puritans at play, see Dennis Brailsford, *Sport and Society: Elizabeth to Anne* (London: Routledge and Kegan Paul, 1969); Robert W. Malcolmson, *Popular Recreations in English Society, 1700–1850* (Cambridge: Cambridge University Press, 1973), 5–14; Joachim Ruhl, "Religion and Amusements in Sixteenth and Seventeenth Century England: 'Time Might Be Better Bestowed, and Besides We See Sin Acted,'" *British Journal of Sport History* 1, no. 2 (September 1984): 125–165.

23. James Tait, "The Declaration of Sports for Lancashire," *English Historical Review* 32 (October 1917): 561–568.

24. William J. Baker, *Sports in the Western World,* rev. ed. (Urbana: University of Illinois Press, 1988), 80–81.

25. On the Puritans in New England, see Hans-Peter Wagner, *Puritan Attitudes toward Recreation in Early Seventeenth-Century New England* (Frankfurt am Main: Peter Lang, 1982); Bruce C. Daniels, *Puritans at Play: Leisure and Recreation in Colonial New England* (New York: St. Martin's Press, 1995); Nancy L. Struna, *People of Prowess: Sport, Leisure, and Labor in Early Anglo-America* (Urbana: University of Illinois Press, 1996).

26. For the historiographical shift on Puritan attitudes toward sport, see Daniels, *Puritans at Play,* 3–15 (for Mencken, see 1–2), and Guttmann, *Whole New Ball Game,* 23–26.

27. Edmund S. Morgan, *The Puritan Dilemma: The Story of John Winthrop* (Boston: Little, Brown, 1958), 8–12.

28. See Nancy Struna, "Puritans and Sport: The Irretrievable Tide of Change," *Journal of Sport History* 4, no. 1 (Spring 1977): 10–13; and Struna, *People of Prowess,* 84–86.

29. On taverns and sports," see Struna, *People of Prowess,* 142–164; see also Steven J. Overman, *The Influence of the Protestant Ethic on Sport and Recreation* (Aldershot: Avebury, 1997).

30. Daniels, *Puritans at Play,* 97–99; Struna, *People of Prowess,* 79–80.

31. Daniels, *Puritans at Play,* 168; and Samuel Eliot Morison, *Harvard College in the Seventeenth Century,* 2 vols. (Cambridge: Harvard University Press, 1936), 1:117.

32. Daniels, *Puritans at Play,* 207–208.

33. Quoted in David Hackett Fischer, *Albion's Seed: Four British Folkways in America* (New York: Oxford University Press, 1989), 147.

34. Ibid., 148–151. For a more detailed account of the Rowley scene, see Struna, *People of Prowess,* 74–76.

35. Thomas J. Wertenbaker, *Princeton, 1746–1896* (Princeton: Princeton University Press, 1946), 194.

36. Ronald A. Smith, *Sports and Freedom: The Rise of Big-Time College Athletics* (New York: Oxford University Press, 1988), 9. T. H. Breen, "Horses and Gentlemen: The Cult of Gambling among the Gentry of Virginia," *William and Mary Quarterly* 34 (April 1977): 239–257; Fischer, *Albion's Seed,* 361.

37. Elliott J. Gorn, "'Gouge and Bite, Pull Hair and Scratch': The Social Significance of Fighting in the Southern Backcountry," *American Historical Review* 90 (February 1985): 18–43.

38. Ibid.; see also Elliott J. Gorn and Warren Goldstein, *A Brief History of American Sports* (New York: Hill and Wang, 1993), 26–29.

## 2. The Road to Brawnville

1. See Chapter 7, "New Standards for Old Sports," in my *Sports in the Western World* (Urbana: University of Illinois Press, 1988).

2. Arthur C. Cole, "Our Sporting Grandfathers: The Cult of Athletics at Its Source," *Atlantic Monthly* 150 (July 1932): 91; William G. McLoughlin, *The Meaning of Henry Ward Beecher: An Essay on the Shifting Values of Mid-Victorian America, 1840–1870* (New York: Alfred A. Knopf, 1970), 12. For a more pleasant, playful image of the elder Beecher, see Marie Caskey, *Chariot of Fire: Religion and the Beecher Family* (New Haven: Yale University Press, 1978), 5–6, 17–18, 24.

3. Henry Ward Beecher, "Athletic Sports," *Herald of Health and Journal of Physical Culture* 8 (September 1866): 113. Beecher might well have been parodying his father's contemporary, John Pierpont, who had described his "bodily exercise" just a month earlier in the same journal. Minister of the Hollis Street Unitarian Church in Boston, Pierpont eschewed gymnastics, billiards, and even boating, but regularly walked, puttered at carpentry, took a cold shower daily, and kept a fastidious record of all his physical activities that "profiteth a great deal": "Personal Habits," *Herald of Health and Journal of Physical Culture* 8 (August 1866): 79–80.

4. Thomas Wentworth Higginson, *Out-Door Papers* (Boston: Lee and Shepard, 1886), 19, originally published as "Saints, and Their Bodies," *Atlantic Monthly* 1 (March 1858): 582–595.

5. Edward Everett Hale, *A New England Boyhood and Other Bits of Autobiography* (Boston: Little, Brown, 1900), 29–31. For the German Lutheran origins of gymnastics, see Mandell, *Sport,* 158–162, and Bruce L. Bennett, "The Curious Relationship of Religion and Physical Education," *Journal of Health, Physical Education and Recreation* 41 (September 1970): 69–71.

6. Hale, *New England Boyhood,* 200–201; Mary Thatcher Higginson, *Thomas Wentworth Higginson: The Story of His Life* (Boson: Houghton Mifflin, 1914), 25–27.

7. Edward E. Hale, Jr., *The Life and Letters of Edward Everett Hale,* 2 vols. (Boston:

Little, Brown, 1917), 1:44. For Hale's reference to "tumultuous throngs," see Hale, *New England Boyhood*, 200; for Higginson's football reminiscences, see M. Higginson, *Thomas Wentworth Higginson*, 25, 27; and Thomas Wentworth Higginson, *Cheerful Yesterdays* (Cambridge, MA: Riverside Press, 1900), 61. For the medieval and early modern history of the game, see Baker, *Sports in the Western World*, 47–48, 119–123, 127–128.

8. Quoted in Elliott J. Gorn, *The Manly Art: Bare-Knuckle Prize Fighting in America* (Ithaca, NY: Cornell University Press, 1986), 62.

9. Gorn, *Manly Art*, 63, 96.

10. Hale, *Life and Letters*, 1:287. For a succinct explanation of the movement of American Protestant thought from Puritanism to liberalism by way of revivalistic evangelicalism, see Lloyd J. Averill, *American Theology in the Liberal Tradition* (Philadelphia: Westminster Press, 1967), 54–60.

11. Hale, *Life and Letters*, 1:138, 167. Thomas Wentworth Higginson once referred to a vigorous leader seizing "the rudder of the age, as he grasped the oar, the bat, or the plough": Higginson, *Out-Door Papers*, 8.

12. Hale, *New England Boyhood*, 178, and *Life and Letters*, 1:24, 39.

13. Sydney E. Ahlstrom, *A Religious History of the American People* (New Haven: Yale University Press, 1972), 398, 400–401; see also Daniel W. Howe, *The Unitarian Conscience: The Harvard Moral Philosophers, 1805–1861* (Cambridge, MA: Harvard University Press, 1970).

14. Ahlstrom, *Religious History*, 403–414, 418–420; Martin E. Marty, *Righteous Empire: The Protestant Experience in America* (New York: Dial Press, 1970), 78–88.

15. See George M. Marsden, *The Evangelical Mind and the New School Presbyterian Experience* (New Haven: Yale University Press, 1970).

16. Marty, *Righteous Empire*, 91–94; see also Marsden, *Evangelical Mind*, 31–58; Timothy L. Smith, *Revivalism and Social Reform: American Protestantism on the Eve of the Civil War* (New York: Harper and Row, 1965).

17. For a specific example of abolitionist-antislavery disagreement involving Lyman Beecher and Charles G. Finney, see McLoughlin, *Meaning of Henry Ward Beecher*, 13.

18. Ahlstrom, *Religious History*, 399.

19. Henry Ward Beecher, *Seven Lectures to Young Men, on Various Important Subjects; Delivered before the Young Men of Indianapolis, Indiana, during the Winter of 1843–4* (Indianapolis, 1844). By 1925 this volume had gone through no fewer than ten editions. For the best critical studies of Beecher, see Clifford E. Clark, Jr., *Henry Ward Beecher: Spokesman for a Middle-Class America* (Urbana: University of Illinois Press, 1978); and McLoughlin, *Meaning of Henry Ward Beecher*.

20. See Clifford E. Clark, Jr., "The Changing Nature of Protestantism in Mid-nineteenth Century America: Henry Ward Beecher's *Seven Lectures to Young Men*," *Journal of American History* 57 (March 1971): 832–846. For commentary on Beecher's turning conservative (opposing labor unions, defending big business, displaying signs

of racism and jingoism) in his later years, see McLoughlin, *Meaning of Henry Ward Beecher,* 9–33.

21. Henry Ward Beecher, *Eyes and Ears* (Boston: Ticknor and Fields, 1862), 203–206; Beecher, "Athletic Sports," 113–115.

22. Henry Ward Beecher, "Uses of the Human Body," *Herald of Health and Journal of Physical Culture* 10 (July 1867): 9.

23. W. R. Greg, quoted in Bruce Haley, *The Healthy Body and Victorian Culture* (Cambridge, MA: Harvard University Press, 1978), 117.

24. For Kingsley's patriotism, see William J. Baker, "Charles Kingsley on the Crimean War: A Study in Chauvinism," *Southern Humanities Review* 4 (Summer 1970): 247–256.

25. T. C. Sandars, "Two Years Ago," *Saturday Review,* 21 Feb. 1857, 176; Frances Kingsley, *Charles Kingsley: His Letters and Memories of His Life,* 2 vols. (London: Kegan Paul, 1879), 2:74; R. B. Martin, *The Dust of Combat: A Life of Charles Kingsley* (London: Faber and Faber, 1959), 219. See also Malcolm Tozer, "Charles Kingsley and the 'Muscular Christian' Ideal of Manliness," *Physical Education Review* 8 (1985): 35–40.

26. See William E. Winn, "*Tom Brown's Schooldays* and the Development of "Muscular Christianity," *Church History* 29 (1960): 64–73. For the roots of the Tom Brown type of literature, see Gerald Redmond, "The First Tom Brown's Schooldays: Origins and Evolution of 'Muscular Christianity' in Children's Literature, 1762–1857," *Quest* 30 (1978): 4–18.

27. See "Thomas Hughes and the Public Schools," in Asa Briggs, *Victorian People: A Reassessment of Persons and Themes, 1851–67* (Harmondsworth: Penguin, 1965), 148–175. On Hughes's differences with Thomas Arnold, see esp. 159–166; see also P. J. Goodwin, "Thomas Arnold: So What?" *Physical Education Review* 7 (1984): 12–31.

28. Thomas Hughes, *Tom Brown at Oxford,* originally published in 1862.

29. Malcolm Tozer, "Thomas Hughes: 'Tom Brown' versus 'True Manliness,'" *Physical Education Review* 12 (1989): 44–48.

30. Charles Kingsley, *Health and Education* (New York: Appleton, 1874), 86.

31. For "public school" athleticism, see David Newsome, *Godliness and Good Learning: Four Studies on a Victorian Ideal* (London: John Murray, 1961); and J. A. Mangan, *Athleticism in the Victorian and Edwardian Public School: The Emergence and Consolidation of an Educational Ideology* (Cambridge: Cambridge University Press, 1981). For a good but brief overview, see Richard Holt, *Sport and the British: A Modern History* (Oxford: Clarendon Press, 1989), 74–86.

32. On Britain's role in the emergence of modern organized sport, see Robert W. Malcolmson, *Popular Recreations in English Society, 1700–1850* (Cambridge: Cambridge University Press, 1973); and J. H. Plumb, *The Commercialisation of Leisure* (Reading: University of Reading Press, 1973); see also Holt, *Sport and the British,* 12–73, and Richard D. Mandell, *Sport: A Cultural History* (New York: Columbia University Press,

1984), 132–157. For the imperial dissemination of British sport and sporting attitudes, see J. A. Mangan, *The Games Ethic and Imperialism: Aspects of the Diffusion of an Ideal* (London: Viking, 1986).

33. For example, see the scene in Lyman Beecher's parsonage in Litchfield, Connecticut: Caskey, *Chariot of Fire*, 28–30.

34. For easy passage into the massive bibliography documenting Anglo-American connections and interactions in the nineteenth century, see Charles S. Campbell, *From Revolution to Rapprochement: The United States and Great Britain, 1783–1900* (New York: John Wiley and Sons, 1974).

35. Higginson, *Out-Door Papers*, 7.

36. Hale, *Life and Letters*, 1:314; 2:30, 43–44.

37. Moses Coit Tyler, *The Brawnville Papers; Being Memorials of the Brawnville Athletic Club* (Boston: Fields, Osgood, 1869), 154. On the Jamaican issue, see Bernard Semmel, *Jamaican Blood and Victorian Conscience: The Governor Eyre Controversy* (Boston: Houghton Mifflin, 1963). For Tyler's stint in England, see Tyler, *Glimpses of England; Social, Political, Literary* (London: G. P. Putnam's Sons, 1898).

38. *Herald of Health and Journal of Physical Culture* 8 (1866): "English Pluck" (August): 56–58; "Muscular Christianity" (September): 97–99; "Concerning a Muscular Christian" (October): 120–122.

39. William Blaikie, "American Bodies," *Harper's Weekly* 27 (December 1883): 770. For Tyler's response to *Tom Brown's Schooldays*, see "English Pluck," 58; "Muscular Christianity," 98–99; *Brawnville Papers*, 161.

40. Higginson, *Out-Door Papers*, 14–15.

41. Tyler, "Muscular Christianity," 98, reprinted in *Brawnville Papers*, 161.

42. Hale, *Life and Letters*, 1:171. For the forces of urban growth in Hale's Boston, see Stephen Hardy, *How Boston Played: Sport, Recreation, and Community, 1865–1915* (Boston: Northeastern University Press, 1982), 21–40; for the English story, see Bruce Haley, *The Healthy Body and Victorian Culture* (Cambridge, MA: Harvard University Press, 1978).

43. E. Anthony Rotundo, "Body and Soul: Changing Ideals of American Middle-Class Manhood, 1770–1920," *Journal of Social History* 16 (Fall 1983): 29, 33; see also Stephen Nissenbaum, *Sex, Diet, and Debility in Jacksonian America: Sylvester Graham and Health Reform* (Westport, CT: Greenwood Press, 1980).

44. "Gymnastics," *Herald of Health and Journal of Physical Culture* 8 (September 1866): 112; O. B. Frothingham, "The Sacredness of the Body," *Herald of Health and Journal of Physical Culture* 9 (January 1867): 9.

45. J. C. Holbrook, "The Body as the Servant, and Not as a Lord," *Herald of Health and Journal of Physical Culture* 10 (October 1867): 171; Henry Ward Beecher, "The Human Body a Temple of the Holy Ghost," *Herald of Health and Journal of Physical Culture* 9 (June 1867): 272; see also Tyler, "Muscular Christianity," 98–99: "Muscular

Christianity is Christianity applied to the treatment and use of our bodies. It is an enforcement of the laws of health by the solemn sanctions of the New Testament."

46. Tyler, *Brawnville Papers*, 163–164.

47. James C. Whorton, *Crusaders for Fitness: The History of American Health Reformers* (Princeton: Princeton University Press, 1982), 7–8, 15.

48. Tyler, *Brawnville Papers*, 20.

49. Ibid., 30.

50. "Rev. Dr. Kirk on Physical Culture," *Herald of Health and Journal of Physical Culture* 6 (August 1865): 42; M. L. Holbrook, "Physical Culture for Youth," *Herald of Health and Journal of Physical Culture* 5 (May 1865): 129.

51. M. Higginson, *Thomas Wentworth Higginson*, 69. For good commentary on Higginson, see John A. Lucas, "Thomas Wentworth Higginson—Early Apostle of Health and Fitness," *Journal of Health, Physical Education, and Recreation* 42 (February 1971): 30–33.

52. M. Higginson, *Thomas Wentworth Higginson*, 138–139; Thomas Wentworth Higginson, *Letters and Journals of Thomas Wentworth Higginson, 1846–1906*, ed. Mary Thatcher Higginson (Boston: Houghton Mifflin, 1921), 90. Higginson tells of one young divine who lost his parish because he swam across the Merrimac River, and another because he beat a parishioner in a game of tenpins: *Out-Door Papers*, 5–6.

53. Higginson, *Out-Door Papers*, 5–6.

54. Higginson, "A Letter to a Dyspeptic," *Out-Door Papers*, 70. In "Saints, and Their Bodies," Higginson mentioned the boyhood memories evoked by athletic games (p. 17) and "a certain stigma of boyishness" that often accompanied the playing of games (p. 22). For Veblen's view, see his *Theory of the Leisure Class: An Economic Study of Institutions* (New York: New American Library, 1953, orig. pub. 1899), 167–171.

55. Higginson, *Out-Door Papers*, 30. In varying degrees, Edward Everett Hale, Henry Ward Beecher, and Mose Coit Tyler all agreed with Higginson in this romantic acclaim of nature. See, especially, Hale, *Life and Letters*, 1:71–72, 87–101, 114–120, 216–217. For Higginson on Emerson, see M. Higginson, *Thomas Wentworth Higginson*, 81–82, 270.

56. M. Higginson, *Thomas Wentworth Higginson*, 256–257, 376–377.

57. Thomas Wentworth Higginson, *Concerning All of Us* (New York: Harper and Brothers, 1892), 121.

58. Higginson, "Saints," *Out-Door Papers*, 20. Higginson died in 1911 at the age of eighty-seven.

## 3. Praying and Playing in the YMCA

1. "Muscular Christianity," *North Carolina Presbyterian*, 2 Jan. 1866, 186. For a similar view from the North, see Horace Bushnell, "The Age of the Homespun," *Work and Play; or Literary Varieties* (New York, 1864), 387–388.

2. Abiel Abbot Livermore], "Gymnastics," *North American Review* 86 (1855): 51–69.

3. Moses Coit Tyler, "Muscular Christianity," *Herald of Health and Journal of Physical Culture* 8 (September 1866): 97–98.

4. Thomas Wentworth Higginson, "Saints," "Dyspeptic," and "Barbarism and Civilization," *Out-Door Papers* (Boston: Lee and Shepard, 1886), 19, 71, 109–110; Henry Ward Beecher, "Athletic Sports," *Herald of Health and Journal of Physical Culture* 8 (September 1866): 113. For English comparisons in the middle-class control of urban leisure, see Peter Bailey, *Leisure and Class in Victorian England: Rational Recreation and the Contest for Control, 1830–1885* (London: Routledge and Kegan Paul, 1978); and Richard Holt, *Sport and the British: A Modern History* (Oxford: Clarendon Press, 1989), 136–148. For clear echoes of "rational recreation" in the United States, see "Recreation," *Herald of Health and Journal of Physical Culture* 4 (August 1864): 78.

5. See "Amateurism and the Victorians" in Holt, *Sport and the British,* 74–134; for the American acceptance of that mentality, see Ronald A. Smith, *Sports and Freedom: The Rise of Big-Time College Athletics* (New York: Oxford University Press, 1988), 165–174.

6. Catharine Beecher, *Physiology and Calisthenics for Schools and Families,* p. iv, quoted by Linda J. Borish, "The Robust Woman and the Muscular Christian: Catharine Beecher, Thomas Higginson, and Their Vision of American Society, Health, and Physical Activities," *International Journal of the History of Sport* 4 (September 1987): 144; Eliza Archard, "Muscle and Womanhood," *Herald of Health and Journal of Physical Culture* 10 (December 1867): 267. For an argument that vigorous ball games were "not well adapted to girls," see M. L. Holbrook, "Physical Culture for Youth," *Herald of Health and Journal of Physical Culture* 5 (May 1865): 129.

7. For a sterling exception, see Moses Coit Tyler, *The Brawnville Papers; Being Memorials of the Brawnville Athletic Club* (Boston: Fields, Osgood, 1869), 189–190: "The point on which the woman question turns is: What do you consider woman to be?" According to the fictitious Judge Fairplay, only if woman was considered a mindless, cackling, silly goose would she be "going out of her sphere" to participate in sports. For reflections on male-female differences in physical training, see Thomas Wentworth Higginson, *Concerning All of Us* (New York: Harper and Brothers, 1892), 122–123, and *Out-Door Papers,* 126–127.

8. Moses Coit Tyler, "English Pluck," *Herald of Health and Journal of Physical Culture* 8 (August 1866): 56–58; and Tyler, *Brawnville Papers,* 131.

9. Higginson, *Out-Door Papers,* 5; see Livermore, "Gymnastics," 53–59, and M. L. Holbrook, "Physical Culture," *Herald of Health* 4 (December 1864): 183–185.

10. For this process of feminization, see Ann Douglas, *The Feminization of American Culture* (New York: Knopf, 1977); Mary P. Ryan, *The Cradle of the Middle Class: The Family in Oneida County, New York, 1790–1865* (Cambridge: Cambridge University Press, 1981); and Barbara Welter, *Dimity Convictions: The American Woman in the*

*Nineteenth Century* (Athens: Ohio University Press, 1976), esp. the chapter entitled "The Feminization of American Religion," 83–102.

11. Quoted from Trollope's *Domestic Manners of the Americans* (New York, 1949, p. 75), in Welter, *Dimity Convictions*, 88.

12. Much of the following is taken from Clyde Binfield, *George Williams and the YMCA: A Study in Victorian Social Attitudes* (London: Heinemann, 1973).

13. Ibid., 120.

14. Ibid., 185, 273–274, 277.

15. Ibid., 276, 298. For other references to the amusement question in the early years of the YMCA in England, see 162–163, 300–301, 567; cf. Doreen M. Rosman, *Evangelicals and Culture* (London: Croom Helm, 1984), 3, for Sydney Smith's *bon mot* against "these gloomy people" who "hate pleasure and amusements."

16. For the contours of what radical journalist William Cobbett called "the puritanical school" (*Cobbett's Annual Register*, 20–27 Feb. 1802) in early nineteenth-century England, see Thomas Walter Laqueur, *Religion and Respectability: Sunday Schools and Working Class Culture, 1780–1850* (New Haven: Yale University Press, 1976); Brian Harrison, *Peaceable Kingdom: Stability and Change in Modern Britain* (Oxford: Clarendon Press, 1982); Ford K. Brown, *Fathers of the Victorians: The Age of Wilberforce* (Cambridge: Cambridge University Press, 1961); K. S. Inglis, *Churches and the Working Classes in Victorian England* (London: Routledge and Kegan Paul, 1963); and Rosman, *Evangelicals and Culture.*

17. On Finney's impact, see Binfield, *George Williams*, 17–21, 210–212; and J. E. Hodder Williams, *The Life of Sir George Williams, Founder of the Young Men's Christian Association* (New York: Association Press, 1906), 30–36.

18. Williams, *Life*, 35.

19. Ibid., 32.

20. Charles Howard Hopkins, *History of the YMCA in North America* (New York: Association Press, 1951), 18, 23–24; Cleveland E. Dodge, *"YMCA": A Century at New York (1852–1952)* (New York: Newcomen Society, 1953), 9–11.

21. Lawrence W. Fielding and Clark F. Wood, "The Social Control of Indolence and Irreligion: Louisville's First YMCA Movement, 1853–1871," *The Filson Club History Quarterly* 58 (April 1984): 219–236.

22. See Hopkins, *History of the YMCA*, 25–32, 34–39.

23. *Young Men's Magazine* 1 (May 1857): 25.

24. *Young Men's Magazine* 1 (August 1857): 148–151; (October 1857): 255. The editors of this magazine were less tolerant of "the fascinating seductions of the theatre, the casino, the gin-palace, and the gambling-saloon": (June 1857): 78.

25. Owen E. Peuce, ed., *The Hundred-Year Book: A Synoptic Review of Association History* (New York: Association Press, 1944), n.p., 1867 items; *The Watchman* 2 (November 1875): 4.

26. Elmer L. Johnson, *The History of YMCA Physical Education* (Chicago: Association Press, 1979), 22–25; cf. Hopkins, *History of the YMCA*, 32–34, and *Hundred-Year Book,* n.p., 1856 and 1857 items.

27. *Young Men's Magazine* 1 (July 1857): 137.

28. For "The YMCAs and the Civil War," see Hopkins, *History of the YMCA*, 84–98.

29. See Mayer N. Zald, *Organizational Change: The Political Economy of the YMCA* (Chicago: University of Chicago Press, 1970), 28–38.

30. Richard C. Morse, *My Life with Young Men* (New York: Association Press, 1918), 67; Dodge, "*YMCA,*" 19.

31. Johnson, *YMCA Physical Education,* 31–34; Morse, *Life with Young Men,* 67; J. Gardner Smith, "History of Physical Training in New York City and Vicinity in the Young Men's Christian Associations," *American Physical Education Review* 4 (1899): 303–308.

32. Smith, "Physical Training in New York City," 304; *Hundred-Year Book,* n.p., 1870 item; *The Watchman* 2 (March 1876): 6; Johnson, *YMCA Physical Education,* 38.

33. See L. L. Doggett, *History of the Boston YMCA* (Boston: privately published by the YMCA, 1901), and William B. Whiteside, *The Boston YMCA and Community Need: A Century's Evolution, 1851–1951* (New York: Association Press, 1951); I. E. Brown, *Young Men's Christian Association Buildings* (Chicago: W. W. Vanarsdale, 1885); M G. Ross, *The YMCA in Canada: The Chronicle of a Century* (Toronto: Ryerson Press, 1951).

34. Amid the massive bibliography on Moody and his evangelical tactics, probably the most balanced critique is James F. Findlay, Jr.'s *Dwight L. Moody: American Evangelist, 1837–1899* (Chicago: University of Chicago Press, 1969).

35. Morse, *Life with Young Men,* 74; Richard C. Morse, *History of the North American Young Men's Christian Associations* (New York: Association Press, 1913), 122–124. For Sankey's point of view, see Ira D. Sankey, *My Life and the Story of the Gospel Hymns* (New York: Bigelow and Main, 1906).

36. *Hundred-Year Book,* n.p., 1866 item; Morse, *Life with Young Men,* 66.

37. P. W. Coke, ed., "Some Significant Gleanings from the History of the Young Mens' Christian Association of Chicago" (1940), YMCA Collection, Box 7, Folder 4, Chicago Historical Society.

38. Hopkins, *History of the YMCA,* 188; on Hemmingway, see Johnson, *YMCA Physical Education,* 36.

39. John R. Patterson, "Recollections of Early Days of the Chicago YMCA" (1940), YMCA Collection, Box 7, Folder 4, Chicago Historical Society.

40. G. F. Thompson, "History of Physical Work in the YMCA," Association *Seminar* 12 (May 1904): 307; Hopkins, *History of the YMCA,* 247. See also William E. Wood, *Manual of Physical Exercises* (New York: Harper and Brothers, 1867).

41. In some cases, people were simply mesmerized by the circus crowd. Circus apparatus should be avoided "as you would a trick mule," warned one gym director. "When

they come in the 'actors' begin to 'act,' the others watch them because they cannot imitate, and all real beneficial work is at an end": Thomas C. Diggs, "Some Gymnasium Don'ts," *Young Men's Era* 17 (5 Feb. 1891): 90.

42. Johnson, *YMCA Physical Education,* 34–35; Doggett, *Boston YMCA,* 50.

43. D. D. Brink, *The Body Builder* (New York: Association Press, 1916), 10; "Short Stories about Physical Directors: Robert J. Roberts," *Young Men's Era* 19 (25 May 1893): 663–664; cf. Luther H. Gulick, "Robert J. Roberts and His Work," in *Home Dumb Bell Drill,* ed. R. J. Roberts (Springfield, MA: Springfield College pamphlet, 1894).

44. Johnson, *YMCA Physical Education,* 39–41; Hopkins, *History of the YMCA,* 249–250; Morse, *Life with Young Men,* 264; cf. Morse, *History,* 167–169.

45. Morse, *Life with Young Men,* 263–264.

46. Zald, *Organizational Change,* 44.

47. See Lawrence W. Fielding and Clark F. Wood, "From Religious Outreach to Social Entertainment: The Louisville YMCA's First Gymnasium, 1876–1880," *The Filson Club History Quarterly* 60 (April 1986): 239–256.

48. *Young Men's Christian Association Monthly Bulletin* 6 (Bangor, ME), June 1888.

49. *Hundred-Year Book,* p. 53.

50. Owen E. Pence, *The YMCA and Social Need: A Study in Institutional Adaptation* (New York: Association Press, 1939), 47, 75.

51. For that larger "culture of professionalism," see Robert Wiebe, *The Search for Order, 1877–1920* (New York: Hill and Wang, 1967); Paul Boyer, *Urban Masses and Moral Order in America, 1820–1920* (Cambridge, MA: Harvard University Press, 1978); Burton Bledstein, *The Culture of Professionalism: The Middle Class and the Development of Higher Education in America* (New York: W. W. Norton, 1976); Barbara Ehrenreich, *Fear of Falling: The Inner Life of the Middle Class* (New York: Harper Collins, 1989).

52. Dwight L. Moody and Robert McBurney were on the first board of trustees: *Hundred-Year Book,* n.p., 1885 item.

53. For the early history of Springfield College, see Leonard L. Doggett, *A Man and a School* (New York: Association Press, 1943).

54. Hopkins, *History of the YMCA,* 251–253; Morse, *Life with Young Men,* 265.

55. Johnson, *YMCA Physical Education,* 57–58.

56. For Roberts's views on competitive sports, see his many articles in *Young Men's Era:* "Hints to Competitive Workers," *Young Men's Era* 17 (5 Feb. 1891): 90; "The Boston Gymnasium," 18 (11 Feb. 1892): 182–183; "Value of Simple Work," 18 (24 March 1892): 373; "Competitive Athletic Work," 18 (2 June 1892): 693–694; "Boxing in Association Gymnasiums," 19 (21 Dec. 1893): 1425.

57. Roberts was born in 1849, Gulick in 1865.

58. Hopkins, *History of the YMCA,* 253.

59. Ibid., 246.

60. *The Watchman* 15 (3 Oct. 1889).

61. *Young Men's Era* 7 (8 Oct. 1891): 633. For more on the baseball question, see William J. Baker, "Disputed Diamonds: The YMCA Debate over Baseball in the Late 19th Century," *Journal of Sport History* 19 (Winter 1992): 257–262.

62. L. B. Smith, "Baseball," *Young Men's Era* 18 (2 June 1892): 692; O. E. Ryther, "Athletics," *Young Men's Era* 18 (16 June 1892): 758–759; *Young Men's Era* 18 (22 Sept. 1892): 1204. In 1892, J. Gardiner Smith connected specialization and prize winning as the beginnings of professionalism; see his "Athletic Problem in the Young Men's Christian Association," *Physical Education* 1 (April 1892): 33–35.

63. For the following, see William T. Ellis, *"Billy" Sunday: The Man and His Message* (Philadelphia: John C. Winston, 1914), 24, 31–34, 38, 40–44, 46–47.

64. Ibid., 70, 75, 77, 138–139.

65. See Ronald A. Smith, *Sports and Freedom: The Rise of Big-Time College Athletics* (New York: Oxford University Press, 1988), 165–174.

66. See William J. Baker, *Sports in the Western World* (Urbana: University of Illinois Press, 1988), 127–131.

67. Paul C. Phillips, "Rugby Football," *Young Men's Era* 17 (8 Oct. 1891): 632; cf. Luther H. Gulick, "Foot-ball Debate," *The Triangle* 1 (December 1891): 131–133.

68. "Foot Ball at the Association Training School, Springfield, Mass.," *The Triangle* 1 (February 1891): 6–8; "Foot Ball," *The Triangle* 1 (December 1891): 125–131; Hopkins, *History of the YMCA,* 259.

69. Gulick, "Foot-Ball Debate: Athletics at Chicago University," *Young Men's Era* 18 (10 Nov. 1896): 1431. Numerous invitations for Stagg to speak at churches, colleges, and clubs are in the A. A. Stagg Papers (Box 109, Folder 2) in the Department of Special Collections at the Joseph Regenstein Library, University of Chicago; for manuscript examples of Stagg's addresses, see Box 109, Folders 3 and 7; for a proud YMCA report on Stagg's sermonic efforts, see "Stagg at Rochester," *Young Men's Era* 18 (10 March 1892): 310.

70. "Physical Department," *Young Men's Era* 18 (20 Oct. 1892): 1332.

71. James B. Naismith, *Basketball: Its Origin and Development* (New York: Association Press, 1941), 22. On Naismith, see Bernice Larson Webb, *The Basketball Man: James Naismith* (Lawrence: University Press of Kansas, 1973); and John Dewar, "The Life and Professional Contributions of James Naismith," Ed.D. diss., Florida State University, 1965.

72. Naismith, *Basketball,* 23.

73. See Johnson, *YMCA Physical Education,* 86–97; for the geographical diffusion of basketball, see Naismith, *Basketball,* 100–160.

74. Johnson, *YMCA Physical Education,* 78; cf. Lawrence W. Fielding and Brenda G. Pitts, "The Battle over Athletic Priorities in the Lousiville YMCA, 1892–1912," *Canadian Journal of History of Sport* 20 (December 1989): 64–89.

75. Fielding and Pitts, "Battle," 80; J. Gardner Smith, "Physical Training in New York City," 303–308; Bangor YMCA *Monthly Bulletin* 12 (November 1893): 1.

76. See Steven A. Riess, "Sport and the Redefinition of American Middle-Class Masculinity," *International Journal of the History of Sport* 8 (May 1991): 5–27, esp. 16–17; E. Anthony Rotundo, "Body and Soul: Changing Ideals of American Middle Class Manhood, 1770–1920," *Journal of Social History* 16 (Fall 1983): 23–38.

77. Mary S. Sims, *The Natural History of a Social Institution—the Young Women's Christian Association* (New York: The Womans Press, 1936), 33, 40, 42.

78. Thomas Hughes, *Memoir of a Brother* (Boston: James R. Osgood, 1873), 18; Hughes, *The Manliness of Christ* (Boston: Houghton, Osgood and Co., 1880), 2–5, 20–21.

## 4. Sweetening the Gospel with Sport

1. See Paul Boyer, *Urban Masses and Moral Order in America, 1820–1920* (Cambridge, MA: Harvard University Press, 1978); and Robert Wiebe, *The Search for Order, 1877–1920* (New York: Hill and Wang, 1967).

2. For examples of this more ideological, or theological, explanation of the social gospel, see Robert T. Handy, ed., *The Social Gospel in America, 1870–1920: Gladden, Ely, Rauschenbusch* (New York: Oxford University Press, 1966); and Handy, *A Christian America: Protestant Hopes and Historical Realities* (New York: Oxford University Press, 1984), 134–158. The earliest standard history nicely blends sociological and theological causes: Charles Howard Hopkins, *The Rise of the Social Gospel in American Protestantism, 1865–1915* (New Haven: Yale University Press, 1940). For the Canadian social gospel in terms of Christian principles, see Roger Hutchinson, "The Canadian Social Gospel in the Context of Christian Social Ethics," and Benjamin G. Smillie, "The Social Gospel in Canada: A Theological Critique," in *The Social Gospel in Canada*, ed. Richard Allen (Ottawa: National Museums of Canada, 1975), 286–342.

3. Washington Gladden, *The Christian Pastor and the Working Church* (New York, 1898), 408–409.

4. Richard Holt, *Sport and the British: A Modern History* (Oxford: Clarendon Press, 1989), 138; Tony Mason, *Association Football and English Society, 1863–1915* (Sussex: Harvester Press, 1980), 24–25.

5. Holt, *Sport and the British*, 138, 264; and H. A. Harris, *Sport in Britain* (London: Paul, 1975), 76; cf. C. A. Lansbury, "Straight Bat and Modest Mind," *Victorian Periodicals Newsletter* 49 (Spring 1976): 9–18.

6. For more detail, see Holt, *Sport and the British*, 136–148; and James Walvin, *Leisure and Society, 1830–1950* (London: Longman, 1978), 1–125; for heavier documentation, see Hugh Cunningham, *Leisure in the Industrial Revolution, c. 1780–1880* (London: Croom Helm, 1980); Peter Bailey, *Leisure and Class in Victorian England: Rational Recreation and the Contest for Control, 1830–1885* (London: Routledge and Kegan Paul, 1978); and Chris Waters, *British Socialists and the Politics of Popular Culture, 1884–1914*

(Manchester: Manchester University Press, 1990). For an important shift in the nature of the "leisure question" around 1800, however, see Waters, p. 11.

7. W. S. Rainsford, *A Preacher's Story of His Work* (New York: Outlook, 1904), 60; and Rainsford, *The Story of a Varied Life: An Autobiography* (New York: Doubleday, Page, 1922), 64; cf. K. S. Inglis, "English Nonconformity and Social Reform, 1880–1900," *Past and Present 13* (April 1958): 83.

8. K. S. Inglis, *Churches and the Working Classes in Victorian England* (London: Routledge and Kegan Paul, 1963), 74–76, 78.

9. See Peter d'A. Jones, *The Christian Socialist Revival, 1877–1911: Religion, Class, and Social Conscience in Late-Victorian England* (Princteon: Princeton University Press, 1968).

10. Waters, *British Socialists and Popular Culture*, 86–87, 135–35; cf. Stanley Pierson, "John Trevor and the Labour Church Movement in England, 1891–1900," *Church History* 29 (1960): 463–478.

11. Owen Chadwick, *The Victorian Church*, Part 2 (New York: Oxford University Press, 1970), 317–318.

12. G. P. T. Finn, "Racism, Religion and Social Prejudice: Irish Catholic Clubs, Soccer and Scottish Society, I: The Historical Roots of Prejudice," *International Journal of the History of Sport* 8 (May 1991): 81–82. Individual clergymen, not churches, promoted sport in central Scotland: N. I. Tranter, "The Patronage of Organised Sport in Central Scotland, 1820–1900," *Journal of Sport History* 16 (Winter 1989): 227–247.

13. Holt, *Sport and the British*, 253–256.

14. Morris Mott, "The British Protestant Pioneers and the Establishment of Manly Sports in Manitoba, 1870–1886," *Journal of Sport History* 7 (Winter 1980): 25–36; cf. Gerald Redmond, "Some Aspects of Organized Sport and Leisure in Ninteenth-Century Canada," in *Sports in Canada: Historical Readings*, ed. Morris Mott (Toronto: Copp Clark Pitman, 1989), 83–85.

15. See David Brown, "Athleticism and Selected Private Schools in Canada," Ph.D. diss., University of Alberta, 1984.

16. Alan Metcalfe, *Canada Learns to Play: The Emergence of Organized Sport, 1807–1914* (Toronto: McClelland and Stewart, 1987), 41. For remarkably similar activities and pronouncements by a Congregationalist minister in Winnipeg, 1894–1900, see Morris Mott and John Allardyce, "'Curling Capital': How Winnipeg Became the Roaring Game's Leading City, 1876–1903," *Canadian Journal of History of Sport* 19 (May 1988): 5.

17. See Gerald Redmond, *The Sporting Scots of Nineteenth-Century Canada* (East Brunswick, NJ: Associated University Presses, 1982), 137–38.

18. *Canadian Churchman*, 1 Nov. 1900, 661, quoted in David Howell and Peter Lindsay, "Social Gospel and the Young Boy Problem 1895–1925," in Mott, *Sports in Canada*, 223.

19. *Canadian Epworth Era,* August 1901, 233, quoted in ibid., 222–223.

20. Metcalfe, *Canada Learns to Play,* 44, 59, 65.

21. David Francis Howell, "The Social Gospel in Canadian Protestantism, 1895–1925: Implications for Sport," Ph.D. diss., University of Alberta, 1980, 69, 121–125, 128. For later developments of the social gospel in Canada, see Richard Allen, *The Social Passion: Religion and Social Reform in Canada, 1914–28* (Toronto: University of Toronto Press, 1971), 3–17.

22. Washington Gladden, *Recollections* (Boston: Houghton Mifflin, 1909), 35.

23. Jacob Henry Dorn, *Washington Gladden: Prophet of the Social Gospel* (Columbus: Ohio State University Press, 1966), 29, 45, 47–48.

24. Dorn, *Gladden,* 46–48; Gladden, *Recollections,* 169.

25. Washington Gladden, *Amusements: Their Uses and Abuses* (North Adams, MA: James T. Robinson, 1866), 7, 9–10. Tyler distributed copies of the pamphlet to clergymen in the town of Rockford, Illinois (Dorn, *Gladden,* 47–48), suggesting that Gladden might well have mailed him a packet. He should have, for this sermon-pamphlet appeared in November 1866, on the heels of three articles by Tyler—"English Pluck," "Muscular Christianity," and "Concerning a Muscular Christian"—in the *Herald of Health and Journal of Physical Culture* 8 (August–October 1866). Gladden's terms, phrases, and general perspective strongly suggest that he read and was influenced by Tyler's essays.

26. Quoted in Dorn, *Gladden,* 57–58.

27. *Independent* 25 (2 Jan. 1873): 16, quoted in Dorn, *Gladden,* 57.

28. Quoted in Dorn, *Gladden,* 101.

29. Washington Gladden, *The Christian Way: Whither It Leads and How to Go On* (New York: Dodd, Mead, 1877), 106–112; "Christianity and Popular Amusements," *Century* 29 (January 1885): 392; *The Church and the Kingdom* (New York: Fleming H. Revell, 1894), 8.

30. Washington Gladden, *The Christian Pastor and the Working Church* (New York: Charles Scribner's Sons, 1898), 412.

31. Washington Gladden, *Social Salvation* (Boston: Houghton Mifflin, 1902), 10; and Gladden, *The Church in Modern Life* (Boston: Houghton Mifflin, 1908), 219–220; cf. Susan Curtis, *A Consuming Faith: The Social Gospel and Modern American Culture* (Baltimore: Johns Hopkins University Press, 1991), 45–47.

32. Washington Gladden, "The Church and Social Reform," *Christian Literature* 14 (1895–1896): 73.

33. Gladden, "Christianity and Popular Amusements," 387.

34. Dorn, *Gladden,* 99; Gladden, "Christianity and Popular Amusements," 386; and Gladden, *Christian Pastor,* 412–413.

35. For the churches' more general social service programs, see Henry F. May, *Protestant Churches and Industrial America* (New York: Harper and Row, 1967), 182–203;

and Aaron I. Abell, The *Urban Impact on American Protestantism, 1865–1900* (Cambridge, MA: Harvard University Press, 1943), 137–165. For an overview of Protestantism and play, see Richard A. Swanson, "The Acceptance and Influence of Play in American Protestantism," *Quest* 11 (December 1968): 58–70, an article derived from Swanson's "American Protestantism and Play: 1865–1915," Ph.D. diss., Ohio State University, 1967. For surveys of church recreation, see Rufus Rockwell Wilson, "Institutional Church and Its Work," *Outlook* 54 (29 Aug. 1896): 384; Henry A. Atkinson, *The Church and the People's Play* (Boston: Pilgrim Press, 1915); Richard Henry Edwards, *Christianity and Amusements* (New York: Association Press, 1915); Herbert Wright Gates, *Recreation and the Church* (Chicago: University of Chicago Press, 1917); "Recreation as a Function of the Church," *The Playground* 14 (August 1920): 283–290; and Albert Ben Wegener, *Church and Community Recreation* (New York: Macmillan, 1924).

36. Like basketball, softball was invented in the 1890s. See Terrence Cole, "'A Purely American Game': Indoor Baseball and the Origins of Softball," *International Journal of the History of Sport* 7 (September 1990): 287–296.

37. George Willis Cooke, "The Institutional Church," *New England Magazine* 14 (August 1896): 653–655; "Berkeley Temple, and Kindred Local Work," in *Triumphs of the Cross: or, the Supremacy of Christianity as an Uplifting Force,* ed. E. P. Tenney (Boston: Balch Brothers, 1895), 536–539; "Berkeley Temple's Tenth Anniversary," *Outlook* 57 (20 Nov. 1897): 730–731; Gladden, *Christian Pastor,* 402–403; Stephen Hardy, *How Boston Played: Sport, Recreation, and Community, 1865–1915* (Boston: Northeastern University Press, 1982), 57.

38. Hopkins, *Rise of the Social Gospel,* 105.

39. Quoted in Roy Rosenzweig, *Eight Hours for What We Will: Workers and Industrial Leisure in an Industrial City, 1870–1920* (Cambridge: Cambridge University Press, 1983), 57.

40. Ibid., 55. For Sullivan's popularity, see Elliott J. Gorn, *The Manly Art: Bare-Knuckle Prize Fighting in America* (Ithaca, NY: Cornell University Press, 1986), 224–227, 245–247; and Michael T. Isenberg, *John L. Sullivan and His America* (Urbana: University of Illinois Press, 1988).

41. Gates, *Recreation and the Church,* 124–125.

42. John L. Scudder, "The Tabernacle Church, and People's Palace," in Tenney, ed., *Triumphs of the Cross,* 524–525.

43. Ibid., 522, 525; Cooke, "Institutional Church," 658; Gladden, *Christian Pastor,* 404–405.

44. Scudder, "Tabernacle Church," 521–523; "Recreation as a Function of the Church," 289.

45. Rainsford, *Varied Life,* 67, 338; and Cooke, "Institutional Church," 456; cf. W. S. Rainsford, "What Can We Do for the Poor?" *The Forum* 40 (April 1891): 119.

46. See Rainsford's own accounts in *Preacher's Story* and *Varied Life,* and a full de-

scription of St. George's program in George Hodges and John Reichert, *The Administration of an Institutional Church* (New York: Harper and Brothers, 1906); cf. William Kirkus, "New York Mission Work of the Protestant Episcopal Church," in Tenney, ed., *Triumphs of the Cross*, 530–533; Cooke, "Institutional Church," 656–659; and Abell, *Urban Impact on American Protestantism*, 147–150.

47. Rainsford, *Preacher's Story*, 48–49, 58.

48. Ibid., 7–16; *Varied Life*, 114–115, 302.

49. Rainsford, *Preacher's Story*, 22; *Varied Life*, 133.

50. As Walter Rauschenbusch put it, "The starting point of the social movement is the conviction of the inherent worth of a human being": from "The Ideals of Social Reformers," *American Journal of Sociology* 2 (July 1896–May 1897): 202–219, in Handy, ed., *Social Gospel in America*.

51. Rainsford, *Varied Life*, 108–109, 152–153; *Preacher's Story*, 166, 217. For "efforts to formulate an adequate Christian sociology" in universities, seminaries, and institutes, and to put "sociology in the service of religion" around the turn of the century, see Hopkins, *Rise of the Social Gospel*, 105–106, 162–170, 257–279.

52. Rainsford, *Preacher's Story*, 61–69; *Varied Life*, 145, 175–176, 178, 191.

53. Rainsford, *Varied Life*, 180–183; *Preacher's Story*, 106–109; cf. Rainsford, *The Reasonableness of the Religion of Jesus* (Boston: Houghton Mifflin, 1913), 204–262, and Washington Gladden's similar contention that "the whole world is redeemed" in an exerpt from his *Church and the Kingdom* (1894) in Handy, ed., *Social Gospel in America*, 115.

54. Rainsford, *Varied Life*, 181, 183, 195.

55. Ibid., 200, 208–2ll; notes by Henry Potter and John Reichert in Hodges and Reichert, *Administration of an Institutional Church*, xi and xix–xx.

56. Rainsford, *Varied Life*, 200–201.

57. See chapters "The Social Gospel" and "Christianizing the Social Order" in James Thayer Addison, *The Episcopal Church in the United States, 1789–1931* (New York: Charles Scribner's Sons, 1951), 280–289, 320–329; cf. May, *Protestant Churches and Industrial America*, 182–187.

58. Rainsford, *Varied Life*, 249, 256; Kirkus, "New York Mission Work," 533.

59. Rainsford, *Varied Life*, 215, 218; Hodges and Reichert, *Administration of an Institutional Church*, 221, 230.

60. Rainsford, *Varied Life*, 251, 302, 308; and *Preacher's Story*, 160; Hodges and Reichert, *Administration of an Institutional Church*, 16.

61. Rainsford, *Varied Life*, 271, 302. According to Rainsford, Morgan was a religiously conservative person who was more comfortable with a simple "plan of salvation" than with liberal reform: ibid., "My Senior Warden," 277–292.

62. Hodges and Reichert, *Administration of an Institutional Church*, 230–231; Harold Seymour, *Baseball: The People's Game* (New York: Oxford University Press, 1990), 63; Gladden, *Christian Pastor*, 406; Kirkus, "New York Mission Work," 533.

63. *New York Times,* 13 June and 11 Dec. 1904; Wegener, *Church and Community Recreation,* 125. For problems in enforcing the Sunday School Athletic League's written and unwritten codes of conduct, see Gates, *Recreation and the Church,* 106–109.

64. C. Waldo Cherry, "The Church's Method of Reaching Men," *Auburn Seminary Record* 1 (March 1907): 28–29; Gates, *Recreation and the Church,* 106; "Recreation in the Church," *Literary Digest* 53 (29 July 1916): 256; "The Sunday School Athletic Association in Hagerstown, Maryland," *Playground* 16 (June 1922): 98; Ross W. Sanderson, "An Experiment in Church Cooperation," *Playground* 19 (August 1925): 251–252.

65. For turn-of-the-century statistical surveys that support this negative assessment, see Boyer, *Urban Masses and Moral Order,* 138–139; but see Le Roy E. Bowman, "Community Recreation," in *Christianity and Social Advernturing,* ed. Jerome Davis (New York: Century, 1927), 280, for much more positive answers to questionnaires in the 1920s. For "some churches with recreational features," see Abell, *Urban Impact on American Protestantism,* 147–161; and Wegener, *Church and Community Recreation,* 239–243.

66. Seymour, *Baseball,* 62; *Harper's Weekly* 33 (13 July 1889), 551; "Church Work in Philadelphia," *Outlook* 55 (17 April 1897): 1086; C. Allyn Russell, "William Bell Riley: Architect of Fundamentalism," *Minnesota History* 43 (Spring 1973): 20.

67. Scudder quoted in Cooke, "Institutional Church," 658.

68. Edwards, *Christianity and Amusements,* 17.

69. "Recreation as a Function of the Church," 287; Wegener, *Church and Community Recreation,* 242; Gates, *Recreation and the Church,* 134.

70. Gates, *Recreation and the Church,* x, 22, 117.

71. See Jay P. Dolan, *The American Catholic Experience: A History from Colonial Times to the Present* (Garden City, NY: Doubleday, 1985).

## 5. When Dixie Took a Different Stand

1. Pete Daniel, *Standing at the Crossroads: Southern Life since 1900* (New York: Hill and Wang, 1986), 4; Samuel S. Hill, Jr., *The South and the North in American Religion* (Athens: University of Georgia Press, 1980), 10.

2. *Raleigh News and Observer,* 6 Dec. 1903, quoted in Frederick A. Bode, *Protestantism and the New South: North Carolina Baptists and Methodists in Political Crisis, 1894–1903* (Charlottesville: University Press of Virginia, 1975), 18–19. For religious homogeneity in the South, see George B. Tindall, *The Ethnic Southerners* (Baton Rouge: Louisiana State University Press, 1976), 1–21; Charles Reagan Wilson, *Baptized in Blood: The Religion of the Lost Cause, 1865–1920* (Athens: University of Georgia Press, 1980), 2–3; Hill, *South and North,* 126–130; and Kenneth K. Bailey, *Southern White Protestantism in the Twentieth Century* (New York: Harper, 1964), 17–18.

3. E. Merle Coulter, *The South during Reconstruction, 1865–1877* (Baton Rouge: Louisiana State University Press, 1947), 300.

4. *Cincinnati-American Christian Review,* October 1875, quoted in William R. Hogan, "Sin and Sports," in *Motivations in Play, Games and Sports,* ed. Ralph Slovenko and James A. Knight (Springfield, IL: Charles C. Thomas, [1967]), 127; cf. Rufus B. Spain, *At Ease in Zion: Social History of Southern Baptists, 1865–1900* (Nashville: Vanderbilt University Press, 1961), 22.

5. Compare the virtual absence of any mention of a southern social gospel in a 1940 classic, Charles Howard Hopkins, *The Rise of the Social Gospel in American Protestantism, 1865–1915* (New Haven: Yale University Press, 1940), to a chapter entitled "Voices from the New South" in a book edited by Hopkins and Ronald C. White, Jr., almost forty years later, *The Social Gospel: Religion and Reform in Changing America* (Philadelphia: Temple University Press, 1976), 80–100. Examples of revisionism include John Lee Eighmy, "Religious Liberalism in the South during the Progressive Era," *Church History* 38 (September 1969): 359–372; Eighmy, *Churches in Cultural Captivity: A History of the Social Attitudes of Southern Baptists* (Knoxville: University of Tennessee Press, 1972), 57–92; Dewey W. Grantham, *Southern Progressivism: The Reconciliation of Progress and Tradition* (Knoxville: University of Tennessee Press, 1938); and J. Wayne Flynt, "Southern Protestantism and Reform, 1890–1920," in *Varieties of Southern Religious Experience,* ed. Samuel S. Hill (Baton Rouge: Louisiana State University Press, 1988), 135–157. For the debilitating factor of race on religious thought in the South, see William G. McLoughlin, *Modern Reivalism* (New York: Ronald Press, 1959), 136.

6. See Wilson, *Baptized in Blood;* and Bode, *Protestantism and the New South,* 17; cf. Carl N. Degler, *Place over Time* (Baton Rouge: Louisiana State University Press, 1976).

7. David Edwin Harrell, Jr., "The Evolution of Plain-Folk Religion in the South, 1835–1920," in Hill, ed., *Varieties of Southern Religious Experience,* 46; Victor I. Masters, *The Country Church in the South* (Atlanta: Home Mission Board of the Southern Baptist Convention, 1916), 15–21; and H. V. Morse and Edmund DeS. Brunner, *The Town and Country Church in the United States* (New York: George H. Doran Co., 1923), 26.

8. W. J. Cash, *The Mind of the South* (New York: Vintage, 1941), 52–56; Dickson D. Bruce, Jr., *Violence and Culture in the Antebellum South* (Austin: University of Texas Press, 1979). For variations on a single competitive theme, compare lowcountry gentlemen in T. H. Breen, "Horses and Gentlemen: The Cultural Significance of Gambling among the Gentry of Virginia," *William and Mary Quarterly* 34 (April 1977): 239–257, with backcountry mountaineers in Elliott J. Gorn, "'Gouge and Bite, Pull Hair and Scratch': The Social Significance of Fighting in the Southern Backcountry," *American Historical Review* 90 (February 1985): 18–43. On the ethics of honor, see Bertram Wyatt-Brown, *Southern Honor: Ethics and Behavior in the Old South* (New York: Oxford University Press, 1982); cf. Wyatt-Brown's *Yankee Saints and Southern Sinners* (Baton Rouge: Louisiana State University Press, 1985).

9. Ted Ownby, *Subduing Satan: Religion, Recreation, and Manhood in the Rural South, 1865–1920* (Chapel Hill: University of North Carolina Press, 1990), 104–105.

10. Dale A. Somers, *The Rise of Sport in New Orleans, 1850–1900* (Baton Rouge: Louisiana State University Press, 1972), 13. For the lack of church-sponsored sport in the South, see Ownby, *Subduing Satan*, 122–143; for similar reservations about recreational activities among northern Methodists, see "Church Amusements," *Christian Advocate* 72 (28 Oct. 1897): 6; and *Christian Advocate* 74 (27 June 1899): 19.

11. Quoted in Coulter, *South during Reconstruction*, 303–304.

12. Ibid., 297; Sam S. Jones, *Sam Jones' Revival Sermons* (New York: Fleming H. Revell, 1912), 141. For more on Jones, see Edward L. Ayers, *The Promise of the New South: Life after Reconstruction* (New York: Oxford University Press, 1992), 173–178.

13. *Alabama Christian Advocate*, 22 Nov. 1894.

14. Somers, *Rise of Sport in New Orleans*, 56, 172; Randy Roberts, "Boxing," in *Encyclopedia of Southern Culture*, ed. Charles Reagan Wilson and William Ferris (Chapel Hill: University of North Carolina Press, 1980), 1214–1215; Jeffrey T. Sammons, *Beyond the Ring: The Role of Boxing in American Society* (Urbana: University of Illinois Press, 1988), 6–10.

15. Paul Magriel, "Tom Molineaux: Career of an American Negro Boxer in England and Ireland, 1809–18," *Phylon* 12 (December 1951): 320–336; and Carl B. Cone, "The Molineaux-Cribb Fight, 1810: Wuz Tom Molineaux Robbed?" *Journal of Sport History* 9 (Winter 1982): 83–91.

16. Ayers, *Promise of the New South*, 312.

17. *Christian Advocate*, 11 Feb. 1897; cf. 18 Feb. and 25 March 1897 editorials against pugilism. Spain, *At Ease in Zion*, 172; cf. Hunter Dickinson Farish, *The Circuit Rider Dismounts: A Social History of Southern Methodism, 1865–1900* (Richmond: Dietz Press, 1938), 353.

18. Ownby, *Subduing Satan*, 83; *New Orleans Daily Picayune*, 5 Feb. 1882, quoted in Somers, *Rise of Sport in New Orleans*, 166.

19. Sammons, *Beyond the Ring*, 12–15; Michael T. Isenberg, *John L. Sullivan and His America* (Urbana: University of Illinois Press, 1888), 311–319.

20. Sammons, *Beyond the Ring*, 20.

21. Coulter, *South during Reconstruction*, 301–302; Ayers, *Promise of the New South*, 310–311. For an overview, see John DiMeglio, "Baseball," in Wilson and Ferris, eds., *Encyclopedia of Southern Culture*, 1210–1211.

22. Farish, *Circuit Rider Dismounts*, 352; *Alabama Christian Advocate*, 10 Sept. 1903.

23. Ayers, *Promise of the New South*, 311; Farish, *Circuit Rider Dismounts*, 352.

24. Spain, *At Ease in Zion*, 171; W. T. Ussery, "Ethics of Base Ball," *Tennessee Baptist Reflector*, 22 Oct. 1903, quoted in William A. Link, *The Paradox of Southern Progressivism, 1880–1930* (Chapel Hill: University of North Carolina Press, 1992), 117. For another tirade against the "idleness, vice and general demoralization" of professional baseball, see "Let It Go for Good," *Christian Advocate*, 6 Oct. 1892.

25. Somer, *Rise of Sport in New Orleans*, 132–136.

26. Ownby, *Subduing Satan*, 83; John P. Ralls, "Baseball: What of It?" *Alabama Christian Advocate*, 10 Sept. 1903; Link, *Paradox of Southern Progressivism*, 55.

27. *Christian Advocate*, 30 April 1887, quoted in Farish, *Circuit Rider Dismounts*, 339.

28. *Alabama Christian Advocate*, 25 Aug. 1887 and 15 Oct. 1903, quoted in Link, *Paradox of Southern Progressivism*, 56.

29. Link, *Paradox of Southern Progressivism*, 117.

30. *Christian Advocate*, 11 Nov. 1897; for commentary on the *Christian Advocate*'s national impact, see Hal D. Sears, "The Moral Threat of Intercollegiate Sports: An 1893 Poll of Ten College Presidents, and the End of 'the Champion Football Team of the Great West,'" *Journal of Sport History* 19 (Winter 1992): 222–224.

31. *Wesleyan Christian Advocate*, 30 Nov. and 13 Dec. 1893; for context, see J. Steven Picou, "Football," in Wilson and Ferris, eds., *Encyclopedia of Southern Culture*, 1221–1224.

32. *Alabama Christian Advocate*, 22 Nov. 1894. For a midwestern version of this pietistic critique of football, see Sears, "Moral Threat of Intercollegiate Sports," 211–226.

33. "Our State University," *Wesleyan Christian Advocate*, 30 Nov. 1892; cf. Farish, *Circuit Rider Dismounts*, 344; and Spain, *At Ease in Zion*, 172.

34. *Christian Advocate*, 27 Dec. 1894, 10 and 24 Dec. 1896, 10 Nov. 1898, and 20 July 1899.

35. Bailey, *Southern White Protestantism*, 26–27; C. Vann Woodward, *Origins of the New South, 1877–1913* (Baton Rouge: Louisiana State University Press, 1951), 446; *Alabama Christian Advocate*, 14 Dec. 1893; *New Orleans Christian Advocate*, 3 Feb. 1887, quoted in Farish, *Circuit Rider Dismounts*, 346.

36. "Amenities and Moralities of Football," *Alabama Christian Advocate*, 4 Jan. 1894.

37. *Wesleyan Christian Advocate*, 14 Nov. and 19 Dec. 1894.

38. Unless otherwise indicated, all this information on Vanderbilt is taken from Paul K. Conkin's excellent institutional history: *Gone with the Ivy: A Biography of Vanderbilt University* (Knoxville: University of Tennessee Press, 1985).

39. *Alabama Christian Advocate*, 22 Nov. 1894.

40. This story is largely reconstructed from Jim L. Sumner, "John Franklin Crowell, Methodism, and the Football Controversy at Trinity College, 1887–1894," *Journal of Sport History* 17 (Spring 1990): 5–20; Earl W. Porter, *Trinity and Duke, 1892–1924* (Durham: Duke University Press, 1964); and John Franklin Crowell, *Personal Recollections of Trinity College, North Carolina, 1887–1894* (Durham: Duke University Press, 1939).

41. For Yale football in the late nineteenth century, see Ronald A. Smith, *Sports and Freedom: The Rise of Big-Time College Athletics* (New York: Oxford University Press, 1988), 84, 113.

42. On North Carolina Methodist leadership in the crusade against liquor, see Dan-

iel Jay Whitener, *Prohibition in North Carolina, 1715–1945* (Chapel Hill: University of North Carolina Press, 1945), 63–65, 107–108; cf. Ownby, *Subduing Satan,* 170–173, 208–209.

43. For another of the many turn-of-century comparisons of football to Roman gladiatorial contests, see Smith, *Sports and Freedom,* 198.

44. Sumner, "Football Controversy at Trinity," 18.

45. "A Weather Prediction for Colleges," *Wesleyan Christian Advocate,* 6 Nov. 1895.

46. George Washington Paschal, *History of Wake Forest College,* 3 vols. (Wake Forest: Wake Forest College, 1935–1943), 2:309–317; 3:109–111. Thanks to J. Edwin Hendricks, Wake Forest professor of history, for photocopies of this reference.

47. George J. Stevenson, *Increase in Excellence: A History of Emory and Henry College* (New York: Appleton-Century-Crofts, 1963), 191–192; Minutes, Emory and Henry College Board of Trustees, 11 June 1895 and 7 June 1915. Thanks to Eugene Rasor, professor of history at E&H, for photocopies.

48. Archie Vernon Huff, *Greenville: The History of the City and County in the South Carolina Piedmont* (Columbia: University of South Carolina Press, 1995), 320; David Duncan Wallace, *History of Wofford College, 1954–1949* (Nashville: Vanderbilt University Press, 1951), 108–109; Alfred Sandlin Reid, *Furman University: Toward a New Identity, 1925–1975* (Durham: Duke University Press, 1976), 22; *Greenville Daily News,* 2 Oct. 1903 and 18 Sept. 1914. Thanks to Steve Richardson, Furman reference librarian, for photocopies.

49. *Religious Herald,* 25 Feb. 1897, quoted in Hogan, "Sin and Sports," 129; John Wendell Bailey, *Football at the University of Richmond, 1878–1948* (Richmond: privately published, 1949), 27; W. Harrison Daniel, *History of the University of Richmond* (Richmond: University of Richmond Print Shop, 1991), 63. Thanks to Martin Ryle, professor of history at Richmond, for these references.

50. *Mississippi Baptist,* 8 Jan. 1903, quoted in Hogan, "Sin and Sports," 129; Richard Aubrey McLemore and Nannie Pitts McLemore, *The History of Mississippi College* (Jackson, MS: Hederman Brothers, 1977), 174–175; biographical entry, "Dan Xenophon Bible," by Charles R. Middleton in *Biographical Dictionary of American Sports: Football,* ed. David L. Porter (Westport, CT: Greenwood, 1987), 46–47.

51. Eugene W. Baker, *To Light the Ways of Time: An Illustrated History of Baylor University, 1845–1986* (Waco: Baylor University, 1987), 106.

52. Sumner, "Football Controversy at Trinity," 19.

53. For the impact of World War I on American sport, see John Rickards Betts, *America's Sporting Heritage, 1850–1950* (Reading, MA: Addison-Wesley, 1974), 136–139.

54. See Ownby, *Subduing Satan,* 194–212, and Ayers, *Promise of the New South,* 409–441; see George Brown Tindall, *The Emergence of the New South, 1913–1945* (Baton Rouge: Louisiana State University Press, 1967), 33–110.

55. Albert Ben Wegener, *Church and Community Recreation* (New York: Macmillan, 1924), 240–243.

56. *Raleigh (NC) News and Observer,* 7 May 1922; "The Olympic" (editorial), *Durham Morning Herald,* 2 May 1922.

57. *Durham Morning Herald,* 2, 3, 4 May 1922; Marmaduke R. Clark, "State Olympics as a Basis for National Olympic Teams," *The Playground* 16 (September 1922): 260–261.

58. *Charlotte Observer,* 23 April 1922.

59. H. G. Bissinger, *Friday Night Lights: A Town, a Team, and a Dream* (New York: Harper Collins, 1991), 28–29, 35–36.

60. Andrew Doyle, "'Causes Won, Not Lost': College Football and the Modernization of the American South," *International Journal of the History of Sport* 11 (1994): 240–247.

61. Charles S. Johnson, *Growing Up in the Black Belt: Negro Youth in the Rural South* (Washington, DC: American Council on Education, 1941), 138, 141; cf. Harry V. Richardson, *Dark Glory: A Picture of the Church among Negroes in the Rural South* (New York: Friendship Press, 1947), 120.

62. Hill, *South and North,* 100; "The Attitudes of Negro Ministers," *American Review of Reviews* 73 (March 1926): 310.

63. For the religious symbolism of the Great Exodus, see Pete Daniel, *Standing at the Crossroads: Southern Life since 1900* (New York: Hill and Wang, 1986), 77–78.

## 6. God and Country Games

1. S. W. Pope, *Patriotic Games: Sporting Traditions in the American Imagination, 1876–1926* (New York: Oxford University Press, 1997). My conceptual framework comes from Benedict Anderson, *Imagined Communities: Reflections on the Origin and Spread of Nationalism* (London: Verso, 1883); Eric Hobsbawm, "Mass-Producing Traditions: Europe, 1870–1914," in *The Invention of Tradition,* ed. Eric Hobsbawm and Terence Ranger (Cambridge: Cambridge University Press, 1983), 263–307 (for focus on sport, see 288–290, 298–302, 305–306); see also Hobsbawm, *Nations and Nationalism since 1780: Programme, Myth, Reality* (Cambridge: Cambridge University Press, 1990), 101–130.

2. E. J. Hobsbawm, *The Age of Empire, 1875–1914* (New York: Pantheon, 1987), 163.

3. Walter Rauschenbusch, *The Social Principles of Jesus* (1916), excerpt in *The Social Gospel in America, 1870–1920,* ed. Robert T. Handy (New York: Oxford University Press, 1966), 376.

4. Richard Henry Edwards, *Christianity and Amusements* (New York: Association Press, 1915), 147–148; cf. Howard Wright Gates, *Recreation and the Church* (Chicago: University of Chicago Press, 1917), 72–79; and Allan Hoben, "Ethical Value of Organized Play," *Biblical World* 39 (March 1912): 187.

5. James Thayer Addison, *The Episcopal Church in the United States, 1789–1931* (New York: Scribner, 1951), 281; Aaron Ignatius Abell, *The Urban Impact on American Protestantism, 1865–1900* (Cambridge, MA: Harvard University Press, 1943), 251.

6. Le Roy E. Bowman, "Community Recreation," in *Christianity and Social Adventuring*, ed. Jerome Davis (New York: Century, 1927), 276.

7. Wells, "Country Pastor," 243–244; Eastman, "Rural Recreation," 236; Elizabeth Wootton, "Much in Little—Canooga, N.Y.," in *Churches of Distinction in Town and Country*, ed. Edmund De Schweinitz Brunner (New York: Doran, 1923), 42–46. For the Roman Catholic Church in rural America, see Edwin V. O'Hara, *The Church and the Country Community* (New York: Macmillan, 1927).

8. Clarence E. Rainwater, *The Play Movement in the United States* (Chicago: University of Chicago Press, 1922), 15, 22–23; Henry S. Curtis, "Vacation Schools and Playgrounds," *Harper's Monthly Magazine* 105 (June 1902): 22–29; Jerry G. Dickason, "The Origin of the Playground: The Role of Boston's Women's Clubs, 1885–1890," *Journal of Leisure Sciences* 6, no. 1 (1983): 83–98. For the best overview, see Dominick Cavallo, *Muscles and Morals: Organized Playgrounds and Urban Reform, 1880–1920* (Philadelphia: University of Pennsylvania Press, 1981).

9. "A Brief History of the Playground Movement in America, I," *Playground* 9 (April 1915): 4–5; Gates, *Recreation and the Church*, 57.

10. Henry S. Curtis, "Vacation Schools and Playgrounds," *Harper's Monthly Magazine* 105 (June 1902): 27.

11. Henry S. Curtis, *The Practical Conduct of Play* (New York: Macmillan, 1915), 212. On teamwork as a civic virtue inculcated in team sports, see Cavallo, *Muscles and Morals*, 92–106, and Susan Curtis, *A Consuming Faith: The Social Gospel and Modern American Culture* (Baltimore: Johns Hopkins University Press, 1991), 24–25.

12. Curtis, "Vacation Schools and Playgrounds," 27–28.

13. Cavallo, *Muscles and Morals*, 27–29; cf. Cary Goodman, *Choosing Sides: Playground and Street Life on the Lower East Side* (New York: Schocken, 1979), 35–38.

14. Bruce Bennett and Mabel Lee, "This Is Our Heritage," *Journal of Health, Physical Education, and Recreation* 31 (April 1960): 27. For the origins of high school sports, see Benjamin Rader, *American Sports: From the Age of Folk Games to the Age of Televised Sports* (Englewood Cliffs, NJ: Pentice Hall, 1990), 225–229.

15. Ethel Josephine Dorgan, *Luther Halsey Gulick, 1865–1918* (New York: Columbia University Teachers College, 1934), 71–92; *New York Times*, 18 Feb. 1904; Warren Hugh Wilson, *The Farmer's Church* (New York: Century, 1925), 131. For more on the PSAL, see J. Thomas Jable, "The Public Schools Athletic League of New York City: Organized Athletics for City Schoolchildren, 1903–1914," in *The American Sporting Experience: A Historical Anthology of Sport in America*, ed. Steven A. Riess (West Point, NY: Leisure Press, 1984), 219–238; and Steven A. Riess, *City Games: The Evolution of American Urban Society and the Rise of Sports* (Urbana: University of Illinois Press, 1989), 160–164.

16. Henry S. Curtis, *Play and Recreation for the Open Country* (Boston: Ginn and Co., 1914), 150. For the best secondary sources on this subject, see John Springhall, *Youth, Empire and Society: British Youth Movements, 1883–1940* (London: Croom Helm, 1977); Michael Rosenthal, *The Character Factory: Baden-Powell and the Origins of the Boy Scout Movement* (New York: Pantheon, 1984); and David I. MacLeod, *Building Character in the American Boy: The Boy Scouts, YMCA, and Their Forerunners, 1870–1920* (Madison: University of Wisconsin Press, 1983).

17. Rosenthal, *Character Factory,* 18, 21–22, 31; Springhall, *Youth, Empire and Society,* 55, 58.

18. MacLeod, *Building Character,* 130–145; Tim Jeal, *The Boy-Man: The Life of Lord Baden-Powell* (New York: William Morrow, 1990), 515–516.

19. Frederick W. Cozens and Florence S. Stumpf, *Sports in American Life* (Chicago: University of Chicago Press, 1953), 98–100; Curtis, *Play and Recreation,* 224; Ralph A. Felton, *Serving the Neighborhood* (New York: Interchurch World Movement, 1920), 75; "Recreation as a Function of the Church," *Playground* 14 (August 1920): 285; Norman E. Richardson, *The Church at Play: A Manual for Directors of Social and Recreational Life* (New York: Abingdon Press, 1922), 127.

20. Thorstein Veblen, *The Theory of the Leisure Class: An Economic Study of Institutions* (New York: New American Library, 1953, orig. pub. 1899), 170; Theodore Roosevelt, *The Strenuous Life: Essays and Addresses* (New York: Century, 1900), 8, 20–21. For Roosevelt's views on the benefits of athletics, see his "Value of an Athletic Training," *Harper's Weekly* 37 (23 Dec. 1893): 1236.

21. Hobsbawm, *Age of Empire,* 163.

22. Richard D. Mandell, *Sport: A Cultural History* (New York: Columbia University Press, 1984), 159–165; cf. William J. Baker, *Sports in the Western World* (Urbana: University of Illinois Press, 1988), 100–102.

23. Mandell, *Sport,* 167; Hobsbawm, "Mass-Producing Traditions," 302.

24. Quoted in Mandell, *Sport,* 175–176.

25. On Belgium, see Jan Tolleneer, "Gymnastics and Religion in Belgium (1892–1914)," *International Journal of the History of Sport* 7 (1990): 335–347; and "The Dual Meaning of 'Fatherland' and Catholic Gymnasts in Belgium, 1892–1914," *International Journal of the History of Sport* 12 (1995): 94–107. On France, see Richard Holt, *Sport and Society in Modern France* (London: Macmillan, 1981).

26. John Sugden and Alan Bairner, *Sport, Sectarianism and Society in a Divided Ireland* (Leicester: Leicester University Press, 1993), 28; cf. W. F. Mandle, *The Gaelic Athletic Association and Irish Nationalist Politics, 1884–1924* (London: Christopher Helm/ Gill and Macmillan, 1987); and Richard Holt, *Sport and the British: A Modern History* (Oxford: Clarendon, 1989), 238–246.

27. Conor Cruise O'Brien, "1891–1916," and David Greene, "Michael Cusack and the Rise of the GAA," in *The Shaping of Modern Ireland,* ed. Conor Cruise O'Brien

(London: Routledge and Kegan Paul, 1960), 15, 74–84; Sugden and Bairner, *Sport, Sectarianism and Society*, 32.

28. Sugden and Bairner, *Sport, Sectarianism and Society*, 29.

29. Holt, *Sport and the British*, 253–262; cf. Chris Harvie, "Sport and the Scottish State," in *Scottish Sport in the Making of the Nation: Ninety Minute Patriots?* ed. Grant Jarvie and Graham Walker (Leicester: Leicester University Press, 1994), 43–57.

30. W. J. Murray, *The Old Firm: Sectarianism, Sport and Society in Scotland* (Glasgow: John Donald, 1984); Murray, *Glasgow's Giants: One Hundred Years of the Old Firm* (Edinburgh: Mainstream, 1988), 17–29; G. P. T. Finn, "Racism, Religion and Social Prejudice: Irish Catholic Clubs, Soccer and Scottish Society, I: The Historical Roots of Prejudice," *International Journal of the History of Sport* 8 (May 1991): 72–95; Finn, ". . . II: Social Identities and Conspiracy Theories," *International Journal of the History of Sport* 8 (December 1991): 370–397; Joseph M. Bradley, "Football in Scotland: A History of Political and Ethnic Identity," *International Journal of the History of Sport* 12 (April 1995): 81–98.

31. Harvie, "Sport and the Scottish State," 44; and Holt, *Sport and the British*, 249; cf. Gareth Williams, "How Amateur Was My Valley: Professional Sport and National Identity in Wales, 1890–1914," *British Journal of Sports History* 2 (December 1985): 248–269.

32. Holt, *Sport and the British*, 264; *Encyclopedia Brittanica*, vol. 6 (1891), 578–579.

33. Holt, *Sport and the British*, 263–265; Kipling quoted in Coral Lansbury, "A Straight Bat and a Modest Mind," *Victorian Newsletter* 49 (Spring 1976): 9–18.

34. The best biographical treatment of Coubertin is John J. MacAloon, *This Great Symbol: Pierre de Coubertin and the Origins of the Modern Olympic Games* (Chicago: University of Chicago Press, 1981).

35. Pierre de Coubertin, *The Olympic Idea*, ed. Carl-Diem-Institut (Stuttgart: Verlag Karl Hofmann, 1967), 57, 131.

36. For commentary on the religious aspects of the ritual and dogma of the modern Olympics, see Siegfried von Kortzfleisch, "Religious Olympism," *Social Research: An International Quarterly of Political and Social Science* 37 (1970): 231–236; and John J. MacAloon, "Religious Themes and Structures in the Olympic Movement and the Olympic Games," in *Philosophy, Theology, and History of Sport and Physical Activity*, ed. Fernand Landry and William A. R. Orban (Miami, FL: Symposia Specialists, 1978), 161–169.

37. MacAloon, *This Great Symbol*, 141–142.

38. Kortzfleisch, "Religious Olympism," 234; Coubertin, *Olympic Idea*, 118; John Hoberman, *The Olympic Crisis: Sport, Politics, and the Moral Order* (New Rochelle, NY: Caratzas, 1986), 38.

39. MacAloon, *This Great Symbol*, 141; Walter Umminger, *Supermen, Heroes, and Gods*, trans. James Clark (London: Thames and Hudson, 1963), 33–34. For a slightly

different translation of Coubertin's Berlin speech, see Ove Korsgaard, "Sport as a Practice of Religion: The Record as Ritual," in *Ritual and Record: Sports Records and Quantification in Pre-Modern Societies*, ed. John Marshall Carter and Arnd Kruger (Westport, CT: Greenwood, 1990), 115.

40. MacAloon, *This Great Symbol*, 141–142; Coubertin, *Olympic Idea*, 22.

41. MacAloon, *This Great Symbol*, 258–259. For Coubertin's rejection of that "particularly vicious form of nationalism" associated with French thinkers Charles Maurras and Maurice Barres, see 111–112.

42. Coubertin, *Olympic Idea*, 3.

43. Ture Widlund, "Ethelbert Talbot: His Life and Place in Olympic History," *Citius, Altius, Fortius: The International Society of Olympic History Journal* 2, no. 2 (1994): 7–14. For an alternate view, see David C. Young, "On the Source of the Olympic Credo," *Olympika: The International Journal of Olympic Studies* 3 (1994): 17–25.

44. Kortsfleisch, "Religious Olympism," 234.

45. Guttmann, *The Olympics: A History of the Modern Games* (Urbana: University of Illinois Press, 1992), 83; see also Guttmann's *The Games Must Go On: Avery Brundage and the Olympic Movement* (New York: Columbia University Press, 1984).

46. *The Era*, 22 Nov. 1894.

47. Elmer L. Johnson, *The History of YMCA Physical Education* (Chicago: Association Press/Follett, 1979), 145–177; for athleticism in the British empire, see J. A. Mangan, *The Games Ethic and Imperialism: Aspects of the Diffusion of an Ideal* (New York: Viking, 1986), and Allen Guttmann, *Games and Empires: Modern Sport and Cultural Imperialism* (New York: Columbia University Press, 1994).

48. For context, see Paul Varg, *Missionaries, Chinese, and Diplomat: The American Protestant Missionary Movement in China, 1800–1952* (Princeton: Princeton University Press, 1958); and Thomas McCormick, *China Market: America's Quest for Informal Empire, 1893–1901* (Chicago: University of Chicago Press, 1967). For the work of the YMCA in China specifically, see D. Willard Lyon, *The First Quarter Century of the YMCA in China, 1895–1920* (Shanghai: Association Press of China, 1920); and Shirley S. Garrett, *Social Reformers in Urban China: The Chinese YMCA, 1895–1926* (Cambridge, MA: Harvard University Press, 1970).

49. M. G. Ross, *The YMCA in Canada: The Chronicle of a Century* (Toronto: Ryerson, 1951), 276; cf. C. W. Bishop, *The Canadian YMCA in the Great War* (Toronto: Canadian National Council, 1924).

50. Johnson, *History of YMCA Physical Education*, 182.

51. See Pope, *Patriotic Games*, 145–150.

52. Nancy K. Bristow, *Making Men Moral: Socail Engineering during the Great War* (New York: New York University Press, 1996), 38; Wanda Ellen Wakefield, *Playing to Win: Sports and the American Military, 1898–1945* (Albany: State University of New York Press, 1997), 26; Pope, *Patriotic Games*, 150, 201n56.

53. Bristow, *Making Men Moral,* 4–5, 31.

54. Wakefield, *Playing to Win,* 27.

55. Johnson, *History of YMCA Physical Education,* 185–190; James Naismith, *Basketball: Its Origin and Development* (New York: Association Press, 1941), 151.

56. Johnson, *History of YMCA Physical Education,* 175–176, 180.

57. Ibid., 190, 196–197.

## 7. For God, the Gipper, and the Green

1. John R. Tunis, "The Great God Football," *Harper's Monthly Magazine* 157 (November 1928): 442–252.

2. For the history of Notre Dame, see Arthur J. Hope, *Notre Dame: One Hundred Years* (South Bend: Notre Dame University Press, 1948); and Thomas J. Schlereth, *The University of Notre Dame, 1919–1933: A Portrait of Its History and Campus* (Notre Dame: University of Notre Dame Press, 1991).

3. Quoted from *The Scholastic,* 11 June 1921, in David Joseph Arthur, "The University of Notre Dame, 1919–1933: An Administrative History," Ph.D. diss., University of Michigan, 1973.

4. For pre-Rockne sport, see Chet Grant, *Before Rockne at Notre Dame: Impression and Reminiscence* (South Bend: Icarus Press, 1978); Arthur, "University of Notre Dame," 308; and Hope, *Notre Dame,* 240–248. For Rockne's contribution to the myth that Notre Dame was athletically unaccomplished prior to his matriculation, see *The Autobiography of Knute K. Rockne,* ed. Bonnie Skiles Rockne (South Bend: Bobbs-Merrill, 1931), 70–71.

5. Michael R. Steele, *Knute Rockne: A Bio-Bibliography* (Westport, CT: Greenwood, 1983), 102. For bigotry as a background to Notre Dame's emergence as a football power, see Jerry Brondfield, *Rockne: The Coach, the Man, the Legend* (New York: Random House, 1976), 26–27.

6. Arthur, "University of Notre Dame," 343; Murray Sperber, *Shake Down the Thunder: The Creation of Notre Dame Football* (New York: Henry Holt, 1993), 207–212. On the quality of Catholic higher education in the 1920s, see Sperber's comments on pp. 67–70. For background to Notre Dame–Michigan hostilities, see Francis Wallace, *Knute Rockne* (Garden City, NY: Doubleday, 1960), 36–39; for Rockne's ongoing conflict with Yost, see Steele, *Knute Rockne,* 9, 166.

7. See Leonard J. Moore, *Citizen Klansmen: The Ku Klux Klan in Indiana, 1921–1928* (Chapel Hill: University of North Carolina Press, 1991). For the connection between religious fundamentalism and the Klan, see William E. Leuchtenburg, *The Perils of Prosperity, 1914–32* (Chicago: University of Chicago Press, 1993), 203–224.

8. Hope, *Notre Dame,* 371–378; and Sperber, *Shake Down the Thunder,* 157–162.

9. O'Hara's line appeared in a campus *Religious Bulletin,* 17 Nov. 1924, quoted in

Arthur, "University of Notre Dame," 359; the "Indiana native" is Elmer Davis, whose *Have Faith in Indiana* (1926) is quoted in Hope, *Notre Dame*, 389.

10. *New World*, 29 Aug. and 3 Oct. 1930.

11. *New World*, 17 Jan., 4 April, and 22 Aug. 1930; Arthur, "University of Notre Dame," 137.

12. Hope, *Notre Dame*, 389.

13. For Rockne on Chicago, see *Autobiography*, 60; Steele, *Knute Rockne*, 3–14, is the most detailed critical study of his early life; see James D. Whalen's item in *Biographical Dictionary of American Sports: Football*, ed. David L. Porter (Westport, CT: Greenwood, 1987), 504–507.

14. Thomas B. Littlewood, *Arch—A Promoter, Not a Poet: The Story of Arch Ward* (Ames: Iowa State University Press, 1990), 34–35. For Rockne's coaching principles and tactics, see his *Coaching: The Way of the Winner* (New York: Devin-Adair, 1933; orig. pub. 1925, repr. 1931).

15. See Francis Wallace, *The Notre Dame Story* (New York: Rinehart, 1949), 145–152, and Sperber, *Shake Down the Thunder*, 144–145.

16. Littlewood, *Arch*, 3–23.

17. Wallace, *Notre Dame Story*, 146.

18. Littlewood, *Arch*, 45.

19. For a list of Rockne's student press assistants, see Wallace, *Rockne*, 15; cf. Sperber, *Shake Down the Thunder*, 179–180; and Wallace, *Notre Dame Story*, 154.

20. Wallace, *Notre Dame Story*, 154, 188; Sperber, *Shake Down the Thunder*, 81.

21. Randall Poe, "The Writing of Sports," *Esquire*, October 1974, 173; Wallace, *Notre Dame Story*, 47.

22. Littlewood, *Arch*, 25; Sperber, *Shake Down the Thunder*, 164.

23. Sperber, *Shake Down the Thunder*, 146, 198, 215, 264, 285–286; Wallace, *Notre Dame Story*, 182, 205, 209, 214, 242, 250–251; Steele, *Knute Rockne*, 29, 191.

24. Sperber, *Shake Down the Thunder*, 164.

25. Alexander M. Weyand, *The Saga of American Football* (New York: Macmillan, 1955), 135. Weyand captained an Army team that lost to Notre Dame, 7–0, in 1915 when Rockne was an assistant coach.

26. Hope, *Notre Dame*, 290–291, 442–451. Father O'Hara's official title in the 1920s, "Prefect of Religion," combined the roles of moral monitor, counselor, and spiritual advisor of students. See Thomas T. McAvoy, *Father O'Hara of Notre Dame* (South Bend: Notre Dame University Press, 1967).

27. Arthur, "University of Notre Dame," 346–347, 359; Weyand, *Saga of American Football*, 135.

28. Hope, *Notre Dame*, 445; Wallace, *Notre Dame Story*, 225–227; Eugene "Scrap-iron" Young, *With Rockne at Notre Dame* (New York: G. Putnam's Sons, 1951), 97–100.

29. Wallace, *Rockne*, 144. For the Praying Colonels, see "Praying Football Team of

Centre College" and "Centre College, Ky., Gives Harvard a Tussle," *Literary Digest* 67 (11 Dec. 1920): 39, 91–92.

30. Quoted in Sperber, *Shake Down the Thunder,* 344.

31. Quoted from campus *Religious Bulletin,* 14 Nov. 1930, in Hope, *Notre Dame,* 446–447.

32. Wallace, *Rockne,* 144; Weyand, *Saga of American Football,* 135.

33. Hope, *Notre Dame,* 425; Delos W. Lovelace, *Rockne of Notre Dame* (New York: Putnam's, 1931), 142–146.

34. Rockne, *Autobiography,* 272–275; *New World,* 7 Nov. 1930.

35. Hope, *Notre Dame,* 333; cf. Arch Ward, *Frank Leahy and the Fighting Irish: The Story of Notre Dame Football* (New York: Putnam's, 1944), 38, 225. For the death, by natural causes, of "many a beloved campus personality" in the 1920s, see Hope, *Notre Dame,* 378–384.

36. Charles Fountain, *Sportswriter: The Life and Times of Grantland Rice* (New York: Oxford University Press, 1993), 10–32; cf. Sperber, *Shake Down the Thunder,* 173–182. The Biblical source is Revelations 6:1–8.

37. *New World,* 24 Jan. 1930; Wallace, *Notre Dame Story,* 196, 232, and *Rockne,* 225–232; Robert Harron, *Rockne: Idol of American Football* (New York: Burt, 1931), 155–156, 163; Harry A. Stuhldreher, *Knute Rockne, Man Builder* (New York: Grosset and Dunlap, 1931), 80–91.

38. See George Mosse, *Fallen Soldiers: Reshaping the Memory of the World Wars* (New York: Oxford University Press, 1990); and Paul Fussell, *The Great War and Modern Memory* (New York: Oxford University Press, 1975).

39. Hope, *Notre Dame,* 334–335.

40. Patrick Chelland, *One for the Gipper* (Chicago: Henry Regnery, 1973), 195; Rockne, *Autobiography,* 236 (see pp. 217–236 for an entire chapter on "Gipp the Great"); cf. George Gekas, *Gipper: The Life and Times of George Gipp* (South Bend: And Books, 1987). For critical correctives, see Sperber, *Shake Down the Thunder,* 105–113.

41. For the dubious basis of this myth, see Chelland, *One for the Gipper,* 190–192, and Wallace, *Rockne,* 88.

42. Quoted in Wallace, *Rockne,* 270.

43. Steele, *Knute Rockne,* 135.

44. Christy Walsh, "Happy Landing," in *Knute Rockne on Football,* ed. Christy Walsh (New York: Individual Publications, 1931), 3. For later references to the rosary, see Hope, *Notre Dame,* 427; and Wallace, *Notre Dame Story,* 74. For a critical assessment of this myth, see Sperber, *Shake Down the Thunder,* 353.

45. For one of the earliest straightforward but ill-informed reports, see Lovelace, *Rockne of Notre Dame,* 205–206. For later, more critical accounts, see Wallace, *Rockne,* 254, and especially Sperber, *Shake Down the Thunder,* 240.

46. Quoted in Sperber, *Shake Down the Thunder,* 361.

47. "'Rock' Is of the Ages," *New Republic* 66 (15 April 1931): 222; Steele, *Knute Rockne*, 105–109. For a recent approximation of the Rockne reverence in the South, see Charles Reagan Wilson, "The Death of Bear Bryant: Myth and Ritual in the Modern South," *South Atlantic Quarterly* 86 (Summer 1987): 282–295.

48. Paul Gallico, *The Golden People* (Garden City, NY: Doubleday, 1965), 152; Cannon quoted in Wallace, *Notre Dame Story*, 143.

49. "'Rock' Is of the Ages," 221.

50. Benjamin Rader, "Compensatory Sport Heroes: Ruth, Grange, and Dempsey," *Journal of Popular Culture* 16 (1983): 11–22.

51. For the importance of statistics and records in modern sport, see Allen Guttmann, *From Ritual to Record: The Nature of Modern Sports* (New York: Columbia University Press, 1978). Specifically for the 1920s, see Warren L. Susman, *Culture as History: The Transformation of American Society in the Twentieth Century* (New York: Pantheon, 1974), 141–149.

52. Hope, *Notre Dame*, 428. For a good summary of Rockne's religion, see Steele, *Knute Rockne*, 101–109.

53. For Rockne on manliness, see his "Football, a Man's Game," *Mentor* 17 (November 1929): 24–27; *New York Times*, 2 April 1922; Wallace, *Notre Dame Story*, 156–158; Gallico, *Golden People*, 146. For a summary, see Steele, *Knute Rockne*, 97–101.

54. Littlefield, *Arch*, 27; Steele, Knute *Rockne*, 100.

## 8. Sunday Games

1. "Morals of Wheelmen," *New York Times*, 16 May 1899.

2. "Guardians of the Sabbath," *Christian Advocate* 71 (3 Sept. 1896): 5; *The Era*, 10 Nov. 1892, quoted in Elmer L. Johnson, *The History of YMCA Physical Education* (Chicago: Association Press/Follett, 1979), 50–51. For the larger social significance of cycling, see Steven A. Riess, *City Games: The Evolution of American Urban Society and the Rise of Sports* (Urbana: University of Illinois Press, 1989), 62–65.

3. "The World's Sporting Impulse," *Review of Reviews* 14 (July 1896): 58–63.

4. S. G. McConnell, "The Moral Side of Golf," *Outlook* 65 (2 June 1900): 299–301; cf. a more severe indictment of Sunday golf by the Reverend A. Elmendorf in the *New York Times*, 17 April 1922.

5. Joseph Lee, "Sunday Play," *Playground* 4 (October 1910): 221–232.

6. *Playground* 13 (September 1919): 226.

7. Richard Henry Edwards, *Christianity and Amusements* (New York: Association Press, 1915), 111–112; Lyman Abbott, "Letters to Unknown Friends," *Outlook* 103 (25 Jan. 1913): 159.

8. See J. Thomas Jable, "Sport, Amusements, and Pennsylvania's Blue Laws, 1682–1973" (Ph.D. diss., Pennsylvania State University, 1974), 117–118.

9. "Our Sunday and Anti-Sunday Laws," *Literary Digest* 86 (12 Sept. 1925): 32–33;

John S. Gilkeson, Jr., "The Rise and Decline of the 'Puritan Sunday' in Providence, Rhode Island, 1810–1926," *New England Quarterly* 5 (March 1986): 81; Harold Seymour, *Baseball: The Early Years* (New York: Oxford University Press, 1960), 211; and Seymour, *Baseball: The Golden Age* (New York: Oxford University Press, 1971), 362.

10. William C. White, "Bye, Bye, Blue Laws," *Scribner's Magazine* 94 (August 1933): 108.

11. Steven A. Riess, "Professional Sunday Baseball: A Study in Social Reform, 1892–1934," *Maryland Historian* 4 (Fall 1973): 100; Seymour, *Baseball: The Golden Age*, 362–363; Jable, "Sport, Amusements," 123.

12. *New York Times*, 24 April 1904; Riess, "Professional Sunday Baseball," 100–101; Jable, "Sport, Amusements," 122.

13. Harold H. Ela, "New England Sunday Observance," *Christian Advocate* 75 (5 Oct. 1900): 12.

14. "Sunday and Anti-Sunday Laws," 33; Jable, "Sport, Amusements," 122; J. E. Erickson and James H. McCrocklin, "From Religion to Commerce: The Evolution and Enforcement of Blue Laws in Texas," *Southwestern Social Science* Quarterly 45 (1964): 50–58.

15. *Bishop Whipple's Southern Diary, 1843–1844* (1937), 98–99, quoted in Dale A. Somers, *The Rise of Sport in New Orleans, 1850–1900* (Baton Rouge: Louisiana State University Press, 1972), 10; Hunter Dickinson Farish, *The Circuit Rider Dismounts: A Social History of Southern Methodism, 1865–1900* (Richmond: Dietz Press, 1938), 336–337; "From Minnesota," *Christian Advocate* 70 (16 May 1895): 314.

16. Samuel Lane Loomis, *Modern Cities and Their Religious Problems* (New York: Arno Press, 1970; orig. pub. 1887), 104, quoted in Jable, "Sport, Amusements," 108; see 188–190 for the Sabbath in urban context.

17. "Sunday and Anti-Sunday Laws," 33; Jable, "Sport, Amusements," 155. Milwaukee lost its major league franchise in 1902: Seymour, *Baseball: The Early Years,* 321. For urban-rural differences on the Sunday question, see Foster Rhea Dulles, *America Learns to Play: A History of Popular Recreation, 1607–1940* (New York: Appleton-Century, 1940), 204–207.

18. John D. Buenker, *Urban Liberalism and Progressive Reform* (New York: Scribner, 1973), 172–173.

19. Jable, "Sport, Amusements," 123; "Sunday and Anti-Sunday Laws," 32; *New Orleans Christian Advocate,* 29 April 1880; Louis B. Weeks, "The Scriptures and Sabbath Observance in the South," *Journal of Presbyterian History* 59 (Summer 1981): 271.

20. *The Legislative Journal of the Commonwealth of Pennsylvania for the Session of 1913,* vol. 1, 479, quoted in Jable, "Sport, Amusements," 128.

21. *Worcester Evening Guardian,* 1 May 1877, quoted in Roy Rosenzweig, *Eight Hours for What We Will: Workers and Leisure in an Industrial City, 1870–1920* (Cambridge: Cambridge Univeristy Press, 1983), 177; White, "Bye, Bye, Blue Laws," 107.

22. Georgetown student letter, 27 Aug. 1936, from the Georgetown University Li-

brary, quoted in Betty Spears and Richard A. Swanson, *History of Sport and Physical Activity in the United States* (Dubuque, IA: William C. Brown Co., 1983), 85; Jable, "Sport, Amusements," 126; David Voigt, *American Baseball* (University Park: Pennsylvania State University Press, 1983), 215.

23. *New World,* 28 March 1930.

24. *New World,* 15 Aug. and 31 Oct. 1930; Caspar Whitney, "Recreation on Sunday," *Outing* 53 (17 April 1897): 382.

25. Catherine Swift's *Eric Liddell* (Minneapolis: Bethany House, 1990) is informative, though religiously motivated.

26. See William T. Ellis, *"Billy" Sunday: The Man and His Message* (Philadelphia: John C. Winston, 1914); William G. McLoughlin, *Billy Sunday Was His Real Name* (Chicago: University of Chicago Press, 1955); Lyle H. Dorsett, *Billy Sunday and the Redemption of Urban America* (Grand Rapids, MI: Eerdmans, 1991).

27. For Sunday's own account of his conversion, see *Billy Sunday Speaks,* ed. Karen Gullen (New York: Chelsea House, 1970), 213–214.

28. "Billy Sunday Called Out for Last Time" (6 Nov. 1935), "Sunday Was Great Fielder but Feeble with the Ash," and "William Ashley Sunday," unidentified clippings from the National Baseball Hall of Fame and Museum archives, Cooperstown, New York (thanks to Peter Kelly, research associate); *Billy Sunday Speaks,* 204.

29. Georges Lechartier, "Americans and Sport," *Living Age* 310 (10 Sept. 1921): 663; Ellis, *"Billy" Sunday,* 70, 75, 77, 138–139; Bruce Barton, "Billy Sunday—Baseball Evangelist," *Collier's: The National Weekly,* 26 July 1913, pp. 7–8, 30; "Billy Sunday's War on the Devil in New York," *Literary Digest* 117 (27 Jan. 1934): 21.

30. *Billy Sunday Speaks,* 203; "Calls Baseball Cleanest Sport" (January 1909) and "Base Ball Evangelist: Billy Sunday's Successful Career as Player and Preacher" (2 Jan. 1908), unidentified clippings, Baseball Hall of Fame; William A. Sunday, "Keep the Sabbath Undefiled," ibid.

31. Seymour, *Baseball: The Golden Age,* 361. On Rickey, Arthur Mann, *Branch Rickey, American in Action* (Boston: Houghton Mifflin, 1957), is uncritical but useful; cf. Rickey's telling of his own story, with Robert Rieger, in *The American Diamond: A Documentary of the Game of Baseball* (New York: Simon and Schuster, 1965).

32. Quoted in Seymour, *Baseball: The Golden Age,* 410–412.

33. See the chapter entitled "The Tragic Career of Carl Mays," in Fred Lieb, *Baseball As I Have Known It* (New York: Coward, McCann and Geoghegan, 1977), 127–137; Seymour, *Baseball: The Golden Age,* 264–268.

34. See Ray Robinson, *Matty, an American Hero: Christy Mathewson and the New York Giants* (New York: Oxford University Press, 1993); Lieb, *Baseball As I Have Known It,* 139–146; Steven A. Riess's entry in *Biographical Dictionary of American Sports: Baseball,* ed. David L. Porter (Westport, CT: Greenwood, 1987), 390–391.

35. Charles C. Alexander, *John McGraw* (New York: Viking, 1988), 101.

36. Robinson, *Matty,* 11–12, 93.

37. Ibid., 52–53.

38. Ibid., 183; Seymour, *Baseball: The Golden Years,* 363.

39. Manuscript letter from James Naismith to Frances(?) Naismith, 10 Aug. 1916, quoted in John Dewar, "The Life and Professional Contributions of James Naismith," Ph.D. diss., Florida State University, 1966.

40. Jable, "Sport, Amusements," 128–129, 196–197; "Our Sunday and Anti-Sunday Laws," 33; Guy Lewis, "World War I and the Emergence of Sport for the Masses," *Maryland Historian* 4 (Fall 1973): 109–122; Seymour, *Baseball: The Golden Years,* 359, 364.

41. Riess, "Professional Sunday Baseball," 103; Seymour, *Baseball: The Golden Years,* 364.

42. William T. Manning, "The Place of Athletics in an Educational Program," pamphlet reprinted from the *Proceedings of the Twentieth Annual Convention of the National Collegiate Athletic Association,* New York, 30 Dec. 1925; "Manning Extols Value of Sport," *New York Times,* 31 Dec. 1925; *New York Herald Tribune,* 4 Jan. 1926.

43. *Montreal Gazette,* 8 Jan. 1926.

44. Manning, "Place of Athletics," 2; *Brooklyn Eagle* quoted in "Polo as Prayer," *Literary Digest* 88 (23 Jan. 1926): 32.

45. *New York World,* 7 Jan. 1926; *New York Herald Tribune,* 7 Jan. 1926. Some of the correspondence on this issue can be found in Box 6, Folder 32, and Box 12, Folder 3, Bishop Manning Papers, General Theological Seminary Library, New York City. For the *Literary Digest* survey, see "Should Christians Play on Sunday?" *Literary Digest* 88 (30 Jan. 1926): 27–28, 57–58.

46. Jable, "Sport, Amusements," 140–141. For the story of commercialized amusements, see David Nasaw, *Going Out: The Rise and Fall of Public Amusements* (New York: Basic Books, 1993); cf. Gilkeson, "Rise and Decline of the 'Puritan Sunday,'" 87–90. For a sterling example of this class bias from a liberal set of assumptions, see Caspar Whitney, "Blue Laws and Wise Laws," *Outing* 53 (December 1908): 383.

47. Quoted in "Polo as Prayer," 32.

48. "Lifting the Ban on Sunday Sports," *Literary Digest* 99 (1 Dec. 1928): 29–30; William E. Brown, Jr., "Sunday Baseball Comes to Boston," *A Review of Baseball History,* pamphlet provided by the Baseball Hall of Fame Archives, 83–85.

49. White, "Bye, Bye, Blue Laws," 108; Jable, "Sport, Amusements," 151.

50. Jesse Frederick Steiner, *Americans at Play: Recent Trends in Recreation and Leisure Time Activities* (New York: McGraw-Hill, 1933), 179–180; Riess, "Professional Sunday Baseball," 104–105.

51. John A. Lucas, "The Unholy Experiment—Professional Baseball's Struggle against Pennsylvania Sunday Blue Laws, 1926–1934," *Pennsylvania History* 38 (April 1971): 163–175; "Pennsylvania Bans Sunday Baseball as Unholy," *Literary Digest* 94 (30 July 1927): 28–29.

52. Lucas, "Unholy Experiment," 173–174; "Pennsylvania Changes Archaic Blue Laws," *Literary Digest* 116 (25 Nov. 1933): 18.

53. Lucas, "Unholy Experiment," 174; Jable, "Sport, Amusements, 170.

54. Julian S. Myrick, *History of the Sports Bay* (New York, privately printed, n.d.); *Modern Sport and the Cathedral of St. John the Divine* (New York, privately printed, n.d.); see Manning, "The Place of Athletics," p. 3; and Manning, "The Church and Wholesome Play," *Playground* 20 (January 1927): 537.

55. *The World*, 7 Jan. 1926; *Montreal Gazette*, 8 Jan. 1926; *New York Herald Tribune*, 7 Jan. 1926; G. I. Rickard to William T. Manning, 31 Dec. 1925, Box 12, MSS M316p, Bishop Manning Papers, General Theological Seminary. Marshall's comments are from photocopies of *The Churchman* and *The Diocesan Bulletin* of St. John the Divine (1926, exact dates unknown) in the St. John the Divine Cathedral Archives.

56. Myrick, *History of the Sports Bay*, p. 3; for Sherrill, see Richard D. Mandell, *The Nazi Olympics* (Urbana: University of Illinois Press, 1987), 27, 70–76.

57. William T. Manning to John McEntee Bowman, 27 Nov. 1926, and Manning to A. F. Belli, 22 Oct. 1926, in St. John the Divine Cathedral Archives; Joe D. Willis and Richard G. Wettan, "Religion and Sport in America: The Case for the Sports Bay in the Cathedral Church of St. John the Divine," *Journal of Sport History* 4, no. 2 (Summer 1977): 189–207; G. T. Hodges to William T. Manning, 31 Jan. 1927, St. John the Divine Cathedral Archives.

58. J. S. Myrick to William T. Manning, 13 Nov. 1930, St. John the Divine Cathedral Archives; Will Wedges, "Setting the Pace," *New York Sun*, 28 Jan. 1936.

59. See Jesse F. Steiner, *Research Memorandum on Recreation in the Depression* (New York: Arno Press, 1972), 57–59, 80; and Steiner, *Americans at Play*, 165–180.

60. Willis and Wettan, "Religion and Sport in America," 203–205.

## 9. Playing on the Fringe

1. For the contours of this "recreation ideology," see Richard Ian Kimball, *Sports in Zion: Mormon Recreation, 1890–1940* (Urbana: University of Illinois Press, 2003), 23–56; and Ruth Andrus, "A History of the Recreation Program of the Church of Jesus Christ of Latter-Day Saints," Ph.D. diss., University of Iowa, 1962.

2. Kimball, *Sports in Zion*, 66–71.

3. Thomas G. Alexander, *Mormonism in Transition: A History of the Latter-Day Saints, 1890–1930* (Urbana: University of Illinois Press, 1986), 145–146; Kimball, *Sports in Zion*, 68.

4. Ernest L. Wilkinson, ed., *Brigham Young University: The First One Hundred Years*, 4 vols. (Provo, UT: Brigham Young University Press, 1975), 2:336.

5. Ibid., 1:67–68.

6. Ibid., 1:282–283, 378.

7. Ibid., 1:483, 3:447.

8. Ibid., 2:319–320, 334–335.

9. Alexander, *Mormonism in Transition*, 146.

10. Kimball, *Sports in Zion*, 105.

11. Edward R. Kantowicz, *Corporation Sole: Cardinal Mundelein and Chicago Catholicism* (South Bend: University of Notre Dame Press, 1983), 183–188; *New World*, 24 Jan. and 24 Oct. 1930, 9 Oct. 1931.

12. See Gerald R. Gems, "Sport, Religion, and Americanization: Bishop Sheil and the Catholic Youth Organization," *International Journal of the History of Sport* (August 1993): 233–241; Roger L. Treat, *Bishop Sheil and the CYO* (New York: Julian Messner, 1951), 21–23. Herbert M. Kraus Co. article on Sheil (ca. 1958, typescipt), Sheil Papers, Box 4, Folder 26, and miscellaneous clippings re St. Viator's baseball team, Sheil Papers, Box 4, Folder 11, Archdiocese of Chicago Archives, Chicago, Illinois.

13. Radio address, Summer 1939, Shiel Papers, Box 1, Folder 5, Archdiocese of Chicago Archives.

14. *New World*, 25 July 1930.

15. Treat, *Bishop Sheil and the CYO*, 109; transcript of Bishop Sheild's Radio Address, Summer 1939, Sheil Papers, Box 1, Folder 5, Archdiocese of Chicago Archives.

16. *New World*, 5 and 26 Sept. 1930; 3 March, 21 July, 4 Aug. 1933; Treat, *Bishop Sheil and the CYO*, 78–79.

17. *New World*, 17 March 1933; Treat, *Bishop Sheil and the CYO*, 78–79.

18. Gerald R. Gems, *Windy City Wars: Labor, Leisure, and Sport in the Making of Chicago* (Lanham, MD: Scarecrow Press, 1997), 183; *New World*, 28 Feb. 1930, 4 Dec. 1931; *Chicago Tribune*, 6 Dec. 1931; *New World*, 17 Feb. 1933.

19. See Lloyd Wendt, *Chicago Tribune: The Rise of a Great American Newspaper* (Chicago: Rand McNally, 1979); cf. *New World*, 28 March 1930.

20. Treat, *Bishop Sheil and the CYO*, 112; see also Arch Ward, "Talking It Over," *Chicago Tribune*, 4 Dec. 1931.

21. *New World*, 23 Oct. 1931; *Chicago Tribune*, 16 Oct. 1931; Treat, *Bishop Sheil and the CYO*, 86.

22. *New World*, 9 Oct. and 20 Nov. 1931; *Chicago Tribune*, 31 Oct. 1931.

23. Treat, *Bishop Sheil and the CYO*, 69–71.

24. *Chicago Tribune*, 28 Dec. 1931; *New World*, 6 Jan. 1932 and 13 and 27 Jan. 1933; Bishop Sheil's Radio Address, Summer 1939, Sheil Papers, Box 1, Folder 5, Archdiocese of Chicago Archives.

25. Kantowicz, *Corporation Sole*, 189–193.

26. Ibid., 239–240; see *Be the New Apostles: Go Out and Change the World!*, the service directory of the Catholic Youth Organization, Archdiocese of New York, 1989–1990.

27. Much of the following is taken from Peter Levine, *From Ellis Island to Ebbets Field: Sport and the American Jewish Experience* (New York: Oxford University Press,

1992); and Steven A. Riess, ed., *Sports and the American Jew* (Syracuse: Syracuse University Press, 1998). For an older historiography, see Stanley Frank, *The Jew in Sport* (New York: Miles, 1936); Harry U. Ribalow, *The Jew in American Sports* (New York: Bloch, 1952); and Robert Slater, *Great Jews in Sports* (Middle Village, NY: Jonathan David Publishers, 1983).

28. Riess, *Sports and the American Jew*, 2–9; Benjamin Rabinowitz, *The Young Men's Hebrew Associations (1854–1913)* (New York: Jewish Welfare Board, 1948).

29. See Levine, *Ellis Island to Ebbets Field*, 11–25.

30. On Jews in boxing, I borrow liberally from Steven A. Riess, "Tough Jews: The Jewish American Boxing Experience, 1890–1950," in Riess, *Sports and the American Jew*, 60–104; and Levine, *Ellis Island to Ebbets Field*, 144–189. The Benny Leonard quote is from Levine, 149.

31. Budd Schulberg, "The Great Benny Leonard," *The Ring*, May 1980, 32–37, quoted in Levine, *Ellis Island to Ebbets Field*, 155. For more on Benny Leonard, see Ribalow, *The Jew in American Sports*, 112–133.

32. These details on Ross come largely from Levine, *Ellis Island to Ebbets Field*, 170–180; and Ribalow, *The Jew in American Sports*, 157–171.

33. See Steven A. Riess's summary in *Biographical Dictionary of American Sports: Basketball and Other Indoor Sports*, ed. David L. Porter (Westport, CT: Greenwood Press, 1989), 459–460.

34. Levine, *Ellis Island to Ebbets Field*, 158.

35. Ibid., 161–164.

36. Riess, "Tough Jews," 92–103.

37. See Robert Soderman's entry on Fleischer in Porter, ed., *Biographical Dictionary: Basketball and Indoor Sports*, 381–382.

38. Quoted in Levine, *Ellis Island to Ebbets Field*, 30. Unless otherwise indicated, the following account of Jews in basketball comes from this source, pp. 26–80.

39. For early basketball as a community activity, see Ted Vincent, *Mudville's Revenge: The Rise and Fall of American Sport* (Lincoln: University of Nebraska Press, 1994), 246–247.

40. For the SPHAs, in addition to Levine, see Vincent, *Mudville's Revenge*, 243–244, 248–249, 251–253, 280–282.

41. For the Original Celtics, see Robert W. Peterson, *Cages to Jumpshots: Pro Basketball's Early Years* (New York: Oxford University Press, 1990), 69–79.

42. For the CCNY story, see Sherry Gorelick, *City College and the Jewish Poor: Education in New York, 1800–1924* (New Brunswick, NJ: Rutgers University Press, 1981); and James Traub, *City on a Hill: Testing the American Dream at City College* (Reading, MA: Addison-Wesley, 1994).

43. See Linda Borish, "Jewish American Women, Jewish Organizations, and Sports, 1990–1940," and Gerald R. Gems, "The Rise of Sport at a Jewish Settlement House: The Chicago Hebrew Institute, 1908–1921," in Riess, ed., *Sports and the American Jew*, 105–131, 146–159.

44. For Jews in baseball, see Levine, *Ellis Island to Ebbetts Field*, 87–143.

45. On Meyer, see Ribalow, *The Jew in American Sports*, 42–46; and Levine, *Ellis Island to Ebbets Field*, 126–127.

46. See Hank Greenberg, *Hank Greenberg: The Story of My Life*, ed. Ira Berkow (New York: Times Books, 1989).

47. See William Simon, "Hank Greenberg: *The* Jewish American Sports Hero," in Riess, ed., *Sports and the American Jew*, 185–207; and Levine, *Ellis Island to Ebbets Field*, 132–143.

48. Levine, *Ellis Island to Ebbets Field*, 209–214; Ribalow, *The Jew in American Sport*, 172–221.

49. For the following, see Levine's "'Where Have You Gone, Hank Greenberg?' Sport and the American Jewish Experience since World War II," in *Ellis Island to Ebbets Field*, 235–269.

50. For a firsthand account of Brandeis's origins (without a single mention of sports), see Israel Goldstein, *Brandeis University: Chapter of Its Founding* (New York: Bloch, 1951).

51. Unless otherwise indicated, this story is taken from William Simons's "Brandeis: Athletics at a Jewish-Sponsored University," *American Jewish History* (March 1995): 65–81; and James Whitters, "QB No Longer Passed Over," *Boston Globe*, 5 Aug. 2005.

52. Abram L. Sachar, *A Host at Last* (Boston: Atlantic Monthly Press, 1976), 59.

53. Ibid., 281–282. For Grange, see David L. Porter, ed., *Biographical Dictionary of American Sports: Football* (Westport, CT: Greenwood, 1987), 216–218.

54. For Friedman, see Porter, *Biographical Dictionary: Football*, 193–195. The Sachar-to-Friedman exchange comes from Sachar's interview with William Simons, quoted in Simons, "Brandeis: Athletics," 68. In 1953 Leonard Bernstein was appointed to the Mann Chair in Music at Brandeis: *New York Times*, 11 May 1953.

55. "The Longest Yard," *Brandeis Review* 28, nos. 1–2 (2005): 14; Benny Friedman's interviews with Elli Wohlgelernter, 5 Sept. and 6 Oct. 1980, in the American Jews in Sports Collection at the William F. Wiener Oral History Library of the Jewish Committee, cited in Simons, "Brandeis: Athletics," 69.

56. Between 1950 and 1952, at least thirty-seven colleges and universities abolished their varsity football programs, invariably because of the expense: *New York Times*, 9 Feb. and 31 Dec. 1952.

## 10. Making a Pitch for Jesus

1. See Tony Ladd and James A. Mathisen, *Muscular Christianity: Evangelical Protestants and the Development of American Sport* (Grand Rapids, MI: Baker Books, 1999), 69–94.

2. Frank Deford, "Religion in Sport," *Sports Illustrated*, 19 April 1976, 88–102; "The

NOTES TO PAGES 194–198

Word According to Tom," 26 April 1976, 54–69; "Reaching for the Stars," 3 May 1976, 42–60.

3. Sydney E. Ahlstrom, *A Religious History of the American People* (New Haven: Yale University Press, 1972), 950; Winthrop Hudson, *Religion in America: An Historical Account of the Development of American Religious Life* (New York: Charles Scribner's Sons, 1981), 385. For religion in the interwar years, see Robert T. Handy, "The American Religious Depression, 1925–1935," *Church History* 29, no. 1 (1960): 3–16.

4. The most thorough treatment of this change in fundamentalism is Joel A. Carpenter, "The Renewal of American Fundamentalism, 1930–1945" (Ph.D. diss., John Hopkins University, 1984); for Wyrtzen, see George Sweeting, *The Jack Wyrtzen Story* (Grand Rapids, MI: Zondervan, 1960).

5. "Wanted: A Miracle of Good Weather and the 'Youth for Christ' Rally Got It," *Newsweek,* 11 June 1945, 84. On Dodds, see Mel Larson, *Gil Dodds: The Flying Parson* (Grand Rapids, MI: Zondervan, 1948); and James A. Mathisen, "Reviving 'Muscular Christianity': Gil Dodds and the Institutionalization of Sport Evangelism," *Sociological Focus* 23 (August 1990): 233–249.

6. Gene Farmer, "Best Indoor Mile," *Life,* 16 Feb. 1948, 96. For factual data on Dodds, see Ian Buchanan's entry in *Biographical Dictionary of American Sports: Outdoor Sports,* ed. David L. Porter (Westport, CT: Greenwood, 1988), 455–456.

7. For Billy Graham's youthful enthusiasm for sport, see John Pollock, *Billy Graham: The Authorized Biography* (New York: McGraw-Hill, 1966), 3–4. The Charlotte story is told in Marshall Frady, *Billy Graham: A Parable of American Righteousness* (Boston: Little, Brown, 1979), 173–174.

8. William H. Chafe, *The Unfinished Journey: America since World War II* (New York: Oxford University Press, 1986), 112–119.

9. Ibid., 119; Ahlstrom, *Religious History,* 950–956.

10. For "the revival of revivalism" in the 1950s, see Ahlstrom, *Religious History,* 956–960.

11. See Pollack, *Billy Graham,* 62–63, for the Zamperini story.

12. Ahlstrom, *Religious History,* 951–952; see also A. Roy Eckardt, *The Surge of Piety in America: An Appraisal* (New York: Association Press, 1958); and Martin E. Marty, *The New Shape of American Religion* (New York: Harper, 1959).

13. *Christian Century* 69 (13 Aug. 1952); "The Games at Helsinki," *America: National Catholic Weekly Review* 87 (9 Aug. 1952): 449–450.

14. "Brethren Minister Wins Olympic Pole Vault," *Christian Century* 69 (30 July 1952): 893; Harry T. Paxton, "That Big-Talking, Pole-Vaulting Parson," *Saturday Evening Post,* 19 Jan. 1952, 22ff. See Richards's inspirational autobiography, *The Heart of a Champion* (Westwood, NJ: Fleming H. Revell Co., 1959); cf. Francis P. Bowles's entry in Porter, *Biographical Dictionary: Outdoor Sports,* 521–523.

15. Norman Vincent Peale's enormously successful *The Power of Positive Thinking* was published in 1952.

16. "Bibles and Basketball Aid in Formosa Mission," *United Evangelical Action,* 15 March 1952, 43, and various items from the Special Collections of the Billy Graham Archives, Wheaton College, quoted in James A. Mathisen, "'Muscular Christianity': The Development and Institutionalization of Modern Evangelical Sport Ministries," conference paper presented at Wheaton College, June 1991, 12–13. For one version of evangelical anticommunism, see Richards, *Heart of a Champion,* 145.

17. James A. Mathisen, "From Muscular Christians to Jocks for Jesus," *Christian Century* 109 (1–8 Jan. 1992): 12–13; Mathisen, "'Muscular Christianity': Development and Institutionalization," 13–14.

18. Bill Allen, "Fellowship of Athletes Talks Up Christianity," *Christian Science Monitor,* 29 June 1972; Brian W. W. Aitken, "The Emergence of Born-Again Sport" (manuscript in possession of author), 3–4.

19. "FCA at Twenty Five," *Christian Athlete* 23 (July–August 1979): 3; Arthur Mann, *Branch Rickey: American in Action* (Boston: Houghton Mifflin, 1957), 6–7.

20. "The Fellowship of Christian Athletes," chapter photocopied from an unidentified source in the Baseball Hall of Fame Archives, Cooperstown, New York; "FCA at Twenty Five," 5.

21. George Vecsey, "The Fellowship of Christian Athletes, A Love Cult that Continues to Grow," *New York Times,* 22 Aug. 1971; "FCA at Twenty Five," 9–16; Deford, "Religion in Sport," 91–93; Allen, "Fellowship of Athletes."

22. *Athletes in Action,* Fall 1985, p. 5, quoted in Brian W. W. Aitken, "The Emergence of Born-Again Sport," *Studies in Religion* 18 (Autumn 1989): 391–405; Deford, "Religion in Sport," 90.

23. Aitken, "Emergence of Born-Again Sport," 393; Deford, "Religion in Sport," 90.

24. Aitken, "Emergence of Born-Again Sport," 393–394.

25. Dana Scarton, "Faith Takes the Playing Field," *Pittsburgh Press,* 8–13 Sept. 1991; Jane Leavy, "The Lord of the Locker Room," *Washington Post,* 28 July 1988; "TV Halftime Evangelism," *Christianity Today* 37 (17 March 1993): 86; "Two Hundred Make Spiritual Waves in Dallas," *Sporting News,* 8 March 1975.

26. Deford, "The Word According to Tom," 69.

27. M. J. Wilson, "Sports Undergoing a Faith-Lifting?" unidentified newspaper article from the Baseball Hall of Fame Archives; "Fellowship of Christian Athletes Part of '76 Tourney," *Daily Sentinel,* Grand Junction, Colorado, also from Baseball Hall of Fame Archives, n.d.

28. Gary Swan, "Baseball Chapel Offers Alternative to Players," *San Francisco Chronicle,* 14 Aug. 1990; Jim Bouton, *Ball Four* (New York: Dell, 1970).

29. Wilson, "Sports Undergoing a Faith-Lifting?"; Petrocelli quoted in Joe Falls, "More and More Athletes Turn to Religion," *Parade Magazine,* 23 April 1978.

30. Watson Spoelstra, "How 'Real Hell-Raiser' Found God," *National Tattler* (Chicago), 8 Dec. 1974.

31. Glass quoted in Carol Flake, *Redemptorama: Culture, Politics, and the New Evan-*

*gelicalism* (Garden City, NY: Doubleday, 1984), 105; see Donald Meyer, *The Positive Thinkers: Religion as Pop Psychology from Mary Baker Eddy to Oral Roberts* (New York: Pantheon, 1965).

32. Tom Landry with Gregg Lewis, *An Autobiography: Tom Landry* (New York: HarperCollins, 1990), 116–120, 175; Bob St. John, *The Man Inside . . . Landry* (Waco, TX: Word Books, 1979), 96–103.

33. Landry with Lewis, *Autobiography,* 173–174. For a critical appraisal of Landry's religion, see Skip Bayless, *God's Coach: The Hymns, Hype, and Hypocrisy of Tom Landry's Cowboys* (New York: Simon and Schuster, 1990); cf. Peter Gent's fictionalized account, *North Dallas Forty* (New York: Morrow, 1973).

34. Wilson, "Sports Undergoing a Faith-Lifting?"; Jerry Kramer, *Instant Replay: The Green Bay Diary of Jerry Kramer,* ed. Dick Schaap (New York: New American Library, 1968), 31.

35. Kramer, *Instant Replay,* 124, 129, 154, 172, 196.

36. Ibid., 129.

37. Roy Blunt, Jr., "Temple of the Playing Field," *Esquire,* December 1976, 111.

38. Tim Wendel, "Role of Religion Spans a Century," *USA Today,* 8–14 June 1994.

39. "Man with a Mission," *Sporting News,* 28 April 1973; Falls, "More and More Athletes"; Spoelstra, "How 'Real Hell-Raiser' Found God"; Linda Kay, "When Christianity Goes into the Locker Room," *Chicago Tribune,* 17 Oct. 1982.

40. Phil Elderkin, "Religion and Baseball," *Christian Science Monitor,* 2 Aug. 1977; Spoelstra, "How 'Real Hell-Raiser' Found God."

41. *New York Times,* 6 July 1975; Barry Sparks, "Baseball Chapel Real Hit with Big League Players," *Grit,* 17 Oct. 1982.

42. Tom Callahan, "'The Lord's Player' Becoming More Common in Sports," *Lincoln Star,* 23 May 1991.

43. George Vecsey, "Religion Becomes an Important Part of Baseball Scene," *New York Times,* 10 May 1981; Tim Wendel, "Religion in the Clubhouse: Divine or Devisive?" *USA Today Baseball Weekly,* 8–14 June 1994; Hank Hersch, "The Gospel and Gaetti," *Sports Illustrated,* 21 Aug. 1989, 42–47.

44. Peter Becker, "At Play in the Fields of the Lord," *M Inc.,* August 1991, 74.

45. "Thanks, Waddy" and "Religion in the Clubhouse," *Sporting News,* 9 Aug. 1982 and 4 June 1984.

46. Dana Scarton, "Faith Takes the Playing Field" and "Christian Fellowship Finds a Home in the Locker Room," in "The New Testament: Christianity's March on Sports," reprinted from *Pittsburgh Press* (8–13 Sept. 1991), 3–6, 14–16; Diego Ribadeneira, "They Play and Pray," *Boston Globe,* 25 Jan. 1996.

47. See Mark D. Howell, *From Moonshine to Madison Avenue: A Cultural History of the NASCAR Winston Cup Series* (Bowling Green, OH: Bowling Green State University Popular Press, 1997); and Joe Menzer, *The Wildest Ride: A History of NASCAR (or How a*

*Bunch of Good Ol' Boys Built a Billion-Dollar Industry Out of Wrecking Cars)* (New York: Simon and Schuster, 2001).

48. Menzer, *Wildest Ride,* 22, 43. For a critical assessment of the moonshine myth, see Ted Ownby, "Manhood, Memory, and White Men's Sports in the Recent American South," *International Journal of the History of Sport* 15, no. 2 (August 1998): 110–111.

49. Peter Golenbock and Greg Fielden, eds. *NASCAR Encyclopedia* (St. Paul, MN: MBI Publishing Co., 2003), xxii; Yanessa Hua, "God and Drivers on the NASCAR Circuit Ministries Offer Prayers at Races that Could End in Death," *San Francisco Chronicle,* 27 June 2005.

50. Hua, "God and Drivers"; Menzer, *Wildest Ride,* 48.

51. Menzer, *Wildest Ride,* 50; cf. Robert Lipsyte, "NASCAR and Religion," *Relgion and Ethics Newsweekly,* 23 Feb. 2001.

52. Robert H. Boyle, "Oral Roberts: Small But Oh, My!" *Sports Illustrated,* 30 Nov. 1970, 64; for biographical details on Roberts, see Daniel Edwin Harrell, Jr., *Oral Roberts: An American Life* (Bloomington: Indiana University Press, 1985).

53. David Kucharsky, "It's Time to Think Seriously about Sports," *Christianity Today* 20 (7 Nov. 1975): 19; quotation from Granville Oral Roberts, *Oral Roberts University, 1965–1983: "True to a Heavenly Vision"* (New York: Newcomen Society, 1983), 15.

54. Jerry Sholes, *Give Me That Prime-Time Religion: An Insider's Report on the Oral Roberts Evangelistic Association* (New York: Hawthorn Books, 1979), 109–110; Roberts quoted in Boyle, "Oral Roberts," 64.

55. Sholes, *Prime-Time Religion,* 111–113; Boyle, "Oral Roberts," 64.

56. Kucharsky, "Time to Think Seriously," 19–20; Flake, *Redemptorama,* 97–98.

57. Michael Jaffe, "Scouting Reports: NAIA," *Sports Illustrated,* 19 Nov. 1990, 109.

58. Flake, *Redemptorama,* 98; Harrell, *Oral Roberts,* 363–364; Jaffe, "Scouting Reports," 108–109; Boyle, "Oral Roberts," 64.

59. Jaffe, "Scouting Reports," 108.

60. T. Kreider, "Gospel on the Gridiron: Evangelical Crusaders," *Saturday Evening Post,* November 1978, 48.

61. For Falwell's account of the founding of Liberty University, see his *Strength for the Journey: An Autobiography* (New York: Simon and Schuster, 1987), 304–321.

62. Douglas Lederman, "Libery University Seeks Success in Football to Spread Fundamentalist Message," *Chronicle of Higher Education* 35 (15 March 1989): 32.

63. Leigh Montville, "Thou Shalt Not Lose," *Sports Illustrated,* 13 Nov. 1989, 89; Sally Jenkins, "Liberty U. Hits First, Saves Later," *Washington Post,* 5 Oct. 1985; Barry Jacobs, "Building from the Ground Up," *New York Times,* 21 March 1989. For some later departures from these rigid rules, see "Is Liberty Losing Freedom by Playing Virginia's Tune?" *Christianity Today* 37 (19 July 1993): 46–47.

64. Falwell, *Strength for the Journey,* 91; John Capouya, "Jerry Falwell's Team," *Sport* 77 (September 1986): 74.

65. Falwell, *Strength for the Journey,* 303. For Worthington's story prior to his coming to Lynchburg, see J. Devaney, "Bible in the Bullpen," *Saturday Evening Post,* 2 May 1964, 28–29.

66. Montville, "Thou Shalt Not Lose," 87.

67. Peter King, "The Beginning of the End," *Sports Illustrated,* 14 Oct. 1991, 72.

68. Lederman, "Liberty University Seeks Success," 29.

69. Jacobs, "Building from the Ground Up"; Lederman, "Liberty University Seeks Success," 32.

70. This information is gleaned from a telephone interview with Liberty Sports Information Director Todd Wetmore, 18 December 2000.

71. George Vecsey, "Big Dreams Starting to Come True for Liberty and Falwell," reprinted from the *New York Times* in the *Bangor Daily News,* 17 March 1994.

72. Ladd and Mathisen, *Muscular Christianty,* 167.

## 11. Athletes for Allah

1. Kenneth Cragg, *The Call of the Minaret* (New York: Oxford University Press, 1956), 5.

2. Malcolm X with Alex Haley, *The Autobiography of Malcolm X* (New York: Ballentine Books, 1965), 212–220, 251.

3. Malcolm X with Haley, *Autobiography of Malcolm X,* 339.

4. Jack Olsen, *Black Is Best: The Riddle of Cassius Clay* (New York: G. P. Putnam's Sons, 1967), 98, 104.

5. Thomas Hauser, *Muhammad Ali: His Life and Times* (New York: Simon and Schuster, 1991), 14–15, 89.

6. Olsen, *Black Is Best,* 177–178; Hauser, *Muhammad Ali,* 97.

7. David Remnick, *King of the World: Muhammad Ali and the Rise of an American Hero* (New York: Random House, 1998), 207–208.

8. Cannon quoted in ibid., 102–104.

9. Hauser, *Muhammad Ali,* 83.

10. Ibid., 14.

11. For "the angry politics of race and religion" behind this event, see Thomas R. Hietala, "Muhammad Ali and the Age of Bare-Knuckle Politics," in *Muhammad Ali, the People's Champ,* ed. Elliott J. Gorn (Urbana: University of Illinois Press, 1995), 128–136.

12. Bill Russell with Tex Maule, "I'm Not Worried about Ali," *Sports Illustrated,* 1 June 1967, 19–21. For Ali's explanation ("Why am I resisting? My religion, of course"), see Muhammad Ali with Richard Durham, *The Greatest: My Own Story* (London: Granada, 1977), 208–209.

13. For Ali's religious change, see David K. Wiggins, "Victory for Allah: Muhammad Ali, the Nation of Islam, and American Society," in Gorn, *Muhammad Ali,* 88–116.

14. Hauser, *Muhammad Ali,* 516.

15. Kareem Abdul-Jabbar and Peter Knobler, *Giant Steps: The Autobiography of Kareem Abdul-Jabbar* (New York: Bantam, 1983), 141.

16. Kareem Abdul-Jabbar with Mignon McCarthy, *Kareem* (New York: Warner, 1990), 243–244; Hauser, *Muhammad Ali,* 178.

17. Abdul-Jabbar and Knobler, *Giant Steps,* 139–141; Abdul-Jabbar with McCarthy, *Kareem,* 244.

18. Abdul-Jabbar and Knobler, *Giant Steps,* 165–167; see Peter C. Bjarkman's entry on Abdul-Jabbar in *Biographical Dictionary of American Sports: Basketball and Other Indoor Sports,* ed. David L. Porter (Westport, CT: Greenwood, 1989), 2–4.

19. Abdul-Jabbar and Knobler, *Giant Steps,* 168–169.

20. Ibid., 169, 181.

21. Abdul-Jabbar with McCarthy, *Kareem,* 168–169; Abdul-Jabbar and Knobler, *Giant Steps,* 224.

22. Ibid., 264–272; Abdul-Jabbar with McCarthy, *Kareem,* 294–295.

23. Abdul-Jabbar with McCarthy, *Kareem,* 294–295, 322.

24. Ahmad Rashad with Peter Bode, *Rashad: Vikes, Mikes, and Something on the Backside* (New York: Viking, 1988), 41, 49.

25. Rashad with Bode, *Rashad,* 9, 35, 38.

26. See Stan W. Carlson's entry on Rashad in *Biographical Dictionary of American Sports: Football,* ed. David L. Porter (Westport, CT: Greenwood, 1987), 485–486.

27. Rashad with Bode, *Rashad,* 147.

28. Ibid., 9, 147–148.

29. Hakeem Olajuwon with Peter Knobler, *Living the Dream: My Life and Basketball* (Boston: Little, Brown, 1996), 27–28, 207–208.

30. Ibid., 27, 197–198, 207–208.

31. Ibid., 212.

32. Ibid., 216.

33. For Abdul-Rauf's physical malady and early athletic achievements, see Rick Reilly, "Quest for Perfection," *Sports Illustrated,* 15 Nov. 1995, 80–84. This is the dominant source of the next two paragraphs.

34. Robert Lipsyte, "Athletes Standing Up as They Did Before," *New York Times,* 17 March 1996.

35. Peter May, "Rauf Gets Fire and Support," *Boston Globe,* 12 March 1996.

36. "After the Singing and Boos, Bulls Roll," *New York Times,* 17 March 1996; *Washington Post,* 17 March 1996.

37. "NBA Suspends Star of Nuggets," Associated Press item in the *Bangor Daily News,* 16 March 1996.

38. Gerald Eskenazi, "Brutal, Reverent, Blissful Tyson," *New York Times,* 18 March 1996.

39. For Tyson's childhood, see Peter Heller, *Bad Intentions: The Mike Tyson Story* (New York: New American Library, 1989), 6–12. For the following two paragraphs, in addition to Heller see Phil Berger, *Blood Season: Tyson and the World of Boxing* (New York: William Morrow, 1989).

40. Heller, *Bad Intentions*, 232.

41. "Tyson Has Prison Meeting with Shabazz," *New York Times*, 19 March 1993; Pete Hamill, "The Education of Mike Tyson," *Esquire*, March 1994, 98–99; Ron Fimrite, "One for the Books," *Sports Ilustrated*, 10 April 1995, 102.

42. Donald McRae, *Dark Trade: Lost in Boxing* (London: Headline, 1996), 362–363; "Tyson's Name Is Still Mike Tyson," *New York Times*, 2 April 1993.

43. Jonah Blank, "The Greater Struggle," *U.S. News and World Report*, 30 June 1997, 9; Hamill, "Education of Mike Tyson."

44. Hamill, "Education of Mike Tyson."

45. Steve Wulf, "Two Champs Are Back," *Time*, 3 April 1995, 56.

46. *Boston Sunday Globe*, 26 March 1995; John Sedgwick and Allison Samuels, "He's Back," *Newsweek*, 21 Aug. 1995, 62–68. On King, see Jack Newfield, *Only in America: The Life and Crimes of Don King* (New York: William Morrow, 1995).

47. Richard Hoffer, "Out of Darkness," *Sports Illustrated*, 3 April 1995); Valerie Burgher, "Boxer Rebellion," *Village Voice*, 29 June 1995, 15; Steve Rushin and Sonja Steptoe, "Second Chance," *Sports Illustrated*, 3 July 1995.

48. Mark Kram, "The Tiger King," *Esquire*, April 1996, 75; cf. Robert E. Johnson, "*Ebony* Interview with Mike Tyson," *Ebony*, September 1995, 78–81.

49. *New York Times*, 13 August 2000; cf. *The Times* (London), 18 June 2000.

50. Holyfield quoted in Tom Mashberg, "God Is My Quarterback," *Boston Sunday Herald*, 19 Jan. 1997.

51. Donald McRae, "Straight to the Heart of Boxing's Holy Warrior." I am grateful to McRae for a photocopy of this item, newspaper and date unidentified; Blank, "Greater Struggle," 9.

52. Hauser, *Muhammad Ali*, 505.

53. This information, and that in the following paragraphs, is gleaned from Jerome Vaughn, "Analysis: Football Players at One Michigan High School Train and Fast during Holy Week of Ramadan," National Public Radio transcript, 31 Oct. 2003, and Samuel G. Freedman, "For Fasting and Football, a Dedicated Game Plan," *New York Times*, 26 Oct. 2005.

## 12. Teammates and Soul Mates

1. Much of this story comes from Julie Byrne's fine study, *O God of Players: The Story of the Immaculata Mighty Macs* (New York: Columbia University Press, 2003).

2. Ibid., 130.

3. For Jackson's youth, see Phil Jackson with Charles Rosen, *Maverick: More than a Game* (New York: Playboy Press, 1975), 11–23; and Phil Jackson and Charley Rosen, *More than a Game* (New York: Simon and Schuster, 2002), 26–30.

4. Phil Jackson and Hugh Delehanty, *Sacred Hoops: Spiritual Lessons of a Hardwood Warrior* (New York: Hyperion, 1995), 45.

5. Ibid., 108–110. For Jackson's earlier exposure to Native American culture, see Jackson with Rosen, *Maverick,* 17–18.

6. Jackson with Rosen, *Maverick,* 161, 171–172, 176.

7. Jackson and Delehanty, *Sacred Hoops,* 32.

8. Ibid., 36, 46, 58. On the theme of guilt in Jackson's experience, see Jackson with Rosen, *Maverick,* 61, 117, 122, 127, 141, 146–147, 196.

9. Jackson and Delehanty, *Sacred Hoops,* 4–6; Ron Liber, "Zen and the Art of Teamwork," *Fortune,* 25 Dec. 1995, 218.

10. Frank Deford, "Father Phil," *Sports Illustrated,* 1 Nov. 1999, 82–91, quotation on 89; David Shields, "The Good Father," *New York Times Magazine,* 23 April 2000, 61; Jackson and Delehanty, *Sacred Hoops,* 11–12; cf. Roland Lazenby, *Mindgames: Phil Jackson's Long Strange Journey* (Chicago: Contemporary Books, 2001), 13–15.

11. Shields, "Good Father," 61.

12. Jackson and Rosen, *More than a Game,* 105–109; Liber, "Zen and the Art of Teamwork," 218; Lazenby, *Mindgames,* 133.

13. Deford, "Father Phil," 89, 91.

14. Ibid., 85.

15. Shields, "Good Father," 60; Allison Samuels and John Leland, "My White Father," *Newsweek,* June 19, 2000, 56–57.

16. See Jackson and Rosen, *More than a Game,* 256.

17. Linda Kay, "When Christianity Goes into the Locker Room," *Chicago Tribune,* 17 Oct. 1982.

18. Leonard Koppett, *Sports Illusion, Sports Reality: A Reporter's View of Sports, Journalism, and Society* (Urbana: University of Illinois Press, 1994), 21.

19. Jane Leavy, "Scott McGregor and the Pulpit Pitch," *Washington Post,* 29 July 1988; "Prayers and the Pros—an Expanding Link," *Los Angeles Times,* 25 Jan. 1992.

20. William Wagner, "Never Say Die," *Inside Sports,* January 1997, 38–42; Diego Ribadeneira, "They Play and Pray," *Boston Globe,* 25 Jan. 1996.

21. Leigh Montville, "Trials of David," *Sports Illustrated,* 29 April 1996, 90–104.

22. Peter Becker, "At Play in the Fields of the Lord," *M Inc.,* August 1991, 75–76.

23. Gary Swan, "God and Baseball," *San Francisco Chronicle,* 14 Aug. 1990; Michelle Green, "Musclebound for Glory," *People Weekly,* 14 Oct. 1991, 64.

24. Hank Hersch, "The Gospel and Gaetti," *Sports Illustrated,* 21 Aug. 1989, 42–47, quotation on 47; Martin E. Marty, "Trinitarian Free Throw," *Christian Century* 101 (19 Feb. 1984): 231.

25. "Sports and Religion, Their Links More than Coincidental," *Elkhart, Indiana, Truth,* 2 Feb. 1991; Dana Scarton, "Van Slyke Learns Hard Way that He Wasn't Born to Be Wild," *Pittsburgh Press,* 8–13 Sept. 1991; Jane Leavy, "The Lord of the Locker Room," *Washington Post,* 28 July 1988.

26. Rick Reilly, "Save Your Prayers, Please: Organized Worship Has No Place at Football Games," *Sports Illustrated,* 4 Feb. 1991, 86; "Sports and Religion."

27. Bud Collins, "Giants' Victory Was Simply Divine?" *Boston Globe,* 1 Feb. 1991.

28. Curry Kirkpatrick, "Boom Boom," *Sports Illustrated,* 18 Sept. 1989, 24.

29. Dana Scarton, "Faith Takes the Playing Field," *Pittsburgh Press,* 8–13 Sept. 1991; George Vecsey, "As They Look Past Their Riches, Athletes Are Turning to Religion," *New York Times,* 29 April 1991; Tom Callahan, "'The Lord's Prayer' Becoming More Common in Sports," *Lincoln (Nebraska) Star,* 23 May 1991.

30. Michael Sokolove, "The Last Straw," *New York Times Magazine,* 15 April 2001, 26–31, 58–58, 62–63.

31. Jim Bouton, *Ball Four: My Life and Hard Times Throwing the Knuckleball in the Big Leagues* (New York: World, 1970), 369; Becker, "At Play in the Fields of the Lord," 77.

32. Dana Scarton, "Athletes, Media Often Disagree Whether Gospel Should Be Spread," *Pittsburgh Press,* 8–13 Sept. 1991; Roy Blount, Jr., "Temple of the Playing Fields," *Esquire,* December 1976, 111–113, quotation on 198.

## 13. Gods and Games Today

1. See Christopher H. Evans and William R. Herzog II, eds., *The Faith of Fifty Million: Baseball, Religion, and American Culture* (Louisville: Westminster John Knox Press, 2002). For the best account of the Black Sox scandal, see Eliot Asinof, *Eight Men Out: The Black Sox Scandal and the 1919 World Series* (New York: Holt, Rinehart, and Winston, 1963).

2. David Riesman and Reuel Denney, "Football in America: A Study in Culture Diffusion," in *Individualism Reconsidered,* ed. David Riseman (New York: Free Press of Glencoe, 1954), 242–257; Jacques Barzun, *God's Country and Mine: A Declaration of Love Spiced with a Few Harsh Words* (Boston: Little, Brown, 1954), quoted in *Bartlett's Familiar Quotations,* 16th ed., ed. Justin Kaplan (Boston: Little, Brown, 1992). See also Kathryn Jay, *More than Just a Game: Sports in American Life since 1945* (New York: Columbia University Press, 2004), 40–47; Randy Roberts and James Olson, *Winning Is the Only Thing: Sports in American Life since 1945* (Baltimore: Johns Hopkins University Press, 1989).

3. Paul V. Bryant and John Underwood, *Bear: The Hard Life and Good Times of Alabama's Coach Bryant* (Boston: Little, Brown, 1975), 10–11.

4. For a condensed report from a source beholden to sport, see "For the Record," *Sports Illustrated*, 8 May 2006, 18, 20.

5. Susannah Meadows and Evan Thomas, "What Happened at Duke?" *Newsweek*, 1 May 2006, 40–51.

6. See Robert Lipsyte, "The Emasculation of Sport," *New York Times Magazine*, 2 April 1995, 50–57.

7. *New York Times*, 4 May 2006; Jack Curry, "Brotherly Love for Bonds? Yeah, Right," *New York Times*, 6 May 2006; Mark Fainaru-Wada and Lance Williams, "The Truth about Barry Bonds and Steroids," *Sports Illustrated* 13 March 2006, 38.

8. Linda Head Flanagan, "What Does It Take to Coach Girls' Track?" *Newsweek*, 8 May 2006, 14.

# ACKNOWLEDGMENTS

For assistance in the making of this book, I am grateful for references and suggestions from Jerry Nadelhaft, Howard Segal, Chuck Korr, Jack Higgs, Allen Guttmann, Steve Pope, Don McRae, and Ron Smith. Early versions of the manuscript benefited immensely from critiques by Ben Rader, John Salmond, James Lewis, and Randall Balmer. My mate, Tina, read and corrected the entire manuscript; daughter Christina Baker Kline momentarily laid aside her novel, *The Way Life Should Be,* to assist ole Dad. Sons-in-law David Kline and Will Pitts guided me through the mysteries of iMac.

A sabbatical leave from the University of Maine and a generous research grant from the Lilly Foundation, administered through the Louisville Institute for the Study of Protestantism and American Culture, provided time reasonably free from distractions. I am especially grateful to Mac Warford for putting me in touch with the Lilly Foundation. A Visiting Research Fellowship at Fitzwilliam College, Cambridge University, enabled me to complete the research, and also to receive critical but encouraging comments on papers presented to a Cambridge Divinity School seminar and to Tony Badger's American history seminar at Clare College.

Other presentations evoked useful comments at annual conferences of the North American Society of Sports History and at public gatherings at Tusculum College, the University of Tennessee, St. Olaf College, and Furman University. Based on the research for this book, a series of lectures at the University of New South Wales in Sydney, Australia, resulted in a volume entitled *If Christ Came to the Olympics* (Sydney: University of New South Wales Press, 1990).

My literary agent, Beth Vesel, Harvard editor Joyce Seltzer, and copyeditor Donna Bouvier have been unfailingly patient, kind, and effective, professionals without peer. They are, as my Maine neighbors would put it, wicked good.

# INDEX